Y0-CBO-219

THE FISCAL, LEGAL, AND POLITICAL ASPECTS OF STATE REFORM OF ELEMENTARY AND SECONDARY EDUCATION

THE FISCAL, LEGAL, AND POLITICAL ASPECTS OF STATE REFORM OF ELEMENTARY AND SECONDARY EDUCATION

Edited by

VAN D. MUELLER
University of Minnesota-Twin Cities
Minneapolis, Minnesota

and

MARY P. McKEOWN
Maryland State Board for Higher Education
Annapolis, Maryland

Sixth Annual Yearbook of the American Education Finance Association 1985

BALLINGER PUBLISHING COMPANY
Cambridge, Massachusetts
A Subsidiary of Harper & Row, Publishers, Inc.

International Standard Book Number: 0-88730-045-6

Library of Congress Catalog Card Number: 85-22901

Printed in the United States of America

Library of Congress Cataloging-in-Publication Data

Main entry under title:

The Fiscal, legal, and political aspects of State reform of elementary and secondary education.

(Sixth annual yearbook of the American Education Finance Association)
Includes bibliographies and index.
1. Education—United States—Finance—Yearbooks.
2. Education and state—United States—Yearbooks.
3. State aid to education—United States—Yearbooks.
I. Mueller, Van D. II. McKeown, Mary P. III. Series: Annual yearbook of the American Education Finance Association ; 6th.
LB2825.F525 1985 379.1'22'0973 85-22901
ISBN 0-88730-045-6

CONTENTS

LIST OF FIGURES AND TABLES

Figures

Tables

INTRODUCTION

Van D. Mueller and Mary P. McKeown

The National Commission on Excellence in Education's April 1983 report, *A Nation at Risk*, put education in the headlines. In strong, clear language it described an education system in chaos (p. 5):

> . . . the education foundations of our society are presently being eroded by a rising tide of mediocrity that threatens our very future as a Nation and a people. What was unimaginable a generation ago has begun to occur—others are matching and surpassing our educational attainments. . . . We have, in effect, been committing an act of unthinking, unilateral, educational disarmament.

The months since April 1983 encompass the most intense and potentially far-reaching period of educational reform in the history of the United States. Propelled by a steady stream of national studies (ECS 1983), several large-scale research reports (Goodlad 1983; Sizer 1984; Boyer 1983), numerous state task force reports (ECS 1984) and considerable media attention, the majority of states undertook measures to substantially revise their elementary and secondary education systems.

In this sixth annual yearbook of the American Education Finance Association, an attempt is made to analyze these school reform implementation efforts from several policy perspectives, e.g., fiscal, legal, programmatic, and political. The book includes sections covering the national reform movement, case studies of state reform development and implementation, and concerns about the newest reforms and their implications for the future of the schools.

THE NATIONAL REFORM MOVEMENT

The first section, The National Reform Movement, is devoted to a discussion of the current status of school finance reform in the states, legal trends and issues regarding education reform, the political context of school reform, and the implications of school reform for programmatic excellence and access. Chapter 1, by John Augenblick, describes the school financing reforms of the 60s and 70s and asserts that "school financing reform is unlikely to slow down in the years ahead." Augenblick points out that the quest for adequate and equitable funding has been rejuvenated by the desire to improve the effectiveness of the schools. School financing policy issues are likely to shape and be shaped by continued school improvement.

Recent trends in education law, especially as related to the new fervor for education quality are summarized and synthesized by J.U. O'Hara in Chapter 2. This chapter includes discussion of the roles of the major legal actors in educational law: the federal government, the judiciary, and state legislatures. O'Hara forecasts that education law during the next era will be centered in the state legislatures and on the local boards of education. The unwillingness of the courts to engage in academic questions, appears to give state legislatures great flexibility in making statutory changes in school programs.

The political context of school reform is the focus of Chapter 3 authored by Lorraine McDonnell and Susan Fuhrman. The authors point out that it is the political context that determines whether school reform even reaches the states' policy agenda or, later, how broadly new policy initiatives may be conceived. Educational reform is occurring now in most states because of a dramatic shift in the political incentives of state policymakers. In short, the risks to legislators and governors of acting decisively were very low and the political costs of not acting were indeed higher. McDonnell and Fuhrman offer several concerns about the speed with which new reform legislation is being enacted and the resultant gaps between policy and research knowledge. Additional questions are raised concerning the questionable capacity of local school districts to implement many of the far-reaching reforms and whether the political climate supportive of school reform can be maintained long enough to resolve these difficult problems.

Perhaps the national focus on educational excellence and the emphasis on quality of student, teacher, and school performance has led to the majority of school reform initiatives. As outlined by Arthur Stellar in Chapter 4, these reform efforts include strategies as diverse as general school improvement programs, effective schools projects, student and teacher competency tests, revised teacher certification standards and changes in graduation requirements. It is concluded that policymakers and educators can move forward with a sense of optimism about the ability of schools to make a difference.

STATE CASE STUDIES OF EDUCATION REFORM IMPLEMENTATION

In Section II, seven state case studies of education reform implementation are presented. Each of the states reflect unique responses to the school reform initiation, advocacy, and implementation. The state case study authors have addressed the political process undergirding the school reform efforts in their states while providing a description of the context for reform, reform issues and actions, and implementation strategies. Since many of the reforms have had a short life span, analysis or assessment of impact is tentative. The first signs of reform impact are noted however and reflect differentially on issues such as centralization/decentralization and revenue shifts between state and local sources. A brief preview of the seven case studies follows.

Diane Massell and Michael Kirst describe school reform in California in Chapter 5. According to the authors, the 1983 Hughes-Hart Education Act is the most comprehensive reform package in California history. This act involved $800 million in new state funds that purchased over eighty substantive reforms. The California reform activities are characterized by the appearance of new and committed state education policy leadership, accompanied by a rebounding state economy and a rekindled public support for the schools. The California Business Roundtable influence on the reform agenda and a falling-off of the traditional influence of educator groups are important elements in the California political climate for school reform.

As shown by Kern Alexander in Chapter 6, school reform in Florida received its major thrust from actions by Governor Graham and several legislative leaders. Alexander concludes that based on the 1983 Florida experience, educational reform cannot be left in the hands of the business community. The business community's collective power is described as detrimental to public schools with antecedents going back as far as 1830 in Florida. The author also observes that during the 1983 and 1984 legislative activities regarding school reform, there was a tendency of the organized teacher profession to act in opposition to its own self-interest. The union's opposition to master teacher and merit pay initiatives led them to forego major funding initiatives proposed by reform leaders.

In Chapter 7, Barry Sullivan and Tim Mazzoni address educational reform in Minnesota by asserting that the national excellence movement has had "little effect on the policy contours of Minnesota education." Reform initiatives in Minnesota are characterized as improvement increments rather than major restructuring. The important reform initiators were the legislature, governor and several quasi-governmental groups (Citizen's League, Minnesota Well-Spring, etc.). Minnesota reforms are described as fostering bottom-up capability and stress incentives rather than mandates. The approach has been methodical and included pilot testing and demonstration models rather than edicts or "quick-fix" solutions.

Educational reform in New York gained its impetus from the State Board of Regents. Chapter 8, authored by James Ward and Charles Santelli, provides an analysis of the political economy of school reform as a state-local partnership with a strong possibility of the state becoming the dominant partner. The development of the Regents' Action Plan was supported by the organizations representing school boards and teachers. The authors raise several important questions in regard to school reform implementation. The most significant is whether New York will provide sufficient financial resources to permit full development reform of proposals. The importance of professionalization of the teacher cadre to school reform and improvement is noted.

In Chapter 9, authors Charles Achilles, Zelma Lansford, and William Payne emphasize the critical importance of gubernatorial advocacy to educational reform in Tennessee. Key elements in school reform included passage of a Comprehensive Education Reform Act, a new education governance law and an increase in the state sales tax. The 1984–85 state appropriation for education represented a 23 percent increase over 1983–84. The substance of the broad-based reform initiatives include teacher career ladders, funding for new math and science teachers, purchase of computers for school use, renewed emphasis on basic skills teaching and provision of discipline alternatives for high school students.

The enactment of career ladder legislation is the focal point of public school reform in Utah. Chapter 10 authors Betty Malen and Roald Campbell provide an analysis of the fiscal and legal implications of this new provision for Utah. While *A Nation at Risk* spawned dialogue in many states, it spurred action in Utah. According to Malen and Campbell, "The national momentum permeated the Utah context and provided the impetus for the Utah response to public school reform." Disagreements between the state teacher organization and legislative reform leaders over the career ladder approach to educational reform appear to be receding. The authors conclude that the career ladder policy may be a persuasive way to demand increased financial aid for the schools because it focuses on the concern about availability of quality teachers.

Chapter 11 presents the final state case study. Deborah Verstegen, Richard Hooker, and Nolan Estes present an analysis of Texas educational reform legislation. The authors describe the Texas educational reform legislation as representing a comprehensive shift in education policymaking from the local to the state level. The results of this shift in control are seen particularly in the areas of pupil and teacher standards and curriculum and oversight. Texas state fiscal policy still permits substantial local discretion. The role of the Select Committee on Public Education (SCOPE) and its chair, H. Ross Perot are described and analyzed. The Texas reforms finally enacted in special legislative session are characterized by increased student, teacher, and administrator accountability; increased state funding; and increased state control by a restructured state board of education.

STATE REFORM ISSUES: IMPLICATIONS FOR THE FUTURE

The third and concluding section consists of two chapters bringing state and equity perspectives to the assessment of current and future school reform efforts.

In Chapter 12, Kent McGuire provides a state perspective of the implications for future school reform. He presents several issues related to traditional school finance issues such as equity and adequacy and reframes them in the context of excellence and school improvement. These issues include: (1) the current focus of reform and the manner in which specific reform initiatives are likely to impact teachers and students; (2) the complexities associated with improving education and the challenges created for state policymakers; and (3) the problems related to equity and adequacy which undergird the current education reforms. McGuire identifies the gap between what is currently known about school effectiveness and change in education and the content and structure of many state reform initiatives. The importance of linking school financing improvements to educational reforms is emphasized.

The effects of recent school reform initiatives on the equity of school finance systems is discussed in Chapter 13 by David Long. His discussion is more conceptual than empirical due to the lack of actual data on reform effects. Long asserts that the current movement for education reform is on excellence rather than on equity and access. Issues discussed in this chapter include: (1) whether or not fiscal and educational disparities prevent poor low-spending school districts from implementing education reform to the same extent as wealthy high-spending school districts and (2) whether children who are at academic risk will benefit from reforms that require them to pass tests or take additional courses for promotion or graduation. Specific reform/equity issues discussed include raising teachers' salaries, improving working conditions for teachers, increasing instructional time, reforming instructional and administrative practices, increasing requirements for promotion and graduation, and administering school reform by state educational agencies. Finally, the author states very strongly his belief that inequalities between school districts may be exacerbated by state funded educational reform and the result will lead to some children actually being harmed by the school reforms if equity issues are ignored.

CONCLUSIONS

This book's readers should share in the challenging task of understanding the issues of school reform. We feel that the focus of this book is broad enough to encompass the fiscal, legal, and political aspects of school reform from both theoretical and process dimensions. The chapter authors are scholars with research interests and/or direct experience in school reform. The seven state case studies illustrate well the variation that exists across our nation. Certainly school reform is being implemented in an uneven manner. Will the reforms lead to true improvement for children and youth? Doyle and Hartle express the future of reform clearly: " . . . if the schools do not improve, the finger of blame can be pointed at the states. Today they have the opportunity, the responsibility, and the motive (economic growth) to change and improve education (1984: 69).

REFERENCES

Boyer, Ernest L. 1983. *High School: A Report on Secondary Education in America.* New York: Harper & Row.

Doyle, Denis P. and Terry W. Hartle. 1984. "Excellence in Education: The States Respond." Paper prepared for AEI's Public Policy Week, Washington, D.C., December 5.

Education Commission of the States. 1983. *A Summary of Major Reports on Education.* Denver, Colo.: Education Commission of the States.

Goodlad, John I. 1983. *A Place Called School: Prospects for the Future.* New York: McGraw-Hill.

National Commission on Excellence in Education. 1983. *A Nation at Risk.* Washington, D.C.: U.S. Government Printing Office.

Sizer, Theodore R. 1984. *Horace's Compromise: The Dilemma of the American High School.* New York: Houghton Mifflin.

Task Force on Education for Economic Growth. 1984. *Action in the States: Progress Toward Education Renewal.* Denver, Colo.: Education Commission of the States.

I THE NATIONAL REFORM MOVEMENT

1 THE CURRENT STATUS OF SCHOOL FINANCING REFORM IN THE STATES

John Augenblick

INTRODUCTION

Since April 1983, policymakers have paid a tremendous amount of attention to elementary and secondary education in this country. Most of this attention has been directed toward recommending changes in the way the education enterprise is organized in order to improve the public schools. While some of the proposed changes cost very little to implement, others are very costly. Most of the highly publicized national reports that examined the quality of the schools avoided discussing how recommended improvements would be funded. Following on the heels of the national reports, nearly 250 commissions and study groups were established by states, school districts, and private organizations to examine the quality of the schools (Task Force on Education for Economic Growth 1984). Many of these study groups echoed the findings of the national reports, agreeing that improvements were needed, recommending similar changes, and dealing indirectly with how such changes would be funded. Some study groups called for basic changes in the organization of schools and sought large increases in their funding.

A number of states began in the 1984 legislative sessions to tackle the issue of school improvement and how proposed changes would be funded. In most cases, improvements focused on the curriculum, time spent in school, graduation requirements, and teachers. The most costly changes were made in states that traditionally spent relatively low amounts on education; those changes were funded by increases in state taxes, most notably the sales tax.

States have tended to address the issues of school improvement and school financing independently. Funds for school improvement have been allocated outside of formulas used to distribute the vast majority of state educational aid. While the strategy of funding school improvements separately has been successful in the short run, it is likely to be less successful in the long run for two reasons: (1) isolating the funding of improvements, such as teacher salary increases, may threaten the availability of funds in the future, particularly if the improvements do not yield anticipated results quickly, and (2) providing funds outside of traditional formulas may lead to inequities in the distribution of improvements similar to those found in per pupil expenditures before school financing systems began to be reformed. School improvement and school financing are inextricably linked. Improvements that have significant cost should ultimately be funded by school financing systems; by the same token school financing systems must be capable of addressing school improvement.

Over the last thirty years numerous efforts have been made to improve schools. In the late 1950s, efforts focused on desegregation, curriculum development, and teacher training. In the 1960s, programs for special, high-cost pupil populations were implemented widely. In the 1970s, school financing reform dominated the attention of policymakers. Each of these movements was stimulated by a specific event, often litigation.

The *Brown* case of 1954 stimulated the effort to desegregate the schools. The passage of the Elementary and Secondary Education Act, in 1965, stimulated interest in and a significant response to the needs of pupils with special needs. The *Serrano* case of 1971 initiated the school financing reform movement. The release of *A Nation at Risk* in 1983 served as the stimulus of the current effort to improve the quality of the schools. In fact, each of these movements evolved in a particular social and economic context, which had roots extending much further back in time. Each was buffeted by other events such as the launching of Sputnik in 1957, the civil rights movement of the 1960s, the tax limitation and competency testing movements of the 1970s, and the poor fiscal condition of the states in the early 1980s. While each of these movements focused on a particular aspect of the educational system, all had to deal to some extent with school financing systems because all increased the cost of education and all required that resources be redistributed.

School financing reform has been going on in this country for eighty years, beginning in the first years of this century with the studies of Cubberley and continuing with more or less vigor as new ideas (such as property tax reduction or declining enrollment) and new champions (such as Paul Mort or Charles Benson) reinvigorated it. For many people, the decade from 1968 to 1978 represents the high point of school financing reform. During this period the courts heard a plethora of cases, tremendous growth in research was stimulated by federal and foundation funds, and diverse groups worked together in an appropriate political environment. In addition, the availability of state funds fueled substantial changes in the structure of state school aid systems (Fuhrman 1982). School financing systems became more complex in an attempt to make the distribution of state aid more sensitive to the characteristics of pupils and school districts that affect the cost of providing educational services.

A primary purpose of school financing reform was to equalize the resources available for education across the numerous school districts of each state; however, school financing reform had many other objectives, some of which were more explicit than others. Taxpayer equity was a major objective. While reducing property taxes became the primary method of achieving this goal, states improved their property assessment systems, implemented property tax circuit breakers, developed new ways of measuring the fiscal capacity of school districts, and limited the expenditure and tax authority of school districts. Another objective of school financing reform was to assure that adequate resources were available for education. States developed sophisticated indicators of need, measured more carefully the excess costs of serving special pupil populations, studied geographic price differences, and began to define "basic" education and its costs.

Precise assessments of the accomplishments of the school financing reform activities of the 1970s are difficult to make (Hickrod and Goertz 1983). Early examinations led to the conclusion that school finance reform achieved more in terms of taxpayer equity than in terms of pupil equity (Carroll 1979). Assessment of the impacts of school financing reform was difficult because: (1) school financing reform had multiple objectives, some of which could not be defined easily and many of which conflicted with each other, and (2) so many other events were taking place in the social, economic, and political context of the states that it was difficult to link outcomes to specific stimuli (Brown and Elmore 1983).

Whatever school financing reform achieved, it apparently did not result in a perception that the schools were performing adequately. Policymakers became convinced that more money would not necessarily improve the schools. Perhaps more importantly, the public shifted its attention from equity to excellence, an elusive concept to define and an objective that was only tangentially part of the school financing reform agenda.

In order to understand how school financing and school improvement may be related in the future, the current status of school financing in the states will be reviewed together with (1) some of the demographic and economic trends of the last five years (the context of school finance); (2) recent changes in school financing systems; and (3) future issues that school financing systems must address.

DEMOGRAPHIC AND ECONOMIC TRENDS DURING THE LAST FIVE YEARS

It is sometimes difficult to determine whether school financing reform has been a cause or an effect of demographic and economic changes. For example, pupil enrollments typically are viewed as being out of the control of policymakers. While schools financing systems are removed completely from birth trends, they are not isolated completely from decisions families make about where to live and whether to enroll their children in public schools. In fact, some approaches to school financing, such as vouchers, could have dramatic effects on enrollment trends in public schools. When school financing systems are considered broadly, in terms of the magnitude of support provided, the allocation of funds, and their approach to taxation, they can be viewed as having some impact on numbers of pupils and teachers, teacher salary levels, state and local taxes, and so on. Even where school financing systems have little impact as a cause, they must respond to demographic and economic changes. During the past five years, numerous changes have occurred that may have been influenced by school financing systems or to which school financing systems must respond.

Pupils and Teachers

Between 1979 and 1984, the average daily membership (ADM) of the country's public schools continued to drop, from 41.9 million to 38.5 million, a decline of 8 percent. In fact, the decline from 1979 to 1984 was greater than in the previous five years. In six states (Connecticut, Delaware, Mayland, Massachusetts, Minnesota, and Pennsylvania) enrollments decreased by more than 15 percent. In six states (Arizona, Idaho, Nevada, Texas, Utah, and Wyoming) enrollments increased during the last five years. The enrollment decline was greater between 1979 and 1984 than between 1974 and 1979 in thirty-seven states (Augenblick 1984a). Every school financing system in the country is sensitive to enrollment levels because they are based on classroom units or because they permit enrollment averaging over time, alleviating the fiscal impact of declining enrollment.

Enrollment declines are not expected to continue at the same pace in the future. Enrollment in elementary schools is expected to begin increasing soon and enrollment in secondary schools is expected to increase within the next decade. Only nine states are expected to lose school-age population between 1985 and 2000. It is also expected that the percentage of minority pupils will increase steadily from a level of 25 percent in 1980 (Odden, McGuire, and Belsches-Simmons 1983).

During the last five years, the number of teachers also began to decline. Between 1979 and 1984, the number of teachers dropped by 3.6 percent. Decreases in numbers of teachers occurred in twenty-nine states; the decrease exceeded 15 percent in three states. In contrast, between 1974 and 1979, the number of teachers dropped in only fourteen states. In some states, reductions in the number of teachers have followed the decline in numbers of pupils by a few years. Finally, in some states, the number of teachers has increased as enrollments have declined, presumably in order to decrease pupil-teacher ratios (Augenblick 1984b).

As a result of changes in the numbers of pupils and teachers, pupil-teacher ratios have changed; between 1979 and 1984, the national average pupil-teacher ratio dropped from 19.4 to 18.5. In 1979, twenty states had pupil-teacher ratios that exceeded 20.0 while sixteen states had pupil-teacher ratios that were less than 18.0. In 1984, only ten states had pupil-teacher ratios greater than 20.0 while in twenty-five states pupil-teacher ratios were below 18.0 (Augenblick 1984b).

Changes in pupil-teacher ratios have tremendous impacts on school financing systems because (1) ratios determine the primary cost of delivering services; (2) ratios are often directly included as parameters in formulas; and (3) ratios inherently reflect the tension between how many teachers are employed and how much teachers are paid.

Expenditures and Teacher Salaries

During the last five years, expenditures for public schools have grown from $86.2 billion to over $126.8 billion. Current expenditures per pupil in average daily attendance (ADA) have increased from $1,917 to $3,173, an increase of nearly 66 percent (National Education Association 1983 and 1979). This increase has outstripped inflation despite the fact that spending for public schools is declining as a proportion of the Gross National Product (GNP) and total personal income. Wide variations exist in the average per pupil spending levels of the states. In five states (Alaska, Connecticut, New Jersey, New York, and Wyoming), spending exceeds $4,000. In five states (Alabama, Arkansas, Mississippi, Tennessee, and Utah), spending is less than $2,300. Some of these differences reflect price variations, school size, service differences, and other influences.

Teacher salaries, of course, account for a large share of all costs, and both the number of teachers and their salary levels are major factors in determining total expenditures. Between 1979 and 1984, an average teacher's salary grew from $15,057 to $22,019, an increase of 46.2 percent. In 1984, average teachers' salaries ranged from a low of $15,895 in Mississippi to a high of $36,564 in Alaska. In nineteen states average teacher salaries were higher than the national average; in eleven of those states, growth in the average salary exceeded the national average during the last five years. In seventeen of the thirty-one states with below average salaries, growth during the last five years was also below average (National Education Association 1983 and 1979).

Traditionally, states have played only a small role in setting the level of teacher salaries. In a few states, such as Texas, the legislature establishes a statewide minimum salary schedule, although districts are free to supplement the minimum levels specified. States may require that teachers be paid in relation to their training and/or experience although actual salary levels will be determined by local school districts. In some states, a portion of the new funds provided by the state may be earmarked for salary increases, as was done in 1984 in Arkansas, or for distribution under merit pay or career ladder plans, as was done in Tennessee also in 1984.

State and Local Support for Schools

One of the most obvious changes that has taken place during the last five years is the increase in state support for education, despite the dire condition of many states' budgets. In 1981 and 1982, state budgets were particularly weak in the area of education. Actions taken in 1982 and 1983 to deal with state fiscal problems tended to increase state revenues and to reduce state spending in areas other than elementary/secondary education (Gold 1984). Generally, state support for public schools has become a much more important part of state budgets, despite the fact that between 1978 and 1983 there was only a slight increase, from 34.5 to 35.4 percent, in the average percentage of all state expenditures devoted to public schools. In 1983, support for public schools consumed over 40 percent of state general fund expenditures in twenty-one states while it consumed less than 30 percent of such expenditures in twelve states; in 1978, school aid consumed more than 40 percent of state general fund expenditures in fifteen states and required less than 30 percent of such expenditures in fifteen states (Augenblick and Van de Water 1983).

In 1984, on average, states provided 49 percent of all revenue for public schools; in 1979, the states provided 47.3 percent of all revenue. The variation among the states in the percentage of revenue provided by the state is narrowing. A few states still provide a very low percentage of funds; in Nebraska, New Hampshire, Oregon, and Wyoming, the state provides less than 30 percent of all school revenues. In Alaska, Hawaii, Kentucky, New Mexico, and Washington, the state provides more than 70 percent of all school revenue (National Education Association 1983 and 1979). This steadily increasing proportion of all school revenues provided by states has set the stage for some of the states' actions taken in 1984 that increased their influence over the educational system. In California, Florida, North Carolina, and South Carolina, implementation of changes in teacher qualifications and pay was easier because the state provided the majority of all funds for education. Fundamental changes in the educational system, at least those mandated by state legislatures, are more difficult to implement in states that provide a relatively small share of all school revenues.

Compared to their incomes, states' expenditures for public schools have decreased slightly over the past few years. Of the twenty-six states where there has been such a decrease during the last five years, seven (Alabama, Illinois, Maryland, Massachusetts, New Hampshire, Rhode Island, and Wisconsin) provide low support relative to income while two (Delaware and Utah) provide high support. Of the twenty-four states where state support has increased relative to income, eight (Alaska, Hawaii, Idaho, Kentucky, New Mexico, Oklahoma, Washington, and West Virginia) provide high support relative to income while six (Connecticut, Missouri, Nebraska, Ohio, South Dakota, and Virginia) provide low support (Augenblick and Van de Water 1983).

In 1984, the states provided 59 percent of the new funds available to public schools but once again the proportion differs. Ten states provided more than 100 percent of all new funds, indicating that increases in state aid exceeded increases in total support and that state aid made up for losses in other sources. In six states, state support accounted for between 75 and 100 percent of all new school aid. In fourteen states, new state aid provided between 50 and 75 percent of all new support for schools. New state aid accounted for between 25 and 50 percent of new school funds in thirteen states. In seven states new state funds provided less than 25 percent of all new funds for schools (Augenblick 1984a).

Comparisons of these figures to those of earlier years indicate the growing importance of the states in providing support for schools: between 1978 and 1981, only ten states provided over 75 percent of the new funds for schools; this number grew to eleven states for the period 1981–82, fourteen states for the period 1982–83, and sixteen states for the period 1983–84. By the same token, there has been a decrease in the number of states providing less than 25 percent of the new funds for schools: Between 1978 and 1981, fifteen states were responsible for less than 25 percent of the new funds for schools, more than twice the number of states with that level of commitment in the period 1983–84 (Augenblick 1984a).

Table 1-1. Annual Rates of Increase in Different Taxes Between 1973 and 1981.

	Type of Tax			
Period	*Property*	*Sales*	*State Income*	*Federal Income*
	%	%	%	%
1973-79	7.8	12.3	13.3	11.9
1978-81	4.0	9.6	12.0	16.4

Source: Author calculations based on Table 17 in *Significant Features of Fiscal Federalism in 1981-82* (Washington, D.C.: Advisory Commission on Intergovernmental Relations, 1983), p. 16.

One of the most important stimuli of school financing reform in the 1970s was the reduction of property taxes. At the time, property taxes were the most unpopular of all taxes and most policymakers viewed them as regressive, placing a relatively higher burden on low income individuals. Dramatic increases in property values, in some cases linked to reassessment, combined with a perception that school expenditures were out of control, led to concern about the level of property taxes. Between 1971 and 1981, property taxes increased from $36.7 billion to $72.0 billion; however, despite this increase, property taxes declined from 15 percent of all state and local tax revenues to 11 percent. During the same period, property taxes decreased from 1.98 percent of market value to 1.26 percent of market value, on average (Augenblick, 1984c). The figures in Table 1-1 indicate the annual growth in property taxes relative to other taxes between 1973 and 1981.

In part, this reduction in property tax revenue resulted from limitations imposed on property assessments, restrictions on property tax rates or rate increases, and controls placed on local government spending. Currently, thirty-nine states use one or more types of limitations to control the spending and taxing authority of local governments, including school districts: In thirty-four states, property tax collections are limited; in thirteen states there are limits on property tax rates; in eleven states there are revenue or expenditure limitations; and in five states there are limits on property assessment increases. In addition, thirty-two states use circuit breakers (mathematical adjustments to taxes to relate tax burden to income) to limit the burden of property taxation relative to family income, although in only seven of those states are all homeowners and renters eligible for the appropriate reduction (Advisory Commission on Intergovernmental Relations 1983).

Some people argue that the future of school financing depends on increasing property taxes because states may be unwilling to commit vast new resources to education, even though states are recovering from the difficult fiscal situation of a couple of years ago and have more funds available. States also may be reluctant to increase the share of all school revenues they provide without taking more control of how funds are spent. Continued improvements in the administration of the property tax system may permit increases in reliance on property taxes without threatening the taxpayer equity achieved by school financing reform. Others argue that the trend of reducing property taxes should be continued until they are eliminated. At that point, states more easily could change school financing systems in fundamental ways, such as by creating voucher or family choice systems (Finn and Doyle 1985).

RECENT CHANGES IN THE METHODS USED BY STATES TO SUPPORT SCHOOLS

During the last five years, the changes made in school financing systems have been neither as fundamental nor as frequent as the changes made a decade ago. Several states have modified aspects of their school financing systems, three states have responded to court requirements, and a few states have provided funds aimed at improving the quality of the educational system, although such funds were typically provided outside of school financing formulas.

General Modifications in School Financing Systems

In 1984, as has been the case for some time, the most popular approach states used to provide basic support for schools was the foundation program. Twenty-two states used this system, under which the state sets both a minimum expenditure level and a required tax effort and pays the difference between the expenditure level and the amount that districts raise at the required tax rate. The simplest and most used version of this system specified the minimum expenditure level in dollar per pupil terms, as was done in Iowa, Maryland, Massachusetts, and New Mexico; more complex versions specified the minimum in terms of dollars per classroom unit, as was done in Idaho and Wyoming, or in terms of pupil-teacher ratios and minimum statewide salary schedules, as was done in Louisiana (McGuire and Dougherty 1984). Several states, including Alaska and Illinois, are developing education cost models to determine base costs rather than relying on statewide average expenditure figures or state appropriations to determine foundation levels (Brackett, Chambers, and Parrish 1983); however, such models have not been implemented yet.

In ten states, the basic aid program was some form of a guaranteed tax base approach (McGuire and Dougherty 1984). Under this system, the state specified a rate at which it will match local taxes; the rate varies inversely with the wealth of school districts. The state essentially allows school districts to behave as if they had the wealth of some designated district, typically the district of average wealth. The basic difference between this approach and the foundation program is that the state does not specify the spending level beyond which state aid will not be available. In reality, due to other restrictions, no state aid system is open-ended. For example, Colorado used the guaranteed yield approach, assuring each school district that a specified amount per pupil per mill of tax effort would be generated; however, this guarantee applies only up to a spending level referred to as the authorized revenue base, an amount strictly controlled by the state since 1973.

Fourteen states combined these approaches and put them into multiple tiers, usually by providing a guaranteed tax base on top of a foundation program. These multitiered systems specify a minimum spending level, with an associated minimum tax effort requirement, while helping to equalize the ability of districts to provide funds beyond the minimum level; they permit the state to meet its objectives of adequacy and equity while also promoting local control, at least over spending. In Utah, for example, the state operated a foundation program and a two-tiered guaranteed yield system that provided $1,103 per pupil at a required local effort of $23.25 million of property tax plus $17 per pupil per million dollars for the next two million dollars beyond 23.25 mills and $4 per pupil per mill for the next 8 mills beyond 25.25 mills in 1983–84 (McGuire and Dougherty, 1984).

The states also used a number of different approaches in providing support for high cost programs, such as special education, compensatory education, and bilingual education. Twenty-seven states treated such programs categorically, separate from the basic aid program.

These states tended to provide either a fixed amount per classroom unit, as was done in Missouri, or per pupil, as was done in Virginia, or a percentage of the excess cost of providing such services, as was done in Minnesota. The other states integrated the funding of special, high cost programs into the basic aid program through the use of pupil weights, as was done in Florida, or classroom unit factors, as was done in Wyoming. Under these approaches, either the counting of pupils in high cost programs is weighted to reflect the relationship between the cost of the special program and the cost of the regular program or the number of pupils eligible to be counted as a classroom unit is lower for special programs than for the basic program.

Since 1980, only three states have made fundamental changes in their school financing systems that are not related to court requirements. In 1980, Arizona created a new system that merged all state school aid into a block grant program, provided state support for capital outlay, and limited local property taxes (Odden and Augenblick 1981). In 1981, Oklahoma revamped its school financing system, creating a two-tiered pupil-weighted system. In 1984, Texas reorganized its multitiered system, replacing a foundation program driven by pupil-teacher ratios and a statewide salary schedule with a pupil-weighted system. A number of other significant changes, however, have been made by states to improve their school financing systems. Two states modified the way by which the relative wealth of school districts was determined: Income was combined with property wealth in Vermont and Pennsylvania. Prior to 1980, Connecticut, Kansas, Maryland, Missouri, Rhode Island, and Virginia combined income and property in measuring the fiscal capacity of school districts. Three states, Missouri, Ohio, and Texas, incorporated "price indices" into their formulas to recognize regional cost variations. Alaska and Florida already used such a factor. Finally, a number of states initiated studies that may result in school financing changes in the future. Such studies have been undertaken in Alaska, Colorado, Illinois, Kentucky, Maine, Michigan, Montana, Nevada, New Hampshire, and Wisconsin.

Court Mandates Changes in School Financing Systems

Seven states have been required by the courts to change their school financing systems. In four of these states (California, Connecticut,

New Jersey and Washington), legislative action was taken more than five years ago. In three states (Arkansas, West Virginia, and Wyoming) legislative action has been taken since 1982.

In Arkansas in 1983, a pupil-weighted foundation program replaced a number of separately funded programs. Under the new program, districts were required to spend no less than 70 percent of new state funds to raise teachers' salaries. School financing reform was combined with school improvement through the Quality Education Act, which raised high school graduation standards, reduced class size, extended the length of the school day and the school year, required periodic testing of pupils and teacher competency testing, and required school improvement plans from all school districts. The program was funded by an increase in the state sales tax, which allowed state aid to grow by 41 percent over a two year period, and increases in property taxes in approximately one-third of the state's 367 districts (Odden 1984).

In West Virginia, the state embarked in 1983 on a long-term plan to equalize educational resources around the state. The purpose of the plan was to assure that every pupil would be exposed to a similar set of basic resources, which were defined very specifically in terms of staffing levels, personnel qualifications, materials, and other "inputs." West Virginia is viewed as having gone further than any other state, including Washington, in defining the basic needs of the educational system.

Wyoming implemented a new school financing system in 1983. Perhaps the most controversial part of the plan was a recapture provision under which districts must impose a uniform property tax rate and return to the state a portion of the collected revenues that exceed the foundation level. Recapture was based on a sliding scale; the greater the excess of revenues over the foundation level, the larger the proportion of funds that must be returned to the state.

Changes Designed to Promote School Improvement

A number of states have begun to provide large amounts of funds to improve the quality of education programs. In 1983, Mississippi, one of the first states to make such an effort, infused millions of new dollars into its educational system with much of the new funds designed to increase services, lower pupil-teacher ratios, and raise teacher salary levels. In 1984, a number of other states began making improvements in their education systems. Tennessee, in a widely publicized effort, raised teacher salaries in an effort to attract highly qualified personnel, created a career ladder program for teachers as a retention incentive, provided funds for teacher aides, and funded a series of categorical programs designed to expand and improve education services. South Carolina passed legislation that increased high school graduation requirements; created a comprehensive pupil testing program; raised teacher salaries; provided fiscal incentives for teachers, administrators, and schools; and made other improvements. California, Florida, and Texas passed programs with similar components to improve education. Florida and Texas emphasized teacher pay and more state control over the educational program while California provided incentives to lengthen the school year and expanded its support of school initiated improvement (Odden 1984).

Many other states created less comprehensive programs designed to promote school improvement by raising promotion and graduation standards; increasing teacher certification requirements; providing incentive funds for higher performing teachers, administrators, or schools; strengthening the curriculum through more stringent requirements, textbook review, or curricular research; lengthening the school day or school year; increasing technical assistance; lowering pupil-teacher ratios; and so on. A portion of the funds supporting these efforts flow through traditional school finance formulas; many of the states making improvements in 1984 also expanded basic funding and funding of categorical programs. But much of the funding for the new, highly targeted efforts, particularly those focusing on teacher pay and fiscal incentives for high performance, was allocated outside of the equalization formulas used to provide the bulk of school support.

THE FUTURE OF SCHOOL FINANCING REFORM

School financing reform is unlikely to slow down in the years ahead. In fact, given the attention that education is receiving and the increasing share of state budgets that schools are consuming, school financing is likely to be of even greater interest in the future. The sluggishness of school financing reform in the early 1980s was related to the rapid, unanticipated deterioration of the states' fiscal conditions.

Although some recent school financing changes have already been described (Kirst 1983), school financing reformers have been reluctant to take an in-depth look at what happens to resources in schools and classrooms. This situation needs to change if school financing research is to be valuable in an era of fiscal constraint.

Circumstances already have begun to change. The states already have begun to recover from the fiscal doldrums of the early 1980s. The states, however, cannot guarantee good fiscal conditions. Many states now have become the major source of revenue for public schools; and education always is dependent on state support. Further, education's need for support will increase in the future as enrollment declines soften, teacher salary issues take center stage, and improvements are made in the services provided to special pupil populations.

School financing reform will continue in the future in part because the courts still are actively involved in reviewing the status of school financing systems. The courts played a more active role after the *Rodriquez* case, which reduced the likelihood that a single federal court decision would, in one blow, require change throughout the country. Recent decisions in Arkansas and West Virginia have resulted in bold efforts to link educational improvement and educational financing. The courts are reviewing school financing systems in Connecticut, New Hampshire, and New Jersey. Other states, such as Texas, are in the early stages of litigation. While the courts should not be expected to play the same role in the future that they played during the last decade, the legal presence will serve as a source of tension in the world of school financing.

The most important change likely to occur in school financing is that states will begin moving away from simply reimbursing districts for previous expenditures. The public's increasing demand for accountability combined with more conservative fiscal management will create the biggest challenge for school financing systems: to provide incentives for improvements in the efficiency and effectiveness of schools while assuring that resources, in terms of both "macro" objects such as money and "micro" objects such as curriculum or time, are distributed equitably. This balance may be difficult to achieve.

The most important issue that school financing systems will have to address in the next few years is teacher salaries. As noted previously, states have played an indirect role in determining teacher salary levels. Many states are considering actions similar to those taken in Tennessee, in 1984, that put the state into the business of evaluating teachers and paying a portion of their salaries. This practice raises numerous issues, one of which concerns the equity of providing what amounts to flat grants to teachers. The simple approach of having the state pay the full cost of a statewide career ladder may result in more state aid flowing to relatively wealthy districts, which attract high quality teachers by paying higher salaries. New approaches need to be found to make school financing systems more sensitive to teacher pay issues, including both how teachers are paid and how much they are paid.

The nation is in the midst of a school financing revolution. This is not a fad. Reform will continue in the future and will both shape and be shaped by school improvement. The quest for adequate and equitable funding has been rejuvenated by the desire to improve education's effectiveness.

REFERENCES

Advisory Commission on Intergovernmental Relations. 1983. *Significant Features of Fiscal Federalism, 1981–82 Edition.* Washington, D.C.

Augenblick, John. 1984a. "The States and School Finance: Looking Back and Looking Ahead." *Phi Delta Kappan* 66, no. 3 (November): 196–201.

____. 1984b. "Teacher Salaries and the States." Denver: Augenblick, Van de Water & Associates.

____. 1984c. "The Importance of Property Taxes to the Future of School Finance." *Journal of Education Finance* 9, no. 3 (Winter): 384–393.

Augenblick, John and Gordon Van de Water. 1983. *State Support for Education, 1982–83.* Denver: Augenblick Van de Water & Associates.

Brackett, John, Jay Chambers, and Thomas Parrish. 1983. "The Legacy of Rational Budgeting Models in Education and a Proposal for the Future." Project Report 83-A21. Stanford: Institute for Research on Educational Finance and Governance.

Brown, Patricia R., and Richard F. Elmore. 1982. "Analyzing the Impact of School Finance Reform." In *The Changing Politics of School Finance*, edited by Nelda H. Cambron-McCabe and Allan Odden, pp. 107–138, Cambridge, Mass.: Ballinger Publishing Company.

Carroll, Stephen. 1979. *The Search for Equity in School Finance: Results from Five States.* Santa Monica: The Rand Corporation.

Finn, Chester E., Jr., and Denis T. Doyle. 1985. "As States Take Charge of Schools: A New Plan." *Education Winter Survey, The New York Times*, January 6, 1985.

Fuhrman, Susan. 1982. "State-Level Politics and School Financing." In *The Changing Politics of School Finance*, edited by Nelda H. Cambron-McCabe and Allan Odden, pp. 53-70. Cambridge, Mass.: Ballinger Publishing Company.

Gold, Steven D., and Corina L. Eckl. 1984. "State Fiscal Conditions Entering 1984." Denver: National Conference of State Legislatures.

Hickrod, George Alan, and Margaret E. Goertz. 1983. "Introduction: Evaluating the School Finance Reforms of the 1970s and Early 1980s." *Journal of Education Finance* 8, no. 4 (Spring): 415-418.

Kirst, Michael W. 1983. "A New School Finance for a New Era of Fiscal Constraint." In *School Finance and School Improvement Linkages for the 1980s*, edited by Allan Odden and L. Dean Webb, pp. 1-15. Cambridge, Mass.: Ballinger Publishing Company.

McGuire, Kent, and Van Dougherty. 1984. "School Finance at a Glance, 1983-84" (Chart). Denver: Education Commission of the States.

National Commission on Excellence in Education. 1983. *A Nation at Risk.* Washington, D.C.: U.S. Government Printing Office.

National Education Association. 1980. *Estimates of School Statistics, 1979-80.* Washington, D.C.: National Education Association.

_____. 1984. *Estimates of School Statistics, 1983-84.* Washington, D.C.: National Education Association.

Odden, Allan. 1984. *Education Finance in the States: 1984.* Denver: Education Commission of the States.

Odden, Allan, C. Kent McGuire, and Grace Belsches-Simons. 1983. *School Finance in the States: 1983.* Denver: Education Commission of the States.

Odden, Allan, and John Augenblick. 1981. *School Finance Reform in the States: 1981.* Denver: Education Commission of the States.

Task Force on Education for Economic Growth. 1984. *Action in the States, Progress Toward Education Renewal.* Denver: Education Commission of the States.

2 NATIONAL LEGAL TRENDS

J. U. O'Hara

Discussing recent legal trends and predicting future legal trends is a very difficult task, which is caused primarily by the complexity of the U.S. legal system. Law is rarely a black or white subject; it is better described in terms of shadows and penumbras. Since the United States' legal structure is developed along both federal and state lines, at least two different lines of authority may develop on issues. In addition, state courts and legislatures frequently differ on issues, creating the possibility for another fifty different resolutions to the same problems. This complexity is acute in education since each state has preeminence in delivering educational services to its citizens, but the U.S. Congress and federal courts play a large role in developing the relationships between state and student and/or teacher. With this caveat, this chapter reports recent trends in U.S. education law, especially as it is related to the new fervor for "quality" education.

Education law during the late 1960s and early 1970s involved primarily philosophical issues. The courts, asked to address some basic social issues in our country, accepted this task, discussed the concepts of equality and liberty, and officially recognized the constitutional rights of students. During this period individuals went to courts and asked them to solve perceived injustices. Education law was centered in the federal courts and involved litigation between and among teachers, students, administrators, and parents asking for delineation of federal constitutional rights.

Throughout the 1970s the legal impact on education came mainly from the U.S. Congress. Before this time, federal regulation of education had been relatively minimal, but the same hand that began granting funds in the 1950s began regulating in the 1970s. During this time education faced the Lau regulations, the Buckley Amendment, Title IX, P.L. 94–142 and the more general type of regulations, such as OHSA, Title VI, and Title VII. The legislation was enacted primarily to ensure rights that had been delineated earlier by the federal courts.

FEDERAL INVOLVEMENT

During the 1960s and 1970s many important federal decisions were made about education, including in the 1970s policy and implementation decisions made by the U.S. Congress and federal administrative agencies. Now, in the 1980s the major substance of education law apparently will not be dealt with in the federal arena.

During the 1980s the U.S. Congress has done little proactively in the area of education, maintaining its dollar amount of funding and thereby reducing the percentage of funding granted to states under P.L. 94–142[1] and repealing the statute for education of the gifted.[2] Congress did develop the Department of Education,[3] whose very existence is a continued source of Administration debate.

The most noted exception to this inactivity is the recent passage of the Equal Access Act.[4] This federal statute prohibits any

> public secondary school which receives Federal financial assistance and which has a limited open forum to deny equal access or a fair opportunity to, or discriminate against, any students who wish to conduct a meeting within that limited open forum on the basis of the religious, political, philosophical, or other content of the speech at such meeting.[5]

The statute defines a "limited open forum" as any "offering to or opportunity for one or more noncurriculum related student groups to meet on school premises during noninstructional time,"[6] which is defined as that "time set aside by the school before actual classroom instruction begins or after actual classroom instruction ends."[7] According to the statute, school administrators retain full authority to maintain order and discipline on school grounds, protect the well-being of students and faculty, and ensure that student attendance at meetings is voluntary. The statute does not subject school systems to loss of federal funds if its requirements are violated, and it does not specifically outline other methods of enforcement.[8]

Even this piece of legislation, however, may have little or no impact on education nationally. The Third Circuit Court of Appeals recently overturned a district court's ruling allowing for similar access to students in the Williamsport, Pennsylvania School District.[9] The U.S. Supreme Court could determine the constitutionality of the Equal Access Act when it hears the appeal of this case, since any decision could be analogized to cover the Equal Access Act.[10]

Congressional inactivity persists in the face of numerous challenges to improve the quality of education nationwide. Taken with current budget concerns, little could happen to change the direction of this trend.

JUDICIAL INVOLVEMENT

During the 1960s and 1970s the courts made many policy decisions that impacted education. The early court decisions of the 1980s indicate an increased willingness to give local districts autonomy on most issues unless there is a constitutional or statutory violation. Recently in *Board of Education of Rogers v. McCluskey,*[11] the U.S. Supreme Court made it clear that local school boards will not be scrutinized on every decision they make. In *Rogers*, the Court overruled a lower court that, in its opinion, replaced the board's construction of a board rule with its own. The Court ruled that decisions will not be scrutinized unless unreasonable. By analogy the decision could be extended to other school officials. The courts will become involved only when school officials' actions are not reasonable. This decision, as well as the lack of federal involvement, indicates that the major substance of education and education law will be determined by the states and the local school boards. This contention can be tested in three areas of litigation: right to an education, educational malpractice, and educational questions.

Right to an Education

In 1973, the U.S. Supreme Court handed down a watershed opinion for education law. In *San Antonio School District v. Rodriguez,*[12] the Court ruled that the right to education was not a fundamental right under the U.S. Constitution.[13] The decision hinged on the fact that education is not found explicitly or implicitly in the Constitution, thus not granting any right to individuals, and leaving the power in the hands of the state and the people according to the Tenth Amendment. The history and impact of this opinion are well known. The decision sparked criticism and may have marked the beginning of the end to federal legislative and judicial involvement in education.

The 1982, the U.S. Supreme Court held in *Plyler v. Doe*[14] that the State of Texas could not exclude from the public schools undocumented alien children illegally residing in the state. The Court determined that Texas was in violation of the Equal Protection Clause of the Fourteenth Amendment when it refused to provide these children with the same educational services that were provided to other children residing in the state. In the decision the Court applied a stricter level of scrutiny than would have been expected under *Rodriguez*.[15] *Rodriguez* would have indicated that in order to justify a differentiation that would result in the loss of educational benefits the state must show only that the distinction was rationally based on a legitimate state interest: a traditional equal protection analysis for interests that are not of constitutional proportions. The distinction based on the children's status of illegal aliens did not trigger a stricter level of scrutiny. Nonetheless, the Court in *Plyler* did apply a slightly stricter level of scrutiny to the Texas statute in question.[16] Although still not recognizing education as a constitutionally protected right, the Court determined that the case involved an "area of special constitutional sensitivity"[17] requiring that the state distinction be rationally related to the furtherance of "some substantial goal of the State."[18] The Court emphasized that the children had no culpability in the matter because they did not control their parents' decision to enter the country illegally. In addition, the Court also emphasized that the opportunity to attend school was very important. In language reminiscent of *Brown v. Board of Education of Topeka*,[19] written nearly thirty years earlier, the Court stated:

> [E] ducation provides the basic tools by which individuals might lead economically productive lives to the benefit of us all. In sum, education has a fundamental role in maintaining the fabric of our society. We cannot ignore the significant social costs borne by our Nation when select groups are denied the means to absorb the values and skills upon which our social order rests.[20]

Thus, almost ten years after *Rodriguez*, the U.S. Supreme Court may have softened slightly the impact of its earlier decision. It is too early to determine the significance of this decision and whether the stricter level of scrutiny will be applied generally in education decisions. As one commentator has suggested (McCarthy 1983):

> Based on the precedent established in *Plyler*, possibly courts in the future will be more inclined to apply the intermediate test in assessing equal protection challenges to state school finance plans and to other classifications affecting the receipt of educational benefits. Although the total denial of an education was at issue in *Plyler*, this decision will likely be relied upon in subsequent challenges to various disparities in public school opportunities within states. If the Supreme Court should declare that state action resulting in educational inequities as well as complete deprivation must be justified as advancing a substantial state objective, a new era in educational litigation will be launched.

Nonetheless, the *Plyler* decision so far has not had the explosive or immediate impact that *Rodriguez* had, nor is it clear that the intermediate level of scrutiny would be applied under a different set of facts. The plight of the children in this case was deemed to be tragic; through no fault of their own they were being totally excluded from the educational system. *Plyler* appears to be one of the very few cases in which the courts are willing to become involved. In light of other events in the decade, the intermediate level of scrutiny used in *Plyler v. Doe* may be an isolated incident of judicial activism.

Educational Malpractice

Educational malpractice refers to negligence on the part of an educational professional. Negligence is the omission to do something that a reasonable person, guided by ordinary considerations, would do, or the doing of something that a reasonable and prudent person would not do. To recover in a negligence action, the plaintiff must prove that a duty was owed to the plaintiff, the defendant breached that duty through negligence, and the negligence was the proximate cause of the plaintiff's injuries (Prosser 1971).

The seminal case in educational malpractice is *Peter W. v. San Francisco Unified School District.*[21] *Peter W.* received a high school diploma from the San Francisco schools. Although a California statute requires graduates to be able to read at over the eighth grade level,[22] *Peter W.* was functionally illiterate at the time of his graduation. He sued the district for not teaching him basic skills and allowing him to graduate. The lower court's dismissal of the action was upheld by the California Court of Appeals, which discussed at length the "duty" requirement as it exists in negligence law and found no legal duty on which to base an action. Also, the court concluded there was no workable standard of care against which to gauge a district's or teacher's actions to determine reasonability. In addition, the court noted that the degree of certainty that the plaintiff had suffered an injury, the extent of the injury, and the establishment of a causal link between defendants' conduct and plaintiff's injuries were all highly problematic. The court also noted that it could not recognize the cause of action for public policy reasons including the possible strain on the public school system and the possible flood of litigation that might be created.

Even after this case, some have suggested that educational malpractice claims may replace physical injury suits as the biggest legal threat to education (Connors 1981), and litigation still continued at the same pace. Nonetheless, the courts so far have been adamant about not recognizing the cause of action. Courts in Maryland,[23] New York,[24] California,[25] and Alaska[26] have all rejected educational malpractice suits. The rejections of these claims, as was the opinion in *Peter W.*, have been based primarily on three considerations: "the absence of a workable rule of care against which defendant's conduct may be measured, the inherent uncertainty in determining the cause and nature of any damages, and the extreme burden which would be imposed on the already strained resources of the public school system to say nothing of the judiciary."[27] Although these may be valid points, the courts' reluctance may be explained better as a desire not to become entwined in the educational workings of the public schools.

The courts' refusals to accept educational malpractice as a valid cause of action may benefit schools by denying actions that may result in monetary damages. Nonetheless, the court's refusals may not benefit the educational profession. Although the *Peter W.* decision may have been meant as a defense of public education, its language is a good example of the court's reluctance to interfere in education. The result was an insult to the educational profession in this situation.

> Few of our institutions, if any, have aroused the controversies, or incurred the public dissatisfaction, which have attended the operation of the public schools during the last few decades. Rightly or wrongly, but widely, they are charged with outright failure in the achievement of their educational objectives; according to some critics, they bear responsibility for many of the social and moral problems of our society at large. Their public plight in these respects is attested in the daily media, in bitter governing board elections, in wholesale rejections of school bond proposals, and in survey upon survey.[28]

This gallant protection of the public school system by the judiciary has been criticized by the commentators (Hooker 1982):

> This defense of the schools cannot be maintained indefinitely. Just as the courts effectively addressed the issue of equality of educational opportunity . . . the courts must not confront the issue of equality of educational quality. This will require a more thorough examination of the performance of educators, holding them to a standard of care in the delivery of their services as is typically applied in other professions. The responsibilities of educators then will become commensurate with the privileges and advantages of the profession that educators presently enjoy.

"Failure to learn," the type of educational malpractice issue presented in *Peter W.*, is not likely to be recognized as a valid cause of action in the near future. Although dismissals of the cause of action are usually couched in terms of "duty" and "causation," the primary reasons appear to be the unwillingness of the court to inject its presence into the educational workings of the school. In *Donohue v. Copiague Union Free School District,*[29] the court made this idea more apparent in noting that recognition of this cause of action would require the courts to make judgments on the validity of broad educational policies and might eventually require the court's hand in reviewing the implementation of policies.

Educational Questions

Historically the courts have refused to intrude on issues that are strictly academic in nature, leaving these areas to the discretion of the educational experts. Educational areas include the assignment of grades, promotion to the next grade, academic requirements, and academic dismissals. The courts have deferred to the educational experts in these areas unless a showing of malice, arbitrariness, or bad faith has been made.

In *Board of Curators of University of Missouri v. Horowitz,*[30] the United States Supreme Court drew a sharp distinction between academic dismissals and disciplinary dismissals. In that case, Charlotte Horowitz was dismissed from the University of Missouri Medical School shortly before her graduation on the grounds that she lacked personal hygiene and did not relate well to patients and colleagues. Horowitz had received high scores on the admissions tests and academically was in the top of her class. The school, however, required more of their candidates than these objective criteria. The Supreme Court upheld her dismissal. In doing so the court did not decide whether students facing academic dismissals were entitled to procedural due process but held that if due process is required, it is of a different nature than the due process required for disciplinary decisions. Regarding the actual substance of the grading procedure, the court noted that lower courts have stated or implied that academic dismissals can be overturned if shown to be made in bad faith, to be malicious, or to be arbitrary or capricious. However, courts will not evaluate otherwise purely academic decisions.[31]

Primary and secondary schools cases focus more on the validity of grading, testing, promotion, and graduation requirements than the validity of academic dismissals. Nonetheless, the general rule as set forth in *Horowitz* can be applied to issues in public elementary and secondary schools. In sum, the courts will not second guess an academic decision made by educational experts but instead will defer to the educators unless there is a showing of malice, arbitrariness, or bad faith. Schools are organized to insure that correct academic decisions are made; thus, the scoring and subjective scrutiny teachers give to their students' work is acceptable unless it can be shown that the grading was arbitrary or unreasonable. At that point, the decisionmaking process itself will be questioned.

In *Sandlin v. Johnson,*[32] four students questioned the school's decision not to promote them from the second to the third grade. The basis for the denial was the students' failure to complete the requisite level on the Ginn reading series. The court refused to scrutinize the decision made, deferring to the educational authorities. "Decisions by educational authorities which turn on evaluation of the academic performance of a student as it relates to promotion are peculiarily within the expertise of educators and are particularly inappropriate for review in a judicial context."[33]

In *Brookhart v. Illinois State Board of Education,*[34] the court was asked to scrutinize the state's requirement of passing a minimum competency test for high school graduation. The Seventh Circuit refused to second guess the substance of this regulation. "The School District's desire to ensure the value of its diploma by requiring graduating students to attain minimal skills is admirable, and the courts will interfere with educational policy decisions only when necessary to protect individual statutory or constitutional rights."[35]

In sum, academic decisions are fairly sacrosanct from a court's perspective. Such decisions are scrutinized only when they are challenged as unreasonable. Basically, academic decisions have been found to be unreasonable only when there is no connection between the academic performance and academic penalty, when they are arbitrary, capricious, or malicious. This long-standing hands-off policy continues into the 1980s.

STATE INVOLVEMENT

States, unlike the federal government, have inherent "police powers," the sovereign prerogative of the state to impose restrictions upon private rights as long as these restrictions are reasonably related to the public welfare. Although parents have a recognized natural right to control their children, the state, as part of its police power, may preempt that right when the state's interest in preserving the general welfare overrides the parents' interests. The state as *parens patriae* may also restrict the parent's right to control to guard the child's well-being.[36] Thus the state can require that a child attend school, thereby subordinating the natural rights of the parents to custody and control of their children to the state's interest in an educated citizenry. In this context, the constitutionality of statutes like compulsory attendance statutes is now beyond question. As Justice Reynolds in *Meyers v. Nebraska*[37] stated: "The power of the state to compel attendance at some school and to make reasonable regulations for all schools is not questioned."[38]

In the 1980s, the states may use that sovereign prerogative to bolster education. Although many states are not increasing their funding of education, states are increasing their regulation of education in response to recent national attacks on education. Most of the new state regulations deal either with the quality of the school program, teacher competency, or student competency. The remainder of this chapter will discuss these issues.

Quality of School Programs

In an attempt to respond to the attacks on education, some states have made statutory changes in school programs. In public schools, requirements such as curriculum, qualifications of staff, and facilities may be mandated simply. Dealing with private schools, however, is more difficult for legislatures. To ensure that an adequate education is provided to all students, many states include in the accreditation process quality regulations that are used to determine a "school" for the purposes of compulsory attendance statutes. Recently an objection to this type of state regulation has been raised. Those who object contend nonpublic schools cannot fulfill their distinctive educational goals if the requirements for accreditation preclude them from independently determining the content and style of their own programs. The most frequent and compelling argument raised is that the requirements contained in, and the process of, state accreditation unduly burden the free exercise of religion by mandating how a school must carry out the congregation's religious duty of educating its children. In mediating this controversy the U.S. courts have spoken most recently on the competing interest of parents and the state in the field of education and the free exercise of religion.

Even though the free exercise of religion is guaranteed by the First Amendment, the government is not rendered powerless to regulate. Although the right to religious beliefs is absolute, the right to act on those beliefs is not. The government still has the authority to regulate actions, even if religiously motivated, to protect the safety and peace of all of its citizens. When government regulations enacted for a valid purpose interfere with religious activity, a balance between the two competing interests must be struck; a reconciliation must be reached that requires the weighing of the respective interests involved.[39] The constitutional right to free exercise of religion must be balanced against the state's need to legislate for the common good. Generally the balance is struck so that when a religious activity is directly interfered with, the power to regulate is allowed to be exercised only when necessary to a compelling governmental concern, and in a manner that is the least restrictive or burdensome to the activity.

This balancing of interests approach is by its nature extremely fact oriented and does not lend itself well to rigid definition or litmus-type tests. The U.S. Supreme Court set forth a basic balancing analysis in *Wisconsin v. Yoder.*[40] This test has been used frequently in cases where a state had exercised its power to regulate for the purpose of educating its citizens and those regulations were contested on the basis of infringing on free exercise of religion. The type of analysis involves a determination of whether the activity interfered with, was motivated by, and was central to a legitimate and sincerely held religious belief; the regulation burdened the parties' free exercise of religion, and if so, to what extent; and the state had an interest that would be furthered by the regulation commensurate with the burden caused by it.

These issues were presented in *State ex rel. Douglas v. Faith Baptist Church of Louisville.*[41] In this case, the trial court had granted an injunction against the Faith Baptist Church's operation of an elementary and secondary school for their failing to comply with the state's accreditation requirements. Those requirements included a prescribed core curriculum, specified material and equipment, health and safety regulations, and the filing of attendance and biannual reports. The Faith Christian School was in operation without accreditation contrary to the Nebraska statute. The Faith Christian School used the Accelerated Christian Education method of instruction under the supervision of nonaccredited teachers. The school refused to file any reports with the state or subject itself to state inspection for the purposes of accreditation. The church argued that the operation of the school was an extension of religion over which the state could have no legitimate authority. Thus, it was the process of accreditation itself that was objectionable to the church, not any of the underlying requirements. The Supreme Court of Nebraska, using the *Yoder* analysis, found the system of accreditation was necessary to protect the state's interest in education. The requirements the state imposed for accreditation were not unreasonable nor unduly burdensome to the free exercise of religion. The court concluded: "Although parents have a right to send their children to schools other than public institutions, they do not have the right to be completely unfettered by reasonable government regulations as to the quality of the education furnished."[42]

Similar holdings have been made in other states; the finding appears to be a good summary of the current state of the law. In sum, rulings thus far indicate that state legislatures have the authority to regulate for the purposes of ensuring quality in education in both public and private schools. This general rule will continue to be crucial during the 1980s as state legislatures emerge preeminent in their attempts to regulate schools to improve educational quality.

Teacher Competency

Assessment of teacher competency has received increased public and legislative attention during the past decade and is one way in which states have used substantive quality regulations in an attempt to improve education. Certification requirements are a state prerogative; as long as the requirements are reasonably related to the state's interest in students receiving an education and do not otherwise violate a person's rights, they have been upheld. The requirement of use of certified teachers in schools has been found to be a valid regulation even in light of First Amendment claims.

In 1979, a Gallup poll surveyed citizens to determine what U.S. schools should do to rate an "A" in performance. The number one response was to improve the quality of teachers. Also the survey asked: "In addition to meeting college requirements for a teacher's certificate, should those who want to become teachers also be required to pass a state board examination to prove their knowledge in the subject(s) they will teach before they are hired?" Eighty-five percent of those polled answered in the affirmative. Eighty-five percent also answered yes to the question: "After they are hired, do you think teachers should be tested every few years to see if they are keeping up to date with developments in their field?" (Townsel 1983).

By 1982, thirty-six states tested teacher competency in some way as part of the certification process. Eleven of these states used the National Teacher Examination as an entry level certification requirement. The most objection to competency tests for teacher certification purposes has come from minority groups who have alleged that the tests are racially discriminatory.

This argument was tested in *United States v. State of South Carolina.*[43] Since 1945, the state of South Carolina has required a minimum score on the National Teachers Examination to certify teachers and determine the amount of state aid payable to local school districts. Local districts have used the scores to make selection and pay level decisions. Historically, more blacks than whites have failed to achieve the minimum score required for minimal certification. For example, in 1969–1970, 41 percent of blacks apparently failed to achieve a passing score in comparison to 1 percent of white applicants. The court was presented with both a Title VII[44] and Fourteenth Amendment claim. However, the court addressed only the discrimination claim under Title VII to rule in favor of the state requirement. The court determined that the test was a valid assessment of a teacher's knowledge. As such, the state had a rational reason to administer the test and the reason was rationally related to the state's interest in educating students. The court held that, even though the use of scores on the National Teacher's Examination had a disparate impact on racial minorities, a valid business purpose existed and thus was not a violation of Title VII.

South Carolina's use of the same exam was again challenged in *Newman v. Crews.*[45] There, the test was being used to determine certification levels, promotions, and pay raises. Black teachers predominated the lower certification levels and more frequently were denied pay raises because of lower scores on the exam. The issue of discrimination under Title VII was raised again. The court recognized that use of the exam had a disproportionate impact on black teachers, but found that the requirement served a legitimate employment objective of the state and the district. The court found that the exam was a valid gauge of a teacher's subject matter knowledge and might be less discriminatory than subjective evaluations. Thus, the use of the exam was in furtherance of the state's interest in upgrading its schools.

In sum, a state can enact an employment practice even though the practice has a disparate impact on a racial minority if that practice serves the legitimate employment objectives of the state. This general rule reiterates the larger concept that states have the authority to regulate for the purposes of ensuring quality in education as long as the regulation and the state's interest in assuring quality education to its citizens are reasonably related.

Student Competency

Up to this point the only state quality initiatives discussed have been input initiatives: state certification and accreditation requirements. In addition to these initiatives, some states have enacted output initiatives such as substantive graduation requirements or competency testing as a graduation requirement.

By 1984, thirty-seven state legislators had enacted student minimum competency legislation (Logar 1984) with legislation pending in another four states.[46] In fifteen states,[47] students are required to take and pass minimum competency tests before receiving a high school diploma; in seven states,[48] minimum competency tests are administered and the results are used for studies only; in eight states,[49] tests are administered and the local district decides how to deal with the results; and the remaining seven states, have differing requirements for testing and using results.

The primary use of the minimum competency test is that of an additional requirement for graduation. The testing requirement in this capacity has been challenged by students. Among the challenges that students might and have presented are that withholding a diploma based on the test results:

- constitutes a denial of equal protection of the laws if the program functions in an arbitrary or capricious manner,
- denies students due process of law if implemented with insufficient phase-in time or if it covers material not covered in the curriculum,
- constitutes discrimination on the basis of race or ethnicity,
- denies handicapped students an appropriate education in violation of state and federal statutes, and
- represents discrimination on the basis of handicap in violation of state or federal civil rights statutes.

Probably the most noted case dealing with challenges of the first three types is *Debra P. v. Turlington.*[50] In 1976, the Florida Legislature passed an act that set minimum high school graudation requirements beginning with the 1978–79 school year. In 1978, the statute was amended to require students to pass a functional literacy examination before they were allowed to graduate.[51] The Fourth Circuit Court of Appeals found the implementation of the requirement of passage of the functional literacy test on the class of 1979 without warning or time to prepare violated the students' procedural due process rights because a property interest in their diploma was denied without notice in some cases. The test also was found to be racially discriminatory since some students who were required to pass the test for graduation had been denied equal educational opportunities in their district in previous years. The cure for this ill, however, was only to delay the implementation of the testing requirement. Substantively the requirement was questioned by the court of appeals as "fundamentally unfair in that it may have covered matters not taught."[52] The court, however, clearly specified that the decision did not mean they were trying to set graduation requirements for the state but only were trying to guarantee that the requirements the state chose be fair. The case was remanded to the district court to determine if the test was instructionally valid and if the subjects tested were actually taught in the schools. The district court, after hearing a substantial amount of evidence, found that the tested subjects and skills were

> included in the official curriculum and that the majority of the teachers recognize them as being something they should teach. . . . Although the instruction offered in all the classrooms of the district might not be ideal, students are nevertheless afforded an adequate opportunity to learn the skills tested on the SSAT-II before it was issued as a diploma sanction.[53]

A similar result was reached in *Anderson v. Banks,*[54] in which the students questioned the use of the California Achievement Test as a valid requirement for high school graduation.

The other typical area of litigation in the area of minimum competency testing involves handicapped students. Two reported court decisions on these issues exist. Although the outcome of these cases differs due to differing fact situations, some general conclusions can be gleaned from the cases when read together. Statutory rights of handicapped students are not violated by requirements to pass a minimum competency test to qualify for a high school diploma. However, if these students are included in the testing requirement, sufficient provisions must be made to ensure that handicapped students also have an adequate opportunity to prepare and to participate successfully in the testing program. The adequacy of the opportunity provided to these students is measured, not as it would be for general students but, by looking at the individualized needs of each handicapped student.

In *Brookhart v. Illinois State Board,*[55] the court dealt with a competency test required by the Peoria School Board that was formally approved in 1978 and implemented with the 1980 graduating class. Under the program, a student had five opportunities to pass a three-part test prior to graduation. Any student who did not pass all three parts of the test was given the opportunity to retake the failed portion of the exam, which was administered once a semester. Remedial materials and course work were made available to all students in need of them. Students who were unable to pass all three portions of the test by their twenty-first birthday or who choose not to retake the exam were awarded a "Certificate of Program Completion" rather than a standard diploma. The program was challenged under the Education for All Handicapped Children Act, P.L. 94–141.[56] In response, the Seventh Circuit Court of Appeals stated:

> Denial of diplomas to handicapped children who have been receiving the special education and related services required by the Act, but are unable to achieve the educational level necessary to pass the [minimum competency test], is not a denial of a "free appropriate public education."[57]

Similarly the New York Court of Appeals found no violation of P.L. 94–142 in a state imposed minimum competency requirement in *Board of Education of Northport-East Northport Union Free School District v. Ambach.*[58] The court found that "under the circumstances of this case the petitioning students had no reasonable expectation of receiving a high school diploma without passing competency tests."[59]

Neither court found discrimination under Section 504 of the Rehabilitation Act.[60] The Seventh Circuit determined that the content of the test did not have to be substantively altered to accommodate students' handicaps; nor was it discrimination to refuse handicapped students who could not pass the test a standard diploma.

The courts, however, have found some merit in the plaintiffs' due process arguments in relation to the provisions of P.L. 94–142. In *Brookhart*, the court determined that some of the plaintiffs had not been afforded adequate notice to prepare for the minimum competency test. However, not all handicapped students' programs must be geared toward passing the test either. The court stated:

> Though we are unable on this record to define "adequate notice" in terms of a specific number of years, the School District can be assured that the requirement would be satisfied if one of the following two conditions for adequate notice is met. The School District can, first, ensure that handicapped students are sufficiently exposed to most of the material that appears on the [minimum competency test], or second, they can produce evidence of a reasoned and well-informed decision by the parents and teachers involved that a particular high school student will be better off concentrating on educational objectives other than preparation for the [minimum competency tests].[61]

Thus, to be "appropriate" under P.L. 94-142 or provide sufficient due process guarantees, not all handicapped students' programs must have as their ultimate objective passage of the minimum competency test.

In sum, the states are free to enact reasonable graduation requirements including the passing of a minimum competency examination. Equal protection guarantees are not violated if the programs are reasonable and do not function in an arbitrary or capricious manner. Due process guarantees are not violated if the students have been given sufficient opportunity to learn the material upon which they are tested. Minorities' civil rights are not violated, although graduation requirements normally have a disparate impact. Finally, handicapped students are not discriminated against nor denied their right to an appropriate education since graduation requirements do not have to be substantively altered to accommodate handicapped students and since a student's educational program does not have to result in passing the exam to be appropriate.

CONCLUSIONS

Education law during the late 1960s and early 1970s involved primarily philosophical issues. The U.S. courts were asked to address some basic social issues. The courts accepted this task and discussed the concepts of equality and liberty and officially recognized the constitutional rights of students. During this period, individuals went to courts and asked the courts to solve perceived social injustices. Education law was centered in the federal courts and involved litigation between and among teachers, students, administrators, and parents, who asked for delineation of federal constitutional rights.

The next phase of education law was played out in a different arena. Throughout the 1970s the legal impact on education came mainly from the U.S. Congress. Before this time federal regulation of education had been relatively minimal. But the same hand that began granting funds in the 1950s began regulating in the 1970s. During this time education faced the Lau regulations, the Buckley Amendment, Title IX, P.L. 94–142, and the more general type of regulations, such as OSHA, Title VI, and Title VII. The legislation was enacted primarily to insure the rights that had earlier been delineated by the federal courts.

Education law during the coming decade appears to be centered in the state legislatures and on the local boards of education. The other primary actors in the field (the federal Congress and administrative bodies and the judiciary) seem to be willing to adopt a hands-off approach and allow educational practice and policy to be determined by the state and local districts unless deemed unreasonable or in violation of statutory or constitutional rights.

The U.S. Congress has played a very inactive role over the last few years. It has not been willing to approach education from a national perspective and address the problems that have come recently into the public consciousness. Although Congress has made some increased spending provisions for math and science programs, Congress also has maintained its dollar level of funding for handicapped programs and thereby decreased the federal percentage of funding for programs for handicapped students. The only active part Congress has played in education recently has been the passage of the Equal Access Act, the constituionality of which is currently in question.

The courts also are currently engaged in a hands off policy toward schools. The courts still are unwilling to find a federal constitutional right to an education even though the rhetoric of that line of cases recently has been softened, to recognize educational malpractice as a valid cause of action, and to engage educational questions, especially when they are academic judgments. In sum, recent cases indicate that the courts are willing to become involved only when school officials actions are not reasonable or if they clearly violate statutory or constitutional provisions.

State legislatures, however, have begun to take a more active role in education. Some states, in an attempt to respond to recent attacks on education, have made statutory changes in school programs. Changes that have been enacted include upgrading curriculum requirements, staff qualifications, and graduation requirements. The courts have upheld these legislative attempts at improving education in spite of challenges made on such grounds as race discrimination, discrimination against the handicapped, infringement on the free exercise of religion, and denials of due process. The courts virtually have given the legislatures free rein as long as there is evidence that the state's programs are related to the state interest in providing education to its citizens. As such, during the 1980s the arena for change, if any is to occur, is in the state legislatures.

NOTES TO CHAPTER 2

1. P.L. 94-142, 20 U.S.C. §§1101 et seq. (1978).
2. P.L. 95-561, 20 U.S.C. §§2701 et seq. (1978), repealed (1980).
3. P.L. 96-88, 20 U.S.C. §§3401 et seq. (1984).
4. P.L. 98-377, 20 U.S.C. §§4071 et seq. (1985).
5. 20 U.S.C. §4071(a) (1985).
6. Id. §4071(b) (1985).
7. Id. §4072(4) (1985).
8. Id. §4071(e) (1985).
9. 563 F. Supp. 697 (M.D.Pa. 1983), *rev'd*, 741 F.2d 538 (3d Cir. 1984), *cert. granted*, 105 S.Ct. 1167 (1985) (No. 84-773).
10. P.L. 98-377, 20 U.S.C. §§4071 et seq. (1985).
11. 458 U.S. 966 (1982).
12. 411 U.S. (1973).
13. 441 U.S. at 35.
14. 457 U.S. 202 (1982).
15. 411 U.S. (1973).
16. Tex. Educ. Code, §21.031 (Vernon Supp. 1982).
17. 457 U.S. at 226.
18. Id. at 224.
19. 347 U.S. 483 (1954).
20. 457 U.S. at 221.
21. 60 Cal. App. 3d 814, 131 Cal. Rptr. 854 (1976).
22. California Education Code §8573.
23. *Hunter v. Board of Educ. of Montgomery County*, 439 A.2d 582 (Md. 1982).
24. *Hoffman v. Board of Educ. of City of New York*, 49 N.Y.2d 121, 424 N.Y.S.2d 376, 400 N.E.2d 317 (1979); *Donohue v. Copiague Union Free*

School District, 47 N.Y.2d 440, 418 N.Y.S.2d 375, 391 N.E.2d 1352 (1979).

25. *Peter W. v. San Francisco Unified School District*, 60 Cal. App. 3d 814, 131 Cal. Rep. 854 (1976).
26. *D.S.W. v. Fairbanks North Star Board School District*, 628 P.2d 554 (Alaska 1981).
27. *Hunter*, 439 A.2d at 584.
28. 60 Cal. App. 3d at 825, 131 Cal. Rptr. at 861.
29. 47 N.Y.2d 440, 418 N.Y.S.2d 375, 391 N.E.2d 1352 (1979).
30. 435 U.S. 78 (1978).
31. 435 U.S. at 91. Also *State ex rel. Miller v. McLeod*, 605 S.W.2d 160 (Mo. App. 1980).
32. 643 F.2d 1027 (1981).
33. Id. at 1024.
34. 697 F.2d 179 (7th Cir. 1983).
35. Id. at 182.
36. *Prince v. Massachusetts*, 321 U.S. 158 (1944).
37. 262 U.S. 390 (1923).
38. 262 U.S. at 402.
39. Konigsberg v. State Bar of California, 366 U.S. 36 (1961).
40. 406 U.S. 205 (1972).
41. 207 Neb. 802, 301 N.W.2d 571 (1981), *appeal dismissed*, 434 U.S. 803, (1981), *aff'd sub nom.*, In Re Contempt of Liles, 217 Neb. 414, 349 N.W.2d 377 (1984).
42. 301 N.W.2d at 579.
43. 445 F. Supp. 1094 (D.S.C. 1977), *aff'd mem.*, 434 U.S. 1026 (1978).
44. 42 U.S.C. §§2000e et seq. (1970).
45. 651 F.2d 222 (4th Cir. 1981).
46. Iowa, Minnesota, North Dakota, and South Dakota, id.
47. Alabama, Arizona, California, Delaware, Florida, Georgia, Maine, Maryland, Nevada, New York, North Carolina, Oregon, Tennessee, Utah, Vermont, Virginia, and Wyoming, id. at 39.
48. Arkansas, Kentucky, Louisiana, Missouri, Nebraska, New Jersey, and Rhode Island, id.
49. Colorado, Idaho, Indiana, Kansas, Massachusetts, Michigan, New Hampshire, and Washington, id.
50. 655 F.2d 397 (5th Cir. 1981), *on remand*, 564 F. Supp. 177 (M.D. Fla. 1983), *aff'd*, 730 F.2d 1405 (11th Cir. 1984).
51. Fla. Stat. Ann. §232.246 (West Supp. 1980).
52. 644 F.2d 397 at 404.
53. 564 F. Supp. at 186.
54. 540 F. Supp. 761 (S.D. Ga. 1982).
55. 534 F. Supp. 725 (C.D. Ill, 1982), *rev'd*, 697 F.2d 179 (7th Cir. 1983).

56. 20 U.S.C. §§1401 et seq. (1978).
57. 697 F.2d 183.
58. 436 N.Y.S.2d 564, *modified*, 458 N.Y.S.2d 680, *aff'd.*, 469 N.Y.S.2d 669, 457 N.E.2d 775 (Ct. App. 1983), *cert. denied*, 104 S. Ct. 1598 (1984).
59. 469 N.Y.S.2d at 669, 457 N.E.2d at 775.
60. 29 U.S.C. §§794 et seq. (1978).
61. 697 F.2d at 187.

REFERENCES

Conners, Eugene T. 1981. *Educational Tort Liability and Malpractice.* Bloomington, Ind.: Phi Delta Kappa.

Hooker, Clifford. 1982. "Maryland High Court Rules Out Educational Malpractice Suits: *Hunter v. Board of Education of Montgomery County.*" *Education Law Reporter* 2: 625-630.

Logar, Antoinette. 1984. "Minimum Competency Testing in Schools: Legislative Action and Judicial Review." *Journal of Law and Education* 3: 35-38.

McCarthy, Martha. 1983. "*Plyler v. Doe:* Issues and Implications." *Education Law Reporter* 7: 235-240.

Prosser, W. 1971. *Handbook on the Law of Torts, 4th ed.* St. Paul: West Publishing Company.

Townsel, Alvin. 1983. "*Whaley v. Anoka-Hennepin:* A New Standard of Tenured-Teacher Competency Assessment in Minnesota." *Education Law Reporter* 11: 755-758.

3 THE POLITICAL CONTEXT OF SCHOOL REFORM

Lorraine M. McDonnell and Susan Fuhrman

How educational problems are addressed by state governments and subsequent policy is translated into practice depend on a variety of educational, organizational, and political factors. The educational dimension influences how a problem is defined and the range of technical solutions available; the organizational environment defines the administrative structures and capacity of implementing agencies. It is the political context, however, that determines whether school reform even reaches the state policy agenda or later and how broadly new policy initiatives are conceived.

During the past two years, not only has school reform reached the policy agendas of most states, but in a number of them, the resulting policy has been comprehensive in scope. In the expectation that educational outcomes can be significantly improved, state policymakers have intervened in every aspect of schooling from the level and kind of resources that support it to the instructional process itself. Student standards, school calendar and attendance, new or expanded instructional programs, teacher recruitment, training, certification, and compensation, administrator selection and compensation, and technology in the schools have each been the subject of either new legislation or state board of education regulations in at least half the states. The scope and rapidity of these actions raise fundamental questions about the political conditions that foster such broad-based reform policy.

In this chapter, we examine three questions:

- Why is education reform occurring now?
- Why has it spread so quickly across the states?
- Why have so many states adopted comprehensive approaches to reform?

In addressing these questions, we take a largely political science perspective and focus on those factors identified from past research as the most likely explanations for major policy innovation. The first section describes the scope of the current school reform movement and outlines the questions it raises about the interaction between problem definition and the manner and speed with which the political system responds. In the second section, we attempt to answer these questions by assessing which factors best explain the role of political context in shaping school reform policy. The concluding section looks ahead to identify how political factors are likely to affect the implementation of school reform measures.

THE STATES AND SCHOOL REFORM POLICY

Even the keenest observer surveying public education in 1982 could not have predicted that, within a year, the condition of the nation's public schools would be a page one story in every major newspaper in the country, and educational reform would move to the top of the policy agenda in a majority of states. At the national level, Ronald Reagan had been elected President on a platform that advocated abolishing the U.S. Department of Education, and federal spending for elementary and secondary education had dropped in real terms from $8.2 billion in 1979 to $6.7 billion in 1982 (Odden et al. 1983: 18).

At the state level, fiscal austerity, resulting from a deep recession and various tax limitation measures had seriously constrained state budgets. Governors showed little interest in educational policy beyond its impact on the total state budget, and a new generation of state legislators held little enthusiasm for a policy area where there were no longer "any goodies to hand out" (Rosenthal and Fuhrman 1981: 104). The client and professional groups that had traditionally come together to lobby in favor of increased funding for education were increasingly less able to present a united front. Teacher collective bargaining had pitted organized teachers against administrators and school boards; groups speaking for special needs students had different concerns than those representing the general education program; and moral issues like sex education and school prayer had further splintered education interest groups. Citizen support for the public schools was also on the wane. Less than a third of all registered voters had school-aged children (U.S. Department of Commerce 1979: 38), and the proportion of public school bond elections that were approved by the voters declined from a high of 74.7 percent in the mid-1960s to around 55 percent in the late 1970s (National Center for Educational Statistics 1981: 75).

Contrasted with this seeming disinterest in more activist educational policy were the problems the public schools faced. Those familiar with the schools recognized that while achievement was improving at the elementary level and in basic skills, it was falling at the secondary level, particularly in higher-order, analytical skills (NAEP 1982). Major teacher shortages loomed, especially in science and mathematics (Guthrie and Zusman 1982: 2–3), and new entrants into teaching scored significantly lower on basic measures of academic ability than those in other occupations requiring a comparable educational level (Vance and Schlechty 1982). Most states had responded to these problems in a limited way, for example, by requiring student competency tests for high school graduation. Yet in 1982, more comprehensive action by either states or the federal government seemed very unlikely.

By the fall of 1983, the picture had changed markedly. Not only had public education moved to center stage in the nation's electronic and print media, but state officials across the country were seriously considering comprehensive reforms that were costly and in the case of performance-based compensation for teachers and administrators, seriously challenged the status quo.

In the spring of 1983, several national commissions comprising government, academic, and business leaders released reports criticizing the state of U.S. schools and recommending a variety of reforms to promote educational excellence. *A Nation at Risk*, issued by the National Commission on Excellence, was the first and most influential largely because Ronald Reagan used its release as an occasion for advancing his administration's educational philosophy. The commission, an eighteen-member panel of university presidents, other educators, and policymakers appointed by Secretary of Education, T.H. Bell, recommended stronger curriculum content; increased course requirements and higher student standards generally; expanded hours of instruction; new approaches to attracting, training, and compensating teachers; and improved leadership and fiscal support. *A Nation at Risk* (1983) was immediately followed by: *Action for Excellence* (1983), a report of an Education Commission of the States task force; *Academic Preparation for College* (1983), released by the College Board; *Making the Grade* (1983), a report of a Twentieth Century Fund task force; *America's Competitive Challenge* (1983) by the Business-Higher Education Forum, and *Educating Americans for the 21st Century* (1983), released by the National Science Board. Although varying in emphasis and specifics, these reports made numerous recommendations along lines similar to the National Commission's about curriculum content, standards, and teaching. Most argued that the nation's future, particularly its economic viability, depended on such educational improvements. Even more attention was focused on education by the publication of a series of scholarly studies in succeeding months. Books by Ernest Boyer (1983), John Goodlad (1984), and Theodore Sizer (1984) assessed the state of American schools and recommended changes, including some far-reaching structural and organizational reforms.

Throughout 1983, and continuing into the following year, state governments enacted major educational reform legislation, and every one increased its educational budget. State revenues for education rose by $4.5 billion during the 1982–83 school year, over $2 billion in real terms. Estimates for 1983–84 projected a minimum of a billion dollars in real spending growth. Eight states that enacted or considered comprehensive educational reforms in 1983 linked those measures to increased budget allocations of 6 to 17 percent (Odden 1984). Almost all states are proposing continued increases in education spending for 1985–86, and virtually all states tackled at least three of the following substantive areas of education reform:

- teacher certification and training—including entrance and exit testing, scholarship programs, and loan programs;
- teacher compensation and career structure—including across-the-board or minimum salary increases, career ladder plans, and other incentive programs;

- governance and finance—including formula revisions and changes in governance structures at the state, local, or intermediate levels;
- school attendance, calendar, and class size—including longer instructional days and years, and revisions in the compulsory school age and in attendance policy;
- graduation standards—including new course requirements and exit-testing policies; and
- curriculum and testing—including more widespread assessments, new programs in computerized instruction, and school-based improvement projects.

As legislatures were enacting these reforms, governors, who had in many cases initiated them or established commissions to do so, were speaking about education and mobilizing public support. Half of the governors made education the top priority in their 1984 state-of-the-state messages.

Not only was it unlikely that education's new found prominence could have been predicted a year earlier, but the rapidity with which reform initiatives spread across the states could scarcely have been foretold. Historically, policies without specific federal fiscal incentives or sanctions have taken as long as fifty years to diffuse throughout the states. Diffusion studies of such "state preserve" policies have found that the mean rate of adoption is sixteen years for the first 25 percent of states, twenty-four years for the first 50 percent, and thirty-one years to reach 75 percent (Welch and Thompson 1980; Gray 1973). Diffusion rates have undoubtedly accelerated in recent years as the electronic and print media have grown in influence, and national organizations have increasingly used these channels in their agenda-setting activities. Even so, a number of educational reforms are spreading at an exceptionally rapid rate. In fact, many are diffusing even more quickly than another recent education initiative: school financing reform.

Twenty-eight states reformed their systems for financing education between 1971 and 1981, fifteen states between 1971 and 1973, and twenty-five by 1977. In other words, school financing reform reached 25 percent of the states within two years, and half within six, for a diffusion rate that was more than twice the expected one for state preserve policies (Brown and Elmore 1982). Yet the most prevalent current educational reform, a revision of course requirements for high school graudation, is spreading even more quickly. By early 1985, forty-one states increased requirements by legislation, regulation, or state board of education policy; three states addressed the issue using guidelines. At least two other states are considering increasing their requirements. One state, New Jersey, acted in 1981; two states, Nevada and Ohio, acted in 1982. The remaining forty-one acted in 1983, 1984, and 1985. Thus, the first 50 percent raised their graduation requirements within three years; within one more year, 75 percent of the states had acted (U.S. Department of Education 1984; *Education Week* 1985).

Reforms that have not reached all the states are also diffusing very rapidly. Half established loan or scholarship aid for prospective teachers, primarily in shortage areas, with these actions all occurring since 1982. In addition, some states with long-established scholarship programs modified or expanded them during this same period. Eighteen states raised minimum teacher salaries or granted across-the-board increases between 1982 and 1984. Seventeen others have such proposals under consideration in 1985. Between 1978 and 1984, twenty-nine states mandated the passage of an examination as a precondition for teacher certification or as a requirement for satisfactorily completing a teacher education program. The first 25 percent acted within five years; 50 percent adopted this reform within seven. Fifteen states acted in 1984 alone (Goertz, Eckstrom, and Coley 1984; Education Week 1985). Similarly, programs based on the effective schools research have been identified in fifteen states; five were enacted between 1979 and 1981 and ten were introduced or overhauled in 1982 and 1983 (Dougherty 1983). It is clear that many current educational reforms are spreading at nearly twice the rate of school finance reform. Some of those not yet reaching half the states appear to be spreading at an even more rapid rate.

Policymakers do not make such far-reaching reforms very often; even more infrequently do they fashion a number of them together in a single piece of legislation. Generally, policymakers act incrementally, making minor modifications rather than radical changes. They often do this because they lack the time to investigate all possible alternatives, are uncertain or fearful of the consequences of new and different approaches, and have a great deal invested in the status quo. Agreement is also much easier, and conflict minimized when debate is confined to small alterations in policy, especially in education where the kind of consensus on societal goals that could set the parameters for major new policy directions is generally lacking (Lindblom 1959).

Even legislatures that have been notably active in education have commonly made reforms in a serial fashion. They have addressed one or two important educational issues each year or session, rather than bundling a set of major items together at one time. For example, the Florida legislature developed a general revision of the school code in 1972. In 1973, the legislature concentrated on early childhood education and basic skills; the next year it passed the Accountability Act of 1976. In 1977, it enacted a compensatory education act (Rosenthal and Fuhrman 1982).

Florida is a striking example of a state that in 1983 deviated from its past incremental approach to educational reform policy. In legislation that year, Florida tackled school standards, the length of the school day, teacher incentives, teacher preparation, and special initiatives for mathematics and science. Accomplishing such sweeping legislation is difficult, even if its components are widely supported. In Florida's case, however, the reform included several highly controversial items, such as merit pay for teachers. The legislation was also extremely specific about a number of schooling issues. For example, it specified the appropriate level of progress towards the doctoral degree for visiting scholars in elementary and secondary schools and required regular writing assignments for high school students.

Florida's program reflects unprecedented legislative intervention into the substance and structure of schooling, even for its traditionally activist legislature. Perhaps an even truer measure of how unique recent reforms are, however, can be seen in the actions of states not traditionally known for their innovativeness. South Carolina's 1984 reform is even more comprehensive in scope than Florda's, and some aspects of its program are extremely innovative, offering significant potential for improving educational practice. In addition to all the areas of reform addressed by Florida, South Carolina's legislation included a major effort in remedial education, a program for disadvantaged four-year-olds, and a variety of incentive grants to be awarded to high-performing schools, teachers, and principals.

A number of other states have also enacted broad-based reforms. Among them are Arkansas, California, North Carolina, Tennessee, and Texas. Yet even those states not enacting such wide-ranging initiatives have addressed several major issues simultaneously. Over a period of two or three years, such states may achieve much of what the most comprehensive ones accomplished in one legislative session.

The school reforms initiated in 1983 and 1984, then, differed in several important ways from past ones. In contrast to earlier post-war reforms, like those of the Sputnik and Great Society eras, these were state, not federally-sponsored. Unlike school financing reform, they were directed at the core processes of schooling—who teaches, what is to be learned, and in some cases, even how it is to be learned. And unlike earlier programs directed primarily at special subgroups (e.g., the poor, limited English-speaking, gifted, and handicapped), these were aimed at all students. Perhaps the greatest difference, however, was their comprehensiveness and the remarkable speed with which these policies spread across the states.

EXPLAINING THE POLITICS OF EDUCATION REFORM

The breadth of recent school reforms and the swiftness with which they were enacted belie traditional images of a slow-moving political system, designed to produce only marginal adjustments in existing policy. Past research on the diffusion of policy innovations suggests four different explanations for this seeming deviation from the norms of routine policymaking.

The first asserts that some state governments are simply more innovative than others and, historically, have always displayed a greater tendency to adopt new policy approaches. Using a large number of policies (between 80 and 180), adopted by the states since the nineteenth century, researchers have calculated innovation scores that measure how quickly after a policy is first adopted by at least one state, a given state adopts it. These scores are then summed and averaged across policies. After examining the demographic, economic, and political correlates of innovation, researchers have concluded that some states exhibit a general innovativeness trait that continues over time and across policy areas (Walker 1969; Savage 1978). Some of these states may aspire to a position of national or regional leadership; others are governed by policymakers and bureaucracies with professional norms that value innovation; while still others owe their innovativeness to strong historical and cultural traditions like progressivism. Although the states show greater similarity today in rates of policy diffusion then they did in the nineteenth and early twentieth centuries, several like California, Minnesota, New York, Ohio, and Washington consistently rank high on innovativeness indicators, while others like Delaware, Georgia, Mississippi, and South Carolina have consistently scored in the lowest quartile of states in their tendency to innovate.

Although this innovativeness factor may help in explaining the school reforms adopted by states like California and New Jersey, it neither explains why so many traditionally noninnovative states (e.g., South Carolina and Texas) recently adopted school reforms, nor why so many chose comprehensive approaches.

A second explanation argues that innovation results from either a crisis or a widespread perception that the current system is not working well. This explanation is synonymous with Cyert and March's notion of problemistic search (1963: 121). Innovation occurs as a product of the search for solutions to a problem or an organization's failure to meet one or more of its goals. Not only does a crisis convince the members of an organization that a search for new approaches is necessary, but it also increases the cost to individual members of opposing innovation. Those who resist adopting the most-favored innovations place themselves in the position of, in effect, favoring a significant weakening or even the demise of the organization (Wilson 1966: 208). Major crises exert a similar effect on policymakers and their attentive publics, if they do not search for and adopt new solutions, they could be held responsible for seriously jeopardizing the public welfare.

It is true that in many important ways, the educational system was not working well and to some extent (e.g., in the secondary schools, in parts of the South), there was a crisis in U.S. education. Yet these problems were neither new nor previously unrecognized. The decline in student achievement had begun in the late 1960s; problems with teacher quality had also continued for a decade or more. In fact, by the time states began to enact school reform measures in 1983, the national decline in academic achievement had already begun to bottom-out and begin a modest improvement (Peterson 1983: 11). In other words, what was called a crisis in 1983, could just as easily have been perceived as such five years earlier; the objective conditions had not significantly worsened and in some cases, had actually improved.

A third explanation posits that innovation results from organizational and fiscal slack (Cyert and March 1963; Nelson 1978). Organizations and governmental agencies that have more resources than they need to perform required functions can devote the excess to experimenting with new approaches. Certainly the costs associated with major school reform meant that some fiscal slack was necessary, and such flexibility was not available in the early 1980s. In fact, fiscal years 1982 and 1983 were described as the worst since the Depression for state governments. The majority of states (29) finished fiscal year 1983 with a budgetary balance equal to 3 percent or less of annual appropriations; eight ended the year with a deficit (Gold 1983). The only reason the fiscal picture was not any worse was that thirty-six states raised taxes and thirty-five cut spending after their initial 1983 budgets were already adopted. Because of the upturn in the national economy and the willingness of state governments to reduce their budgets and increase taxes, fiscal year 1984 was a much better one for the states. The median increase in revenues across all states was estimated to be about 9.8 percent. In other words, by late 1983, state governments were enjoying more fiscal flexibility than they had experienced in several years.

The course of other recent educational reforms suggests that the states' willingness to spend a large proportion of these new monies on school improvement programs provided a necessary, but not sufficient, condition for broad-based reform. Past reforms resulting from fiscal slack (e.g., the compensatory educational programs of the 1960s and school financing reform of the 1970s) were not as comprehensive. They either did not extend into the substance of schooling or were not directed at all students. Consequently, it appears that although organizational slack defines a critical condition for innovation, it does not explain why this one differed from earlier reforms in its comprehensiveness.

A final explanation from past research suggests that innovations are more likely to occur when opposition to them is relatively weak (Mohr 1969). Weak opposition was certainly the case for school reform. Not only was a major, traditional source of opposition not against it, but the business community abandoned its usual resistance to raising taxes for education and campaigned actively for school reform. In states like Arkansas, California, Florida, South Carolina, and Texas, the business community played a major role in designing and enacting school reform measures (Pierce and Sagan 1983). The states' top businessmen served on the commissions and task forces that proposed reform agendas; they raised money for public opinion polls and advertising campaigns to mobilize support among the general public; and they lobbied state legislatures to enact various school improvement programs.

Why did the business community reverse its traditional opposition and decide to play such an active political role in support of public education? The changing nature of the labor pool from which U.S. business must draw its workers provides a major reason. Due to declining birth rates, there will be fewer young people entering the labor market—20 percent fewer students will graduate from high school in 1990 than in 1980. Consequently, employers will have less choice in whom they decide to hire, making it critical that all applicants be well-qualified in basic academic skills. Because technology is changing the nature of many jobs and because people are working longer, workers will also need to learn new job skills over the course of their careers. Thus, business recognized how critical it is that these workers have the basic mathematical and language training needed to provide a foundation for learning other new skills as necessary. In addition, U.S. industry realized that it requires an increasingly productive and skilled work force if it is to remain competitive in the international economy. Finally, business understood that although its own training programs complement the work of the schools, they are not a substitute for it. The job of educating tomorrow's labor force will be done, in the main, by the schools (Timpane 1984). For these reasons, then, business leaders found it in their interest to assume a major role in promoting educational reform.

Somewhat ironically, traditional education interest groups were either peripheral to the lobbying effort or opposed to specific reforms; however, they constituted a weak opposition. For example, many teacher organizations were opposed to compensation based on factors other than seniority and educational attainment; some local school boards viewed many reforms as likely to result in less local autonomy. Nevertheless, many organizations (e.g., the national leadership of the American Federation of Teachers and some individual state teacher organizations and local school board associations) saw the reform movement as an opportunity to obtain more visibility and support for public education generally. Consequently, these groups were willing to compromise and accept some measures they had traditionally opposed, in exchange for others that would provide more resources for schools. In addition, given the overall political climate, strong opposition on the part of the educational establishment was very risky politically. Not only were demands "to do something" about the schools widespread, but the national movement for vouchers and tuition tax credits meant that if the public school establishment had appeared unresponsive, it could have ended-up with much less public support and fewer resources than it had enjoyed traditionally. As a result, not only was opposition to school reform weak, but to an unprecedented extent, it was broadly supported.

The lack of strong opposition to school reform begins to explain why it occurred in the way it did. Yet concentrating only on the notion of weak opposition conceives the reason much too narrowly. To provide answers to our three questions—why now, why so quickly, and why so comprehensive?—we have to expand on this last explanation. To do this, we need to turn it around to focus not so much on the lack of opposition per se but rather on the fact that this lack of opposition was just one indicator the incentives for pursuing reformist policies had changed significantly.

NEW INCENTIVES TO ACT

A combination of factors came together to create a compelling set of incentives for political leaders to act. The first was the direction and intensity of public opinion. Although criticism of the schools was high in 1983, the public also believed that education could be improved and appeared willing to pay for such efforts. Each year for the past sixteen years, the Gallup organization has conducted a national opinion poll to measure public attitudes towards the public schools. One question asks respondents to grade the schools in their communities. The proportion of respondents rating the schools as an A or a B decreased from 48 percent in 1974 to 31 percent in 1983, and similarly, the proportion rating them as a D or an F increased from 11 to 20 percent (Gallup 1983: 39). Nevertheless, as the public intensified its criticism of public education, it also modified its reluctance to support the schools financially. Between 1971 and 1981, the proportion of Gallup Poll respondents who favored raising taxes to support local schools decreased from 40 to 30 percent (Gallup 1981: 37). In the 1983 Gallup Poll, however, the proportion had risen once again to 39 percent (Gallup 1983: 37). By a two-to-one margin (65 percent to 31 percent), respondents in a *Los Angeles Times* poll expressed approval for a one-cent-a-dollar sales tax increase to help improve the schools (Savage 7/3/83 Pt. I: 3).

A number of state-level polls (e.g., in California, Oklahoma, South Carolina, Tennessee, and Utah) documented similar attitudes: Significant majorities supported increased taxes for the public schools as long as the money was specifically used to support quality improvement efforts. This support was quite consistent across political parties, age groups, and even extended to those without children in the public schools. In one state, South Carolina, respondents were asked if they would be more or less likely to vote for legislators who supported a tax increase to improve the quality of public education. Seventy-five percent of those responding said they would be *more* likely to vote for such legislators (South Carolina Governor's Office 1983). In a variety of ways, then, the general public was sending a strong signal that it wanted policymakers to address problems of school quality and that it was willing to pay for such programs.

A second factor conveyed a similar message to state policymakers. Not only was the general public interested in educational reform but business and political elites were also concerned. We have already discussed the role business leaders played in advocating reform in individual states. These same sentiments were echoed at the national level by prominent business leaders who most often linked the need for school reform with their growing concern about the United States' ability to compete in world economic markets. Demands for action were not limited to the business community. National political elites, most notably the Reagan administration, also called upon states and local school districts to improve educational quality. For Reagan, espousing the recommendations outlined in *A Nation at Risk* was a way of showing concern about education while still favoring a reduced federal financial commitment. The effect of this elite pressure was to provide strong, visible support for state policymakers who wished to initiate school reform programs, and to make it very difficult for those who tried to ignore the issue.

The growing cost of public education and the increased state share of these costs created a third force to change the incentive structure of state policymakers. Between 1969 and 1979, total expenditures for public elementary and secondary education increased from \$35 billion to \$87 billion, a nominal increase of 149 percent, or 26 percent when adjusted for inflation (Odden 1984: 2). Perhaps more important than the total increase was the fact that responsibility for funding education shifted among governmental levels, so that state governments now pay, on average, half the total costs of public education (National Center for Education Statistics 1983). This proportion had increased from about 40 percent fifteen years ago. States are now spending, on average, a quarter of their budgets on elementary and secondary education. The size of this expenditure in a time of fiscal retrenchment, combined with public attention on the policy area, created a substantial incentive for policymakers to become concerned about whether they were receiving their money's worth.

These first three factors created the incentives for state policymakers to act. Once policymakers are motivated to act, however, the likelihood an issue will actually move onto the policy agenda is greatly increased if an easily understood solution exists for the problem being addressed (Walker 1977: 431). In other words, policymakers need both a reason to act and a means to do so. The various national commission reports, issued in 1983, provided such a means. They gave the impression that easily understood, simple solutions (albeit some expensive ones) were available. In arguing that if standards were increased and more time were spent in school, students would learn more and that if teachers were paid based on merit, they would perform better, these reports defined the parameters of acceptable policy solutions. On the one hand, they did not question the basic premises or organization of schooling (Peterson 1983). On the other, they made it acceptable for policymakers to tinker with items formerly off-limits, namely, the basis for teacher and administrator compensation.

The somewhat ironic, but nonetheless critical, role the national commissions and particularly, *A Nation at Risk* played in setting the direction and momentum for state-level reform cannot be underestimated. It is true that the federal government spurred the states to act without providing any support for the endeavor. Many of the solutions proposed by the national commissions were also either simplistic or inconsistent with research knowledge about the schooling process (Stedman and Smith 1983; Levin 1983). Nevertheless, by providing seemingly, straightforward policy solutions, these reports made it much easier for state officials to propose and enact legislation quickly. At the same time, they constrained the range of acceptable reform alternatives.

A final factor that helped shift incentives for policymakers were the resources available to those who wished to act. The first of these was the national media attention paid to school reform. Over 700 newspaper articles were written about the recommendations embodied in *A Nation at Risk* (U.S. Department of Education 1984: 13), educational reform appeared as a major story at least once during this period in every national newsmagazine, and the condition of the public schools was highlighted in numerous television programs, including a three hour documentary produced by one of the national networks. Such publicity helped policymakers make their case for school reform and mobilize the public.

A second resource was provided by national organizations that represent state policymakers, like the Education Commission of the States, the National Conference of State Legislatures, and the National Governors' Association. These organizations played a critical role in: translating relevant research into information useful to policymakers; recommending specific policy directions through publications like ECS' *Action for Excellence*; providing technical assistance to states in formulating legislation; and generally, encouraging state action by publicizing information about those states that had already formulated a reform agenda. Just as the media focus on school reform provided a mechanism for mobilizing public support, the constituent organizations provided needed technical expertise and incentives based on the support and recognition of professional peers across the country.

In sum, the scope and rapidity of recent school reform policy can be largely explained by a major shift in the incentive structure of state policymakers, particularly legislators and governors. Not only did their constituents expect action, but policymakers perceived that political rewards could be gained for bold new policy initiatives. And seemingly effective solutions and the resources to promote them were available. To argue that a unique combination of political incentives made policy action compelling is not to ignore that there were risks in acting (especially in states where taxes had to be raised). But the risks associated with not acting and the payoff for acting decisively were much higher than they had ever been for state policymakers.

IMPLICATIONS

The political conditions that facilitated rapid state-level enactment of comprehensive school reform will also shape the implementation of these policies. Four aspects of the current reforms, resulting largely from the interplay between the policies themselves and the political process that produced them, bear special attention as state and local level implementation proceeds. The first is the high level of public expectation generated in the course of enacting these reforms. Clearly, the degree to which educational reform has captured the public's attention over the past two years is unlikely to continue; other problems and issues will replace it as part of a fairly predictable issue-attention cycle (Downs 1972). The mobilization of support needed to raise taxes in some states and the size and visibility of reforms in many others mean, however, that the public is likely to have a longer-than-average issue-attention span. As a result, positive outcomes will be expected and policy performance scrutinized carefully.

Yet many of the predicted effects of school reform such as increased student achievement and better qualified teachers are longer term ones with little likelihood of occurring in any significant way for five to ten years. If the policymakers who promoted school improvement initiatives are to maintain support for these programs and for themselves as elected and appointed officials, they will need to demonstrate that reasonable progress is being made in achieving such outcomes. The most effective way to do this is to hold local districts and schools accountable to a set of interim goals, based on factors assumed to be affected by the reform policies and positively related to desired ultimate outcomes. These might include: increased high school enrollments in science, mathematics, and advanced placement classes, amount of instructional time spent on core subjects, amount of writing and homework assigned, decreased dropout rates, and increased school attendance.

Such intermediate effects measures are critical not just for policymakers and administrators to include in their implementation strategies, but they should also be a part of scholarly evaluations of recent school reforms. Without diminishing the importance of improved test scores, both policymakers and researchers will need to show the public that, while school reform is a slow, complex process, steady progress can be made in meeting ultimate policy objectives. Otherwise, the potential for public backlash and withdrawal of support is great.

Because of the haste and urgency with which they were enacted, a second characteristic of recent reforms is the extent to which many of the most significant ones go beyond current research knowledge about what really works. Many of the school-based improvement programs included in state reform strategies are derived from the school effectiveness research. Despite some weaknesses in study design and methods, this research has provided policymakers with guidance about the factors that distinguish effective schools and classrooms from less effective ones (for reviews of this research, see: Cohen 1983; Murnane 1981; Purkey and Smith 1983). These studies provide systematic evidence about those factors that can be manipulated by the policy system and that are most likely to result in improved schools. Even for these research-based strategies, however, serious questions remain about their applicability on a widespread basis, particularly in secondary schools (Farrar, Neufield, and Miles 1984; Purkey and Smith 1985) and in schools with more affluent students.

The gap between policy and research is even greater in another major area of educational reform: teacher policy. For example, little empirical data exist on what constitutes effective incentives for teachers and principals at different points in their careers. We also have no systematic information on whether differential pay systems for teachers and principals work as intended. Research to identify the elements of a fair and accurate evaluation system is also in its early stages (Wise et al. 1984). This lack of adequate information has already become evident in the difficulties Arkansas, Florida, and Tennessee are now experiencing in implementing their performance-based compensation systems, with the problems clearest in the area of teacher evaluation. The most likely effect of this disjuncture between policy and research will be the need to modify reform policies throughout the implementation process. Perhaps more than is usually the case, the success of these policies will depend on the ability of state officials to adjust their original strategies in the light of local experience.

A third characteristic of recent reforms is their approach to educational change. In mandating tighter standards for teacher and student performance and in initiating school improvement programs, state policymakers are continuing a twenty-five year tradition of using top-down policy to attempt to change practice in local schools and classrooms. Yet a decade of research on program implementation and the educational change process has shown that the manner in which a policy is translated into practice depends on a variety of factors over which state and local officials often have little control (for a review of the educational change literature, see Fullan 1982). Because of pressures to obtain quick results and the emphasis of the national commissions on top-down, regulatory approaches, many recent state initiatives underestimate the variability of local responses and the time it takes to adapt administration and practice to new policies (e.g., see Cuban 1984 on the California experience). In addition, the fact that groups representing education practitioners did not actively support a number of state initiatives suggests that the sense of local ownership critical to successful implementation is absent in many states.

Where this is the case, state and local officials may need to devise ways to encourage practitioners to buy into new state-initiated programs during the implementation process. In some instances, this may mean revising policies to accommodate practitioner concerns. Policymakers may be reluctant to do this, simply because the education establishment was not part of the political coalition supporting the original policy. Despite the lack of political incentives for making these accommodations, however, policymakers may find they have no choice: such compromises are necessary if they are to maximize the likelihood their policy intentions are reflected in local practice.

A final characteristics of recent reforms, affecting their implementation, is the large number of new responsibilities they place on state and local agencies. One need only think of a local superintendent who must now establish school-based improvement programs, implement a number of new student standards, and at the same time, make certain that teachers, principals, and schools are evaluated in ways never done before. Similarly, state departments of education (SEAs) now face significant new responsibilities, particularly in the areas of assessment and technical assistance. Implicit in the current reform movement is a model of schooling that assumes not just that a given level of inputs or resources should be associated with greater student achievement but that the way these resources are used is equally important in increasing the likelihood of improved student performance. Consequently, many SEAs are now charged with moving beyond simply "counting things" and testing students to assessing the schooling process itself and measuring educational quality in all its complexity. Additionally, the new demands reform policies place on local districts mean they will need more extensive technical assistance than SEAs have historically been able to provide. Yet the traditional reluctance of state legislatures to spend funds on administration has meant that many new reform initiatives have not been accompanied by a proportionate increase in either SEA funding or in technical assistance resources for local districts.

Encouraging a sense of ownership among practitioners will help create the desire to translate state-level reforms into local practice. But policymakers also need to help build the capacity to transform that willingness into appropriate local action. Although some states integrated capacity-building mechanisms into their original reform policies, many did not. These states may find that a "second-round" of reform legislation is necessary to modify policies in light of operating experience and as the need to build greater institutional capacity becomes more obvious.

CONCLUSIONS

In examining the political context of recent school reforms, we found that their broad scope and rapid diffusion across the fifty states are largely explained by a dramatic shift in the political incentives of state policymakers. Strong signals from both the general public and national elites made it clear, particularly to legislators and governors, that the risks of acting decisively were very low, and in fact, the political costs of not acting were even higher. The speed with which new legislation was enacted, however, has meant that potentially serious problems like the significant gaps between policy and research knowledge and the lack of local capacity have been deferred to the implementation phase. The question remaining, then, is whether the political conditions that led to the legislative enactment of school reforms can be sustained long enough to resolve these more difficult problems.

REFERENCES

Boyer, Ernest L. 1983. *High School.* New York: Harper & Row.

Brown, Patricia, and Richard Elmore. 1982. "Analyzing the Impact of School Finance Reform." In *The Changing Politics of School Finance*, edited by Nelda Cambron-McCabe and Allen Odden, pp. 107–137. Cambridge, Mass.: Ballinger.

Business-Higher Education Forum. 1983. *America's Competitive Challenge.* Washington, D.C.: Business-Higher Education Forum.

Cohen, Michael. 1983. "Instructional, Management, and Social Conditions in Effective Schools." In *School Finance and School Improvement*, edited by Allen Odden and L. Dean Webb, pp. 17–50. Cambridge, Mass.: Ballinger.

College Board. 1983. *Academic Preparation for College.* New York: College Board.

Cuban, Larry. 1984. "School Reform by Remote Control: SB 813 in California." *Phi Delta Kappan* 66 (November): 213–215.

Cyert, Richard N. and James G. March. 1963. *A Behavioral Theory of the Firm.* Englewood Cliffs: Prentice-Hall.

Dougherty, Van. 1983. *State Programs of School Improvement: A 50-State Survey.* Denver: Education Commission of the States.

Downs, Anthony. 1972. "Up and Down with Ecology—The 'Issue-attention Cycle.' " *Public Interest* 28 (Summer): 38–50.

Education Week IV, no. 20 (February 6, 1985).

Farrar, Eleanor, Barbara Neufeld, and Matthew B. Miles. 1984. "Effective Schools Programs in High Schools: Social Promotion or Movement by Merit?" *Phi Delta Kappan* 65 (June): 701–706.

Fullan, Michael. 1982. *The Meaning of Educational Change.* New York: Teachers College Press.

Gallup, George H. 1981. "The 13th Annual Gallup Poll of the Public's Attitudes Toward the Public Schools." *Phi Delta Kappan* 63, no. 1 (September): 33–47.

_____. 1983. "The 15th Annual Gallup Poll of the Public's Attitudes Toward the Public Schools." *Phi Delta Kappan* 65, no. 1 (September): 33–47.

Goertz, Margaret, Ruth Ekstrom, and Richard Coley. 1984. *The Impact of State Policy on Entrance into the Teaching Profession.* Princeton: Educational Testing Service.

Gold, Steven D. 1983. Presentation at the National School Finance Reform Conference. September 26. Spring Hill Center, Wayzata, Minnesota.

Goodlad, John I. 1984. *A Place Called School.* New York: McGraw-Hill.

Gray, Virginia. 1973. "Innovation in the States: A Diffusion Study." *American Political Science Review* 67, no. 4 (December): 1174–1185.

Guthrie, James W., and Ami Zusman. 1982. *Mathematics and Science Teacher Shortages: What Can California Do?* Berkeley: Institute of Governmental Studies, University of California.

Levin, Henry M. 1983. "About Time for Educational Reform." Stanford: Institute for Research on Educational Finance and Governance.

Lindblom, Charles. 1959. "The Science of Muddling Through." *Public Administration Review* 19, no. 2 (Spring): 79–88.

Murnane, Richard J. 1981. "Interpreting the Evidence on School Effectiveness." *Teachers College Record* 83, no. 1 (Fall): 19–36.

National Assessment of Educational Progress. 1982. *Reading, Science and Mathematics Trends: A Closer Look.* Denver: Education Commission of the States.

National Commission on Excellence in Education. 1983. *A Nation at Risk.* Washington, D.C.: U.S. Government Printing Office.

National Center for Education Statistics. 1981. *Digest of Education Statistics.* Washington, D.C.: Government Printing Office.

_____. 1983. The Condition of Education. Washington, D.C.: U.S. Government Printing Office.

National Science Board Commission on Precollege Education in Mathematics, Science, and Technology. 1983. *Educating Americans for the 21st Century.* Washington, D.C.: National Science Foundation.

Nelson, Barbara J. 1978. "Setting the Public Agenda: the Case of Child Abuse." In *The Policy Cycle*, edited by Judith V. May and Aaron Wildavsky, pp. 17–41. Beverly Hills: Sage Publications.

Odden, Allan, C. Kent McGuire, and Grace Belsches-Simmons. 1983. *School Finance Reform in the States 1983.* Denver: Education Commission of the States.

Odden, Allan. 1984. *Education Finance in the States: 1984.* Denver: Education Commission of the States.

Peterson, Paul E. 1983. "Did the Education Commissions Say Anything?" *Brookings Review* (Winter): 3–11.

Pierce, Neal R., and Deborah Sagen. 1983. "Business Increasingly Sees Quality Education as Vital to Its Interests." *National Journal* 15, no. 42 (October): 2109–2113.

Purkey, Stewart C., and Marshall S. Smith. 1983. "Effective Schools: A Review." *Elementary School Journal* 83 (March): 427–452.

_____. 1985. "School Reform: The District Policy Implications of the Effective Schools Literature." *Elementary School Journal* 85 (January): 353–389.

Rosenthal, Alan, and Susan Fuhrman. 1981. *Legislative Education Leadership in the States.* Washington, D.C.: Institute for Educational Leadership.

_____. 1982. "State Legislatures and Education Policy: An Overview." *Educational Horizons* 61 (Fall): 4–9.

Savage, David. 1983. "Most Willing to Pay More for Better Schools." *Los Angeles Times.* July 3: Pt. 1, 1.

Savage, Robert L. 1978. "Policy Innovativeness as a Trait of American States." *The Journal of Politics* 40, no. 1 (February): 212–224.

Sizer, Theodore. 1984. *Horace's Compromise: The Dilemma of the American High School.* Boston: Houghton-Mifflin.

South Carolina Governor's Office and Department of Education. 1983. "The Public Viewpoint: Education in South Carolina."

Stedman, Lawrence C. and Marshall S. Smith. 1983. "Recent Reform Proposals for American Education." *Contemporary Education Review* 2 (Fall): 85–104.

Task Force on Education for Economic Growth. 1983. *Action for Excellence.* Denver: Education Commission of the States.

Timpane, Michael. 1984. "Business Has Rediscovered the Public Schools." *Phi Delta Kappan* 65 (February): 389–392.

Twentieth Century Fund Task Force on Federal Elementary and Secondary Education Policy. 1983. *Making the Grade.* New York: The Twentieth Century Fund.

U.S. Department of Commerce. 1979. *Voting and Registration in the Election of November 1978.* Washington, D.C.: U.S. Government Printing Office.

Vance, Victor S., and Philip C. Schlechty. 1982. "The Structure of the Teaching Occupation and the Characteristics of Teachers: A Sociological Perspective." Paper prepared for the National Institute of Education.

Walker, Jack L. 1969. "The Diffusion of Innovations Among the American States." *American Political Science Review* 63, no. 3 (September): 880–899.

_____. "Setting the Agenda in the U.S. Senate: A Theory of Problem Selection." *British Journal of Political Science* 7 (October): 423–445.

Welch, Susan and Kay Thompson. 1980. "The Impact of Federal Incentives on State Policy Innovation." *American Journal of Political Science* 24, no. 4 (November): 715–729.

Wilson, James Q. 1966. "Innovation in Organizations: Notes Toward a Theory." In *Approaches to Organizational Design*, edited by James D. Thompson, pp. 194–218. Pittsburgh: University of Pittsburgh Press.

Wise, Arthur, Linda Darling-Hammond, Milbrey McGlaughlin, and Harriet Bernstein. 1984. *Teacher Evaluation: A Study of Effective Practices.* Santa Monica: The Rand Corporation.

4 IMPLICATIONS FOR PROGRAMMATIC EXCELLENCE AND EQUITY

Arthur W. Steller

Educators through the decades have emerged repeatedly from avalanches of new jargon and reforms as supreme survivors. School teachers and administrators have, for the most part, endured these movements like one puts up with a common cold—take some minor medication, close the eyelids to get more sleep, and wait it out (two weeks if you go to the doctor or fourteen days if you cure yourself). Rip Van Winkle seems to feel at home in schoolhouses whenever he awakes.

Is the current national reform movement merely a passing fancy? Is this merely the latest *Crisis in the Classroom* (Silberman 1970) that will whip up short-lived innovations? Will all the headlines fade into oblivion before stimulating major improvements in educational programs or opportunities for young people? Will schools change and, if they do, will it be for the better?

Time will provide the ultimate answers to these and other related questions. The bulk of this chapter will attempt to address these matters from the perspective of their implications for programming excellence and access for students. Some background information will be offered first to form an appropriate context, although more encompassing materials can be found elsewhere.

The current reform movement will engulf even those educators accustomed to hunkering down or riding out the wind of change, because it is substantially different than other movements. The rhetoric is so hot and the core message so appealing that it has stimulated massive acceptance. Public attention has followed the excellence movement, more faithfully than other reforms. Politicians, business people, and other key decision makers have enthusiastically embraced the concept of excellence in education that is a sufficiently broad ideal that it can include a variety of recommendations and proposed practices. In fact, this latter attribute may be a major contributing factor to the sustained momentum of this drive. Everyone is for excellence; however, the definitions and opinions on how to make it happen vary. Money has flowed into current educational reforms in a fashion unlike anything that has occurred since the educational revolution following the launching of Sputnik. Governors are in a mad scramble to outdo one another in presenting educational reform packages to their legislatures. Clearly, we are witnessing a unique period in education.

At the same time, there are now more tools available to education than ever before. Educational research has matured to the point that a strong foundation exists for determining the characteristics of an effective school. The utilization of technology is accelerating throughout all aspects of our society, including classrooms. It has become apparent that "Changing Conditions Necessitate Resetting of Priorities and Policies for Schools" (Stellar 1980a). The merging at this juncture of the excellence movement and improved means of pedagogy has forged a powerful force for change. Individual manifestations of this reform movement may be rebuked, but the main thrust for change will not be repulsed.

A NATION AT RISK: THE IMPERATIVE FOR EDUCATIONAL REFORM

The National Commission of Excellence in Education released its investigation into the U.S. educational scene in 1983. The first part of the title, *A Nation at Risk*, reinforced the public perceptions concerning the country as well as its schools. "Our Nation is at risk . . . the educational foundations of our society are presently being eroded by a rising tide of mediocrity that threatens our very future as a Nation and a people" (National Commission 1983). Almost overnight it became a "best seller" and placed education in the national spotlight. The subtitle, *The Imperative for Educational Reform*, is a clarion call for faculty members, administrators, other policymakers, the mass media, parents and students to make wholesale changes in education. A careful reading of the Commission's report suggests that the emphasis is upon the subtitle with the singular goal of reform being paramount.

Following a list of "Indicators of the Risk" and findings, the Commission makes major recommendations and implementing recommendations for five areas—content, standards and expectations, time, teaching, and leadership and fiscal support. Some local school districts and politicians have embraced the specific recommendations as *the yardstick* to assess educational quality.

Certainly, full implementation of the Commission's recommendations would upgrade most school districts; however, it is probably true that few, if any, districts have the resources to address all of the suggestions at once. Long term priorities have to be set. Another reason for developing a long range plan comes from a skeptical view of *A Nation at Risk:* "Blind acceptance of these recommendations could lead to little improvement. Worse yet, a rapid adoption in the hopes of speedy improvement could lead to a disenchantment with reform" (Stedman and Smith 1983). The Commission's investigative efforts have been considered insufficient by some educational researchers accustomed to more rigorous and comprehensive application of research methodology that may also give slight pause to carte blanche endorsement of these recommendations. Another reason to refrain from unilateral and uncritical adoption of the Commission's report is its scant notice paid to educational equalization—a long recognized goal of U.S. education (Tye and Tye 1983). These are the grounds, then, for thoughtful review of the contents of *A Nation at Risk* before wildly plunging ahead.

One of the followup books, *The Superintendent's Can-Do Guide to School Improvement* (Dianda 1984) spends a chapter debunking what it labels school reform myths. The four myths identified are "America is a nation at risk," "America has a high-technology future," "states can finance educational reform," and "more is better." In this piece, superintendents are advised to be skeptical.

Successful superintendents are by nature skeptical, some might even say cynical, hence, this advice seems unnecessary. Furthermore, whether or not this country is actually at risk is an issue decided by perceptions rather than upon factual base. If the public believes the nation is at risk, for all intents and purposes, it is. Everyone in the work force within the foreseeable future will not be utilizing computers and robotics. We are still a long way from a Buck Rogers world dawn to dusk. At the same time, it is irrefutable that advanced technology is becoming more commonplace every day. The alleged myths about whether the states "can" finance educational reform is best rephrased as a question—"will" the states fund reform? The so-called more is better myth will be addressed throughout this chapter due to its complexity. More is better as an overall approach may be unsound according to those with a preoccupation on pedagogical intricacies, but the concept of more is psychologically and politically acceptable to the U.S. people, and that's really what the Commission's report is all about—political reform. The bulk of the work of the Commission consisted of taking testimony from citizens, educators, and experts in the form of hearings and papers. That process alone would yield a political document. The spawning of the Commission by the Secretary of Education, Terrell Bell, with the blessing of President Reagan, sealed that as an outcome. No single report in the history of education has touched off such a tidal wave of reform across this country so its popularity has already been verified.

The trick, of course, for both the practitioner and scholar is to capitalize upon the power of the excellence movement to promote improvements in educational programming that make a real difference for students. Dr. Henry M. Brickell, president of Policy Studies in Education, is among those entrepreneurs who have seized upon *A Nation at Risk* to productively channel school board, administrator, teacher, student and citizen deliberations about the Commission's recommendations through "A Checklist for Excellence" (Brickell and Paul 1983).

Before proceeding to a discussion of the instructional implications of the excellence movement, further groundwork needs to be established in three areas—reasons for reform, financing educational excellence, and educational policymaking. These will be the contributing factors to the success or failure of many of the specific proposals. They form a backdrop for the reforms and, to a certain degree, will influence the ultimate shape of the excellence movement within the nation's classrooms.

REASONS FOR REFORM

It has been common practice in educational circles to gain notoriety for one's ideas by decrying the current status of the quality of education. The titles of books such as *Why Johnny Can't Read* (Flesch 1955), *Why Children Fail* (Holt 1964), and *Crisis in the Classroom* (Silberman 1970), proclaim their contents in no uncertain terms. The first paragraph of many articles in the professional literature begin with derogatory statements about education in general or, at least, in connection with the topic of the essay. Consequently, it should come as no great surprise that the flagship of the excellence movement is called *A Nation at Risk*. This reform movement has accelerated so quickly because it goes beyond the natural inclination for tackling a crisis. The rationale cuts much deeper into the fabric of our society.

One of the motivations for improving education is based upon the assumption that education increases economic productivity. Almost concurrent with the decline on national indicators of the quality of education was a slowdown of economic growth in the United States. These correlations do not prove cause-effect relationships, but to many persons that is enough evidence to construct a prima facie case for raising the productivity of schools.

Wynn DeBevoise, in a wonderfully written booklet entitled *The Contribution of Education to Economic Productivity* (1983), acknowledges the clear relationship between education and economic well-being. He also reminds the reader that "By assuming that certain correlations are clearcut, such as that between level of education, status attainment, and productivity, educators and policymakers may do themselves and the educational system a disservice.

A comprehensive picture of the factors contributing to worker productivity, particularly to the use of knowledge in work, must consider not only educational attainment but also affective traits, cognitive skills, family background, reward and punishment systems in schools and bureaucracies, management techniques, and economic and environmental conditions" (DeBevoise 1983: 9).

Most other recent studies or reports on this topic dwell so heavily on the interdependence of economic growth and education that they often overlook other factors.

The Education Commission of the States created a Task Force on Education for Economic Growth that released its initial report,

"Action for Excellence," in 1983. "It is the thesis of this report that our future success as a nation—our national defense, our social stability and well-being, and our national prosperity—will depend on our ability to improve education and training for millions of individual citizens" (1983: 14).

The Taks Force on Education for Economic Growth has produced a glossy, very readable booklet that is fairly representative of similar endeavors relating education to economic survival. The problem is perceived as one of "educational deficits and blurred goals" with a broad stroke set of recommendations (see Table 4-1) amplified with somewhat more specific action steps and the supporting rationale.

The thrust of the education and economic growth segment of the excellence movement is primarily directed upon the college-bound student. Another viewpoint is provided by a panel of the Committee on Science, Engineering, and Public Policy, a joint committee of the National Academy of Sciences, National Academy of Engineering, and the Institute of Medicine. Their report, *High Schools and the Changing Workplace: The Employers' View* (1984), addresses the largest part of the U.S. labor force—high school graduates. The panel's basic findings and the major core competencies they judge to be required by employers are given in Table 4-2.

Some of the relevant commentaries on economic growth with educational implications are found outside traditional educational readings. In some cases, these reports may carry more weight than their more celebrated cousins. For example, President Reagan issued an invitation to the Business-Higher Education Forum in 1982 to determine ways in which this country's competitive position might be strengthened. This reaction, *America's Competitive Challenge: The Need for a National Response*, makes only one central recommendation: "as a nation, we must develop a consensus that industrial competitiveness is crucial to our social and economic well-being" (1983: 2). While there was just a single idea directed wholly at education—"to provide additional support from the public and private sectors to train secondary school science and math teachers" (1983: 36)—it is likely that this idea will receive strong support, due to its origin.

The competitive edge of the United States has been surpassed in many industrial fields by other countries. The desire to recapture this business leadership compels us to look beyond our borders for possible solutions. Education has followed suit, although this is not a

Table 4-1. Recommendation of the Task Force on Education for Economic Growth.

Action 1. Recommendation

Develop and put into effect as promptly as possible state plans for improving education in the public schools from Kindergarten through grade 12.

- Led by the governor, each state should develop a state plan for education and economic growth.
- Each governor should appoint a broadly inclusive state task force on education for economic growth.
- Each school district should develop its own plan.

Action 2. Recommendation

Create broader and more effective partnerships for improving education in the states and communities of the nation.

- Business leaders, labor leaders, and members of the professions should become more active in education.
- Business leaders should establish partnerships with schools.
- Governors, legislators, chief state school officers, state and local boards of education, and leaders in higher education should establish partnerships of their own.

Action 3. Recommendation

Marshal the resources which are essential for improving the public schools.

- School systems should enrich academic programs and improve management to make the best possible use of resources.
- States and communities should invest more financial, human, and institutional resources in education.
- The federal government should continue to support education.

Action 4. Recommendation

Express a new and higher regard for teachers.

- States and school districts—with full participation by teachers—should dramatically improve methods for recruiting, training, and paying teachers.
- States should create career ladders for teachers.
- States, communities, and media, and the business community should devise new ways to honor teachers.

(*Table 4-1. continued overleaf*)

Table 4-1. continued

Action 5. Recommendation

Make the academic experience more intense and more productive.

- States and school systems should establish firm, explicit, and demanding requirements concerning discipline, attendance, homework, grades, and other essentials of effective schooling.
- States and school systems should strengthen the public school curriculum.
- States should increase the duration and the intensity of academic learning.

Action 6. Recommendation

Provide quality assurance in education.

- Boards of education and higher education should cooperate with teachers and administrators on systems for measuring the effectiveness of teachers and rewarding outstanding performance.
- States, with full cooperation by teachers, should improve the process for certifying teachers and administrators and make it possible for qualified outsiders to serve in the schools.
- States should examine and tighten procedures for deciding which teachers to retain and which to dismiss.
- Student progress should be measured through periodic tests of general achievement and specific skills; promotion from grade to grade should be based on mastery not age.
- States and communities should identify clearly the skills they expect the schools to impart.
- Colleges and universities should raise their entrance requirements.

Action 7. Recommendation

Improve leadership and management in the schools.

- Principals should be squarely in charge of educational quality.
- Pay for principals should relate to responsibilities and effectiveness.
- States should set higher standards for recruiting, training, and monitoring the performance of principals.
- Schools should use more effective management techniques.

Action 8. Recommendation

Serve better those students who are now unserved or underserved.

- States and school districts should increase the participation of young women and minorities in courses where they are underrepresented.

Table 4-1. continued

- States should continue to develop equitable finance measures to insure that education resources are distributed fairly.
- States and school systems should identify and challenge academically gifted students.
- States, school systems, principals, teachers, and parents should work to reduce student absences and failures to finish school.
- State and school systems should specifically include handicapped students in programs for education and economic growth.

Source: Task Force on Education for Economic Growth, *Action for Excellence* (Denver, Col.: The Education Commission of the States, 1983), pp. 10-11.

new phenomenon. In the late 1960s and early 1970s, when the issue was relevancy in the curriculum, England became the focal point. *The Plowden Report* (1967) and its offspring were widely read by Uncle Sam's educators. The rage now is Japan.

Some social scientists and educators have even concluded that "a Japanese high school diploma is the equivalent of an average American bachelor's degree" (Rohlen 1984: 160). This judgment may be questioned, but few observers doubt the academic rigor of the curriculum, the intensity of the schooling, and the high expectations and standards of Japanese education. Part of our country's "more is better" recommendations probably stem from the fact that Japanese students attend school for 240 days a year including Saturdays; Summers often become periods of review and/or drill, an average of two hours per day is spent on homework, and numerous private tutoring schools, called *juku*, are attended by students in addition to the time they spend in public schools. Equality of opportunity is an important ingredient in Japanese schooling, if one can successfully pass through the multiple levels of tests used as periodic gates to advanced learning. The pressure resulting from the ever pervasive examinations is a deterimental side effect that people in the United States would likely wish to avoid replicating. What many in the United States would like to import most from the Japanese educational system is the high standards of achievement and the continually rising economic productivity of this Far Eastern super power.

The Japanese, however, have their own educational reform movement in progress due to their interest in maintaining future economic growth. "From an American perspective, however, what is

Table 4-2. High Schools and the Changing Workplace: The Employers' View.

Findings:

- The major asset required by employers of high school graduates seeking upwardly mobile careers is the ability to learn and to adapt to changes in the workplace. The continual evolution of work functions will require that workers master new knowledge and new skills throughout their lives. The ability to learn will be the essential hallmark of the successful employee.
- The core competencies described in Chapter 2 of this report can provide the basic understanding and skills needed both to perform entry level jobs and to continue the learning process. Technical education, vocational training, and curricula providing specific job skills can enhance a student's employability, but cannot substitute for education in the core competencies.
- A positive attitude and sound work habits are of basic importance. Employers place a high value on reliability and cooperation. At the same time, with increased employee participation in decisionmaking, the ability to offer constructive dissent without hindering teamwork will assume greater importance.

The Core Competencies:

- Command of the English language.
- Reasoning and Problem solving.
- Reading.
- Writing.
- Computation.
- Science and Technology.
- Oral Communication.
- Interpersonal Relationships.
- Social and Economic Studies.
- Personal Work Habits and Attitudes.

Source: Committee on Science, Engineering, and Public Policy, *High Schools and the Changing Workplace: The Employers' View* (Washington, D.C.: National Academy of Sciences, 1984), pp. xi, 20-27.

most astonishing about Japan's scrutiny of its learning system is that our biggest economic competitor is worried at all" (Ranbom 1985: 12). Most United States educators are not aware of the introspection occurring in Japan. "Our examination of the system of learning that has helped catapult Japan into a position of industrial pre-eminence has been superficial at best, telling us more about what is missing in our system than what is present in theirs" (Ranbom 1985: 12).

Nobuo Shimahara makes a cogent, yet decorative, statement about "Japanese Education and Its Implications for United States Education" in a 1985 *Kappan* article (p. 418):

> Above all, it is vital to keep in mind that Japanese education serves as a mirror to reflect education in the United States—not as a prototype to be duplicated in every respect. Selective borrowing of the right elements of the Japanese system of education has the potential to enhance our own schools. Thoughtless replication is to be avoided at all costs.

One reason partly responsible for the acceptance of the excellence movement has to do with the national concern over the number of students matriculating to colleges who are ill prepared for post-secondary education. The simple resolution of raising college entry level requirements is not politically or economically feasible. The increased competition among higher education institutions for the shrinking student population, coupled with open enrollment policies and laws, have combined to keep college entrance barriers from being elevated. An acceptable solution is to stress stronger academic background at the elementary/secondary level without advocating educational access be limited.

In 1980, the College Board began a ten year effort, the Educational Equality Project, to enhance quality in secondary education and equality of access to higher education for all students. Three years later a document entitled *Academic Preparation for College* (Educational Equality Project 1983) was released. It outlines what college entrants should be able to do and what knowledge they need to know in six basic academic subjects: English, the arts, mathematics, science, social studies, and foreign language. The general skills necessary for all college work are also described within the categories of reading, writing, speaking and listening, mathematics, reasoning, and studying. A statement is also presented on an emerging skill—computer competency. "The goal . . . is to provide quality preparation for as many college entrants as possible" (1983: 3). To reach that aim, *Academic Preparation for College* is meant for everyone who cares about how well students are prepared for college (1983: 2).

Preparation for the future is another of the themes of the excellence movement. Another "Report to the American people and the National Science Board" aimed at redressing the serious problems affecting public education was formulated by the National Science

Board Commission on Precollege Education in Mathematics, Science and Technology. The emphasis is contained in the title—*Educating Americans for the 21st Century: A Plan of Action for Improving Mathematics, Science and Technology Education for All American Elementary and Secondary Students So That Their Achievement Is the Best in the World by 1995* (1983). The motivating rationale underlying this report is the Commission's belief that " . . . the Nation's national security, economic strength and quality of life depend on the mathematics, science and technology literacy of all its citizens" (1983: IV).

The stated goal of this Commission's study includes the subtitle of the book along with the phrase " . . . without sacrificing the American birthright of personal choice, equity and opportunity" (1983: v). The omission of these very meaningful concepts from the title provides a significant clue into where the real thrust of this report, as well as most of the others, is headed. Rhetorical splashes like "Excellence and elitism are not synonymous" (1983: vii) are sprinkled throughout, but scant concrete recommendations or elaboration trails along afterwards to bolster these ideas. Another interesting facet of *Educating Americans for the 21st Century* is that it is one of a small number of such efforts to venture forth an estimate of costs which are viewed as an economic investment. The federal cost of the first year are calculated to be at least $1.51 billion being reduced annually until reaching a level of $331 million in the sixth year. "Successful living in the 21st century" will require expenditures of $1.51 billion plus "other, additional costs for the nation—at Federal, state and local levels . . . " (1983: iv).

FINANCING EDUCATIONAL EXCELLENCE/EQUITY

Recent school financing reform that has dealt primarily with equity is now being overshadowed by financing reforms glitterized with the achievement of excellence as the goal of this tug-of-war. A very brief review follows with the author's prediction of the outcome.

According to John Augenblick, "Linking school improvement to school finance will not be easy" because "Funds for school improvement have been allocated apart from the formulas used to distribute the vast majority of state aid to education" and "In the last 15 years more than half of the states have modified their school finance systems to make them more equitable . . ." (Augenblick 1984: 197).

"Financing Education Excellence" is treated by Allan Odden of the Education Commission of the States as a real possibility, especially if reform by addition is balanced with reform by reallocation and internal change. Mr. Odden has estimated that implementing various technical assistance programs would cost about $500 million dollars nationwide, incentive programs—$500 million, and longer school days and year—$40 billion. Other high cost strategies such as raising teacher compensation, adding new programs, or putting a greater reliance upon technology could have a major or minor impact upon funding sources depending upon the specifics of the programming adopted. The basis for Odden's optimism for a continued turnaround in educational financing centers around four factors—"First, the political context has changed. Second, the fiscal condition of the states has improved. Third, the knowledge base for educational reform has changed for the better. Finally, the public has changed; it now supports improvement in the quality of education and is willing to pay for it" (Odden 1984: 311).

Inevitably, policy makers at all levels in the educational decision making process will be faced with choices in their deliberations about applying financial resources to needs. With an exhaustible supply of money to distribute, there will be debate around "excellence versus equity" issues, although politicians, including local school board members, will scramble to build a code for such discussions so as not to offend important constituents on any side of the dilemma. Nevertheless, "Serious tensions exist between equity and educational excellence" (Odden 1984: 315).

Odden appears in the aforementioned article to be desirous of politically merging the excellence movement and the equity movement for financing purposes. While the practical mechanisms for making this happen are lacking, he presents an elegant declamation for this position: "Excellence and equity are integrally linked. Together, they provide the key to improving the position of the United States in the world market, by enabling American workers at 'all' levels to outperform their counterparts in other countries. Together, they are also the embodiment of the American dream, which focuses on maximizing potential rather than on reinforcing advantage" (Odden 1984: 318).

The author of this chapter is less convinced that equity and excellence will marry and result in more money for education, except for one area: teachers' salaries. Many of the reform laws that have raised salaries, in one form or another, have pulled justifying quotations from both sides of the aisle. Raising the salaries of existing staff equally across the board is not a demonstrated step toward excellence, although state capitals ring with the cry that this will aid in recruitment and retention of quality teachers. Raising starting salaries is more likely to contribute to both excellence and equity. Some merit pay plans and career ladders blend both concepts.

One former state policy maker, Theodore Black, who served as a New York State Regent from 1969 to 1980 is concerned that equity not be confused with equality (Black 1982: 177–78):

> Equality connotes a leveling, a sameness, a repression of efforts to improve—all of which are anathema to many Americans. And . . . EQUALITY IS NOT NECESSARILY COMPATIBLE WITH QUALITY, which is the goal of all in education. But if the courts . . . decide that equity cannot be achieved short of equal spending on each student . . . loosing a new force which can doom public education to permanent mediocrity, which in a pluralistic society is fatal.

Funding alone is not the decisive determinate in educational quality, yet it certainly makes a difference. Much of the public believes, like Black, " . . . that the citizens of a school district should not be prevented, inhibited, or discouraged from, or penalized for, committing as much of their own resources as they choose for the improvement of the quality of their children's education in their own public schools" (Black 1982: 189). The rub is that some local school districts cannot fund even an adequate educational program on their own. It is generally recognized that the educational gap between the "haves" and the "have nots" will widen if some intervention if not instigated. Perhaps, unfortunately, the allocation of money is the most expedient means of attending to this matter of equity or quality.

Since funding for education has pragmatic gaps imposed by economic and political realities, fiscal priorities must be set. Something has to give. The fact that the excellence movement has increased the size of education's slice of the governmental pie has relieved somewhat the severity of this problem and the budgetary conflicts between excellence and equity. In the opinion of this writer, however, the sheer momentum of the excellence movement will give preference to higher equality in education over equity in budget battles. This emphasis will gradually affect the largest school expenditure, teachers' salaries, as merit and other incentive measures will progressively provide more growth to salaries than equity.

EDUCATIONAL GOVERNANCE

The governance and control of U.S. education is a matter more defined by question marks and ambiguities than straightforward stipulations. The Association for Supervision and Curriculum Development devoted its November, 1980, issue of *Educational Leadership* (Brandt 1980) to the topic "Who Rules the Schools?" Four years later this journal's question was rephrased to "Education Policy: Who's in Charge?" (Brandt 1984). As it turns out, no single level of government controls education. The issue is more complex because "Educational policy makers often tend to respond more quickly and with more vigor to political demands than to true educational needs" (Steller 1980b: 161).

The federal and state governments have played significant roles in the excellence movement. Some of the relevant concepts in this involvement are touched upon in the following paragraphs.

The Federal Education Department has not grown into the controlling octopus that some feared it might, although it has had a role in promoting educational excellence. Contrary to popular myth, the federal government has had minimal impact on educational excellence through laws, regulations, funds, paperwork, etc. The principal tool in federal influence upon education has come in the form of "Using Education's 'Bully Pulpit'" (McGinnis 1984: 24). Former Secretary of Education, Terrell Bell, left as his legacy the proficient and prolific application of this technique in promotion of the excellence movement.

Cabinet level officials, regardless of their power, are an extension of the President. According to at least one writer, Ronald Reagan has earned "the rarely bestowed mantle of Education President" (Kaplan 1984: 7). This honorary title has been achieved almost entirely on the silver tongues and polished pens of rhetoric. This is evident in

Reagan's six steps to return excellence to U.S. education listed below which were contained in the article "Excellence and Opportunity: A Program of Support for American Education" (Reagan 1984: 13–15).

> First, we need to restore good, old-fashioned discipline.
>
> Second, we must end the drug and alcohol abuse that plagues thousands of our children.
>
> Third, we must raise academic standards and expectations.
>
> Fourth, we must encourage good teaching. One of the best ways to achieve this is to pay and promote teachers on the basis of their competence and merit.
>
> Fifth, we must restore parents and state and local governments to their rightful place in the educational process.
>
> Sixth and last, we must teach the basics.

In spite of the existence of an Education President and an active Secretary of Education, the national interest in education has not manifested itself in more than the normal flow of federal laws, projects, or funding. The excellence movement has been foremost in the 50 state capitols. The recent level of studies, legislation, and policymaking activities to upgrade education from a statewide perspective has been unprecedented. Michael Kirst has written that this spurt continues a pattern of growth in state authority that signifies "The Changing Balance in State and Local Power to Control Education" (1984: 189).

Education Week has articles covering the excellence movement practically every week. Several special inserts have attempted to keep readers up-to-date on reforms. In the April 3, 1985, issue twenty-four of the newspaper format pages were filled with a special report on the finding of an *EW* survey labeled "Changing Course." The survey was devoted to the "States Launching Barrage of Initiatives." Besides finding that governors are "No longer simply patrons, they are policy chiefs" regarding education, *EW* summarized the major state initiatives as given in Table 4–3.

Earlier in this chapter it was pointed out that one of the legs of support for the national excellence movement was the basic assumption that the improvement of education would precipitate economic growth. This motive also permeates most of the state level school reforms. An example is Governor Richard Riley's championing of the passage of "The New Approach to Educational and Economic Excellence in South Carolina" (Riley 1984).

Table 4-3. A Fifty State Survey of Reform Measures (*Since 9/81*).

	Total Number of States Indicating Yes	*Total Number of States Indicating "Under Consideration"*
Career Ladder/Merit Pay	14	24
Salary Increases/New Minimum	18	17
Require Competency Tests	29	10
Revise Certification	28	16
Raised Education-School Standards	19	10
Aid Prospective Teachers	24	13
Add Instructional Time	13	7
Limit Extracurriculars	6	4
Reduce Class Size	13	7
Raised Graduation Requirements	42	6
Require Exit Test	15	4
Stateside Assessment	37	6
Promotional Gates Test	8	3
Mandatory Kindergarten	5	2
Preschool Initiatives	7	8
Raised College Admission Standards	17	3

Source: Joanne Toor, "Summary of Major State Initiatives," *Education Week* (April 3, 1985): special insert between pp. A-2 and A-3.

All state reforms are not popular as Jerome Cramer explains in "Some State Commandments of Excellence Ignore Reality and Undercut Local Control." According to Cramer (1984: 25), the mounting criticism has these objectives:

> (1) The new education changes in some states are based on unreasonable and unrealistic assumptions about public schools. (2) Changes are being made without regard to their impact on school system curriculums or on the availability of teachers. (3) Changes in many parts of the U.S.—especially the South—could erode the tradition of local control of education.

Language employed to denigrate state reforms is couched in terms like "reform by remote control" or "ill-conceived bromides could pass for panaceas."

The criticism of state reforms should not be surprising. For the most part, educators were mere bystanders as bills became laws in the statehouses. Larry Cuban attacks California's school reform bill on that basis: "SB813 became a garbage can in which to toss every bright idea and private bias that noneducators had about school reform" (Cuban 1984: 213). The general consensus about state level reforms is that the discretionary authority of local boards and administrators had been usurped. To a certain degree this is true, of course, which explains why they would resist intrusions into their domains of influence.

Thomas Shannon, executive director of the National School Boards Association, understands that as "we grope our way through the most significant political revolution in eduation in 20 years" there will be those who believe in "A 1985 Fairy Tale" that recants local control is bad and state initiative is good. Shannon presents a more accurate and balanced picture of the relationship between local control and state initiatives as constructive partners. Both have legitimacy in educational governance and administration; their roles are complementary, not competitive (Shannon 1985).

Concerns over the loss of local control in all of the states' educational activity is a common topic at gatherings of school board members and administrators. In some ways the complaints are reminiscent of reactions to enforcement of civil rights laws, Title IX, mandates, handicapped legislation and other such matters which basically were equity related. School authorities don't like to be told what to do, even if it may be something they should be doing without the heavy hand of governmental action. The classical rejoiner for a reformer to this kind of criticism is that "If the schools were doing—(the particular reform can fill in the blank) right in the first place, it wouldn't be necessary to compel them to do it" or "The issue should not be at what level this __________ (fill in the blank) is introduced or who is in charge—the issue is to get the job done!" Once this kind of steamroller gets started, the peaks and valleys of dissimilar school practices tend to be eliminated. Arthur Wise has documented the dangers of such mandates that steal the thunder from local officials in his book, *Legislated Learning* (1979).

The natural compulsion to maintain control over one's destiny will ensure that those arguing in favor of local decision making remain vociferous in their objections. Uniformity has as a consequence the discouragement of innovation which gradually weakens the capacity for an organization to change. Reformers should take note less they sacrifice future gains for immediate returns. For those individuals and schools already doing yeoman work, their eagerness can be dampened when enslaved to someone else's panacea. With the well-being of children, not to mention the nation, at stake, it is relatively easy to dismiss the concerns for manifest destiny or political control were it not for one other factor. Top Down commands for fundamental and massive change are poor substitutes for inspirational leadership and/or participative approaches.

THE PROCESS OF SCHOOL IMPROVEMENT

Ernest Boyer, President of the Carnegie Foundation for the Advancement of Teaching, is no slouch when it comes to educational reform. He is a leading proponent of change. He views U.S. education, especially high schools, as "a troubled institution" (1983: 9). Yet, passion and commitment have not blinded him, like many others, to the complexities inherent with school improvement. Boyer bypasses the easy downhill path of quick fixes. His insightful conception of school revival is decidedly different than most of those identified with the excellence movement. Boyer's basic proposal is reproduced in Table 4-4 without the introductory phrase " . . . we conclude the time has come" conveying his sense of urgency for the task.

Boyer represents the pragmatic reformists—the vision is lifted to lofty heights with the feet firmly on the ground, not planted, but instead shuffling steadily forward. The research on educational change is absolutely voluminous. The bottom line finding is that viewed over the long term, education usually changes rather slowly and is built brick-by-brick-by-brick-by-brick. The reasons for this being an acceptable pace of change, often ignored by many of the quick fix reformers, is that education is a "loosely-coupled institution" and that it has a labor intensified organizational structure.

For those truly serious about the excellence movement, it is necessary to incorporate into one's thinking some *Educational Planning for Educational Success* (Steller 1980c). Numerous educational change models are available from the simple to the complex. One of these frameworks had been designed by Susan Louchs-Horsley and Leslie Hergert (1985: xii) as an outgrowth of their school improvement work for the NETWORK in Andover, Massachusetts. They list seven linear steps, given below, with detailed substeps to transform "Our School As It Is Now" to "Our School As We'd Like It To Be."

Table 4-4. High School Revival and Reform—How Should the United States Proceed?

- To clarify the goals of education.
- To stress the centrality of language and link the curriculum to a changing national and global context.
- To recognize that all students must be prepared for a lifetime of both work and further education.
- To strengthen the profession of teaching in the United States. This means improvement of conditions in the classroom, better recruitment and preparation, better continuing education, and better teacher recognition and rewards.
- To improve instruction and give students more opportunities for service in anticipation of their growing civic and social responsibilities as they become adults.
- To take full advantage of the information revolution and link technology more effectively to teaching and learning in the schools.
- To smooth the transition from school to adult life through more flexible class scheduling and by making available to students new learning places both on and off the campus.
- To reduce bureaucracy in education and give school principals the support they need to lead.
- To recognize that excellence in education is possible only when connections are made with higher education and with the corporate world.
- Finally, the time has come for public schools to be aggressively supported by parents, school boards, and government as well and for the nation's historic commitment to public education to be vigorously reaffirmed by all.

Source: Ernest L. Boyer, *High School: A Report on Secondary Education in America* (New York: Harper Colophon Books, 1983), p. 7.

Step 1: Establishing the School Improvement Project
Step 2: Assessment and Goal Setting
Step 3: Identifying an Ideal Solution
Step 4: Preparing for Implementation
Step 5: Implementing
Step 6: Review
Step 7: Maintenance and Institutionalization

For educators desiring even more structure in their school improvement projects, James Slezak (1984) has compiled a series of detailed forms, checklists, and tasks for many of the activities associated with building effective schools.

The aforementioned use of the term Our School is consistent with the predominant literature on educational change—the best and most sustained educational improvements happen on the individual school level. The March 1985 issue of *Educational Leadership* is devoted to the theme, "Excellence: School by School." That's what educators like Ernest Boyer and John Goodlad have been preaching for years. That's also what educators know best about how to implement change. The excellence movement does have its enlightened section leaders, like Ted Sizer, who understand the subleties of schools and how to foster excellence by climbing reasoned stairsteps with periodic landings for everyone to catch their breath.

Yet, the greatest "movers and shakers" of educational excellence more closely resemble Ross Perot, the Texas billionaire. Their approach to educational reform is to decree what is to be via the power of law and they back it up with stiff regulations supported by sanctions and/or incentives. Perhaps, unfortunately, such leaders appear very adept at manipulating the political process for their purposes. For instance, to sustain the quest for reforms, the Governors of Tennessee and Arizona have considered founding a national citizens' lobby (Toch 1984a: 1).

The latter idea will appeal to groups like the Institute for Responsive Education in Boston or the National Committee for Citizens in Education from Columbia, Maryland. Educators could be left out in the cold, unless they educate or co-opt such organizations or form coalitions with them.

A grassroots counter-revolution is underway sponsored by the Public Education Information Network lead by Harold Berlak of Washington University in St. Louis. The primary concern of this coalition of 180 educators is that the reforms are "top down." Their contention is that "people in each school community must develop their own agendas and specific programs for reform" (Currence 1985: 6). In other words, the control of education should be referred to local leaders to create schools dedicated to the principles of equity, excellence, and democracy.

Real programmatic excellence can best be achieved when principals and teachers have pride in their own personal endeavors on behalf of children. Individual educators with their efficacy intact are a potent incentive for achieving excellence. Teamwork is the capstone for accomplishment.

According to a booklet published by the American Educational Studies Association (Razwid 1984: 14):

> Excellence cannot be mandated. It cannot be imposed on any institution, nor can its participants be coerced into pursuing it. Excellence emerges as a quality of the particular goals and norms chosen, the understandings and expectations created and shared by a group of people. It is the commitments of the participants which is the key. More precisely, institutional excellence is not so much a matter of individual values, as of norms participants share, norms which define the crucially important climate or ethos, the moral order, of a school. The excellence challenge then is a matter of generating an environment conducive to a shared commitment to excellence.

The sheer power and intensity of those politicians, educators, citizens and business leaders pushing the excellence movement down from the apex of our society mitigate against grassroot efforts of educators. The professionals are seen by some reformers as obstacles to be overcome, rather than partners. The public has endorsed many of the concepts and recommendations of reports like *A Nation at Risk* simply because they are impatient with the professional educator. Many educators already know some things they could do to improve their performance, but they have resigned themselves to little more than "getting by." This may seem harsh, however, practitioners see examples of this problem every day.

"Educational excellence . . . demands challenge, sets high expectations, invigorates, assesses performance and holds individuals accountable" (Razwid 1984: 17). One implication of the excellence movement is that unless educators grasp hold of the reins of renewal and improvement, others will determine the fate of the profession and the direction of our schools.

Local school boards who wish to jump on a state's reform bandwagon should be wary of using copycat tactics endorsing reforms in their districts. For those persons occupying the seats of power at any level of the educational enterprise, it is easy to overlook other mainstay actors when caught up in the fevered passions of reform. State reform legislators and politicians may be geographically separate and removed from the clutches of irrate citizens, but local school board members have no immunity. Hence, the National School Boards

Association has proposed "A Process Approach for Assessing Excellence in Education" (see Figure 4-1) to remind board members that "It is important for the board member to understand that every participant in the educational process has clear responsibilities for what happens in the schools" (Van Loozen 1984: 5). Furthermore, local board members are advised to make the "right contacts" politically with other local officials, business and labor; other school boards; state school boards associations and officials; the National School Boards Association; other state and national associations; and federal officials to " . . . provide the leadership to muster public support to answer the Commission's call for excellence, and do so outside of the arena of federal intervention" (Van Loozen 1984: 49-51).

Recent statewide educational reforms have often ignored the harvesting of input from the various stakeholders and clients with a vested interest in the educational system. Consequently, some of the reforms themselves have come under vicious attack from disgruntled persons and groups. For example, the C average requirement for participation in extracurricular activities has come under particularly heavy fire in West Virginia and Texas. Local school boards, due to their public accessibility, would have been hard pressed to pass such demanding policies on the local level. Local boards, however, who believe in this kind of requirement can capitalize upon the state action to reinforce their philosophy. The county board of education whom this author serves did just that by working with coaches to encourage the monitoring and upgrading of the academic performance of student athletes. Astute local boards are taking advantage of selected state reforms to further their own aims and viewpoints.

Few, if any, of the recommendations for educational excellence can become programmatic realities with the mere striking of a gavel. One of the lessons that emerged from the aftermath of innovative projects over the last two decades is that results take time to show up and changes require a long term sustained commitment to gain institutional status. Some states and many school districts have apparently recognized that a core of dedicated people are necessary to keep the flame of excellence lit. One approach that seems to work is a two-tiered system. The first tier is a blue-ribbon coalition or commission that sets parameters, generates political supports, musters resources, and gathers at strategic milestones to publicly assess progress. The second tier is more action-oriented, composed of individu-

Figure 4-1. A Process Approach for Assessing Excellence in Education.

Now, the process model looks like this:

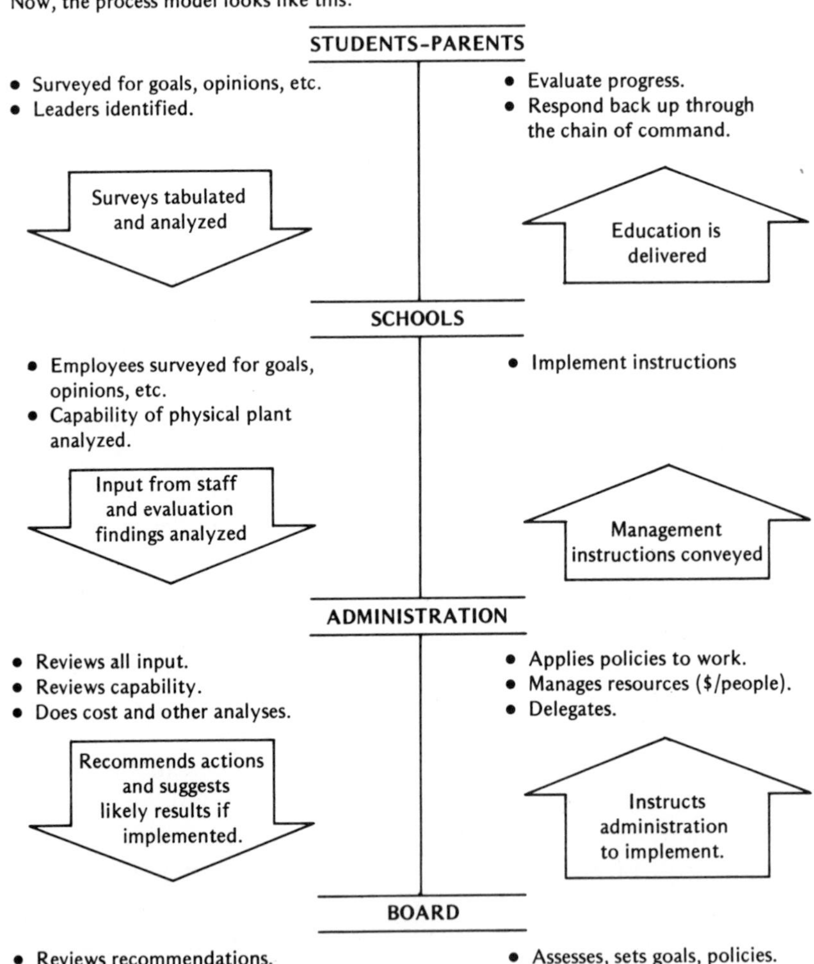

- Reviews recommendations.
- Consults with superintendent.
- Assesses, sets goals, policies.
- Allocates resources.

It is important for the board member to understand that every participant in the educational process has clear responsibilities for what happens in the schools.

As depicted by the accompanying chart, the school board has the essential responsibility, through its policy process, for setting overall goals and objectives for the schools and for review and evaluation of the effectiveness of the schools.

The purpose of using a process approach to meeting these critical board responsibilities is to recognize that administrators, professional staff members, parents, and students are also key participants in the educational process.

Source: Lu Van Loozen, ed., *A Blueprint for Education Excellence: A School Board Member's Guide* (Washington, D.C.: National School Boards Association, 1984), p. 5.

als responsible for implementation who graft the details onto the skeleton. The key is moving people from general acceptance of school improvement to specific actions.

CURRICULUM AND TEXTBOOKS

The excellence movement cannot truly take credit for originating the reexamination of the curriculum and textbooks used in American schools, only for rapidly bringing these matters into focus. The curriculum of most school systems, and, even, state mandated curriculum seems to be in a perpetual state of fluidity. Nearly every educational reform movement, innovation, or funded project addressed the curriculum because it is the very stuff of what makes schooling unique from other kinds of learning processes. The National Commission on Excellence is certainly not the first to call for more than the traditional 3R's or to propose a revised curriculum centered around the "New Basics." Textbooks, too, have their turn in the limelight on a regular basis, if for no other reason than the very practical fact that textbooks often become the curriculum. The renewed efforts to upgrade curriculum and textbooks are generally seen as positive steps by both teachers and the public, although there is obviously no consensus on the exact path to follow.

The reform movement has helped school boards and lay citizens grow in their understanding of the term curriculum, a concept usually discussed without much definition. Prior to all the current reform activity Robert Shutes (1981: 21) demystified some ideas about curriculum by writing:

> Curriculum: one of education's most misunderstood concepts. The public hears the word bandied about so much that it naturally assumes "the curriculum" is a tangible, official document (no doubt locked away in some school board office) that embodies the entire structure of the school program. I'm guessing that eight times out of ten the public is wrong in its assumption. That's because administrators and board members often talk as if they have a clear-cut, written curriculum when all they really have is a set of vague assumptions about what is being taught in their schools.

As indicated in earlier sections of this chapter, other reform authors and panels have decried the lack of comprehensive instructional goals, coherence, and focus that ought to be "in the curriculum."

Many curriculum guides have, in the words of John Goodlad, become little more than a "conceptual swamp" (1984: 49) due to being poorly organized and overly massive. The reform movement has revealed to the public one of education's missing links—the connection between the curriculum and what we want for children as a result of their schooling experiences.

While there are variations state-to-state or report-to-report about what the content of the curriculum should be, there is a growing consensus about some form of a "core curriculum" with less reliance upon electives. The current push stresses common studies for all students with more rigor and increased number of courses in "hard" subjects like math, science, foreign languages, classical literature, computers, etc. Slight mention is made of the arts and humanities or vocational education.

This trend reverses the development of differentiated or relevant curricula designed to keep students interested and enrolled in school. If this "new" curriculum is poorly structured or poorly taught, it could mean losses in equity and access for the less gifted, handicapped, minorities, potential dropouts, and those out of the mainstream for whatever reason. Ideally, curriculum will be constructed and instruction delivered in such a way that all students master the building blocks of skills before being presented with new material. Unfortunately, the pressure for curricular quick fixes will probably mitigate against the latter, preferred approach. Most school districts also lack the resources to produce quality homegrown curricular and instructional materials that are both equity and excellent orientated.

Educators have only begun to scratch the surface with respect to creating the perfect curricular organization. The excellence movement may contribute modest gains to curriculum theory, but this will not be where its major impact will occur. The reformers will stride ahead in more fertile fields. Parents and teachers are aware that "Children simply cannot wait until curriculum is more systematic" (Steller 1983: 74) and will rely upon what they've always relied upon—the "patchwork curriculum." The reformers will not have the patience to sustain their attack upon the fundamental structure of curriculum. They will, however, be able to reorder the priorities of the prevailing curriculum.

One area reformers have found easier to affect is the upgrading of textbooks. Textbook publishers and writers and the special interest groups and censorship boards that function as watchdogs determine to a great extent what is presented to children. Textbooks have much more influence on what is taught than curriculum guides. Textbooks tend to standardize the instructional program across the country. Teachers, principals and supervisors have known this for a long, long time, although it seems to have become acknowledged on a wider scale in the last ten years or so. In many classrooms the textbook is the curriculum.

Critics have turned their pointers directly at the textbook publishers with accusations of superficiality and lowered reading levels. Former Secretary of Education, T. H. Bell, has emphatically stated that textbook companies were "dumbing down" their products to be on par with the least able students. The textbook people counter with claims that they are meeting the market needs which include socio-political pressures and classroom teachers who don't want content that is beyond the skill or comprehension capabilities of their pupils. Some of the criticism of textbooks is valid, however, within a historical perspective it should be noted that regarding "Textbooks: 'There Has Never Been a Golden Age'" (Schuster 1985: 40).

The real problem is quite simply described by P. Kenneth Komoski, executive director of Educational Products Information Exchange Institute: "If instructional materials continue to be developed in order to sell rather than on their ability to facilitate teaching and learning, education will suffer" (1985: 31). Connie Muther reinforces this idea in an article about how educational research affects the selection of instructional materials. She writes: "Textbook authors and consultants seem resigned that current research results cannot be incorporated in depth since publishers must produce what sells. And the unfamiliar won't sell" (1985: 86).

The adoption of textbooks has traditionally been a function of the local school district. While most school boards have policies about the steps to be covered in the selection of textbooks, the rationale has often been as much to avoid conflict of interest as to raise the quality of education. Florida is among a small group of states now calling for more training for members of textbook selection committees. Other state departments of education are looking more carefully about the books that are on the state's approved list. Some large state purchasers of textbooks have even considered forming a "cartel for excellence" to press for better books. Various state officials have been active in communicating their dissatisfactions to textbook publishers. The solutions for upgrading textbooks will come

Table 4-5. School Board Tasks to Achieve Excellence.

To ensure excellence in the school curriculum, a board will undertake these important tasks:

- Develop curriculum and instruction policy that proclaims, generally or specifically, the board's instructional beliefs, expectations, and priorities.
- Shape and reshape goals for instruction, whether they be initially grounded in the Three Rs, the New Basics, Thinking and Problem-Solving Abilities, or otherwise.
- Provide curriculum guidance, including defining what are basics, frills, core curriculum, and electives.
- Support the curriculum with finances specifically targeted toward meeting the school system's instructional goals for excellence.
- Determine staff and financial support for various special instructional programs (gifted students, remedial classwork, alternative schools, shut-in programs, preschool, and so on).
- Provide guidance for and oversee the selection of textbooks and instructional material.
- Balance the curriculum to provide equal opportunity for all learners to perform to the best of their ability and to receive both basic and enrichment instruction.
- Provide for quality teaching by setting high standards for competency and backing them up with adequate resources with which to attract, train, and maintain the most highly skilled administrators and teachers.
- Set competency standards and graduation requirements for students.
- Establish codes for discipline and policies on other issues relative to the learning environment.
- Ensure there is a systematic program for monitoring and evaluating student progress and achievement.
- Monitor innovations in education and provide for regular review of policies.
- Recent research into policy development seems to indicate that clearly written board policies in areas of curriculum development, human resource development and collective bargaining can directly or indirectly affect excellence.
- A school district's instructional program ultimately will reflect the board's view on how to best fit community expectations for education into the dollars the community is willing to approve for education. As such, the instructional program has the potential to be anything from a collection of dry facts to a truly dynamic plan for excellence.
- How far the board is permitted to pursue excellence through its policies, goals and objectives will be determined directly by the level of public support for the board's efforts. This fact puts the premium on involving others in the board's assessment and policymaking activities.

Source: Lu Van Loozen, ed., *A Blueprint for Educational Excellence: A School Board Member's Guide* (Washington, D.C.: National School Boards Association, 1984), pp. 21-22.

Table 4-6. Board Policies Related to Excellence in Curriculum.

Teaching Methods	Instructional Services
School District Goals and Objectives	Academic Achievement
Staff Conduct	Staff-Student Relations
Curriculum Development and Design	Grading
Instructional Goals	Graduation Requirements
Special Programs Administration	Student Assignments to Classes
Instructional Arrangements	Recognition for Accomplishment
Guidance Program	Homework
Commitment to Accomplishment	Testing Program
Class Interruptions	Student/Parent Conferences
School Building Administration	Cocurricular and Extracurricular Programs
Educational Philosophy	Accomplishment Reporting to the Public
Student, Staff and Community Involvement in Decisionmaking	Grouping for Instruction
Scheduling for Instruction	Evaluation of Instructional Programs
	Student Discipline and Conduct

Source: Lu Van Loozen, ed., *A Blueprint for Educational Excellence: A School Board Member's Guide* (Washington, D.C.: National School Boards Association, 1984), p. 23.

from the states or, perhaps, professional associations because of the clout necessary to gain the attention of the textbook publishers.

This is not to say that local school districts cannot significantly upgrade the quality of the textbooks they purchase or their curriculum in the pursuit of excellence. To be successful, school boards must treat these areas with a long term commitment. According to the National Commission on Excellence in Education the current negative conditions in public schools are the result of a twenty year slide. Climbing out of this abyss will take time. Recognizing the implications of this long haul effort the National School Boards Association suggest local school boards undertake the tasks in Table 4-5 and formulate policies of excellence around the topics listed in Table 4-6. Lasting improvements in these areas are often best constructed in an incremental fashion.

EQUITY

Equity has been repeatedly mentioned throughout this chapter in connection with other issues. The historical importance of equity in education requires that its relation to the excellence movement be explored.

Many critics of the excellence reforms base their arguments upon the potential stifling of equity. In the extreme, the reformers are cast as elitists with little concern for the less advantaged, downtrodden, minorities, or even, for fair play. The pragmatists among those advocating equity, knowing that talk is cheap, spotlight the allocation of resources and actual results.

As seen earlier in the brief discussion of state funding, one of their goals is the equal distribution of wealth among school districts. The matter of allocating scarce resources at the state level is made more complex due to the diminishing federal role in mandating that students have equal opportunities and to the accelerating state reform activity. Cynthia Brown, former chief of civil rights for the U.S. Education Department, believes "Lawsuits similar to school-finance suits might be initiated to ensure that scarce resources like math and science teachers are equitably distributed. Such lawsuits would assert that states are liable if students, particularly minority students, suffer disportionately because their school systems are unable to offer the basic program of instruction mandated by the state" (Hertling 1985: 11). This may be especially true in those states who have sanctioned more years of math or science for students, while pushing the standards for teaching credentials upward. The teacher shortages predicted to be on the horizon will exacerbate this problem.

Threats of lawsuits are not likely to relieve the pressure from those state reforms that have defined excellence as a mad rush for superiority. Unfortunately, those who benefit most from equity in education have little else besides such threats to gain the active attention of many state powerbrokers. Without money, votes or public opinion, they are forced to turn to the courts to secure some degree of equity. That is a slow process. The pendulum of educational change is bound to swing back towards equality at some point, but that may be too late for some children. Other means will be needed, if equity is to be part of the current reform movement and not swept away because of it.

The key may very well rest in the hearts of enlightened educators willing to join the great debates over educational reform. The very life work of millions of educators dedicated to the well-being of others is at stake. As much as any professionals, educators have a working knowledge of the debilitating effects of inequities imposed by socioeconomic differences, sexual preferences, racism, ethnic biases, etc. The passions within sincere educators need to be aroused so they lead school renewal towards achieving excellence *and* equity.

The National Coalition of Advocates for Students has prepared a unique report about improving the quality of education in public schools. Some of the language is so strong in tone and negative about schools to the point that it will not win people over to the side of equity, unless they are already predisposed in that direction. Nevertheless, *Barriers to Excellence: Our Children at Risk* (1985) is a book that should be required reading, if that were possible, for all those promoting the excellence movement. The historical role of the public schools as institutions offering opportunities for individuals and society itself to achieve the "American Dream" is an underlying theme of this study.

Recognizing that "Children at risk are capable of success in school and work," the plea for equity is made (National Board of Inquiry 1985: v) because:

> The United States cannot afford to leave underdeveloped the talents of millions of children who happen to be born different by virtue of race, language, sex, or income status. Nor can it ignore, under the pretense of educational excellence, the unfinished national task of offering every child—Black, Hispanic, Native American, Asian and White—a fair chance to learn and become a self-sufficient citizen. The unique promise of this nation has been its commitment to extend opportunity to all—not just some—of its children.

The National Board of Inquiry formed to prepare *Barriers to Excellence* is truly interested in educational excellence with the understanding that *all* children ought to be included in "the mainstream of teaching and learning" and given "access to higher standards of academic performance." Their two major strategies are: (1) removing barriers that schools have placed in the way of student learning and (2) recognizing that many children need extra help to attain the levels of learning of which they are capable. Fourteen overriding recommendations (see Table 4-7) and specific action steps for federal, state and local decision makers are listed to "respond to the needs

Table 4-7. Equity Recommendations from *Barriers to Excellence.*

- To minimize class discrimination in the schools by restoring and expanding support for programs serving economically disadvantaged students, recognizing that it is a false economy to cut programs that work for poor children.
- To reaffirm commitments to nondiscrimination by race by vigorously pursuing efforts to eliminate racially identifiable educational programs and altering school practices that result in minority children dropping out, becoming "push outs," or staying in the educational system but failing to learn.
- To minimize discrimination against students from linguistic minorities by recognizing the importance of bilingual education as a technique that supports their academic development and by moving towards an acceptance of bilingualism as a means of enriching our society.
- To renew commitment to the ideals embodied in Title IX (Education Amendments of 1972) sex discrimination legislation thereby assuring that female students will have an opportunity to develop their talents and skills fully.
- To promote changes in special education that will improve services for children with moderate and severe handicaps while developing more regular education options for children with milder learning difficulties so that they can attend school without being labeled handicapped.
- To end tracking and rigid ability grouping, recognizing that such practices work against the best interests of both the most vulnerable and most able students in the schools.
- To eliminate the use of inappropriate testing practices as a basis for making educational decision which have far-reaching effects upon the futures of young people.
- To broaden curriculum and teaching practices so that they better meet the needs of diverse student populations, based upon the proposition that individual children have differing needs and abilities.
- To move vocational education programs away from the current narrow focus upon job skills and toward the broader goal of preparing young people for a changing world of work.
- To reinstate federal mandates for parent involvement in local programs.
- To remove barriers to parental involvement and create opportunities for parents to participate in decisions about school staffing, education programming, school discipline, and resource allocation.
- To assure students of their due process rights in such matters as school suspension and expulsion.
- To recognize the usefulness and cost effectiveness of high quality early childhood education and child care programs as a means of preventing school failure.

Table 4-7. continued

- To respond to the needs of an increasing number of young people whose chances of remaining in school would be increased if they had help with serious personal and social problems.
- To increase tax equity through state systems of raising revenues that are not dependent on regressive taxes and that insulate property poor districts against excessive local taxes.
- To eliminate inequality in education access, resulting from disparities in funding for schools.
- To raise funding levels for programs serving children at risk so that every eligible child is assured of adequate services.
- To ensure that a comprehensive school-to-work transition program is available for all youth.
- To strengthen counseling services for non-college-bound youth and develop job placement services in high schools.
- To encourage broadly based community councils charged with responsibility for examining what could be done locally to revitalize the local economy and create jobs for youth.

Source: National Board of Inquiry, *Barriers to Excellence: Our Children at Risk* (Boston: The National Coalition of Advocates for Students, 1985), pp. 108-25.

yet to be addressed in realizing the dreams of educational excellence that includes equity for all children."

One of the co-chair persons for the National Board of Inquiry, Harold Howe II (1984), has asserted that educators need "boldness" if we are to succeed in an unflawed approach to excellence. "Giving Equity a Chance in the Excellence Game" is the title of a speech he presented before the Education Writers Association in 1984. He believes the following issues desperately need attention for equity to exist: high school dropout rates, jobs, teaching loads imposed by poor scheduling, freedom for individual schools, building the school's atmosphere, motivating students, fairness in education funding, professional development for teachers, preschool education, and vocational education.

If there were no significant differences in the actual educational results demonstrated by ethnic groups, races, sexes, socioeconomic classes, etc.; equity would simply not be an issue of debate. If all students performed equally well (or equally poorly) without regard to such classifications, public schools would not be accused of inequities. Obviously, there are inequities in educational results. Furthermore, in all probability this problem will become increasingly aggravated with the press for excellence unless solutions are found.

One example of an alarming trend is the recent erosion of educational opportunity and achievement gains made by Blacks. The dramatic progress by Black students actuated since 1960 or thereabouts has fallen off in the last decade according to *Equality and Excellence: The Educational Status of Black Americans*—a project commissioned by the College Board's Office of Academic Affairs. The various indicators and research compiled for this report have not been "in the forefront of the nation's attention. Educators and policymakers who are concerned about equality, as well as fundamental excellence, must put them there" (Darling-Hammond 1985).

The tension between excellence and equity was a topic of discussion among a group of Black educators speaking at the 1985 annual meeting of the Association of Black Foundation Executives. They generally expressed the view that the excellence movement was at odds with the notion of equity, at least in practice. The speakers were apparently not opposed to excellence or higher standards as long as this was not a disguised retreat from equity and equity received attention as well. Mr. Norman Francis, a member of the National Commission on Excellence in Education, was quoted as saying, "I think we have to be part of the total movement, but also an all-black movement" to attain excellence in education for black students (Sirkin 1985: 1).

This last comment is a profoundly insightful statement about the symbiotic relationship between equity and excellence. In the larger context, to survive as a practical and viable goal in U.S. education, equity must live as an organism within the excellence reform movement. To maintain itself as a healthy, growing seedling for educational excellence, care must be taken to blend equity concerns into the current reform movement. Otherwise, the imperative for improvement will become splintered and wither.

STANDARDS, EXPECTATIONS AND REQUIREMENTS

The call for higher standards, expectations and requirements whistling through the various state and national educational reform packages has educators scrambling—some defensively, but numerous practitioners are actually supportive of these ideas in the abstract. The disagreements occur over exactly what such notions mean and what one does to translate and implement them in schools. Surprisingly, many educators will admit that a degree of softness has invaded the profession. Teachers and principals are generally not opposed to higher standards, expectations or requirements, as long as the manifestations of these ideas are not overly cumbersome, imposed from the "outside" and appropriate support is demonstrated. The state educational reforms that are going to be predictably more successful will meet these three criteria among others. Most do not, and they fail or are diluted before they touch students.

Even the staunchest defenders of prevailing educational methods are willing to say that there are schools that need improving when it comes to standards, expectations, and/or requirements. We all know "schools down the street" that could be doing a better job. The easiest way for any of us to change "that school" from a block away might be to suggest that the staff eliminate social promotions, stop accepting substandard work from students, or toss out frivolous electives. Back in our own school we might build a consensus among a critical mass of staff members to promote children on the basis of performance, heighten the minimal levels of acceptable student products, or add more academically rigorous courses to the curriculum. The second approach may be more palatable to educators, but both deal with the same concepts touted in the excellence movement. Most state reforms more closely resemble the former top down method.

Many of the recent reform reports frequently and interchangeably use the terms standards, expectations, and requirements; however, they are not synonymous.

"Requirements determine what must be 'taken' and 'passed' in order to qualify for certain courses or for graduation, but they do not determine the actual levels of performance that must be demonstrated. While standards are also used to determine progress, in the system, they define the actual performance levels which determine success and failure, qualification and disqualification, eligibility and ineligibility" (Spady and Marx 1984: 13). Expectations are based upon assumptions about capacity for performance and are usually quite personalized.

Increasing requirements is the most straightforward, least controversial, and most easily managed of these three improvement strategies. It is partly for these reasons that raising high school graudation requirements has captured the attention of so many state legislatures and local school boards. A legitimate counter argument which usually surfaces is that "more is not always better" or "learning cannot be equated with seat time." People tend to respond to these critics in much the same manner that megavitamin health advocates deal with scientists who say large doses of vitamins have not been proven to make people healthier—"that may be true, but there isn't proof that large doses hurt either." The implications one should draw is that increasing educational requirements is a viable approach at the state or local level and possibly one of the first areas reformers ought to tackle.

In some localities educational standards have been abysmal. The most common instance of low institutional standards is that of promotions from grade to grade. The phenomena of social promotions has crept under the school house door to become standard practice in some school districts. In such situations youngsters are "passed on" for having birthdays rather than mastery of subject matter or for learning academic skills. Prior to the 1900s, standards for promotion were actually higher, although both requirements and expectations were lower. Before the turn of the century, fewer students were promoted because of their chronological age. School requirements were not as complex at that time, nor was everyone expected to finish high school with a diploma. The real key to excellence is the proper mix of requirements, expectations, and standards.

Setting standards is tricky business at best. Thomas Toch describes the experiences of Philadelphia as the superintendent attempted to abandon social promotions in an article entitled "The Dark Side of the Excellence Movement" (1984b: 173–176). The title gives away the plot. The new promotion policy was delayed partly "because the school system had no strategy for working with students who failed to meet the new standards." It was estimated that 40,000 students would have been retained if the policy had been implemented. The most common solution for retainees is to go to summer school. Philadelphia estimated the summer school program would cost sixteen million dollars. High standards can also be expensive.

The financial cost is immaterial to some persons who are concerned about the potential social costs they envision if higher standards result in more dropouts or increased stratification of students. A report from Johns Hopkins University, "Raising Standards and

Retaining Students: The Impact of the Reform Recommendations on Potential Dropouts" (McDill, Pallas, and Natriello 1985), echoes the possibilities of such occurrences—marginal students may fall out or between the cracks with higher standards for promotions. Paradoxically, these researchers noted that "The higher the demand level in the classroom, the more likely students were to report paying attention in class and spending time on homework." In keeping with the definitions stated earlier, this conclusion seems more of a matter of high expectations in the classroom than one of standards. These researchers call for a "balanced emphasis to the ideas of quality and equality of education" and suggest positive alternatives including reducing school size, utilizing individualized instruction, and promoting school climates in lieu of imposing higher standards.

Efforts to raise promotion standards can also face outright contempt and judicial challenge. Over the last several decades, U.S. society has become litigous and education is not exempt from its own share of sue-happy clients. A string of school districts and states have been sued for approving higher standards for grade level promotions and related matters; however, the fear of being sued should not make educators timid about raising standards. According to Earl Hoffman, " . . . the state and federal courts are regularly upholding the responsible decisions of educators and therefore educators should be confident in setting and maintaining their own reasonable standards" (Hoffman 1985: 17).

The courts are not the only ones to back up the concept of higher standards. A recent survey sponsored by the National Institute of Education was publicized in the April/May 1985 issue of *Research in Brief* as "Public Supports Tougher School Standards." Among the findings of this survey of 1200 adults (McKinney 1985) were that:

> Ninety-five percent favor requiring students to pass reading and math tests before they can graduate from high school or be promoted from junior high school. . . . More than 80 percent favor graduation exams even if this would mean their child never received a regular high school diploma because s/he was unable to pass the test.

The current Secretary of Education, William Bennett, acknowledges that raising standards may result in some students on the edge dropping off and out of school, but he maintains that the educationally and economically disadvantaged " . . . are the people who need standards the most, not for purposes of punishment, but for purposes of aspiration, for internalizing those standards" (Hertling 1985: 1).

Some people are not so willing to simply write these children off as statistical casualities. New York City has a series of public alternative high schools for the purpose of dropout prevention. The Public Education Association conducted a two year study in the early 1980s of these programs for high risk youngsters. The findings showed that these efforts helped about 55 percent of those entering students, while others did not continue in school. One particular school, Satellite Academy, demonstrated unique success in lowering the dropout rate and in reaching the highest graduation and persistence rates. The following characteristics were unearthed at Satellite Academy and other effective programs (Foley 1985: 24–27):

- Well-defined student populations
- Principals who are strong academic leaders
- Diversified teachers' roles
- Partial course credit, fast-paced cycles, and learning contracts
- Encouragement of participation
- Student involvement in activities critical to school goals, such as admissions policy and course evaluation
- Clear standards of conduct set in a few commonly agreed-upon, frequently discussed school rules
- Small school size

Another perspective on the issue of standards for promotions comes from a sound pedagogical basis: theories of developmental readiness. Failure to achieve in a particular grade level is often as much a function of developmental readiness as anything else. Continuous progress curricular programs are one means of recognizing this basic psychological principal of human growth. The tradition of grade level assignments has been too strong to be replaced in most schools. Some enlightened and politically savvy educators combine these two systems and manage to keep most everyone happy.

Ralph Frick of Atlanta University has provided a distinctive symbolic way to represent the case for higher standards in terms of grade level promotions that may be more saleable to the public than the typical educational jargon. He suggests viewing retentions and the allocation of time children need to develop as "academic redshirting" (Frick 1985: 24). Football players often sit out a year so that their physical growth during that time will enhance their chances of athletic success. This investment of time is called "redshirting." Dr. Frick believes this idea has academic implications as well.

Raising standards relative to grade level promotions is a basic issue that exemplifies the complexities of higher standards in other aspects of education. Higher standards will bring about excellence for the students able to hurdle these heightened crossbars. Yet, for those with equity concerns on their consciences, every student, even those engulfed within poverty, social discomfort and other handicaps, must be held to high standards of excellence. The floor of student achievement must be raised as well as the ceiling. That's a clear challenge for the excellence movement.

High expectations is one of the causal factors that contribute to an effective school according to the research-based literature on the topic. Superior teachers possess the knack of transmitting to all of their students a belief that they are capable. The students come to believe in themselves. They feel that high achievement is not only possible, but within their grasp. Once thus inspired, these young people set out determined to perform at expected levels. The basic premise that drives effective schools is the conviction by the staff that all children can learn.

The excellence movement and the various state reforms are resolved to arouse people's expectations about the quality of education. The effect upon parents and the general public has gotten underway swimmingly. Subsequently, they have placed pressure upon educators, which is actually a plus for education. Some in the profession would prefer to do without such insistence by a vociferous public upon an improved educational system. This apprehension is misplaced for it is apathy, not interest, that is the enemy of education.

Legislation cannot mandate higher expectations for education. Aspirations and expectations are inherently a part of one's individual values or the mores of the community. Laws and policies can create a charged atmosphere where people rethink their opinions and challenge the status quo. Due to its subjectivity and elusive nature, it is difficult to manage and evaluate higher expectations, per se. It is evident, however, when expectations are low and just as obvious to an observer when they are high. Money cannot buy higher expectations. Leadership and individual desires for higher expectations tend to fix a tone wherein excellence can thrive in a school or district. Local educators and school boards will have to pick up this gauntlet thrown down by the reformers because expectations cannot be raised from the outside.

LEADERSHIP

Implementing change in education has high-stakes consequences for those in leadership roles. Jobs can be lost, if the reforms are unpopular or unsuccessful. Heroes can also be made if things turn out well. The state reforms and national reports have focused attention upon educational excellence and, thereby, opened the door to improvement. Local leadership is indispensable for productive follow-up and classroom applications.

Ron Edmonds and others associated with the effective schools research have cited strong leadership at the school level as one, if not the, key characteristic of instructionally effective schools (Cuban 1983). This often translates into a dynamic principal, although it is conceivable that leadership could emerge from a few persuasive instructors.

The role of the superintendent as an instructional leader has emerged as a "hot topic" over the last five years. Drawing on his or her leadership skills, a superintendent can become a proponent of good teaching, an advocate of children, and a salesperson for educational excellence.

Most state reforms are prescriptive mandates. End products are defined. How to get there is many times ignored. The implication is that local leadership must develop mechanisms to shoehorn the reforms into practice. That is, of course, the hard part of educational reforms.

Regarding instructional program improvement and principals, Gary Phillips of I/D/E/A, has written "Some do, some don't; some will, some won't. But someone must assume a leadership role. . . ." The more ownership all participants—including taxpayers and employers—have in program improvement projects, the more successful the outcome will be. Phillips claims that "A prescription without a process creates problems without improvement" (1983: 1).

Effective leadership generates and maintains the enthusiasm of everyone on the team. The elements of I/D/E/A's school improvement endeavor provide food for thought. They are:

1. Mobilizing new participants and creating new roles for existing participants.

2. Approaching program improvement as a continuous process, not a single event.
3. Expanding collaborative governance.
4. Rewarding quality and celebrating excellence.
5. Envisioning the best we can imagine.
6. Accompanying program improvement with planning improvement in the personal lives of all participants.
7. Using Theory-2 governance.
8. Realizing that any force powerful enough to be a constraint has the potential for being a source of assistance for program improvement.

The mantle of instructional leader has been forced upon principals, superintendents, and other administrators by the current reform movement. Many school executives relish this responsibility and see this opportunity as a convenient way to shed other unwanted burdens and concentrate on what they truly want to do. For many others, heavy retraining will be necessary. New administrative personnel are being subjected to higher standards in certification, graduate schools and employment practices (Stellar 1984: 1).

> The current nationwide demand for improved student achievement carries with it an emerging awareness of the importance of having good school administrators. Colleges of education are being chastised for not producing better leaders through their inservice programs. State departments of education are being called on to raise the certification standards for new administrators.
>
> In addition, school boards are being pressured to hire—or retrain—only those administrators who provide effective educational leadership. School boards are also being alerted to the need for training programs that will support and maintain a cadre of topnotch administrators.

Over the last several years, more and more states are seriously trying to improve administrative leadership within the context of the excellence reforms. Statewide initiatives to establish academies, institutes, seminars, workshops, staff development programs, or other new training ventures for school administrators have occurred in over forty states since 1983. The content may cover how to implement a particular state's reforms, to any administrative skill seen as supportive of the reform movement—at least in terms of excellence. Very little of the content of these programs for administrators appears to be related to equity, except in the broadest sense.

Leadership at the local community level is vital for the excellence movement to constructively influence teachers and learners.

A. Lorri Manasse, in writing about how to recognize and improve conditions for effective principals, states (1984: 13–14):

> In summary, effective schools do have effective principals, but there is no single formula for effective principals. Putting a strong principal into a poor school does not result in instant changes. Progress also requires resources, support and time; and the selection of a particular individual for a particular school requires careful attention to situational factors.
>
> The foregoing discussion about effective principals suggests a number of revisions in existing training, selection, certification and assessment practices. Before embarking on a program to change practices, however, policymakers need to consider some larger implications.
>
> – Effective principals can cause change. . . . districts need to acknowledge the implications of employing leaders who may not be content to operate according to existing expectations and policies.
>
> –Effective principals need a clear direction from the district. . . . support at the district level is essential if individual principals are to pursue excellence in their own buildings.

What Manassee has said about effective principals can be applied equally well to all effective school administrators interested in promoting educational excellence. Likewise, the latter two warnings or implications to school district policymakers are also pertinent for state policymakers in viewing effective superintendents and local school boards—they may rock the boat and they need support.

In the opinion of the writer of this chapter, the public has every reason to be optimistic about the future of education in this country. The leadership of most local school districts and most schools are caring, dedicated people who will take up the cause of excellence and equity and deliver upon the promise.

INSTRUCTIONAL TIME AND ORGANIZATIONAL PATTERNS

The school calendar and organizational patterns of September to June and kindergarten through grade twelve owe their origins to historical contexts far removed from pedagogical knowledge. In fact, most of our school routines, number of periods per day, number of minutes per period, class size, minutes assigned for each elementary subject, scheduling, etc.,—are tradition and culture bound. Neither educational research nor professional judgment has done much to significantly alter what has gone before in these areas.

Some of the national reports on excellence suggest that tracking should be eliminated, promotion and grouping ought to be based upon performance instead of age, larger blocks of instructional time should be available for many subjects, credit by examination offered, students should advance at their own continuous rate of progress, teachers should be organized by teams, etc. Few of these measures have or will become directives by state legislatures of state boards of education as it would not be practicable to impose such practices across an entire state.

In fact, few states have enacted laws or policies dealing with instructional time or organizational patterns with the exception of adding kindergarten or preschool programs, or reducing class size. Thirteen states have added some instructional time to the school day or calendar, but most of these actions are relatively minor or do not involve the high financial cost and the political fallout that would occur if statewide edicts were pronounced. It is not likely that many reforms in these areas will come from the state capitals.

While local school districts are continuously tinkering with organizational patterns, examinations into the use of time have grown more popular in recent times. Some of the ideas most frequently mentioned are listed below:

Using Available Time Better

- Reduce/eliminate classroom interruptions, such as PA announcements, late arrivals, etc.
- Reduce the amount of academic time missed due to assemblies, field trips, athletic contests, etc.
- Eliminate homerooms
- Reduce the amount of "passing time" between classes at the secondary level and reduce the amount of transition time between subjects at the elementary level
- Set clear and consistent standards for student behavior and enforce same
- Improve teachers' classroom management skills

- Reduce "downtime" for students who finish early by providing alternative activities
- Provide independent work for self-pacing of students
- Assign more homework, then check and grade it
- Provide supervised inschool suspension programs

Add More Time

- Expand summer school activities
- Provide extended day programs
- Open school on Saturday for special programs
- Consider longer days—7 hours
- Open tutoring center or homework hotlines for evening work
- Increase the school year to 200 days
- Add early childhood programs for 3 or 4 year olds
- Provide enrichment programs during vacations and holidays

Numerous educators in schools across the country have been working on increasing the "time on task" of students. Time on task has been demonstrated through research to be effective in improving achievement. The ultimate goal with "time on task" is to manage instruction so that each student, according to his/her ability, spends the appropriate time on the appropriate task. This has been labeled "Academic Learning Time."

Time-on-task emphases fall within the first of the above categories and are more likely to be willingly replicated than the ideas in the latter category. Adding more time typically involves adding costs, especially salary costs which is not likely to happen. Therefore, it is a safe prediction that education will be a long ways further down the road before we have a common 200 day school year.

TEACHERS AND OTHER PROFESSIONALS

Any effort to reach for educational excellence and increase achievement rests ultimately on the classroom teacher's shoulders. As stated in the book *Effective Instructional Management* (Zakariya 1983:69):

> Teachers are, of course, a mainstay in the educational enterprise. Teachers interpret a school board's goals and the superintendent's decisions through their daily actions. Not only do teachers directly influence student achievement, but their close contact with students builds rapport and memories that have a residual effect throughout many lives.

State after state has enacted reform legislation pinpointing the need for enhanced performance from teachers and other instructional personnel. While the motives may be in the right place, some hasty and ill-conceived attempts may backfire in the short run. A case in point is the Arkansas basic skills test for teachers. Few persons could persuasively argue that teachers should not have to be competent in basic skills. The offensive manner in which the law was publicized and implemented, however, resulted in a black eye for Arkansas teachers, affecting their morale and undoubtedly the quality of instruction offered their students. The teachers' organizations will also undoubtedly strike back politically in some way that will slow the process of educational reform in that state. Teachers on the whole are not to blame for "the rising tide of mediocrity" or at least the entire burden of blame should not be placed on them.

State legislators may be of a different mind as a majority of the states have passed laws or are seriously considering bills that would raise the standards of teacher training institutions, revise certification requirements upward, require competency tests of teachers, or provide some financial aid to prospective teachers who meet specific criteria. Local school districts should generally welcome these changes as it could very well mean that new staff members will be better trained and more capable than they would be otherwise.

Bills to increase the salaries of teachers have been signed into law in over twenty states in the last few years and proposed in at least another twenty states. Many of these increases have been addressed primarily towards beginning teachers. It is hoped that the establishment of higher beginning salaries will attract more skilled people to education. Part of the rationale for raising salaries statewide is to secure political favor with school employee groups. What is noteworthy about the current reform movement is that much of what was done to raise salaries was either part of a bigger educational reform package or there were some riders attached that added something positive to educational programming. Receiving a raise in salary positively affects teacher morale, thus improving school climate and, it should be expected, pupil gains.

For local school districts, the most challenging new laws are those involving career ladders or merit pay. Tennessee, Florida, and California are the states getting the most national notoriety for their incentive programs, but over a dozen states and many school districts are experimenting with different versions of career ladders or merit pay plans. The most difficult aspect of these schemes is making judgments about who is to move up the ladder or get merit. Few personnel evaluation systems are sufficiently refined to render both summative and formative information that is precise enough to make unquestioned judgments about merit.

Effective incentive plans should at least meet these criteria:

1. the expected performance level to be rewarded must be unambiguous and understood;
2. this goal must be viewed as legitimate and culturally acceptable by those directly involved;
3. the person for whom the reward is meant needs to be given direction on how to achieve the outcome;
4. fairness must be a recognized ingredient in the evaluation procedures; and
5. the reward itself must be abundantly motivating to change behavior.

One of the more fascinating merit pay ideas takes the onus from the individual and places it upon the team in the form of a merit school. A series of school-wide indicators—test scores, records of vandalism, attendance records of students and/or staff, various awards, etc.—are compiled into a profile. Criteria are then set to reward either the school program in some way, i.e., money to purchase a computer, or the rewards are divided among the individuals in the school. Most of the "merit schools" plans stay away from a competitive approach among schools, unless it is somehow done on the basis of improvement.

Education is a labor intensive enterprise with 80 percent or more of most school district budgets going towards personnel costs. Therefore, it is not surprising that most of the national excellence reports recommend wholesale changes in personnel practices. Making recommendations that employees ought to be evaluated more often and more comprehensively is fine, except that the real question of how is untouched. The salaries, scholarships, merit pay plans, financial incentives, award programs, etc., cited throughout the excellence movement literature are attractive tributes for outstanding teachers. Without outside funds, however, most of these financial complements will be little more than rhetorical gewgaw. The complexity of what it would truly take to transform what amounts to three generations of school people is beyond the scope of these reports. Nevertheless, the excellence reports are to be credited for encouraging people to break out of the shackles holding them to outmoded ways of managing people.

One of the more commonly utilized methods of changing the behavior of teachers and other educators is through staff development activities. School districts will have to reset their priorities with more emphasis on in-service programming to upgrade techniques and inspire staff to higher levels of performance. We must reach for excellence pretty much with the current collection of people we have on board. This necessitates high quality staff development programs on a scale and a delivery system unlike anything we have tried up to this point in U.S. education.

As Judith Warren Little states (1984: 101):

> In effect, we are confronted with a tremendous problem, or challenge, of organization, leadership, and scale. It is simply implausible that a small cadre of staff developers in any district will add measurably to the general fund of teachers' knowledge, skill, and enthusiasm, or that programs of the sort just described could be mounted by a district on a scale large enough to exert widespread influence. The lessons are of a different order of magnitude; the guidelines generated by these program examples are properly seen as guidelines for the organization and leadership of professional work in the day-to-day work of teaching.

The excellence movement has also served as a counter-weight to the aspects of collective bargaining that have placed a wedge between many professional educators. Excellence cannot be realized on the grand design envisioned by the reformer unless educators work in tandem. A major and as yet unanswered question is "Can we set in motion a collective commitment to the district's outcome goals and to trying . . . 'in every way possible to help students reach them'?" (Spady and Marx 1984: 20).

FINAL REMARKS

The excellence movement has ignited rich interactions among professionals and others about how to upgrade education. These discussions, while heated at times, are exciting, compelling and meaningful. Regardless of the strategies, programs, or techniques advocated by the various interested parties, the bottom line is that an undiminished profession and field of endeavor is being mobilized to respond to the challenge of being excellent. The resulting manifestations and interpretations of educational excellence will be a manifold of improvements, some better than others. It will take years to sort out the specific effects. The themes covered in this chapter are the ones that should have the most impact over time.

The historical view of the excellence movement will not be written for years, but educational historians have already begun to make some comparisons. For example, Carl Kaestle of the University of Wisconsin rejects the notion of international trade as a sound rationale for educational reform and reminds us of our historical equity concerns (1985: 423):

> There are problems aplenty in U.S. public education, and I don't want my historian's sense of deja vu to sound like indifference or a defense of the status quo. (Personally, I think that the pendulum should swing back somewhat toward academic commitment and training, but for a great many reasons other than to improve our competitive edge in international trade.) Nonetheless, I think that a historical perspective on international comparisons can keep us from being stampeded, from mistaking the rhetoric for the reality of American schooling, and from abandoning other important commitments we have made—commitments to equality of opportunity, to democratic access, and to cultural reconciliation through our public schools.

The excellence movement will surely influence education in the years to come in spite of the naysayers who suggest that it is simply a swing of the pendulum. Kaestle debunks that particular metaphor and substitutes his own—"The real U.S. school system is more like a huge tanker going down the middle of a channel, rock a bit from side to side as it attends first to one slight current and then to another" (Kaestle 1985).

Another scholar, Patricia Albjerg Graham (1985: 24–29) has provided a framework of six "Cautionary Admonitions From Our Educational Past" which could be employed as a contextual evaluation

Table 4-8. Historical Perspective on Reforms—Cautionary Admonitions from Our Educational Past.

1. Even if a statement of educational purpose attracts interest and support, its acceptance in the schools as a guide for educational practice will take a long time.
2. Any statement of educational desideratum must not depend for its success upon its full and total implementation.
3. As we consider educational goals and purposes, we need to be sensitive to the balance between educational aspirations that will primarily benefit the youngster and those that will principally benefit the society.
4. All who set goals for the schools need to recognize schools as the limited, though, important, institutions that they are.
5. We now know much more about education and how children learn and how teachers can be effective in aiding student learning than we previously knew.
6. New goals and purposes for education must involve educators.

Source: Patricia Albjerg Graham, "Cautionary Admonitions From Our Educational Past," *Education Week* 4 (January 30, 1985): 24-29.

and perspective for the excellence movement (see Table 4-8). Massive reforms have a life of their own with a timeless quality that transcends the immediate period of the reform itself.

The historical values of this country ultimately shape various educational reforms and innovations. An ad hoc group of twenty-seven individuals strongly interested in sustaining the current momentum for reform released a report on Thanksgiving Day 1984 to symbolically capture the feelings of obligation to our ancestors that occur on that day. A summary of their recommendations of what needs to be improved and those parties who should be implementors is given in Table 4-9. Their report addresses the fundamental issue of character as it relates to excellence (Thanksgiving Statement Group 1984). As such, this report attends to many of the basic undercurrents of the excellence movement as offered in this chapter.

The sheer momentum for educational excellence described herein will ensure that these reforms will continue for some time. The task ahead is one of applying these concepts in day to day living within schools. One of the reform leaders, Bill Honig (1985: 675), wrote an article whose title says it all—"The Educational Excellence Movement: Now Comes the Hard Part."

Table 4-9. Sustaining the Momentum for Reform in U.S. Education: Allocation of Responsibility for Action.

Responsible Persons and Institutions / *Action Areas*	Good Character	Academic Performance	The Academically Talented	Teachers and Teaching	Curriculum and Textbooks	Choice	Policymaking and Research	Undergraduate Education	Accurate Information
Parents	X	X				X			X
Teachers	X	X	X	X	X				
Local Public Schools	X	X	X	X	X	X	X		X
Public School Districts	X	X	X	X	X	X	X		X
States and State Agencies	X	X	X	X		X	X	X	X
Federal Government		X						X	X
Private Schools	X	X	X	X		X			
Media									X
Education Researchers	X	X					X		X
Institutions of Higher Education			X	X			X	X	X
Private Groups Formally Concerned with Education	X		X	X	X	X	X	X	
Prominent Citizens			X	X			X	X	
Courts	X		X	X		X		X	

Source: Thanksgiving Statement Group, *Developing Character: Transmitting Knowledge* (Chicago: ARL, 1984), p. 34.

The excellence movement, right or wrong in its focus, has afforded the profession a unique window of opportunity to achieve a new renaissance for education. It will take commitment, time, cooperation, and patience. Excellence must also be balanced with equity concerns to generate the support needed for the long haul. The dream and challenge is apparent.

REFERENCES

Augenblick, John. 1984. "The States and School Finance: Looking Back and Looking Ahead." *Phi Delta Kappan* 66 (November): 197–201.

Boyer, Ernest. 1983. *High School: A Report on Secondary Education in America.* New York: Harper Colophon Books.

Black, Theodore M. 1982. *Straight Talk About American Education.* New York: Harcourt Brace Jovanovich Publishers.

Brandt, Ron, ed. 1980. "Who Rules the Schools?", *Educational Leadership* 38 (November): 99–102.

____. 1984. "Education Policy: Who's in Charge?" *Educational Leadership* 42 (October): 3.

Brickell, Henry M., and Regina Paul. 1983. *A Checklist for Excellence.* New York: Policy Studies in Education.

Business-Higher Education Forum. 1983. *America's Competitive Challenge: The Need for a National Response.* Washington, D.C.: American Council on Education.

Committee on Science, Engineering, and Public Policy. 1984. *High Schools and the Changing Workplace: The Employers' View.* Washington, D.C.: National Academy of Sciences.

Cramer, Jerome. 1984. "Some State Commandments of Excellence Ignore Reality and Undercut Local Control," *The American School Board Journal* 171, no. 9 (September): 23–31.

Cuban, Larry. 1983. "Effective Schools Research," *Phi Delta Kappan* 64, no. 10 (June): 695–696.

____. 1984. "School Reform by Remote Control: SB 813 in California," *Phi Delta Kappan* 66, no. 3 (November): 213–215.

Currence, Cindy. 1985. "Grassroots Coalition of Educators Calls for 'Bottom-Up' Reforms," *Education Week* 21 (February): 6, 13.

Darling-Hammond, Linda. 1985. *Equality and Excellence: The Educational Status of Black Americans.* New York: College Board Publications.

De Bevoise, Wynn. 1983. *The Contribution of Education to Economic Productivity.* Eugene, Oreg.: Clearinghouse on Educational Management.

Dianda, Marcella. 1984. *The Superintendent's Can-Do Guide to School Improvement.* Washington, D.C.: Council for Educational Development and Research.

Educational Equality Project. 1983. *Academic Preparation for College.* New York: The College Board.

Flesch, Rudolf. 1955. *Why Johnny Can't Read.* New York: Perennial Library, Harper & Row.

Foley, Eileen. 1985. "What Will Recalibrated Standards Hold for Dropout-Prone Students?," *Education Week* 4, no. 30 (April): 24–27.

Frick, Ralph. 1985. "In Support of Academic Redshirting," *Education Week* 4, no. 17 (January): 24.

Goodlad, John. 1984. *A Place Called School: Prospects for the Future.* New York: McGraw-Hill Book Co.

Graham, Patricia Albjerg. 1985. "Cautionary Admonitions From Our Educational Past," *Education Week* 4, no. 19 (January): 24–29.

Hertling, James. 1985. "States Urged to Assume Civil-Rights Leadership." *Education Week* 4, no. 5 (May): 11.

Hertling, James, and Alina Tugend. 1985. "Bennett Maintains Higher Standards Benefit the Poor," *Education Week* 4, no. 22 (February): 1, 35.

Hoffman, Earl. 1985. "Raising Standards Without Undue Fear of Judicial Reprisal," *Education Week* 4, no. 17 (January): 16–17.

Holt, John. 1964. *How Children Fail.* New York: Dell Publishing Co., Inc.

Honig, Bill. 1985. "The Educational Excellence Movement: Now Comes the Hart Part." *Phi Delta Kappan* 66, no. 10 (June): 676–681.

Howe, Harold. 1984. "Giving Equity a Chance in the Excellence Game," The 1984 Martin Buskin Memorial Lecture delivered April 28, 1984 at the Education Writers Association National Seminar in Philadelphia, Pennsylvania. Reproduced by the National Committee for Citizens in Education.

Kaestle, Carl. 1985. "Education Reform and the Swinging Pendulum," *Phi Delta Kappan* 66, no. 6 (February): 422–423.

Kaplan, George. 1984. "Hail to a Chief or Two: The Indifferent Presidential Record in Education," *Phi Delta Kappan* 66, no. 1 (September): 7–12.

Kirst, Michael. 1984. "The Changing Balance in State and Local Power to Control Education," *Phi Delta Kappan* 66, no. 3 (November): 189–191.

Komoski, P. Kenneth. 1985. "Instructional Materials Will Not Improve Until We Change the System," *Educational Leadership* 42, no. 7 (April): 31–38.

Little, Judith Warren. 1984. "Seductive Images and Organizational Realities in Professional Development," *Teachers College Record* 86 (Fall): 84–102.

Louchs-Horsley, Susan, and Leslie Hergert. 1985. *An Action Guide to School Improvement.* Alexandria, Va.: ASCD and The Network, Inc.

Manasse, A. Lorri. 1984. "How Can We Recognize Effective Principals?" Alexandria, Va.: National Association of State Boards of Education.

McDill, Edward, Aaron Pallas, and Gary Natriello. 1985. "Raising Standards and Retaining Students: The Impact of the Reform Recommendations on Potential Dropouts." Baltimore, Md.: Education Research Dissemination Office, The Johns Hopkins University.

McGinnis, Patricia Gwaltney. 1984. "Using Education's 'Bully Pulpit': National Leadership for Schools," *Education Week* 4, no. 14 (December): 24.

Muther, Connie. 1985. "Revising Research When Choosing Materials," *Educational Leadership* 42, no. 5 (February): 86–87.

McKinney, Kay, ed. 1985. "Public Supports Tougher School Standards," *Research in Brief* (April/May): 1–18.

National Board of Inquiry. 1985. *Barriers to Excellence: Our Children at Risk.* Boston: The National Coalition of Advocates for Students.

National Commission on Excellence in Education. 1983. *A Nation at Risk: The Imperative for Educational Reform.* Washington, D.C.: U.S. Government Printing Office.

National Science Commission on Precollege Education in Mathematics, Science, and Technology. 1983. *Edcuating Americans for the 21st Century.* Washington D.C.: National Science Board.

Odden, Allan. 1984. "Financing Educational Excellence," *Phi Delta Kappan* 65, no. 5 (January): 311–318.

Phillips, Gary. 1983. "Insuring Continuous Improvement of Instructional Programs," *The I/D/E/A Reporter* (Spring): 1–6.

Plowden, Lady Bridget, *et al.* 1967. *Children and Their Primary Schools: Report of the Central Advisory Council in Education.* London: H.M. Stationery Office.

Random, Sheppard. 1985. "Schooling in Japan: The Paradox in the Pattern," *Education Week* 4, no. 22 (February): 12–34.

Razwid, Mary Anne; Charles A. Tesconi, Jr., and Donald Warren. 1984. *Pride and Promise: Schools of Excellence for All the People.* Burlington, Vt.: American Educational Studies Association.

Reagan, Ronald. 1984. "Excellence and Opportunity: A Program of Support for American Education," *Phi Delta Kappan* 66, no. 1 (September): 13–15.

Riley, Honorable Richard W. 1984. "The New Approach to Educational and Economic Excellence in South Carolina." Charleston, S.C.: State of South Carolina.

Rohlen, Thomas P. 1984. *Japan's High Schools.* Berkeley: University of California Press.

Schuster, Edgar. 1985. "Textbooks: 'There Has Never Been a Golden Age,' " *Education Week* 4, no. 4 (March): 40.

Shannon, Thomas. 1985. "A 1985 Fairy Tale," *Phi Delta Kappan* 66, no. 7 (March): 497–500.

Shimahara, Nobuo. 1985. "Japanese Education and Its Implications for U.S. Education," *Phi Delta Kappan* 66, no. 6 (February): 418–421.

Shutes, Robert. 1981. "How to Control Your Curriculum," *The American School Board Journal* 168, no. 8 (August): 1–9.

Silberman, Charles E. 1970. *Crisis in the Classroom.* New York: Random House.

Sirkin, J.R. 1985. " 'All-Black' Education Agenda Advocated," *Education Week* 4, no. 33 (May): 1, 27.

Slezak, James. 1984. *Odyssey To Excellence: How to Build Effective Schools Through Leadership and Management Skills.* San Francisco: Merritt Publishing Company.

Spady, William, and Gary Marx. 1984. *Excellence in Our Schools: Making It Happen.* Arlington, Va.: Far West Laboratory and AASA.

Stedman, L.C., and M.S. Smith. 1983. *Recent Reform Proposals for American Education.* Madison, Wisconsin: Wisconsin Center for Education Research.

Steller, Arthur. 1980a. "Changing Conditions Necessitate Resetting of Priorities and Policies for Schools." In *Updating School Board Policies*, edited by Brenda Greene: 1-4. Washington, D.C.: National School Boards Association.

____. 1980b. "Curriculum Development as Politics," *Educational Leadership* 38, no. 2 (November): 151-158.

____. 1980c. *Educational Planning for Educational Success.* Bloomington, Ind.: Phi Delta Kappan.

____. 1983. "Curriculum Planning," *Fundamental Curriculum Decisions.* Alexandria, Va.: ASCD, p. 74.

____. 1984. "Chart a Course for Selecting New Principals," *Updating School Board Policies* 15, no. 5 (May): 1-8.

Task Force on Education for Economic Growth. 1983. *Action for Excellence.* Denver, Col.: The Education Commission of the States.

Thanksgiving Statement Group. 1984. *Developing Character: Transmitting Knowledge.* Chicago: ARL.

Toch, Thomas. 1984a. "Idea of Citizen's Lobby Is Weighed by Governors," *Education Week* 66, no. 3 (September): 173-176.

____. 1984b. "The Dark Side of the Excellence Movement," *Phi Delta Kappan* 66, no. 3 (November): 173-176.

Tye, B.B., and K.A. Tye. 1983. "Naivete and Snobbery," *Educational Leadership* 41, no. 2 (October): 28-29.

Van Loozen, Lu, ed. 1984. *A Blueprint for Educational Excellence: A School Board Member's Guide.* Washington, D.C.: National School Boards Association.

Wise, Arthur. 1979. *Legislated Learning: The Bureaucratization of the American Classroom.* Berkeley: University of California Press.

Zakariya, Sally Banks. 1983. *Effective Instructional Management.* Arlington, Va.: AASA.

II STATE CASE STUDIES OF EDUCATIONAL REFORM IMPLEMENTATION

5 STATE POLICYMAKING FOR EDUCATIONAL EXCELLENCE
School Reform in California

Diane Massell and Michael W. Kirst

INTRODUCTION

The Hughes-Hart Education Act emerged in 1983 as the most comprehensive school reform package in California legislative history. This act, referred to as Senate Bill 813, granted $800 million in new state funds and purchased over eighty substantive "reforms" for public education. Only one year earlier, the legislature had adjourned in stalemate without providing any supplemental aid to education, despite the fact that school districts were confronting their worst fiscal crisis since the Great Depression. Few observers of the times, including one of S.B. 813's own lead sponsors, would have predicted that a sleeping giant of education reform lay just beneath the surface of California's political agenda.

In this chapter, we explore the political and contextual elements that led to the sudden turnaround in the policy arena. Specifically, we show that the appearance of new and committed state educational policy leadership, accompanied by a rebounding state economy and rekindled public support for the schools, facilitated the development of S.B. 813. Also, secondly, the results of the 1983 policy process are explored.

The chapter begins by examining the contextual factors: the "health" of the public schools in terms of fiscal and quality measures, and California traditions of educational governance and politics. The second section provides an in-depth portrait of the interaction of demands within the political system that shaped the new legislation. In this section we also discuss the legal outcomes and fiscal implications of the bill. The final section concludes the chapter with a report on the first stages of the Act's implementation.

LANDSCAPE FOR REFORM

Over the last decade, a steady erosion in indicators of school quality was concommitent with a dramatic loss of public confidence in and willingness to support the schools in California. By the beginning of 1982, school districts were faced with rising enrollments, a changing student population, and climbing deficits.

Eroding Measures of School Quality

In the 1940s and 1950s, California earned a national reputation for excellence and innovation in its system of public education. Its leadership role persisted through the early 1970s, when the state was still earning high marks on many proxies for school quality such as test scores, per pupil expenditures, teacher salaries, and the like. By the mid to latter part of the decade, however, these measures began a downward slide; and by 1983, California lagged far behind many other states in the nation. Here are just a few of the bleak statistics:

- California's dropout rates increasingly exceed the national average and are currently 3 percent above the national figure.
- California's high school seniors attend school an average of one and one-third years less than their peers nationally because of shorter school days and years.
- California has the second highest pupil-teacher ratio in the country, with one teacher for every 23.1 students.
- California ranks forty-eighth among states in money spent on textbooks per pupil. Reading levels used in the public schools also declined steadily over the years (Guthrie 1984).

At the same time, California opinion surveys chronicled the loss of public confidence in the schools: In 1967, 80 percent of those sur-

Table 5-1. Grades K-12 Total Revenues, 1974-75 through 1983-84 (*in millions*).

Year	State Aid	Federal Aid	Misc. (1/4)	Total Funding	ADA	ADA (1972-73)
1974-75[a]	$2,356.7	$ 550.4	$ 524.4	$ 7,210.5	$1,530	$1,290
1975-76[a]	2,594.4	591.6	391.1	7,587.9	1,650	1,287
1976-77[a]	2,764.6	644.4	495.6	8,654.7	1,843	1,342
1977-78[a]	2,894.9	891.5	485.6	9,516.6	2,045	1,397
1978-79[a]	5,333.4	962.3	551.3	9,425.6	2,207	1,398
1979-80[a]	6,998.5	1,100.4	702.2	10,981.6	2,611	1,525
1980-81[a]	7,348.9	1,064.7	866.3	11,732.8	2,784	1,497
1981-82[b]	7,779.5	882.4	974.9	12,696.5	3,013	1,504
1982-83[b]	8,214.4	885.7	1,104.2	13,074.5	3,110	1,460
1983-84[b]	8,354.6	839.2	1,253.3	13,532.0	3,204	1,411
1984-85[b]	10,147.2	993.3	1,123.4	15,505.9	4,313	1,865

a. Budget.
b. Estimated.
Source: James Guthrie, ed., *Conditions of Education in California 1984* (Berkeley, Policy Analysis for California Education, 1984), p. 6.

veyed assigned the public schools a good or excellent/very good rating; by 1983, only 31 percent would rate them similarly (California Opinion Index 1983). The public expressed their malaise at the ballot box by rejecting school bond issues and by passing the largest property tax relief and limitation measure in the country. Despite the passage of state "bail out" legislation, the 1978 Jarvis-Gann amendment, or Proposition 13, tore $800 million out of school budgets. The schools have not yet regained the purchasing power of pre-Proposition 13 budgets; in fact, since then constant dollars for education have declined 8 percent. California's per pupil expenditure, which ranked among the top ten in the nation in 1961, fell to thirty-sixth place in 1983.

Significant shifts in enrollment trends, teacher salary competitiveness, and pupil demographic trends have exacerbated the problems of declining quality measures. In 1982, after a decade of declining enrollments, the public schools of California experienced a modest pupil increase. This marked the beginning of a long-term enrollment increase that is projected to add more than 91,000 students to the public K-12 system by the 1992-93 school year. This growth, when combined with teacher retirements and attrition, will require the state to hire approximately 100,000 new teachers by 1991. Although salaries for California teachers rank well in the nation, educators are among the lowest paid professionals in the state with an average beginning salary of $13,687. The real purchasing power of this figure falls below both 1960 and 1970 levels (Guthrie 1984).

Between 1978–79 and 1980–81, emergency credentials for teachers rose 167 percent because of shortages in math, science, bilingual, and special education teachers (California Commission for Teacher Preparation and Licensing 1981). The need for bilingual teachers will increase dramatically in the next decade as California's already large limited-English speaking population comprises an even larger proportion of school-aged children (Guthrie 1984).

These new and growing pressures on the public school system, along with the history of decline in quality measures, provided ample fodder for the S.B. 813 debate. Highly publicized state and, in a more general way, national reports chronicled these problems and offered specific policy solutions. These reports heightened public awareness and helped to feed and broaden the public dialogue.

Charting the Course: Educational Governance in California

The legislature, governor, state board of education, and superintendent of public instruction tend to predominate in the governance of education in California. Local school districts do have a considerable degree of decisionmaking authority, but courts have consistently ruled districts to be state agencies that derive their power from the legislature. As a result, the state legislature functions as a kind of "super board of trustees" for the public schools (Encarnation and Mitchell 1983).

The California state legislature adopts an active posture in education policymaking under the view that state law will improve the alleged shortcomings of local officials. It consequently enacts 200 education bills each year and gives California the distinction of the longest education code in the nation (Kirst 1981). Over the years, the legislature has exerted a profound influence over school district budgets and organization as well as employer-employee relations (Encarnation and Mitchell 1983).

Table 5-2. School Enrollment in California—Historical and Projected.

Year	*Public K-12*	*Private Total*
1974-75	4,427,443	412,344
1975-76	4,419,571	421,646
1976-77	4,380,400	433,782
1977-78	4,303,645	451,321
1978-79	4,187,219	477,013
1979-80	4,119,511	497,613
1980-81	4,072,966	507,392
1981-82	4,046,156	528,824
1982-83	4,065,486	532,074
% change 1975-83	-8%	+29%
1983-84	4,081,622	540,890
1984-85	4,128,341	559,957
1985-86	4,196,215	581,606
1986-87	4,278,700	604,788
1987-88	4,365,375	628,752
1988-89	4,421,339	652,669
1989-90	4,559,844	676,212
1990-91	4,692,865	701,165
1991-92	4,838,605	723,348
1992-93	4,983,355	745,362
% change, 1984-93	+22%	+38%

Source: James Guthrie, ed., *Conditions of Education in California 1984* (Berkeley, Policy Analysis for California Education, 1984), p. 4.

The office of Speaker of the Assembly is the Legislature's most powerful position, and with sufficient political strength the office-holder can play an important role in setting the philosophy and fiscal limits that orient educational policy. At the end of the 1980 session, the Assembly elected Democrat Willie Brown to the speakership. Brown rose to power with Republican assistance and despite strong opposition from a majority in his own party. Although he divested the speakers' office of one of its traditional powers, the assignment of bills to committee, he has nevertheless achieved significant strength through notable fundraising achievements, committee appointments, and adept coalition-building (Blackburn 1982). He has successfully outmaneuvered Republican-backed efforts to curb the power of the office. In the process, he has earned the solid support of his Democrat colleagues, who reelected him speaker just one day after the 1984 fall general elections (Fairbanks 1983).

Educational policy in the legislature emanates primarily from four committees: the Senate Education and Ways and Means committees, and the Assembly Education and Finance committees. The Senate and the Assembly regularly contest over the issue of general versus categorical aid for education. Most often the Senate will propose a general aid package and the Assembly will respond by adding on numerous categorical programs (Kirst 1981).

The vastly increased assumption of state fiduciary responsibilities after the passage of Proposition 13 (up from 30 percent to 80 percent of total school resources) put the Legislature in a dominant position in education policy making, but there are too many actors to conclude that the legislature is always preeminent. California ranks high in the formal authority of the governor, who has a line item appropriations veto and extensive appointment authority. The governor usually responds to educational proposals made by the legislature or chief state school officer and rarely initiates his own bills.

The governor, together with the state Senate, appoints the State Board of Education, which establishes major areas of policy for the California Department of Education, the largest bureaucracy in the state. Finally, California has an independent, popularly elected superintendent of public instruction. Although the chief state school officer wields relatively little direct power over the public schools, the individual can be an effective lobbyist for change (Fairbanks 1982). Recent school officers have proven to be such leaders, and have played a crucial role in developing and facilitating the passage of major education legislation in Sacramento. Indeed, as we shall see, all of the traditional policymaking orientations of the legislature, the governor, and the superintendent of public instruction were apparent during the development of S.B. 813.

Interest Group Influence

California has a rich history of interest group dominance, a result, some contend, of the weak party structure pressed upon the state during the Progressive era (Zeigler and Van Dalen 1971). The structure varies by level of education, with higher education primarily represented by the central university system and a small but effective student group. The strength of the university lobby is its unity. Public elementary and secondary education, on the other hand, has a multitude of advocates in Sacramento, which include the 1,043 local education agencies, and categorical and general aid interest groups. In broad terms, the California Teachers Association, the California Federation of Teachers, and the California School Boards Association have focused their lobbying efforts on securing general aid to education and have found sympathetic friends in the similarly oriented Senate. Numerous smaller organizations press for increased categorical program aid and have greater influence in the Assembly. The usual outcome is more money for both general and categorical aid with no clear priorities emerging from the legislature (Kirst 1981).

Although the interest group structure for K-12 education is diverse, it has not prevented the various players from presenting a united front in recent years. In the 1960s, expansive growth allowed educational groups to flourish in the pursuit of their specific interests. In the 1970s, however, a strong of tax expenditure and limitation measures, voter rejection of school bond issues, and declining enrollments forced educators to let go of their growth psychology. The superintendent of public instruction formed the Tuesday Night Group, a collective of traditional education groups (teachers, administrators, boards) and big city school districts. The strategy of this informal group was to "agreed to disagree" in order to obtain as much money for education as possible through omnibus bills. The combined influence of its members and their political information sharing provided the tools for mobilizing a winning coalition of legislators (Kirst and Somers 1981).

During this period, the members of the collective decided to focus their lobbying effort on fiscal matters rather than on the substantive issues that might lead them to conflict (Kirst and Somers 1981). The legislative policy proposals themselves were primarily fiscal in nature and reinforced this perspective. This public education interest group strategy/perspective lingered during the S.B. 813 policy process, despite the distinctly different nature of the proposed legislation. At the same time, new and powerful interest group players, particularly the California business community, rode into the political arena brandishing strong ideas about substantive education issues and moving far beyond fiscal matters.

Status of School Financing

The twin imperatives of fiscal retrenchment and the *Serrano v. Priest* school financing equalization case fueled educational policymaking during the 1970s. In 1971, the California Supreme Court ruled that if wealth-related disparities in school district per pupil expenditures could be proven to exist, then the state's system of school financing would be in violation of the equal protection clauses of the U.S. and state constitutions. In a first attempt to address that tentative ruling, the California state legislature passed S.B. 90, which still remains the core of the state's strategy to equalize expenditures. The bill imposed the "revenue limit," a ceiling on the amount of general purpose monies each district may receive. The legislature devised a sliding scale of increases to the revenue limit in order to eventually "level up" lower spending districts (California Coalition for Fair School Finance 1983).

After the *Serrano II* court affirmed its earlier hypothesis in 1977, the state passed S.B. 65. This bill employed power equalization to redistribute tax revenues from wealthy to poor districts, however, the enactment of Proposition 13 just nine months later invalidated much of this equalization strategy by eliminating 60 percent of local property tax revenues. The state legislature promptly passed S.B. 154, a short-term bailout measure. The next year, S.B. 8 was enacted, a "long-term bailout bill" that simply reaffirmed much of the strategy of S.B. 154. These bills established a "squeeze" mechanism that in general gave districts with revenue limits above the statewide average a smaller cost-of-living increase than those below the average. This mechanism allowed the state to gradually reduce funding disparities (California Coalition for Fair Schools Finance 1983).

In April 1983, the California Supreme Court ruled that the state had adequately complied with *Serrano II* and declared the school financing system constitutional. Using the base revenue limit as the test for compliance, the judge ruled "significant parity" had been achieved since 93.2 percent of the pupils receive funds within a $100 band, adjusted for inflation (California Coalition for Fair School Finance 1983). In essence, as long as the state continued to do what it had been doing, it would remain in compliance. Thus, the April ruling cleared the path for the state legislature to move beyond the questions on which it had focused its attention throughout the 1970s and to turn to other issues in the education policy arena.

THE POLITICS OF EDUCATIONAL EXCELLENCE

The 1983 state legislative session stands in sharp relief to the political landscape of just a few years earlier when education was a less salient issue. There occurred a brief hiatus in educational policy leadership in the state legislature when experienced spokesmen had either been promoted to new committee assignments or had been defeated in their bid for reelection. Observers questioned whether education would continue to attract the same kind of committed leadership (Kirst 1981). The serious erosion of public confidence in the schools and a poor fiscal climate did not auger well for the future. While Proposition 13 had a dramatic impact on the schools, the state's opulent surpluses for many years cushioned the effects of fiscal decline. During the recession of the early 1980s, the surplus continued to dwindle, and in 1982, the state experienced "genuine fiscal crisis"—a $1.5 billion deficit. Budget experts were predicting more of the same for the next fiscal year (Fairbanks 1983). This climate threatened to make educational politics a true zero-sum game for the first time.

New Terrain

In spite of these dismal signs, a corps of dedicated new leaders with agendas for educational reform did emerge in Sacramento. In the fall of 1982, California elected a new chief state school officer and a Republican governor. The Democratic leadership in the Senate and Assembly appointed two new educational committee chairpersons for the 1983 session. These policymakers spoke eloquently for educational reform and seized the initiative that eventually produced the new omnibus legislation. Although they came from different realms of the political spectrum, these players were or would become similarly committed to tying increased state aid for the schools with reform. The new strategy of linking dollars to reform was the crucial political concept that made the omnibus S.B. 813 a feasible alternative.

Not only did leadership change in Sacramento in 1983. Although public confidence in the ability of the schools was at a low ebb, the public's willingness to financially support education increased dramatically. For the first time in many years, a broad-based majority of Californians (64 percent) said they would approve tax hikes for educational purposes, and a majority (66 percent) believed that more aid would improve the quality of education in the schools. In the year that Proposition 13 passed, by contrast, only 24 percent of the public felt that spending increases would improve the quality of education (California Opinion Index 1983). The voters passed five bond issues in the 1982 November elections, leading some to declare the "spirit of Proposition 13" officially on the wane (Brazil 1982).

The California Opinion Index, which was released in July just as the state legislature enacted S.B. 813, also found that the public strongly supported the type of reform measures that were included in the bill, such as the establishment of statewide high school graduation standards, more homework, and revised personnel codes (California Opinion Index 1983). Contributing to the public's awareness of the educational "issue" was the proliferation in 1982 of national and state reports on the decline of educational quality in the public schools. Although the numerous reports emphasized different elements, many of the major conclusions were common to all. Specifically, the reports highlighted the need to devote more time to instruction, to strengthen the academic core of education, and to improve the quality of the teaching force.

These reform themes echoed throughout the 1982 fall elections for the post of state Superintendent of Public Instruction. The message of the successful "traditional-education" platform was clear: establish more rigorous standards, get rid of incompetent teachers, and cut out unnecessary programs. This platform argued that new state aid should be tied to reforms and to the setting of new goals and standards, and it asserted that it was not lack of money but lack of expectations that led to the deterioration of California public schools (PSA 1983). The three-term incumbent talked about basics but contended that fiscal crisis and social changes had caused the schools' decline. The incumbent's agenda won the support of all the major educational interest groups, but the challenger gained the active allegiance and financial support of many members of the California business community—a significant departure in the past practices of this group. These new educational allies would prove to be a potent force in the passage of S.B. 813.

The campaign set the themes and the symbolism and provided a momentum for change. The challenger's platform took concrete shape in the early drafts of S.B. 813, which were fashioned with the new chairperson of the Senate education committee. As a state assemblyman, the new chairperson had introduced several reform bills similar in spirit to the 1983 legislation, such as a minimum competency exam for prospective teachers. In addition to substantive reforms like revisions of the teacher tenure laws, the chairperson focused his energies on securing more general aid to education and on incorporating equalization provisions into the new measure.

The chairperson of the Assembly education committee and a close political ally of the speaker handled the Assembly Democratic package. This package concurred with many major elements in the Senate draft, but the chairman and the Speaker felt that it had overlooked many important items. Consequently, keeping with the tradition of the Assembly to focus on categoricals, the new draft contained a broad number of programs such as dropout prevention and summer school, as well as pilot projects and study proposals.

The anticipated fiscal year 1983 deficits led policymakers to propose several alternative methods and levels of funding for S.B. 813. Speaker Brown suggested a controversial new tax package. The new governor, concerned about maintaining his campaign pledge not to impose additional taxes, originally opted to cut the $900 million recommended by the legislation's advocates to $350 million. As it turned out, neither severely slashing the initial budget request nor raising taxes proved necessary. To the surprise of many experts, the revenue receipts that began rolling in around mid-session indicated that the state would experience a surplus for FY 1983. The budget surplus would allow the governor to uphold his no-tax election promise. This surplus, along with political pressure from Republican colleagues, prompted Governor Deukmejian to up the ante to $800 million. The higher offer, however, was conditional; expounding on the linkage theme, the governor pledged more aid only if the legislative package included more structural reforms. His response was transmitted to the legislature in June as the Conference Committee stood ready to complete its six months of work on S.B. 813; as a consequence, a spate of eleventh-hour reform measures were stapled onto the already large bill. Included in this hectic process, for example, was a radically revised teacher training program that permits local school districts to establish their own training outside the purview of a university. An in-depth analyses of the consequences of these last-minute reform ideas or an assessment of their impact on local school districts did not occur. Although the reforms were added in public committee hearings, the public has scant opportunity or time to respond to the proposed measures.

In sum, S.B. 813 took shape in a two-staged process. The core of the bill, which was developed by the new state superintendent and the Senate chairman, emerged early in the session and largely remained intact throughout the six-month "incubation" period. The rest of the session was essentially an additive process spearheaded by the detailed proposals of the Assembly Democrats and given momentum by the governor's request for more reform.

Linking money to reform was "extremely important, not only from a policy standpoint but, from a political standpoint as well" (Caldwell 1983). By making aid conditional upon reform, advocates of the bill achieved bipartisan consensus. Although the Democrats had a majority in both chambers, they lacked by six votes the two-thirds majority necessary to approve new taxes and most spending bills; thus bipartisan support was imperative. Observers described the talks as "fragile" and largely credit the Senate Chairman and to a newcomer to education with keeping lines open both to Republicans and to freer-spending Democratic legislators and their teacher union allies (Fallon 1983). In the interest of sustaining a consensus to enact S.B. 813, the proponents decided to defer work on categorical programs that earlier had been slated for reform, such as bilingual and special education (Siegel 1984).

A Different Field of Allies

In 1983, the California Business Roundtable (CRT), an organization representing the chief executive officers of more then eighty of the state's largest corporations, emerged to lead the business community's effort to boost aid, and reform, for education. Indeed, without them it is unlikely that such a large-scale statewide effort would have been mounted. CRT clearly influenced the governor and the swing vote Republicans in the Assembly. These activities marked a significant policy departure for CRT, which in the 1970s had focused its state-level lobbying on economic development, housing, and other more directly business-related concerns. Indeed while California's system of public education was deteriorating in the latter part of the decade, CRT's targeting of state and local tax policies helped to weaken education's financial base (Kirst 1984).

CRT turned its attention to education in 1980 as business leaders began to rethink the relationship between education and economic growth. In 1980, CRT formed a Task Force on Jobs and Education headed by Cornell Maier of Kaiser Aluminum and Chemical Corporation. The task force commissioned Berman/Weiler Consultants to conduct a $175,000 study on strategies for "improving student performance." The Request for Proposal that had been issued by CRT embodied a major shift in traditional business intervention in education. CRT wanted to downplay small-scale, somewhat peripheral donation approaches such as Adopt-a-School or equipment contributions. It viewed these as secondary to approaches that intervened directly in the core of financing, academic standards and personnel policies.

Among the reforms recommended by the Berman/Weiler study were:

- minimum statewide graduation standards;
- strengthened state testing;
- required local use of state curriculum guides;
- longer school day and year;
- new technical education programs stressing cooperation with post-secondary institutions;
- deregulated state restrictions on teacher dismissal, layoff, probation, et cetera; and
- revised teacher training concepts (Berman, Weiler 1982).

The organization made clear that it would only support an educational bill that contained some form of these items. CRT viewed teacher salary increases as desirable, but contingent upon the unions' acceptance of other changes. CRT was influential in conveying this linkage theme to the governor, who consequently obtained changes in the bill that required continuing education for all new teachers as a condition for keeping their license, reduced the wages of laid-off teachers working as substitutes, and extended the date by which teachers may be laid off if certain conditions arise (Fallon 1983).

The CRT hired a lobbyist to convey its message in Sacramento by providing frequent testimony and building coalitions. CRT used California Taxpayers, a lobbying group experienced in school reform. The organization also hired consultants to help construct the legislative specifics on teacher dismissal and other personnel issues.

The CRT initiative, coupled with the posture of the new state superintendent and leading legislators, left the public education interest groups in a reactive mode. The business group warned teacher organizations that union opposition to personnel reforms might turn CRT against any new 1983 education bill. The California Teacher's Association, a National Education Association affiliate, declared neutrality in the initial stages but later supported the omnibus legislation. Although the unions won higher beginning salaries for teachers, stricter student discipline authority, and a teacher loan assumption program, their agenda on employee-employer relations in such areas as dismissal was ignored. The once influential Tuesday Night Group was largely reactive throughout the S.B. 813 process.

The CRT and other new allies for education, such as the Junior League, the Masons, and real estate agencies, concerned about property values in near-bankrupt school districts, eclipsed the traditional influence of the educator groups.

The educational associations, which included the school boards associations school administrators, and teacher lobbies, made numerous concessions on structural reforms, lured by the prospects of obtaining new aid to refresh depleted budgets. In many respects the groups' efforts represented a continuation of their posture at the end of the 1970s, when fiscal crises forged collective action on the premise that cohesiveness would allow them to win more state education aid. This tact had enabled them to exert considerable influence over legislation. Unlike the two major "bail-out" bills of that period, however, S.B. 813 was not oriented primarily towards finance; legislators had turned their attention to curriculum and teaching policy, the core of the educational process. Paradoxically, then, many of the substantive issues were shaped by Sacramento insiders whose primary expertise lay in finance, while the professional educators focused on the overall fiscal aspects of the bill (Cuban 1984). The dissolution of professional dominance over education seems to have taken another step in California.

In July 1983, S.B. 813 was overwhelmingly passed into law: The bill received no dissenting votes in the senate, and only two in the assembly. The enrolled bill approved $1.9 billion in second year funding, but for the first time in recent budget history in Sacramento, the governor exercised his "blue pencil" authority to veto the second year continuation funding. The bill included the $800 million allocation, along with $500 million to implement reforms like the longer school year and $600 million for cost-of-living increases. The governor claimed that: "Prudent management requires that we make decisions on augmentations to this funding for 1984–85 during next year's budget deliberations" (Governor's Veto Message 1983).

Despite the concerns Deukmejian's action raised about the future of S.B. 813 for the next school year, a healthy state surplus, and perhaps the political popularity of the measure, allowed the governor and the legislature to reach an easy consensus in the 1984 session for full second year funding.

Seeds of Changes: The Legal and Fiscal Aspects of S.B. 813

S.B. 813 represented one of the first attempts to legislate the multitude of school reform ideas circulating in the national marketplace. The bill had far-reaching effects on professional standards and development, teacher salaries, instructional content, student discipline, the measurement of learning outcomes, and school financing in California. Without listing each component of this comprehensive package, the following highlights some of the more well-known aspects of the bill.

Classroom instruction—The bill:

- provided financial incentives to districts to *increase the length of the school day and the school year* ($257 million appropriated in 1983–84 vetoes, but provided in 1984–85);
- *reestablished statewide high school graduation requirements* of three years of English, three years of social studies, two years of mathematics, two years of science, one year of fine arts or foreign language, and two years of physical education, to commence in the 1986–87 school year;

- provided incentive funds ($400 per pupil) to districts that *improve their prior year scores* on the twelfth grade state achievement test ($7,2 million appropriated in 1983–84; vetoed, but provided in 1984–85);
- established "Golden State" exams to *honor the best students at graduation* ($128,000 for test development in 1983–84);
- provided for the *expansion of pupil testing* ($200,000 appropriated in 1983–84);
- provided, for the first time, *funding for purchase of grades 9–12 instructional materials* ($18.2 million appropriated in 1983–84); and
- *strengthened student discipline laws* that now require, rather than permit, principals to recommend expulsion if the student commits certain aggregious acts.

Teaching—The bill:

- provided funds to school districts that *increase beginning teachers' salaries* to $18,000, adjusted for inflation over three years ($12.3 million appropriated in 1983–84);
- *established a mentor teacher program* that will provide $4,000 stipends for 5 percent of the outstanding teachers in a local education agency who perform additional duties ($30.8 million appropriated in 1983–84);
- *established new teacher competency evaluation criteria*;
- *provided districts with greater flexibility in the lay off and dismissal of teachers* in order to better respond to new state curriculum mandates, lay off incompetent teachers, and respond to budget setbacks; and
- *eliminated unconditional lifetime teaching credentials* and established, for the first time, *continuing education requirements.*

General finance provisions—The bill:

- *brought low-spending districts to within $50 of the prior year average* for 1983–84 and to the actual prior-year average for 1984–85 ($23.5 million appropriated in 1983–84);
- *reduced the "squeeze" on high spending districts*, allowing them to increase expenditures at a faster rate;

- *"folded into" the base revenue limit per pupil some funding adjustments* for special purpose (e.g., increasing teacher salaries) or special circumstances (e.g., declining enrollment); and
- *linked the revenue limit cost of living adjustment to a government cost index* to eliminate the erosion of district purchasing power by inflation.

All told, S.B. 813 allocated $800 million to implement the new reforms. As large as the $800 million in new state aid appears in absolute terms, S.B. 813 provided only an 8 percent boost for the school finance formula, 6 percent for the traditional categorical aids, and 6.7 percent on a per-pupil basis (Odden 1984). In FY 1983-84, the state spent $13.7 billion on total aid to elementary-secondary education, and is estimated to spend $15.6 billion in FY 1984-85 (California Coalition for Fair School Finance 1984). Continuation funding represented only a small proportion of the total state surplus in 1984-85, reflecting the relatively low priority still accorded to elementary-secondary education in California.

Nevertheless, S.B. 813 brought California per pupil expenditures per average daily attendance to within 98 percent of its peak purchasing power in 1979-1980. In 1982-83, the state expended $2,490 per pupil; in 1938-84, this figure was $1,912. This raised the state's national ranking from thirty-sixth to thirty-first place (California Coalition for Fair School Finance 1984).

The appropriated $23.5 million in equalization aid will bring approximately 200 or more districts closer to the statewide changes in the funding provisions enacted by A.B. 65 to meet the court's ruling in *Serrano v. Priest.* The bill eliminates the double "squeeze" mechanism from the formula, which had provided differential cost-of-living adjustments to high- and low-spending districts. S.B. 813 instead provides similar districts (elementary, high school, unified) with similar adjustments. Equalization strategies in the new legislation focus instead on "leveling up" districts that are below the 1983-84 average revenue limit to within $50 of that figure. The effects of this new strategy may be disequalizing (Legislative Analysts' Office 1984):

> The actual statewide average revenue limit, of course, increases when the equalization adjustment is provided; consequently, it is, as a practical matter, impossible to bring revenue limits below the statewide average revenue limit to the average without a corresponding reduction in the revenue limits which fall above the statewide average.

Moreover, several of the new reforms like mentor teacher and longer school days were state reimbursed without regard to local wealth. In other words, the new program dollars are distributed on a flat grant basis, with wealthy local education agencies receiving the same amount of money as poorer ones. The possibility of widely disparate adoptions of the various programs among local school districts may also be a cause for future equity concerns.

Thus, while S.B. 813 does have a strong equalization thrust, it would not pass muster with *Serrano* "hawks" because of (1) the lessening of the "squeeze" mechanism, (2) the distribution of "excellence" dollars on a flat grant basis, and (3) the chance of unequal adoptions.

Summary

In this section a broad-brushed portrait of the S.B. 813 reform process and its outcomes has been developed. The politics of this omnibus measure were characterized by:

- a group of new state players with different political allegiances and an agenda for reform;
- a new tactical strategy of linking state aid to instructional reforms to build a bipartisan coalition;
- several active new advocates for education, including the powerful California big business community;
- the lessened influence of California's typically dominant education community;
- a state surplus; and
- a wide base of public support for reform due in part to the multitude of national and state reports on education.

These conditions—along with the state's strong interventionist traditions—made enactment of a comprehensive, substantive reform bill like S.B. 813 possible in California in 1983.

SCALING THE MOUNTAIN

The 1983 legislation vested primary authority for the implementation of S.B. 813 programs in the hands of the state superintendent of public instruction, giving him a surge of power similar to that enjoyed by his predecessor over a decade ago (Browne 1983). As a consequence, numerous new mandates and directives flowed to the State Department of Education, which had to prepare guidelines, provide instructional guidance, and oversee program implementation. To a department traditionally organized around the administration of categorical programs, these new instructional tasks required a major reorganization effort. In 1982, for example, the department had ten nutritionists and twelve child-care-facility specialists on its staff, but only one half-time specialist in mathematics (Kirst 1984). For the first six months of the administration of the new superintendent, departmental staff concentrated their efforts on a grassroots lobbying campaign that helped to secure enactment of S.B. 813, and they were ill-prepared for the massive job of implementation. The substantial 1983 budget cuts received by the department compounded the problems of reorganization (Browne 1983).

Nevertheless the department has made significant headway in implementing the S.B. 813 mandates. They have already pilot-tested the new eighth grade California Achievement Program test (CAP) and have developed and begun instituting an individual school performance report accountability program. Third, sixth and twelfth graders currently take the state-devised CAP tests to measure progress in reading, writing, and mathematics. S.B. 813 authorized the development of more comprehensive tests in more subject areas (literature, history, science, and advanced mathematics) and the expansion of state testing to the tenth and eighth grades. The new tests will be aimed at assessing "higher-order thinking skills"; the reading exams, for example, will query students about the author's tone or ask them to distinguish between fact and opinion. The superintendent eventually plans to broaden CAP to even more grades and subject areas and to make it an all-purpose "super test" to replace others currently used by districts to assess individual student performance (Fallon 1984).

The superintendent assembled numerous task forces to assist the department in many of its new duties. To accomplish one of his primary goals—curriculum "alignment," whereby state tests are made compatible with textbooks and other instructional material—the superintendent authorized a task force on CAP expansion and another on assessment and accountability practices to work directly with textbook publishers. In addition to providing the department with expertise and guidance, the strong representation of local school professionals on these task forces may also serve to salve the wounds of a strengthened state presence in instructional matters (Fallon 1984).

The department has also taken great strides with its new accountability program which, in addition to assessing school quality, has established statewide goals and standards. While the program continues to use test scores as a proxy for effectiveness, it has added new "quality indicators" such as increased levels of writing and homework assignments, lowered dropout rates, and higher student attendance figures. The department of education has established statewide targets for each area; for example, it set a goal of increasing CAT scores by 5 percent by 1985–86. Finally, through both monetary and nonmonetary programs, the state will recognize those schools with similar populations which "exhibit exemplary achievement" and show the most growth.

Undoubtedly the new assessment standards will play an important role in lobbying efforts for increased funding for education (California State Department of Education 1984).

> Over the next few years, we should be able to retain public support and receive necessary increases in school revenues *if* the public recognizes that we are committed to reforms and *if* we are able to demonstrate results. I believe it is crucial to announce *now* how the public should judge our progress. By defining a comprehensive set of accountability standards, establishing state targets, and initiating improvement efforts at each school and district, we gain the necessary breathing space with the public to prove what we can accomplish. We also avoid being judged solely by test scores alone or other less professionally sound indicators of performance.

On other fronts, the superintendent reports that districts with 90 percent of the state's children and teachers have applied for the mentor teacher program (Honig 1984). The momentum to establish the $18,000 beginning teacher salaries has been stalled somewhat by a technical provision of S.B. 813 requiring districts to certify that their participation in the program did not require them to raise the salaries of other teachers. The compression of the salary schedule would place administrators under difficult pressure to reestablish wage gradations, and consequently many have expressed a reluctance to participate (Legislative Analysts' Office 1984). Technical problems may also hamper the implementation of some other major S.B. 813 reforms; however, since many of them have not yet been implemented or have only been in operation for a few months, assessments based on actual data are limited.

Follow the (State) Leader

S.B. 813 departs significantly from previous state legislation, which dealt primarily with finance formulas and categorical programs in the new legislation, the state has clearly decided that it must go beyond the technical periphery of education into the core of the instructional process to set standards on what should be taught, how it should be taught, and who shall teach it. This more aggressive posture represents a new stage of the trend toward state centralization of educational governance that began in the 1970s.

Woven into the legislation alongside strengthened state control and instructional intervention, however, is another important strand that might be easily overlooked in this somewhat massive bill. Despite the new statewide mandates, many of the reforms, such as the mentor teacher program and the longer school year, are optional. This flexibility is designed to give local school districts the opportunity to choose state programs to suit local circumstance and to work state programs into the local collective bargaining process (Siegel 1984). The significant deregulation of personnel codes wrought by S.B. 813 also puts a great deal of authority back into the hands of local administrators. In short, S.B. 813 also contains room for local discretion and judgment.

Nevertheless the state will have an indisputably strong effect on the instructional process, most notably on curriculum planning and program development. The "curriculum alignment" program, combined with the extensive minimum graduation requirements and the authorized development of "model curriculum" by the state department of education will yield a high degree of uniformity and standardization. S.B. 813 represents part of a growing trend to mandate change rather than to provide technical assistance to schools and school districts. The popularity of mandates derives from their higher visibility (Louis and Corwin 1984), which is an important attribute in the minds of popularly elected bodies like legislatures or state superintendents of public instruction.

Will "remote control" of the classroom by state mandate, however, produce real and positive changes in the classroom or only paper reforms through the manipulation of reporting data? At least one observer believes that only token compliance will result from what he calls the "heavy-handed, top down approach" of S.B. 813 (Cuban 1984). Will strengthened state control of the instructional process violate the "shared moral order" between principals, teachers, students, and parents that effective schools literature suggests is important (Finn 1984)? Will excellent teachers be attracted to a profession where independence and creativity is restricted by state mandate?

Another body of effective schools research, however, does suggest that explicit state goals and high standards are a vital part of school improvement. The 1983 legislation clearly placed its faith in this tenet of the literature.

Conclusion: The Climb Continues

The elements that led to the abrupt turnaround in the California political climate have lingered on since the storm of activity surrounding S.B. 813. For instance, the business group's successful foray into the realm of educational policymaking in 1983 proved not just a momentary venture. Outside the state capital, the CRT group is developing a list of specific academic competencies that high school graduates must attain to succeed in entry-level jobs and to initially qualify for promotion. The policy leaders that emerge in 1983 have continued to be active in education, primarily by fleshing out S.B. 813 and ensuring its continuation.

The public also has demonstrated its ongoing support by approving measures on the November, 1984 ballot that would boost aid to education and by disapproving a measure that could have had a deleterious effect on raising monies for the public schools. Specifically, the voters approved a state lottery that earmarked 34 percent of its proceeds to education, and authorized a $450 million state bond issue to finance school construction. Significantly, the public said "no" to Proposition 36, an initiative constitutional amendment that would have considerably strengthened the tax limitation concepts embedded in the Jarvis-Gann amendment of 1978.

Clearly, the mood of California towards education has changed dramatically since 1982. The giant education reform package resulted from many contextual and political factors. Yet by now, omnibus education reform legislation has arisen in a majority of state capitals across the country, and the similarities as well as the differences are striking. We hope this chapter can be used as a source whereby comparisons, and hopefully patterns, can emerge to serve the inquiry into the nature of change and the direction of education governance.

REFERENCES

Berman, Weiler Associates. 1982. *Improving Student Performance in California: Recommendation for the California Roudtable.* Berkeley: Berman, Weiler Associates.

Blackburn, Daniel J. 1982. "How Willie Brown did it," *California Journal* 13, no. 1 (January): 5-7.

Brazil, Eric. 1983. "A mixed bag of messages from those ballot propositions," *California Journal* 13, no. 12 (December): 442-443.

Browne, Jim. 1983. "SB 813: Who Won and Who Lost?," *Status Report* 1, no. 7 (October): 1-3.

Caldwell, Peggy. 1983. "School Improvement Requires Linking Money to Reform." *State Legislatures* Special Issue 9, no. 9 (October): 27-28.

California Coalition for Fair School Finance. 1983. "Serrano 1983," (May).

____. 1984. "School Finance: 1984-85," (October).

California Commission for Teacher Preparation and Licensing. 1981. *Credential Profile, 1980-81.* Sacramento: Commission for Teacher Preparation and Licensing.

California Opinion Index. 1983. "California's Public Schools," (July).

California State Department of Education. 1984. "Performance Report of California Public Schools."

Cuban, Larry. 1984. "School Reform by Remote Control: SB 813 in California." *Phi Delta Kappan* 66, no. 3 (November): 213-215.

Encarnation, Dennis, and Douglas Mitchell. 1983. "Critical Tensions in the Governance of California Public Educational Finance and Governance," Stanford University.

Fairbanks, Robert S. 1982. "Election analysis," *California Journal* 13, no. 12 (December): 437-452.

____. 1984. "Radical revisions by state mean stiffer courses for students," *California Journal* 15, no. 8 (August): 306-309.

Finn, Chester E. 1984. "Toward Strategic Independence: Nine Commandments for Enhancing School Effectiveness," *Phi Delta Kappan* 66, no. 8 (April): 518-524.

Garcia, Art. 1983. "Interview: Bill Honig," *PSA Magazine* (October): 112-125.

Gold, Steven, and Karen Benker. 1983. "State Fiscal Conditions Entering 1983." Legislative Finance Paper #34. Denver, Colo.: National Conference of State Legislatures.

Governor's Veto Message S.B. 813 1983. Sacramento, Cal.

Guthrie, James, ed. 1984. *Conditions of Education in California 1984.* Berkeley: Policy Analysis for California Education.

Honig, William. 1984. "California Schools on the Move." Paper presented at the Association of California School Administrators Annual Meeting, Sacramento, Calif. October 16, 1984.

Kirst, Michael, and Stephen Somers. 1981. "California Educational Interest Groups," *Education and Urban Society* 13, no. 2. Beverly Hills: Sage, pp. 235-256.

Kirst, Michael W. 1981. "California." In *Shaping Education Policy*, edited by Susan Fuhrman and Alan Rosenthal, pp. 39-55. Washington, D.C.: Institute for Educational Leadership.

____. 1984a. "The California Business Roundtable: Its Strategy and Impact on State Education Policy," *Thrust* (January): 30-33.

____. 1984b. "The Changing Balance in State and Local Power to Control Education," *Phi Delta Kappan* 66, no. 3 (November): 189-191.

Legislative Analysts' Office. *Analysis of the Budget Bill: July, 1984-June, 1985.* Sacramento: Legislative Analyst-California Legislature.

Louis, Karen, and Ronald Corwin. 1984. "Organizational Decline: How State Agencies React," *Education and Urban Society* 16, no. 2 (February): 172-185.

Odden, A., and V. Dougherty. 1984. *Education Finance in the States: 1984.* Denver, Colo.: Education Commission of the States.

Pollard, Vic. 1982. "California's classroom crisis," *California Journal* 13, no. 10 (October): 357-359.

Siegel, Peggy M. 1984. "Legislative Strategies for Enacting Educational Excellence." Washington, D.C.: National Conference of State Legislatures.

Ziegler, Harmon, and Hendrick Van Dalen. 1971. "Interest Groups in the States." In *Politics in the American States*, edited by Herbert Jacob and Kenneth Vines, pp. 122-160. Boston: Little, Brown.

6 EXECUTIVE LEADERSHIP AND EDUCATIONAL REFORM IN FLORIDA

Kern Alexander

A recent newspaper article hailed Florida's public school legislation of 1983 and 1984 as "a dike against the rising tide of mediocrity." Other reports have variously termed the legislative efforts as a "quality revolution," a "return to rigor," a "structural overhaul," and a number of metaphors indicating innovation and change. Such descriptions may be somewhat exaggerated, but they do describe fairly accurately the educational upheaval that occurred during the legislative sessions of 1983 and 1984. In the 1983 session, in particular, substantial changes were made that materially affected the conduct of Florida's public schools.

This chapter gives an account of what happened in Florida, highlights some of the most important innovations, and touches on the political interplay that brought the changes to fruition. First, however, a brief description of Florida's demography, economic condition, and governmental structure is presented.

CULTURAL DIVERSITY

Florida is not a typical southern state. V.O. Key in *Southern Politics* (1949) described Florida as being so eccentric in its politics that it only remotely resembled other southern states. More recent events have confirmed this characterization of Florida as "the different state" (Colburn and Sher 1984: 35). The population of Florida doubled in the last fifteen years, reaching a total of approximately eleven million in 1984. This makes Florida the sixth largest state in the United States. Unlike other southern states, Florida has a large diverse population including substantial numbers of people of Greek, Italian, Polish, Oriental, Jewish and Hispanic descent. By 1980, it was conservatively estimated, Florida's Hispanic population was 860,000 or 8.8 percent of the state's population. The Hispanic population doubled between 1970 and 1980. This figure does not include the 130,000 Cubans who were boatlifted from the Cuban port of Mariel, of whom over 100,000 still remain in Florida. If one considers the Mariel refugees, the normal census undercount, and the daily influx of Spanish-speaking people into Florida, a more reasonable estimate today would place the Hispanic population at over one million (Warren 1984: 321).

Blacks are the largest racial minority in Florida with a population in 1980 of 1.3 million or 13.6 percent of the state's total population. The highest percentages of blacks are found in the northern counties of Florida, a vestige of the pre-Civil War days, and in the core of large cities, with Miami having a high percentage. During the decades of the 1960s and 1970s, substantial progress was made in improving both the political and economic circumstances of the blacks. In spite of these strides forward, however, problems still exist as has been evidenced by the racial strife that has torn at the fabric of Miami during the 1980s.

In addition to its racial and ethnic differences, Florida has the largest percentage of elderly persons of any state; over 17 percent of the state's population is over the age of sixty-five. Even though California and New York have large numbers of older citizens, they both have lower percentages. The elderly tend to cluster in seventeen of Florida's more populous counties in the middle, west coast, and southeastern parts of the State. Over 25 percent of the population of these counties is elderly. In one county, Charlotte, over 45 percent of the population is over sixty years of age, the greatest percentage of any county in the nation (Streib 1984: 309). In viewing such statistics, it is apparent why Florida is unique in the South.

Florida's geographical location and configuration contribute to the state's cultural diversity. As a peninsula extending southward, Florida has a Caribbean presence unlike any other state; yet, it extends nearly 1000 miles north and west into the plantation region of the old south. The Caribbean identity makes Floridians particularly aware of the international political and economic conditions deriving from the Caribbean and Central American cultures. This presence has led the Governor, D. Robert Graham, to assert that much of Florida's future economic vigor may well lie in providing leadership for this geographical region.

The diverse racial and ethnic backgrounds of Floridians also produce educational problems more complex than most other states, and these problems continue to mount as southern Florida is recognized as a haven for the dispossessed and benighted refugees from the Caribbean. These educational problems tend to go unattended by an elderly population that concerns itself with day-to-day existence on fixed incomes. Furthermore, the natural southern conservatism of northern Floridians severely restrains the state government's efforts to provide governmental services, especially funding for public schools.

LOW EDUCATIONAL ASPIRATION

Florida is not a poor state, but it is slightly worse off today than it was a decade ago. The state's great population increase has outstripped its economic growth, thus causing the state's rank among the states in per capita income to decline from nineteen in 1972 to twenty-one in 1982. But, because Florida's population has such a high percentage of elderly, it has a correspondingly low percentage of children of school age per 1000 adults. Florida has a lighter educational burden per capita than any other state, and this situation has become more pronounced during the last decade. Florida's personal income per pupil in average daily attendance in 1982 was $89,695 ranking it third among all states. Only Connecticut and New York had more income per pupil than Florida. By this same measure, Florida ranked ninth among the states in 1972 (Feistritzer 1983). Even with the greater demand placed on the educational system by the state's large percentage of non-English speaking children, and children from low income families, the state's relative fiscal capacity to provide for education is quite good.

The fact that Florida has substantial personal income per pupil, though, does not mean that the state has chosen to spend these resources on public schools. In 1983, for example, the per capital expenditure for public schools was *$565,* ranking Florida forty-fifth among the fifty states.

A combination of forces has traditionally prevented Florida from making a strong fiscal commitment for education. In the northern rural counties of the state, the adult population is characterized by low education levels. In this region blacks and whites who never had the opportunity for a good education, do not now as adults have a strong aspiration for education. The cycle of low income people having little education and a concommitant low educational aspiration for their own children is in effect in most counties of northern Florida. To change this attitude requires outside intervention from a state legislature whose members are cognizant of the value of education. There are exceptions, but generally, this dilemma characterizes the counties of northern and the western panhandle of Florida.

More progressive legislative attitudes toward education usually come from central and southern Florida. However, strong pockets of antitax conservatism exist in these areas of large populations and strong political influence.

The great number of retired persons transplanted from northern states have very little commitment to the education of a new generation of Floridians. Many retirees, living on fixed incomes, would be unable to make much of a tax commitment for education even if they wanted to. In addition, central and southern Florida have a high percentage of absentee property owners who have homes in Florida but whose permanent residences are in other states. These persons, along with owners of large land holdings, truck farmers, and condominium/apartment investors, add up to a paucity of concern for public education.

The demographic conditions that work against a reasonably good tax effort to support education are exacerbated by the nature of the Florida tax base. Florida's tax base is largely two dimensional. The sales tax and tax on real property provide the bulk of the tax base. The personal income tax, a major source of income for most other states, is constitutionally forbidden in Florida. The resulting tax system in Florida is one of the most regressive among the states; only the tax system in Texas is more regressive. Without a graduated personal income tax, the middle and lower income classes tend to bear the brunt of any tax increases to improve education. Thus, those groups for whom public education may give the greatest benefits are most reluctant to support increased funding for education.

A general antitax sentiment was recently exploited by a small group of enterprising real estate entrepreneurs who, in 1983, petitioned for a constitutional amendment that would severely restrict legislative prerogatives in raising tax revenues. Known as Proposition I, this measure would have frozen tax revenues at the 1981 level, allowing for only a modest inflationary increase each year based on total revenues. It would not have allowed for increased revenues to address needs created by population increases. The net effect would have been that the government expenditures per capital would have plummeted. The first year of implementation would have caused a loss of about 20 percent of revenues for public schools, and the state university system could have possibly been required to close the doors of five of its nine campuses. Polls indicated public sentiment for the proposal was strong and Proposition I could well have prevailed had the people actually voted on the issue. Fortunately for public education, the Florida Supreme Court declared that the language was overly broad and, therefore, violated the state constitution.

It was against this demographic and economic backdrop that the educational reform scenario of 1983–84 was superimposed. The alleged decline in the quality of public schools could be addressed only on the same stage with the unfavorable and pervasive antitaxation environment.

QUALITY AND FISCAL COMMITMENT

For some years the general public has apparently harbored a feeling that the quality and rigor of our public schools have been in decline. Parents of school children, themselves, have witnessed less homework, fewer papers being written, and fewer books carried back and forth between school and home. The public became more concerned with evidence showing declines in Scholastic Aptitude Test scores (Feistritzer 1984) and indications that graduates of our high schools were not as capable mathematically as high school graduates from other countries. Nationally average combined SAT scores fell from 937 in 1972 to 893 in 1982. Florida scores declined in the same period from 941 to 889. These conditions coupled with the stagnation of the Gross National Product (GNP) in the late 1970s and the decline of the United State's share of world markets led many to conclude that public schools were the root of the problem. The schools had, it was believed, failed the people. In seeking reasons, many political and industrial leaders did not hesitate to place the blame generally on professional educators and, in particular, on teacher organizations. This blame, coupled with an ongoing barrage of reports and studies by private and parochial school proponents (Coleman 1981; Coons and Sugarman 1978) castigating the effectiveness of public schools, led to a consensus that the ineptness of public schools was hazardous to the health of the nation.

As with most generalizations about social phenomena, particularly with reference to a system as large as the public school system of the United States, evidence supporting virtually all positions could be found. Some evidence indicated that public school educators were culpable, at least to the degree that they were in many instances guilty of a misappropriation of priorities and fuzzy thinking. For example, the conventional wisdom of many professional educators was that the reading difficulty of textbooks should be reduced otherwise the poorer students would fall behind and ultimately drop out. Over time, this view influenced textbook publishing companies to reduce the vocabulary level by dropping the reading level of some books as much as one and one-half grade levels.

Also, somewhere along the way, a philosophy developed in many teacher colleges that all study should be done at school and homework assignments should be curtailed. Reasons for this are hard to identify, but it appeared that some educators accepted the idea that homework would tend to widen the gap between the culturally deprived and middle or upper class children. Or, it was maintained by some teachers, that parental assistance with homework was likely to result in incorrectly done work. Regardless of the reasons, recent evidence reported by the Educational Testing Service (Hertling 1984: 10, 16) shows that homework had, indeed, declined from 4.76 hours per student in 1972 to 4.21 hours in 1980. This same report confirmed that average test scores in vocabulary, reading, and mathematics all declined for males and females. Furthermore, according to this study, high school students had chosen to pursue a less academically oriented curriculum. In 1972, 45.7 percent of the students followed an academic track in high school, and in 1980, this percentage had declined to 38.1 percent. The proportion of schools in which most students were enrolled in the general, nonacademic curriculum nearly doubled from 25.1 percent in 1972 to 47.4 percent in 1980 (Education Week 1984).

However, many other factors outside the public schools may have contributed to the alleged decline in quality. Societal changes may have been factors, but certainly and more directly there has been a reduced public commitment of resources for the public schools. In 1970, expenditures for elementary and secondary education nationwide amounted to 4.2 percent of personal income, and in 1980, the percentage had fallen to 3.7 percent (Johns, Morphet, and Alexander 1983; Feistritzer 1983: Table 32).

In the country, as a whole, between 1973 and 1983, the real income of teachers declined 12.2 percent. Between 1973 and 1981, teachers with bachelor's degrees had their salaries increase only 65.4 percent while salaries for graduates in engineering increased 99.3 percent, sales-marketing 78.3 percent, liberal arts 75.3 percent, chemistry 89.5 percent, math-statistics 85.6 percent, and economics-finance 75.4 percent. The increase in average teachers' salaries, for all teachers, was only 55.0 percent between 1974 and 1981, a smaller percentage increase than for virtually all other state and local government workers (Feistritzer 1983: Tables 41 and 42). In Florida, during the decade between fiscal years 1972 and 1982, government employees' average salaries increased 99.7 percent while average teacher salaries were increasing 87.8 percent (Feistritzer 1983: Table 43).

These factors coupled with additional job opportunities for women, and generally undesirable working conditions for teachers in public schools, may well have helped form a market condition in which less qualified persons are attracted to the teaching profession. In 1973, high school graduates who were future education majors scored 59 points lower than the national average on the combined SAT; by 1983 they scored 82 points lower. Other test data indicated that those individuals in the teaching profession who had higher SAT scores were more likely to leave the profession to seek employment elsewhere. The less able were left in the teaching ranks. In a recent article in the *Scientific American*, Preston (1984) observed that a disproportionate number of "the brightest teachers left the field and many potentially good teachers avoided the field altogether." He concluded that the major reason for this was a decline in the number of school age children and a substantial increase in the elderly population which is much more politically powerful than parents acting on behalf of their children. Contributing to this political phenomenon is the tendency of older people to exhibit great interest in politics and actually go to the polls. He notes that only 40 percent of the persons in the childbearing years between the ages of 25 and 34 voted in congressional elections in 1982 while in the 65 to 74 age category, 66 percent voted. Moreover, Preston's data show that the percentages for the younger adults had declined since 1966 and the older adults had increased (Preston 1984). One could easily see then how Florida, with its very high percentage of elderly, would have great difficulty in improving the tax support for its public schools.

These factors and others have apparently contributed to a decline in the public's fiscal commitment to public schools; a trend that is not easily reversible. In view of these conditions, it is singular and fortunate for public school children that an orchestrated effort to improve public schools developed in 1982–83 and Florida's Governor was the foremost of the state leaders who elevated education to a position of top priority on the state government agenda. Yet, it is also understandable why education reforms were so difficult to achieve and met with such substantial political opposition.

EDUCATIONAL REFORMS

The educational reforms of both the 1983 and 1984 legislative sessions in Florida may be grouped into three general areas: adequacy of funding, quality and rigor of the public school programs, and quality of the teaching force. Efforts to improve the public school system of Florida began before the publication of *A Nation at Risk* and several other national reports addressing the quality of public schooling.

The seeds to improve the public schools in Florida were planted by the voters when they elected Robert Graham governor in 1978. Earlier, as a state representative, Robert Graham had made the improvement of education his primary goal and had pursued this end to substantial success later as a state senator. On becoming governor, Graham began to provide motivation for educational reform beyond the boundaries of the state by chairing the Education Commission of the States and the Southern Regional Education Board. By 1981, Graham's belief in education as the most important governmental tool to improve the state and nation's social and economic condition began to be reflected in legislative attitudes in Florida.

Upon taking office in 1979, Graham found that even the high office of state governor could not bring about much meaningful reform of a major governmental function such as public schools without first creating a public consensus that reform was a necessity. Florida's history and that of U.S. public education has shown that the citizenry will not of their own volition rise up and, through exalted inspiration, require pervasive improvements in the educational system. Even the representatives of the people, the state legislatures, have been slow to demand improvement and reform without some external advocate to shape their opinions and attitudes. In Florida, Graham assumed this advocacy role and began to fire reform ideas at a generally uninspired legislature.

In order to shape consensus more directly, Governor Graham, on October 7, 1981, established The Governor's Commission on Secondary Schools. The twelve members were appointed to include representatives of the legislature, business community, college professors, school administrators, and teacher unions. The Governor charged the commission with the task of examining secondary education and developing specific strategies and plans to improve the quality of public schools in Florida. This commission deliberated for a year and in the Fall of 1982 issued a preliminary report that was very critical of public education in Florida. The first sentence of the report set the tone by launching a bolt at the public schools by charging: "The state's secondary schools had failed to make the connection between our lifestyle, our national security, our economy, our technology, and the quality of education" (Governor's Commission 1983). A vague condemnation to be sure, but one that captured the headlines and caught the abiding interest of the press. The report itself was not a particularly scholarly document. It was rather strident, poorly documented, and unnecessarily vitriolic in its condemnation of educational practices, but nevertheless it served to strengthen Graham's efforts to convince the public and the legislature that public school reform was necessary. The commission's recommendations were mostly along the lines of other state and national reports that began emerging at this time. They called for a reemphasis on quality by increasing the length of the school day and year; stressing mathematics, science, and foreign language; and establishing state-mandated high school graduation requirements. The report also called for a major reorientation of vocational education programs by concentrating on job training and post-secondary programs. The final report of the commission was issued in January, 1983.

Meanwhile during 1983, Governor Graham had proceeded with a campaign of speeches and press conferences that had begun to have their effect on both legislators and the general public alike. By November of 1982, Graham had already formulated his goals and strategies to increase the quality of education. Broadly they were:

- improvement of programs in critical areas such as mathematics, science, and high technology;
- improvement of the coordination between education and industry and the provision of services in educational institutions to support high technology industry;
- reduction of student-teacher ratios in public schools, community colleges, and undergraduate programs;
- provision of special programs for students beyond minimum basis progression through the various levels of education; and
- provision of sufficient funding to minimize remediation at the community college and beginning university levels.

For the 1983 legislative session, Graham's budget called for an increase in funding for public schools including making significant increases for expenditures per pupil and in teachers' salaries; a new emphasis on mathematics, science, and computer education programs; and the development of improved curriculum standards. Another of his initiatives guaranteed that every child would have a textbook for each course to take home every night. This action demonstrated the academic thrust of the reforms.

Specifically, Graham's budget called for funding of summer enrichment mathematics and science programs for high school students, mathematics and science tutorials after school, adjunct faculty programs, in-service training for teachers, and summer camps for computer instruction. But most important, his budget sought appropriations in such magnitude that Florida could move to the upper quartile of the states in pupil funding by the 1985–86 school year. To reach this goal in three years, 1984–86 would require an increase of $232 million as the first installment in the 1983–84 budget and another $634 million increase in the 1984–85 budget.

TWO RAILS TO QUALITY

Graham described his initiatives at improving quality as running on two rails. One rail was the substantive improvements in the quality of the educational programs that were to be closely monitored by annual evaluation reports of quality indicators. These reports would be submitted to the State Board of Education for all three public education delivery systems, the public schools, community colleges, and universities. These indicators were a broad group of productivity measures such as student test scores, process measures such as pupil–teacher ratios, qualifications of teachers, and so forth.

The other rail was to provide the necessary funding, the adequacy of which was to be determined by Florida's deviation from the upper quartile, or twelfth state in the nation, as measured in terms of state and local revenues per pupil. This goal required Florida to move from approximately twenty-third place in revenues per pupil to twelfth in three years and, of equal importance, required that the state make the quantum leap from a rank of thirty-sixth in average teachers' salaries to reach the upper quartile.

One rail of the track could not proceed without the other, quality could not improve without adequate funding, and, similarly, adequacy of funding would require a corresponding improvement in the quality of educational programs.

THE MOVEMENT TOWARD REFORM

As a result of Governor Graham's earlier entreaties and on the initiative of several legislative leaders including Curtis Peterson, president of the Senate, and Lee Moffit, speaker of the House, the legislature had laid its own plans for educational improvement. The House had established a task force to study the mathematics and science needs of secondary schools and the Senate had based a legislative package on many of the Governor's Commission on Secondary Schools' recommendations. Of the two plans, the Senate's gained more attention because it called for state-required graduation standards, increased the length of the school day and school year, and had mathematics and science initiatives. The Senate plan, however, did not call for sufficient appropriations to cover adequately the costs of its proposed innovations. The plan provided only 2 to 3 percent overall increase in funding. The House advanced a plan with substantial funding for teachers' salaries, mathematics and science programs, and for the school districts, to equalize funding.

As the 1983 legislative session progressed, the Senate and the House plans bore little resemblance to each other or to the governor's initiative. Not only were the plans at wide variance in substance but the range of proposed funding was remarkably divergent. Graham's plan continued to state the need for substantial funding and for his several substantive education initiatives. The Senate, anticipating difficult bargaining in conference committee with the House, continued to "low-ball" an appropriations figure. The House kept a budget figure comparable to the governor's. Additionally the Senate plan called for a reduction in property taxes without replacement from the state's general fund. The governor's plan, on the other hand, called for an increase in the required local effort from 3.878 to 4.385 mills. Graham also wanted to allow 1.6 mill to be levied at local discretion while the Senate wanted to allow less than a mill to be levied locally beyond the required local effort.

THE MASTER TEACHER PROGRAM

Of all the educational reforms in the 1983 legislative session, perhaps the most controversial was the master teacher plan. The plan materialized as an important reform effort to retain the best and brightest teachers by offering them both monetary inducements to stay in the classroom. As such, the master teacher plan was designed to be a career ladder. It was not a merit pay plan.

Movement toward a statewide master teacher program began in early 1983 when staff members in the governor's Office initiated a discussion of the efficacy of a master teacher career ladder program in Florida. After initially rejecting the idea, Graham decided to pursue this reform. His staff prepared a plan for possible introduction in the legislature. The idea of such a program had been overlooked as an important legislative objective by the governor's Commission on Secondary Schools. Neither the Senate nor the House had addressed the idea in their hearings and task forces. Also, important in Florida, the teacher unions, school administrators, school boards, and business community had not at this time expressed their attitudes about such a plan. There had been national press coverage of the Tennessee controversy between Governor Lamar Alexander and Tennessee teachers, and the general attitude of the business community supporting work incentive plans was already well known. In Florida, however, no proposals had been advanced for a master teacher plan by the beginning of the 1983 legislative session.

Graham in considering the issue wanted to avoid a Tennessee-type debacle (educational funding increases were denied the public schools in Tennessee through one entire legislative session in an effort to coerce the teacher's organization into accepting Governor Aloxander's master teacher plan). Because of Graham's strong personal belief in the need for increased funding for public schools, the option of holding the state education fund hostage to obtain teacher support was not available.

Before Graham decided to float the master teacher idea, he charged his staff with meeting and negotiating every element of a proposed plan with the two major teacher unions in Florida, the Florida Teaching Profession-National Education Association, the National Education Association affiliate, and Florida Education Association United, the American Federation of Teachers affiliate. Presidents of both unions and their staffs met with the proposal author and the governor's staff on many occasions to reach agreement on a plan to which both unions and Governor Graham could agree. These negotiations began about mid-March 1983 and extended through April, after the legislative session had begun.

Both unions objected to the concept for a master teacher plan, were reluctant to negotiate, and remonstrated directly to Graham. However, to both organizations' credit they did ultimately cooperate in shaping some details and assisted in molding a draft of a plan prepared by Graham's staff. After several meetings there was agreement on several points: There should be at least two levels beyond the level of regular teacher, the associate master teacher and the master teacher; one qualification at associate master level would be an in-field master's degree; teachers should be required to pass a written examination; and, as a part of the career ladder aspect, teachers who became associate or master teachers would be entitled to differentiated work assignments, including additional responsibilities.

On May 13, 1983, Graham called a press conference and announced his master teacher plan. He was accompanied by the Senate president and the speaker of the House, both of whom commented politely about the governor's initiative. It became obvious that a certain amount of interbranch jealousy was increasing between governmental leaders in their efforts to innovate on behalf of the public schools. The governor's announcement had temporarily taken the spotlight from the Senate's RAISE plan, and the announcement had also preempted a planned announcement by the speaker that he would shortly introduce legislation for a merit pay plan.

INCONSTANCY OF THE BUSINESS COMMUNITY

As has been the case historically in Florida, and most other states, the business community is a schizophrenic supporter of public schools; it is virtually always in the forefront in calling for education reform and betterment of public schools through greater efficiency, but it is simultaneously lobbying furiously to avoid tax increases. Such was the case in Florida in 1983. Earlier in the 1983 legislative session the speaker of the House had gained support and passed a bill that would finance the Education Reform Bill with a 2 percent increase in the corporate income tax. The business community had reluctantly agreed to this bill if the speaker's reforms would also include merit pay for teachers.

Near the end of the session the business community, represented by the Associated Industries of Florida, Inc., a lobby group, reneged and refused to support the tax increase even though the speaker had doggedly adhered to his agreement to support merit pay. What happened in Florida was not an unusual business response to public education. The state Chamber of Commerce advanced its support for merit pay and other reforms to improve the quality of education, yet it was reluctant to support a tax increase. The Associated Industries of Florida, a conservative lobbying group of 1600 companies statewide, had in response to the governor's and the legislative reforms, officially adopted a position opposing "any and all tax increases."

In spite of lack of support from the business community on May 11, 1983, the House Education Committee adopted a $500 million education package, including mathematics-science initiatives and a substantial teacher pay raise, but which did not include a merit pay plan. In order not to be completely obstructionist and to capture a possible bargaining chip, the chief lobbyist of Associated Industries indicated that the association would support the Speaker's proposed tax increase if the House would implement a merit pay plan. The Associated Industries position was obviously based on the assumption that teachers should work harder for their pay and that incentive pay could be a device to induce this result. Thus, it was understood that merit or incentive pay would be the *quid pro quo* for the tax increase that the speaker of the House had proposed.

On May 15, 1983, the speaker presented a complete education reform package to the House appropriations subcommittee. It had a merit pay plan calling for bonuses up to $5,000 for teachers found to be meritorious based on the teacher's knowledge as measured by standardized test scores and demonstrated by "superior teaching skills."

The speaker, an experienced legislator, had failed to realize that a portion of the business community represented by Associated Industries never intended to support major reforms if a considerable expenditure was attached. Instead of supporting the Speaker's plan, Associated Industries raised the ante and demanded not only merit pay but in addition a complete overhaul of the public school personnel system, calling for a "performance-based pay system." Associated Industries proposed a nebulous approach to performance pay whereby teachers would be paid more if productive and "fired" if unproductive. The speaker rejected the new requirement and on May 18, 1983, the House Committee on Finance and Taxation voted to provide funding for the Speaker's Plan with a 2 percent corporate income tax. Subsequently, the House voted for a 2 percent corporate income tax increase along with the education package. Yet, it was by no means certain whether the package could be sustained in conference with the Senate that had adamantly refused to increase taxes to cover the reforms it had proposed.

CONFERENCE DISCORD

In the conference committee the representatives of the House and Senate refused to agree on anything. The Associated Industries continued its antitax pressure on members of both houses and was particularly effective in the Senate. The legislative session had been extended beyond its scheduled sixty days and was not being sustained by an executive order of the governor giving the legislature ten more days to complete their business. While the lawmakers wrangled, the governor repeatedly voiced the position that he would veto any bill that did not provide substantial new revenues, in the neighborhood of $300 million, for education. The conference committee reported and both houses voted for a public school budget of only $1.986 billion in state general revenue funds with a required local effort of $3.878 million, the same as the previous year. At this level of appropriation, the innovations originally envisioned by both houses and the governor could not be put into place. In the end, conference committee discord, business community pressure, coupled with the traditional conservatism of the Senate, prevailed and the legislature adjourned with only a continuation budget. The House had succumbed and finally passed an appropriation for public schools that fell $123 million short of the governor's request.

THE GOVERNOR'S CRITICAL CHOICE

Graham at this point had a difficult choice—veto or not to veto. As is always the case, the governor's decision had to be weighed not only in light of educational considerations, but political realities as well. From the outset of his budget preparation process in the fall of 1982, Governor Graham had insisted on improvements for the public schools through his two rail approach, maintaining firmly that the economic and social progress of Florida depended on such an initiative. His state-of-the-state speech in the spring of 1983 had been devoted almost entirely to education, and his proposed budget reflected a tax increase to cover the increased costs of his reform package. Now, however, both houses of the legislature had acted, and, in spite of strong and persuasive leadership from the Speaker of the House, the appropriation bill only called for a continuation budget.

Weighing heavily on the minds of the legislators was the hardcore antitax sentiment that was present in Florida. The Proposition I issue that was looming on the horizon for the November 1984 election, and there was increased activity in the business community that exacerbated the antitax fervor. Also, it was difficult to generate support for educational reform and improvement from the retired, fixed-income elderly who dominated voting in central and southern Florida. The governor's position was also eroded by the lack of support from the teacher unions' leaders who had decided that it would be better to have no salary increases at all than to have to swallow a package of reforms that included the governor's master teacher and the speaker's merit pay plan.

In the final days of the 1983 legislative session, Governor Graham had sought to counteract the antitax influence of the business community, principally led by the Associated Industries lobby, by appealing to the leaders of major companies who made up a special executive committee of the Chamber of Commerce. This effort was partially successful. The group issued a press release endorsing the governor's educational package including an increased appropriation of almost $300 million to be financed by a 1 percent corporate income tax increase and the removal of various sales tax exemptions. This endorsement, however, in the end, had little effect on the legislature and it tended to reinvigorate the opposition of the Associated Industries and other elements of the business community.

The governor's persistence, however, had apparently begun to pay off with a sympathetic press. Several editorials supporting the governor's efforts emerged while condemning the legislature's ineffectiveness in attending to the problems of education. Yet, the political prognostication was generally quite gloomy for the governor's garnering strong support from the legislature, business community, or teacher unions for his educational proposals.

In preliminary consideration of a veto, the governor also had other complications. The extended session of the legislature had continued until June 24 and the end of the 1983 fiscal year was fast approaching. A veto and a special session could interfere with the succeeding school year's planning and operation. Some legislators warned the governor that a veto would be regarded as brinksmanship offensive to the legislature and detrimental to the school children. To further deter the governor's thoughts of a veto, the Senate president had pointedly declared that he had the votes to override such a veto.

In spite of the substantial political risk and difficult timing, Graham decided that needs of the educational system should by right and reason prevail. Regardless of the potential political liabilities, Graham choose to veto the school aids bill and in so doing demonstrated against the legislative effort as "acceptance of mediocrity." The veto covered the $1.9 billion state general revenue for public schools as well as $1.2 billion in local property taxes for public schools.

THE CULMINATION

After the veto, Graham called a special legislative session and moved immediately to capture what he believed to be latent public support for better schools, which was not being reflected in the state capitol by the various powerful lobby groups or by the legislators. He decided on a whirlwind, whistlestop tour of the state by jet, hitting seven populous centers to drum up public support. The response exceeded his expectations. Parents, students, rank-and-file teachers, and even some business leaders came forth with strong denunciations of the legislature's inaction and with vocal support for the governor's program. The press coverage of these events projected an image of strong support for the governor. His strength increased substantially, and the prospects looked good not only for averting an override of the veto but for actually increasing funding for education.

The governor then quickly moved to reach a consensus with the legislative leadership on an acceptable package before the two-day Special Session was to begin on July 12. The major features of the proposed package would include sufficient appropriations to allow scheduled movement toward the governor's coveted upper-quartile goal and the master teacher plan; strengthened mathematics and science curricula and merit pay plans for the speaker; and a lengthened school day and a state-mandated curriculum for the Senate president. An important change was made in the taxation plan whereby the governor substituted a multinational unitary tax for the speaker's corporate income tax increase.

The two day special session went as planned, and the legislative leaders in both houses were able to gain sufficient votes to pass the compromise package in spite of a last ditch stand by the business community led by Associated Industries. The unitary tax plan had caught the big multinational corporations (e.g., IBM, Coca Cola, Harris, Texaco) by surprise. They quickly launched a belated effort to defeat the tax. The Associated Industries lobby never endorsed the funding plan for the schools and right up to the final vote in both houses fought bitterly against the unitary tax and the other revenue initiatives.

PROBLEMS OF IMPLEMENTATION

In order to avert further acrimony with the teacher unions and the business community over the governor's master teacher and the speaker's merit pay plans the governor and the legislative leaders had agreed to create a commission and to delegate to it the responsibility for developing implementation plans for these reforms. This commission, to be known as the Quality Educational Instructional Incentives Council, was established by statute. Its members included representatives from the business community, teacher unions, school administrators, and certain other officials. The council was charged with formulating guidelines and procedures and recommending appropriate implementing regulations to the State Board of Education.

The council, suffering from uncertain leadership, floundered throughout the fall of 1983 making little or no progress on its charges pertaining to either the master teacher or the merit pay plan. Finally in despair, the governor, in December 1983, ordered his staff to work with the Department of Education to develop guidelines and policies for implementation of the master teacher plan. After many meetings, the teacher unions, the governor's staff, Department of Education officials, and others were able in early 1984 to recommend a set of regulations that covered the implementation of most of the master teacher program.

In the spring of 1984 the legislature appropriated an additional sum to devise subject area tests for teachers who wanted to become master teachers. The tests were completed by February 1985 and their administration to teachers began in the spring of 1985. In spite of the teacher unions' opposition to the governor's master teacher plan, the rank and file of the teaching force apparently supported the program as evidenced by the very large number of applications to take part in the program. By February 1985, the list of applicants who met initial application criteria exceeded 30,000 slightly less than one-third of Florida's entire teaching force.

The speaker's merit pay plan did not fare as well. Due largely to the inability of the Quality Educational Instructional Incentives Council to reach agreement, no coherent merit pay regulations could be promulgated. The collapse of the merit plan was imminent and by the convening of the 1984 session of the legislature there was consensus to disband the council and redesign a merit pay plan. Deliberations finally concluded with the creation of a "merit school plan" that was to be implemented by the state Department of Education. Thus far, this program has had limited success and been implemented in approximately half of Florida's school districts.

In final analysis, the governor's initiatives on behalf of the public schools could be judged as largely successful. He had prevailed in the watershed money battle in the 1983 legislative session, maintained movement toward upper-quartile rank among the states, and caused to be enacted the nation's first master teacher program. Also, his desire to improve funding for mathematics and science instruction and laboratories had been implemented. The Speaker's efforts to gain substantial increased funding for the schools had, too, been largely realized and his mathematics and science initiatives had been accommodated. In spite of the Senate president's reluctance to spend money he was able to obtain his primary educational goals of lengthening the school day and having a state-mandated curriculum.

OBSERVATIONS ON THE QUALITY REFORMS

What observations can be made about the extraordinary attention that the public schools received in the 1983 session of the Florida Legislators? Sincere concern for the quality of public schools is certainly attributable to Governor Graham and several of the legislators who believed that assuring the maintenance of a good public school system is perhaps the most important responsibility of state government. These leaders, honestly desiring better public schools, were an obvious and potent force in achieving reform.

More subtle reasons, however, were working for greater quality in public schools. *First*, education is a volatile government enterprise because individuals' aspirations and dreams are tied to it. Social and economic mobility in our culture are to a great extent dependent on education. Kogan (1978: 10) observes that education does and is widely believed to give "economic self-sufficiency," the lack of which may result in a diminished self-esteem and may even be stigmatizing. When persons pursue education collectively for the purpose of acquiring individual goals of social and economic fulfillment, the collective mechanism (the public school) used to achieve the goals may be severely criticized if it does not fulfill expectations. With this great diversity of expectations it is difficult for public schools to be all things to all people. Thus, the result is much public attention and often dissatisfaction (Kogan 1978: 17). This societal response to public education placed subtle pressure on the governor and legislators. As leaders, their interest in reform was accentuated by reports of public dissatisfaction.

Second, the demography of Florida guarantees a generally conservative response to most governmental issues. This conservative view of education emphasizes the individual who must be educated to survive in a system of competition and rewards. Intellectual achievement is a prerequisite to survival in the free market. This view has powerful antiegalitarian motives that constantly press for better education for the more intellectually capable and presumes that the culture will best protect the elite from the leveling impact of the masses. This "Social Darwinism" has been prevelant at the federal level and a similar view has been very apparent in many of the legislative deliberations during the past few years in Florida.

One commentator has observed that the net result of this viewpoint is to first attack progressive education as a perpetrator of all society's evils, to follow suit with cuts in educational expenditures, while simultaneously tightening discipline and introducing a more rigorous curriculum. This was basically the thrust of the Florida Senate in 1983. Critics have charged that the innovations in Florida will result in more dropouts as the system begins to cull the unfit in a social marketplace and that there will be retrogression of the equal educational opportunity that was advanced in the earlier decade. Such a result may be offensive to some but obviously not to those of the more conservative school of thought. At any rate, it must be assumed that the initiatives to increase funding would have a salutary effect on the school programs to make public schools more attractive to all students, including those who may tend to become dropouts.

Third, it is important to observe that the education crisis enunciated in *A Nation at Risk* (1983) was not an education problem per se but a general problem of economic productivity. The crisis began coming into focus as United States products began to slip competitively on world markets, and the public began demanding action by government to better prepare the nation's workforce. These concerns spilled over to Florida. With economic decline, suddenly the private business sector became interested in education. In Florida and nationwide, business and government leaders formed commissions to analyze the problem of the educational system. Predictably, data were gathered that confirmed that problems in the educational system had caused economic stagnation. Also, predictably, the lack of rigor was presumed to be a major contributor to the decline of the public schools. In retrospect there may have been no educational crisis at all, but, instead merely a prevailing perception that there was a crisis. Regardless of what is actual truth, on balance, the public schools will probably be better for the experience.

Fourth, in viewing the Florida legislative experience of 1983, one must conclude that education reform cannot be left in the hands of the business community. The business community cannot provide effective leadership for educational reform because of the heterogeneity of its make-up and the capriciousness of its support. Occasionally an individual business leader will emerge as a reliable force for beneficial reform, but as a general rule, the business community's collective power will be asserted in a manner detrimental to public schools. This phenomenon has antecedents as far back as the 1830s with industry's original opposition to compulsory school attendance laws and general taxation for common schools. The inconstancy of the business community support for public education is most evident in its assertative condemnation of the quality of public education juxtaposed against an equally animated obdurance to increased funding to improve the public schools. Today one can generally rely on the business community to proclaim loudly the benefits of efficiency while, without equivocation, opposing all efforts to increase fiscal support for public schools. The scenario was acted out repeatedly in the midst of Florida's educational reform efforts.

Fifth, another observation that cannot be avoided when looking back at the 1983 and 1984 sessions of the Florida legislature initiatives is the tendency of the teaching profession to act in opposition to its own interest. In her book *The March of Folly*, Barbara Tuchman (1984: 4–5) points out that throughout history leaders and holders of high office have acted contrary to the way reason pointed and enlightened self-interest suggested. She observes that "self-interest is whatever conduces to the welfare or advantage of the body being governed; folly is a policy that in these terms is counterproductive" (Tuchman 1984). In Florida, the leadership of the two teacher unions allowed their contempt for the master teacher and merit pay initiatives to cloud their perspective to the extent that they consistently acted contrary to the interests of the teachers. The union leaders' opposition to master teacher and merit pay was so strong that at times they professed to a willingness to forego the major funding initiatives proposed by the governor and the speaker of the House to defeat the plans. The unions' opposition to these two incentive plans was such that it led them to oppose question, and even oppose, many constructive education reforms and funding increases that the governor and the legislature proposed. The teacher unions' leadership stripped their support away from both the governor and the speaker at a time when their support could have a profound difference.

The position of the teacher unions in neutralizing their own effectiveness to the detriment of public schools is best explained by Tuchman as "wooden-headedness." She says that: "wooden-headedness, the source of self-deception, is a factor that plays a remarkably large role in government. It consists in assessing a situation in terms of preconceived, fixed notions while ignoring or rejecting any contrary signs" (Tuchman 1984: 7).

In Florida, the teacher unions' leaders' preconceived and fixed notions that both master teacher and merit pay plans would be detrimental to the unions' strength and structure created such an ambivalence that they were unable to actually advance the financial interests of their own teacher constituencies. Because of this opposition, the governor was forced to launch out virtually alone, in the Special Session, to gain an increase in state funding that would result in relatively high salary increases for the teachers. Had, though, the teachers acted in concert with the governor, the resulting appropriations could possibly have been much more significant.

Sixth, a final observation regarding the impact of the various initiatives suggests that not enough time has elapsed to truly determine the benefits of the legislative efforts. However, one can already observe certain emerging patterns. Florida reforms have been conscientiously implemented by public school teachers and administrators. Curriculum and class schedules have been revised to meet the new high school graduation standards, student teacher and teacher evaluation processes have been greatly improved as a result of the master teacher plan, mathematics and science programs have been revised and facilities have been improved, and teacher salaries, although still far from competitive and below the upper quartile, are, more competitive. A renewed sense of awareness to provide a more effective teaching force has been witnessed on university campuses. The education reform movement may have an even more important legacy and that is that the public has demonstrated a new awareness of the centrality and importance of the public schools in the well-being of the state and nation. A continuing recognition by legislators and the general public that the quality of public schools is vital to a viable social system and a healthy economy could well be the most durable benefit of the reform movement.

REFERENCES

Colburn, David, and Richard Scher. 1984. "Florida Politics in the Twentieth Century." In *Florida's Politics and Government*, edited by M. Dauer, pp. 35–53. Gainesville, Fla.: University of Florida Press.

Coleman, James. 1981. "Public Schools, Private Schools and the Public Interest," *The Public Interest* (Summer): 64.

Coons, John E., and Stephen D. Sugarman. 1978. *Education by Choice: The Case for Family Control.* Berkeley: University of California Press.

Feistritzer, C. Emily. 1983. *The Condition of Teaching: A State by State Analysis.* Princeton: The Carnegie Foundation for the Advancement of Teaching.

Governor's Commission on Secondary Schools for the State of Florida. 1983. *Secondary Education: A Report to the Citizens of Florida.* January.

Hertling, James. 1984. "Test-Score Decline Caused By Drop in Academic Rigor, Study Finds." *Education Week* 4, no. 15 (December 12): 10, 16.

Johns, R.L., Edgar L. Morphet, and Kern Alexander. 1983. *The Economics and Financing of Education.* Englewood Cliffs: Prentice-Hall, Inc.

Key, V.O., Jr. 1949. *Southern Politics.* New York: Vintage Books.

Kogan, Maurice. 1978. *The Politics of Educational Change.* Glasgow: Fontana.

Phares, Donald. 1984. "The Interstate Distribution of Federal, State, and Local Tax Burdens in the United States," *Journal of Education Finance* 9, no. 4 (Spring): 433–435.

Preston, Samuel H. 1984. "Children and the Elderly in the U.S.," *Scientific American* 251, no. 6 (December): 44–49.

Streib, Gordon F. 1984. "The Ages." In *Florida's Politics and Government*, edited by M. Dauer, pp. 309–320. Gainesville, Fla.: University of Florida Press.

Tuchman, Barbara. 1984. *The March of Folly.* New York: Alfred A. Knopf.

Warren, Christopher L. 1984. "Hispanics." In *Florida's Politics and Government*, edited by M. Dauer, pp. 321–330. Gainesville, Fla.: University of Florida Press.

7 STATE GOVERNMENT AND EDUCATIONAL REFORM IN MINNESOTA

Tim Mazzoni and Barry Sullivan

As defined by the national "excellence movement," current school reform enthusiasms appear to have had little effect on the policy contours of Minnesota education. Interstate comparisons applying criteria from *A Nation at Risk* (National Commission on Excellence in Education 1983) and *Action for Excellence* (Task Force on Education for Economic Growth 1983) rank Minnesota in the bottom half with respect to new enactments for its public schools.[1] Media commentary in the state has often echoed this negative assessment. Legislative response to popular reform proposals has been summed up as follows (Kolderie 1983: 3, Pinney 1984b):

> Increase teacher pay? Yes, more than inflation but less than the major jump recommended by some of the reports. Introduce merit pay? No. Raise graduation requirements? No. Raise college admission requirements? Not much. Require more homework? No. Lengthen the school year? No (though some groundwork was laid for a summer program). Introduce competency tests? Perhaps; but without standards, so that nobody fails!

If educational reform is equated with adoption of such prescriptions, then Minnesota's accomplishments are few indeed. But if the term is given a more neutral meaning, then there have been state initiatives that warrant the label reform. There also has emerged in Minnesota an ever-expanding policy debate on restructuring public education.

This chapter analyzes the Minnesota approach to K-12 educational reform as expressed through enacted legislation, policymaking process, implementation steps, and ongoing debate. Data on these matters were obtained from written records and from participants and other informants. Two sets of intensive interviews were drawn upon. The first (Winter 1984) asked how the education policy system normally functioned; the second (Fall 1984) asked about decisions on selected reform issues.[2] Unless otherwise indicated, all quotations included in this chapter are from the 1984 interviews.

FORCES FOR CHANGE

Policy actors, their relationships, and decisional outcomes are the main concerns of this chapter. Yet the Minnesota reform initiatives also were influenced by broader forces, including the demands of demographic change, the availability of fiscal resources, the concerns of interested publics, and the traditions of the political system.

Declining Enrollment

By the early 1980s, the decline of public school enrollments had been a source of pressures on Minnesota lawmakers for a decade. Enrollment peaked in 1971–72 (916,355 students); then it went steadily down. By the fall of 1982, enrollments had fallen to approximately 725,000 students (Minnesota Department of Education 1982b: 4). The transition from growth to decline was painful for Minnesota's 435 school districts, many of which were small and had meager resources. Enrollment declines often led to program cutbacks, staff reductions, and school closings (Minnesota Department of Education 1982a: 11). The impact of these declines was exacerbated in the 1970s by expanding school responsibilities and by escalating inflation (Peek, Duren, and Wells 1985).

Falling student enrollments not only produced stress for school systems but also posed issues for state government. During the 1970s, the legislature did enact various statutes to ameliorate problems caused by this contraction (Mazzoni 1980: 144–146). But the implications of enrollment decline for educational quality remained a concern of Minnesota lawmakers. Course offerings, teacher morale, community support—all seemed to be eroding in many declining enrollment districts. Then, as the 1980s began, Minnesota schools were hit hard by the state's "worst fiscal crisis in recent history" (Peek and Wilson 1983: 5).

Fiscal Stress

In the summer of 1980, the expansionary politics of surplus, which characterized state education policymaking in the 1970s, rapidly gave way to the redistributive politics of scarcity. For the next two and one-half years, Minnesota lurched from one "revenue shortfall" session to the next. Legislative actions had severe consequences for school funding (Peek and Wilson 1983: 109). State aid was cut by 38.3 percent, $1.52 billion to $.94 billion, between 1981–82 and 1982–83. Even after property-tax revenues were shifted to be available for 1982–83 expenditures, combined state-local revenue, which averaged 6.3 percent annual growth during the 1970s, was 1.9 percent less in 1982–83, $2.07 billion, than in 1981–82, $2.11 billion (Krupey 1984: 6). From the vantage point of school people, as one bluntly put it: "Education took a fantastic beating."

State fiscal trauma in 1980–82 shaped educational reform legislation in 1983–84. The public school lobby redoubled its efforts to pump funds into the state aid formula. Catch-up, not change, was imperative. Legislators concerned about education shared this priority. Improving educational quality, albeit a genuine interest, was not their primary goal. Lawmakers also had been made cautious. They anticipated money would be forthcoming to initiate programs, but they realized the amounts would not be large. Aspirations for reform were tempered by expectations for revenue. Moreover, the prolonged budget crisis, and the patchwork solutions to it, accentuated economic issues on the government's agenda. In policy salience, educational reform simply could not compare with jobs creation, tax relief, and fiscal management in the 1983 and 1984 legislative sessions.

Public Concern

Economic issues also ranked higher than educational issues on the public opinion agenda. A 1984 opinion poll found that Minnesota respondents in naming the state's two or three "most important issues" identified education (16.8 percent) with much less frequency than either taxes (65.4 percent) or unemployment (30.8 percent). Still, even if overshadowed by more compelling issues, education was a public priority, ranking third among nineteen specified categories, just ahead of business climate (12.6 percent) and environment (12.2 percent).[3] Minnesota citizens did favor some national reform prescriptions, especially state competency testing for teachers and students. But they did not want, according to poll data, to lengthen the school year or the school day. And opinion was sharply divided on other proposals—for example, significantly increasing teacher pay, requiring additional homework, and establishing a "voucher system."[4] The last, a particularly contentious proposal, evoked this division: favor (34.5 percent), oppose (28.7 percent), and no opinion (36.8 percent).[5]

Lawmakers were sensitive to the public mood, and they evidently felt constituency pressure on educational issues, the most intense probably being the demand for increased testing. Yet Minnesotans were hardly up in arms about their schools; there was no crisis mentality to prompt consideration of radical change. One 1984 poll reported that 53 percent of its respondents rated Minnesota public schools as doing an "excellent" or "good" job in preparing children for the future (up 17 percent from a 1979 poll response).[6] Another 1984 poll reported even more positive findings to a similar question. Nearly four-fifths (79 percent) of its respondents rated Minnesota public schools "in general" as excellent (23.8 percent) or good (55.2 percent). And 43.2 percent said public school "quality" was better than it was ten years ago, as opposed to 31 percent who said it was worse.[7]

Whatever the necessity of educational reform in the opinion of the general public, it was a mobilizing issue for specialized publics. The early 1980s witnessed in Minnesota a burgeoning of the policy community interested in elementary-secondary education. Old-line school organizations, agency officials, legislators, and their staffs were joined by a host of other actors. Governmental commissions, business and technology alliances, public interest groups, university-based projects, private foundations, and conference centers all sought a voice in reforming the schools. The "ferment" over Minnesota public education, energized in good part by the national debate on the quality issue, brought forth a potpourri of questions, analyses, and recommendations (Peek, Duren, and Wells 1985). But most proposals from this expanded policy community came too late to have much direct influence on the reform statutes enacted in 1983 and 1984.

Political Tradition

Enrollment decline, fiscal stress, public concern, these and other forces impinged on a policy system having well-established traditions (Gieske and Brandt 1977, Citizens League 1983). Minnesota's "moralistic" political culture (Elazar 1966) was reflected in a history of commitment to education (Peek, Duren and Wells 1985). While not having in the early 1980s quite the exalted status of years past, education was still identified by lawmakers as their "number one funding priority." State activism on school issues was balanced, in keeping with Minnesota tradition, by a deference to local autonomy in curriculum implementation and by a fostering of citizen involvement in district decisionmaking (Mazzoni 1980).

Education legislation was typically bipartisan despite the evolution of vigorous two-party competition between the Democratic-Farmer-Labor (DFL) party and the Independent Republican (IR) party. The DFL controlled the legislation from the 1972 to 1982 elections. It controlled the Senate (a 42 to 25 margin in the 1983 session); and, aside from an even split in 1979, it controlled the House as well (a 77 to 57 margin in the 1983 session). The governor's office—and in Minnesota this office is an extremely powerful one (Gieske and Brandt 1977: 242–257)—also was occupied for most of the period by DFL members: Wendell Anderson (1971–76) and Rudy Perpich (1976–78, 1983–85).

Innovative approaches to policy questions were encouraged by a political structure that was "open, issue-oriented, responsive" (Peirce and Hagstrom 1983). Minnesota lawmakers pointed with pride to pioneering legislation in such areas as special education, community education, school finance reform, educational technology, and early childhood services. Rightly or wrongly, these officials thought Minnesota to be a pacesetter in the region and on some issues as offering a model for the country. They were not likely to be swayed from these convictions by reports on the "mediocrity" of the *nation's* schools. And, in considering reform initiatives, they looked first to locally initiated alternatives and ongoing programs.

ARENAS, ACTORS, AND PROCESSES

Minnesota reform initiatives were enacted by the legislature in 1983 (a "budget" session) and in 1984 (a "short" session). State policymakers often referred to these changes as "article 8" reforms, since many initiatives were grouped together in that section of the omnibus educational financing laws of 1983 and 1984. The 1983 article 8 provisions had a threefold emphasis: educational technology, instructional effectiveness, and subject area inservice. The 1984 Article 8 extended several of the earlier initiatives. It also revised substantially Minnesota's Planning, Evaluation, and Reporting (PER) statute. Separate sections in the 1984 omnibus law authorized funding for summer education improvement (article 2), developed a new aid and levy program for early childhood and family education (article 4), and established Programs of Excellence (article 6). Some fiscal and legal information about the reform initiatives are summarized in Table 7-1; their key provisions are described in the Appendix.

Decision Arenas

State educational policy in Minnesota over the past two decades has increasingly become a matter of legislative determination. The reform thrust in 1983 and 1984 exemplified this trend. Initiation, formulation, and enactment occurred in decision arenas within the Minnesota Legislature. The State Board of Education (a nine-member body appointed by the governor) did take complementary action by requiring in 1984 that the number of courses offered by secondary schools be expanded. Yet this requirement, too, was in response to legislative impetus (Pinney, 1984a: 6A).

The State Board had been discussing the minimum program idea for several years and, in 1982, seemed on the verge of mandating it for secondary schools. Then, the board backed off; it enacted a set of recommendations having no force of law. On the minimum program issue, the State Board of Education appeared acutely sensitive to local control sentiments and to pressures from affected subject area interests. A proposal, for example, to improve grades 7-12 science requirements encountered "very strong opposition from the 'elec-

Table 7-1. Selected Educational Reform Initiatives, 1983 and 1984.

Reform Initiative	*Year Enacted*	*Funding*[a]	*Minnesota Statute Citation (1984)*
Educational Improvement			
Subject Area In-service	1983	$ 700,000	121.601
Instructional Effectiveness	1983	1,250,000	121.608–121.609
Academic Excellence Foundation	1983	150,000	121.612
Programs of Excellence	1984	15,000	126.60; 126.62; 126.64
Summer Education Improvement (excluding instruction aid)	1984	6 million[b]	124A.033
Research and Development Grants	1984	150,000	129B.10
Planning, Evaluation, Reporting and Assessment	1984	1,915,000	123.74–123.7431
School Management Assessment Center	1984	25,000	Laws 1984 Chapter 463, Article 8, Section 15
Technology			
Utilization Plan	1983	650,000	129B.33
In-service Training	1983	936,000	129B.34
Demonstration Sites	1983	2,181,000	129B.36
Courseware Evaluation and Subsidy	1983	1,354,000	129B.37–129B.38
Courseware Duplication Rights	1983	225,000	129B.39
Courseware Development	1983	250,000	129B.40
Early Childhood and Family Education	1984	15 million[c] 18 million	121.882

a. Unless noted otherwise, funds are used in Minnesota's 1983–84 biennium.
b. Estimated revenue for FY 1986 from state aid and local levy.
c. Estimated revenue for FY 1986 and FY 1987 from state aid and local levy.
Source: Estimates provided by Minnesota Department of Education Staff, Aid and Levy Office.

tive' areas, especially music, art, home economics, and industrial arts [which] led to a defeat of the recommendation" (Valdez 1984: 15).

Temporizing by the State Board of Education provoked key legislators. They sought not only to acquire more information about course offerings in Minnesota schools but also to prod the board into taking more decisive action. The upshot of this legislative concern in the 1983 session were curriculum reporting requirements for the Commissioner of Education and a directive to the State Board of Education that it adopt rules ensuring a "minimum comprehensive educational program" for Minnesota public school students (Valdez 1984: 15).

In the Minnesota Legislature, the educational reform initiatives were developed largely in two arenas. The first were the subcommittees of the Education Committees that had the authority to write the bills for funding the public schools and related programs. The House Education Finance Division and the Senate Education Aids Subcommittee were the chief originators of the reform initiatives, formulating and aggregating these within the framework of an omnibus aids bill. Subcommittee work did require approval by the Education Committees, and by the House Appropriations, Senate Finance, and Senate Tax Committees. But this approval, especially by the latter committees, was essentially pro forma. The 1983 and 1984 omnibus educational financing bills, including for the first time an inclusion (article 8) on "technology and educational improvement," passed their respective houses without serious modification.

The second decision arena, the one where the Minnesota initiatives were ultimately decided, was the conference committee. By the 1980s, House and Senate disagreements on educational financing issues had become a constant in legislative policymaking, thus making conference committees necessary to resolve these differences. Within the constraints imposed by the need for eventual House and Senate passage (of a nonamendable final report), the ten-member conference committee could add or delete items as it wished in fashioning an acceptable compromise. Whatever the individual merits of the reform articles, they were enacted as relatively minor provisions in complex and costly omnibus legislation, whose adoption depended essentially on the magnitude and distribution of school funding, not on the program content of educational reform.

Influential Politicians

In 1983 several politicians put educational reform on the state policy agenda in Minnesota. One was newly elected Governor Rudy Perpich, who emphasized high technology. Perpich, a DFL member, listened to Minnesota Wellspring, a public-private partnership drawing together leaders from business, labor, government, and education, in formulating his recommendations for the K-12 school system. While primarily directed toward the University of Minnesota, a major teacher training institution, the governor's well-publicized advocacy position gave political visibility to the technology issue. And Perpich's budget message signaled his commitment to funding technology programs in the public schools.

The second group of agenda-setters actors, also DFLers, were the chairpersons of the committee and subcommittee involved with K–12 educational legislation: Representative Bob McEachern, chairperson of the House Education Committee; Representative Ken Nelson, chairperson of the Education Finance Division; Senator Jim Pehler, chairperson of Senate Education Committee; and Senator Tom Nelson, chairperson of the Senate Education Aids Subcommittee. These four legislators assumed leadership for articulating educational reform policy. While they all had come recently to these committee positions, they each had considerable legislative experience, and all had a personal interest in program quality as well as in school financing. "Equally significant," observed an Education Department administrator, "the new leadership determined that legislation should reflect the expertise of professional educators in schools and in the Minnesota Department of Education" (Valdez 1984: 2).

Even prior to the governor's budget message and Wellspring's legislative presentation (both in early 1983), the chairpersons of the educational committees were actively casting about for "creative ideas" to mold into school improvement legislation. Their sense of the public mood, along with their own convictions, persuaded these lawmakers, to quote one, that "something needed to be done." The technology issue offered them a substantive and agreeable point of departure; one that could be modified and extended, combined with other improvement initiatives, and brokered through legislative compromise into a widely accepted reform article.

The same four legislators set the agenda for the 1984 reform statutes. Here their initiation reflected an unusually unified approach, bridging traditional House-Senate rivalries. From their perspective, the growing debate on educational quality (*A Nation at Risk* appeared in Spring 1983) created a "strong environment for school improvement." They wanted to seize this opportunity for leadership; they also did not want to be "upstaged." Although the 1983 legislation established a Legislative Commission on Public Education, the commission came to no resolution on recommendations for the 1984 session. The chairpersons, therefore, decided jointly to issue project LEAD as their reform agenda for that session (Pehler, Nelson, McEachern, and Nelson 1983). "LEAD," said one staffer, "set a general framework that was then divided up with different chairmen and their staffs working on specific interests."

The major exception to all of this was the Early Childhood and Family Education Act of 1984. This act actually had its origins a decade earlier in an experimental grant program. Legislative initiation had come from Jerome Hughes, then chairperson of the Senate Education Committee. The first grants totaled $230,000 divided among six school districts; by the early 1980s, $1.8 million was being awarded to some 30 projects. Throughout the 1970s, it took all of Hughes' power and zeal to keep the program alive. Opposition was formidable in the House. A staffer recalled:

> Year after year, Senator Hughes tried to make this program part of the regular foundation aid formula. But, in several sessions, he had to do everything possible just to ensure its survival as a small grant program. This has always been a "Senate program." It was often not even part of the House education aids bill, as we went to conference committee. Invariably, the Senate would have to give up something in their bill so that the House would accept the Early Childhood and Family Education program.

The state fiscal crises of the early 1980s threatened the grant program with extinction. Although it endured, the legislature did seem ready for a time to scale down support, leaving the fate of the program with local communities.

In the 1984 session, Hughes was finally able to secure a long sought objective. He accomplished this despite no longer having formal authority on the Senate Education Committee (Hughes became president of the Senate in 1982), and the fact that the chairpersons of the educational committees had already "set aside" money for their reform initiatives. Early childhood and family education was not among these initiatives; they, after all, had been around as a grant program since 1974. Still, the Senate Education Aids Subcommittee chairperson did encourage an amendment from Hughes to provide a permanent basis for the early childhood and family education program. The amendment was added to the Senate bill. As usual, no comparable language was in the House bill. Again, the fate of the program was left to the conference committee, and, again, Senator Hughes was successful in convincing conferees. As interpreted by a staff observer: "In the end . . . it was primarily a case of fellow legislators, in a time when state revenues were again growing, deciding to reward a decade of persistence by one of their own."

The priorities of the chairpersons, plus a few other legislators such as Hughes, gave "overall direction" to the process. These lawmakers were the prime movers behind the reform initiatives in Minnesota; they provided the basic cues for other policymaking participants. The legislators were not, though, the only influences. Legislative staff and Education Department specialists collaborated as a "team" with lawmakers in formulating and orchestrating support for reform proposals. Regular interaction built easy familiarity and mutual trust within this policy subsystem.

Educational legislators readily acknowledged their dependence on staff when confronted by complex policy questions. As one chairperson explained: "We rely very heavily on the staff. They are full time; we are citizen legislators and not always around. . . . The more technical your area gets—like school finance—you have a tendency to lean on staff. They have the continuity; you have to be into many other areas." Committee staff worked closely with their respective legislative chairpersons on everything from "brainstorming" about reform alternatives to keeping all those involved abreast of the issues to the drafting of bill language.

The source of policy content for many reform initiatives was the Minnesota Department of Education. The linkage here was not to top-level officials; rather, it was to middle-level managers and curriculum specialists. A handful of these individuals had been wrestling with quality concerns for years. In areas such as educational technology, instructional effectiveness, in-service training, and assessment testing, the department had professionals who had gained credibility for their "realistic" expertise with key legislators and staffs. Several had proposals and alternatives ready and were waiting for a target of opportunity. Once the Minnesota chairpersons of the educational committees had decided to exert leadership and to seek ideas, a "policy window" (Kingdon 1984) was opened for the Department of Education.

Just before the 1983 session, department specialists had been encouraged to communicate directly with legislators and their staffs. When asked to supply lawmakers with "some ideas in a package," they had programs in mind, including the "technology" area and the "effectiveness" area. As one participant described it, legislative leaders established the "form" of the initiatives; the Education Department then filled in the "content." An educational legislator agreed with this assessment, attributing the Minnesota reforms to "policy direction" from the legislature and "idea content" from the department. Both contributions, in his estimation, were equally vital.

To mobilize support for their reform proposals, the core actors in the policy subsystem reached out to involve others. Input from those having a stake in the educational system, such as classroom teachers, was actively solicited, and endorsements were sought from the K–12 organizations. "You can pass any legislation around here," one staff member claimed, "if there is agreement among major lobby groups." Yet while the anticipated reactions of these organizations certainly influenced reform content, they took no active role. In the judgment of an educational legislator:

> Over this two-year period there were very few, if any educational reform proposals put out by any of the groups representing the educational community. Those groups were mainly concerned with funding, and various sorts of funding proposals, and devoted most of their time and energy to that end. There was very little assistance, and only minimal support, in almost all other reform areas pursued.[8]

The lobbying imperative for the 1983 session, from the school groups' view, was to "restore funds to education." Change proposals were "very secondary issues." Their lobbyists did recognize that "the game plan had changed"; that legislative support for greater state aid was contingent on the schools' accepting greater accountability. And they knew that lawmakers could, if necessary, apply the aid formula in the context of an omnibus bill as "leverage" to bring the educational groups into line on the reform articles. Accountability was made palatable, however, because the 1984 Planning Evaluating Reporting (PER) revisions contained only a limited testing mandate. The school district, not the state, remained the constituency for assessment data.

As for Governor Perpich's agenda on technology policy, a sustained commitment to K-12 educational reform in both the 1983 and 1984 legislative sessions did not occur. The centrality of high quality schools, however, did receive much symbolic affirmation. Citing himself as a vivid example, the governor spoke with earnest conviction about the schools being the "passport out of poverty." In his frequent travels as the state's economic development promoter, Governor Perpich hailed Minnesota's educational system, the "brainpower state of the nation." The governor singled out education in major addresses as the "flagship" and "cornerstone" of his development program. He even proclaimed 1984–85 to be the Year of the School in Minnesota.

But policy symbols did not translate into policy leadership. Aside from laudatory rhetoric, comments about the need for expanded foreign language instruction, and early efforts to arouse interest in technology legislation, Governor Rudy Perpich gave school reform low priority among his 1983 and 1984 policy initiatives (St. Paul Pioneer Press 1984: 9A), which stressed job creation, tax relief, "business climate" improvement, and state fiscal management (Alnes 1984). While a few higher education issues did command active, personal attention, the governor reportedly believed that public school supporters could "take care of themselves" in the legislature.

Governor Perpich used his political resources on only a few school-related bills. In the 1983 session, Perpich pushed hard and successfully for a proposal that gave his office sole authority to appoint the Commissioner of Education (Salisbury 1983). Previously, this authority had been shared with the State Board of Education. In the following session, the big educational issue for the governor was a strong desire to establish a state school for the arts. Perpich got from the legislature a bill creating an Arts Education Task Force (Peddie 1984).

Much more visible than Governor Perpich on educational reform issues was his Commissioner of Education, Ruth Randall. Appointed shortly after the 1983 legislative session, Randall had gained the reputation as a "change agent" while a school district superintendent (Pinney 1983). As Commissioner, she pressed her message of change with eloquence and energy, arguing that only a far-reaching transformation could adequately prepare students for the "information age."

Commissioner Randall's vision of "restructured" education was complex and portrayed only in broad-brush strokes. Cental to her vision were "learner outcomes" to drive the delivery system; statewide achievement tests to assess competency, set expectations, and demonstrate accountability; individualized educational plans to allow students to learn and progress at their own pace; and decentralized "participatory management" to facilitate the sharing of power in school-site decisions (Randall 1984).

The commissioner emphasized grassroots communications to flesh out the details of her reform concerns and to enlist support for this thrust. Randall began by pledging that she or an assistant commissioner would visit each of the state's school districts. Early in 1984, an unprecedented attempt was made to organize "town meetings" across the state for citizens to talk about their schools and about "questions of restructuring." Some 15,000 Minnesotans participated in the nearly 300 town meetings. Many more citizens, 176,000 persons, who were mostly students, completed questionnaires or phoned in responses (Minnesota Department of Education 1984a). Despite its questionable status as a representative survey, the "Minnesota Dialogue on Education" provided Commissioner Randall, in her words, with "ideas for policy development." The same she said was true of the ten regional Task Forces on Restructuring Education that discussed "critical issues" facing Minnesota education (Minnesota Department of Education 1984b). But the commissioner, according to the chairperson of an educational committee, "played almost no role in shaping that [1984] legislation."[9] Her policy function was one of long-term agenda setting, raising educator and citizen awareness of a new approach to the state's educational system.

Policymaking Process

By legislative standards, the enactment of Minnesota's reform initiatives was a rather smooth process. Educational policy was sideshow politics. The abrasive political controversies of the 1983 and 1984 sessions were over the state's economic and fiscal problems. Except for technology provisions, the improvement initiatives received almost no media attention. Coverage was so sparse that it appeared, wrote one educational legislator, that in Minnesota "nothing is happening" (Nelson 1984a: 1).

When it came to school legislation, the paramount concern was funding the state aid formula. In 1983, the distribution of the funds was at issue, too, when the legislature substantially modified the financing program. The new Tier Foundation System, as it was named, called for (1) the basic foundation aid and levy; (2) five tiers of party-equalized funding available to school districts; and (3) an unequalized referendum levy (Peek and Wilson 1984: 10). Foundation aids rather than reform initiatives were far more critical. Salience of the aids bill was heightened in the 1983 and 1984 session by the belief that state fiscal retrenchment had fallen heavily on K–12 education. Compared to this priority, reforming Minnesota schools was a peripheral enterprise.

Some reform proposals did generate policy conflict. This was most evident in 1983 when disagreements about general direction, funding emphasis, demonstration sites, and the appropriate state role surrounded the technology issue. Minnesota Wellspring and the Education Department offered competing plans. "In the end," contended a Wellspring official, "the Department of Education is virtually unbeatable; they can amass more lobbies and levers." From a legislator perspective, the issue seemed less adversarial: "We didn't agree with [Wellspring] about how their ideas should be implemented. . . . We refined their ideas and gave them a more realistic approach so that they would have a better chance of being successful."

The question of whether there should be state achievement testing also aroused controversy. Minimum competency standards had been an issue in the mid-1970s, but the issue died out after the legislature in 1976 mandated that every Minnesota school district undertake an annual planning, evaluation, and reporting process. Educational groups could accept this district-oriented form of accountability, and the PER statute for a time effectively preempted the minimum competency issue (Mazzoni 1980: 156–164). Testing resurfaced as a legislative issue in 1983. Widely read national reports had declared performance standards to be the *sine qua non* of educational excellence. Commissioner Randall, in her curriculum report to the Legislature, a report required as part of the 1983 reform article, urged the development of state achievement tests (Randall 1983: 12).

Between the 1983 and 1984 sessions, hearings were held by the House of the PER law. Some testimony must have been disturbing to lawmakers: compliance was spotty; district activity often was symbolic, not substantive; and many school officials thought the process to be a waste of time and money (Minnesota House of Representatives 1983). Educational legislators, however, had no intention of scrapping the "grassroots approach" to accountability. On the contrary, they decided that the law was underutilized; it needed to be strengthened, supported by funding, and made more specific; and it could be the vehicle to pull together reform initiatives on technology and instructional effectiveness. Lastly, in their view, it was a "good alternative" to uniform statewide testing; and, as a staffer commented, "the authors were smart enough to design a package to appeal to local districts."

Conflicts over technology, testing, and other reform initiatives, while real, were not debilitating. The policy subsystem—education legislators, their staffs, and agency specialists—funtioned consensually. A legislator recalled: "We were all moving along the same wavelength." Education Department participants confirmed this assessment: "It was a joint effort with a great sense of ownership; 'you' changed to 'our.'" Reform proposals did need to be refined and aggregated to broaden their appeal. On issues such as educational technology, hundreds of persons were invited to testify and lend support. Appropriate expertise was sought from organizations like the Minnesota Educational Computing Consortium (MECC). Regardless of formal authority, a chairperson of an educational committee could not simply command votes for a bill. Each had to explain his initiatives to other committee members, to accommodate them when possible with language changes and concessions, and ultimately to make conference committee trade-offs so that the reform articles could be incorporated within the much more expansive "package" of omnibus legislation.

Conflict, bargaining, and compromise are the hallmarks of legislative decisions. Yet several factors kept educational reform policymaking in Minnesota from being a contentious process.

First, the financial stakes were small compared to other state issues, and some proposals had a positive valence for nearly all participants. Educational technology, for example, was a popular cause. It was never a question, as one onlooker phrased it, "of whether or if, but of what."

Second, the improvement initiatives had only minor structural implications; they held little prospect of disrupting existing power relationships. Accountability was handled in a "nonthreatening way" by extending the requirements of an existing statute, one with a local district orientation.

Third, despite contrasts in personalities, styles, and preferences, key legislators worked well together in giving direction to educational reform, a pattern of cooperation that extended across party lines.

Policy incrementalism best describes the overall strategy that the Minnesota Legislature took in 1983 and 1984 toward reforming elementary-secondary education.[10] Only a restricted menu of choices was seriously considered, structural change not being among them. The initiatives aimed at improving educational quality were enacted at the margins of the status quo. Some initiatives were both new to the system and imaginative in design. And they did have the potential of stimulating varying degrees of change. Still, they were intended to supplement and strengthen rather than supplant existing programs. The strategy, explained an education legislator, was one of "fine tuning, of providing new incentives for what we already had going on out there . . . Minnesota was already in pretty good shape."

INCREMENTAL CAPABILITY-BUILDING

Interpretation of the impact of the Minnesota reforms must be treated as quite preliminary. Most programs are in the early stages of implementation. The two with the most substantial funding—the early childhood and family education program and the education improvement portion of the summer program—will not commence until the 1985–86 school year. Still, some initial conclusions can be drawn.

As has been suggested, Minnesota's financial investment in K-12 educational reform does not loom at all large when compared to total school funding. As summarized in Table 7–2, projections for the 1986 fiscal year (starting July 1985) show about 27.6 million being allocated to all 1983 and 1984 reforms. This figure assumes extensive participation in the early childhood and family education program and in the improvement portion of the summer program; together, these initiatives account for an estimated 21 million, just over 77 percent of reform funding. Revenues dedicated to "traditional" education activities are projected to be some $2.7 billion.

Table 7–2. Minnesota's Financial Commitment to Educational Reforms Compared with Traditional Programs.

Estimated Entitlements	*Fiscal Year 1984*	*Fiscal Year 1985*	*Fiscal Year 1986*
Traditional Programs			
Foundation Aid	$ 614,500,000	$ 595,200,000	$ 735,800,000
Categorical Aid	272,400,000	285,500,000	311,800,000
Retirement Aids	185,600,000	197,300,000	210,000,000
Tax Relief Aids	382,300,000	369,700,000	380,000,000
Local Levies	942,200,000	1,034,300,000	1,046,700,000
Total	$2,397,000,000	$2,482,000,000	$2,684,300,000
Educational Reforms			
Education Improvement	$1,275,000	$3,423,000	$ 9,294,700
Technology	5,420,000	861,000	3,305,200
Early Childhood and Family Education	—	—	15,000,000
Total	$6,695,000	$4,284,000	$27,599,900

Source: Minnesota Department of Education.

(Table 7-2 calculates revenue from indirect sources, such as state property tax relief aids, as well as from foundation entitlements and other more recognizable aid and levy sources.) If these estimates prove accurate, revenues supporting educational reform will be only about 1 percent of total 1986 funding for Minnesota schools.

The relatively small commitment of funding to reform initiatives, at least in their inception, reflects an incremental strategy toward how change should be instituted in the educational system. This strategy can be detected in themes common to many initiatives. The most obvious are pilot projects and demonstration sites to test out ideas and to expand knowledge, skills, and enthusiasm about a particular reform. The fifteen technology demonstration sites, for example, allow visitors from other schools to examine varied educational technologies being applied in diverse organizational and community settings. Similarly, the twenty-six sites chosen to model "instructional effectiveness" show how principals and teachers can apply findings from the research on effective school characteristics. The research and development grant program, which will fund studies of alternative educational structures and practices, is an example, in a more experimental vein, of implementing change on a limited basis, allowing others to learn from these experiences and to share information on more or less effective innovations.

Minnesota lawmakers have been reluctant to take a prescriptive approach to educational reform. Even the testing requirements added to the PER law and the statutory push given the State Board to stiffen its rules on minimum curriculum do not seriously abridge local discretion. While PER now requires assessments, the chief importance of these tests is to give school staff something substantive to report to their community and to use in future district plans. Furthermore, statewide assessments have been conducted on a voluntary basis for years with most school districts participating. The secondary school curriculum rule does not establish new graduation requirements and many school districts already exceed the minimum course offerings. Only an estimated 5 percent of Minnesota high school students will experience any curriculum change because of the rule. And actual course content will still be the prerogative of local school districts.

Local school officials will decide, too, whether they will participate in the two most costly reform initiatives: early childhood and family education and the improvement portion of summer programs.

Both require a local levy, and the activities occurring under these two programs will be determined primarily by school staff and members of the community. Local control advocates might feel threatened in the future if some reforms were to be expanded. While a tiny program now (a maximum of 100 students for the 1985–86 school year), the Programs of Excellence initiative clearly has this potential, for it allows students to attend public schools outside their district. Large increases in funding for this reform could spur competition among public schools; advocates of vouchers might push to include nonpublic schools in the market of excellent programs.

Minnesota reforms do more than just allow leeway for local decisionmaking in the implementation of state initiatives. Most reforms are positively designed to foster school district capability, and they stress incentives rather than commands to encourage grassroots cooperation.[11] The basic question, according to a legislative author, is "how can we best enhance the learning action in the classroom?" Answers to this question, he adds, "should then percolate up and permeate the rest of the system, constantly redesigning it" (Nelson 1984a: 2). The Minnesota answer has focused on the improvement of schooling inputs as the primary way to enhance student performance. Computer technology, upgraded teacher skills, expanded preschool and summer time, and building-level leadership teams—these and other programs enlarge caability at the local level. Capability building through a decentralized structure typifies Minnesota's educational reforms, not outcome accountability through centralized standards.

Whatever change leverage they may in time exert, the Minnesota initiatives are considered by their legislative sponsors to be incremental "steps" to reforming the L-12 system. "Minnesota was incensed at *A Nation at Risk*," said one participant, "Minnesota is a state that builds on strength." Educational legislators publicly concede that the high-cost alternatives and restructuring issues have yet to be decided (Nelson 1984b). Their approach has been methodical, generally starting with pilot testing and demonstration models instead of (or at least preceding) new state mandates. Global edicts and "quick-fix" solutions have been eschewed by these lawmakers. The guiding commandment seems well stated in the comment of an Independent Republican legislative leader, active in educational reform: "When dealing with institutional change, it's wise to move slowly and deliberately" (Smetanka 1984).

WHITHER REFORM: INCREMENTALISM VERSUS RESTRUCTURING

Educational reform through improvement increments has not been without its Minnesota critics. Applying *A Nation at Risk* prescriptions as a standard, some media commentators have dismissed the legislative initiatives as a "trickle" in the national "tidal wave of school reform" (Minneapolis Star and Tribune 1984: 11A). More inclusive are the reformers who contend that institutional structure is the fundamental barrier to the achievement of excellence in Minnesota public education. As they see it, neither augmenting the amount nor enhancing the quality of inputs into the existing system is likely to do much good.

Among the most trenchant critics is DFL Representative John Brandl, a public affairs professor at the Hubert Humphrey Institute and author of an educational voucher bill. Representative Brandl maintains, as do many other restructuring proponents, that Minnesota's educational problems are far more serious than acknowledged by the legislators responsible for the 1983 and 1984 initiatives. These initiatives, in his opinion, constitute "mere tinkering" at the margins of the central policy of pumping money into the state school-aid formula. More resources should be devoted to grades K-12 education, Brandl argues, "only to the extent that the structure of the system is changed to translate those funds into improved outcomes" (Brandl 1984).

Reforming the public schools through instituting structural change has sparked a hot debate within the education policy community in Minnesota. A growing number of reports, papers, and conferences have addressed structural innovations. Influential advocates have pushed the restructuring issue into prominence amidst the welter of reform proposals crowding the legislative agenda after the 1985 session (Peek, Duren, and Wells 1985).

The debate was triggered by a 1982 report from the prestigious Citizens League, an independent civic research and public interest organization (Wilhelm 1984). The league report called for "rebuilding education" through deregulation, decentralization, and parent choice (Citizens League 1982). The last recommendation—competitive market incentives—was also propounded in many forums by public policy analyst and former league executive director, Ted Kolderie (Kolderie 1982). In 1983, the league encouraged Representative Brandl to introduce legislation creating a voucher option for low-income students. Hearings were held on this bill and on a demonstration district voucher proposal long promoted by the Citizens for Educational Freedom, an organization speaking for private school supporters (Citizens for Educational Freedom 1984). No vote was taken in the legislature on either bill.

Along with the Citizens League, Commissioner Randall was widely and consistently set forth her vision of "restructured education." But this vision, unlike the league's, does not extend to choice proposals that would provide state funding support to nonpublic schools. Another noteworthy voice for structural change is Public School Incentives (PSI), a nonprofit corporation formed to "create alternatives in public school education" (Public School Incentives 1984). Its first major project, which is still underway, was in school-based management. Subsequently, PSI became active on a wide spectrum of change alternatives and had some influence in promoting these alternatives in the legislature. Working with this organization on a foundation grant is Joe Nathan, author of the book *Free to Teach* (Nathan 1983). Nathan become PSI's most visible proponent of employing choice mechanisms to reform Minnesota public education and is the most active policy entrepreneur, of all the restructuring advocates, in trying to forge a viable political coalition.

Most recently, two political heavyweights have weighed in on the restructuring side of the policy debate: the Minnesota Business Partnership and Governor Rudy Perpich. Their legislative influence is sufficient to propel this issue, using Kingdon's distinction (1984), from the "governmental agenda" (issue receiving serious attention) to the "decision agenda" (issue in position for authoritative action).

The Partnership, representing the heads of the state's largest corporations, unveiled its Minnesota Plan in late 1984. This plan had been developed for the Partnership by a California consulting firm, Berman-Weiler Associates, as the final phase of an eighteen month $250,000 study (Berman and others 1984). Their main recommendations call for "major restructuring" of K-12 public education:

- A core curriculum (science, mathematics, social studies, and communications) to be mastered by all students through individualized learning programs by tenth grade completion.

- State-developed, uniform achievement tests to be administered at the end of the sixth and tenth grades; local districts not state government to set graduation requirements.
- Reorganized grades 7–12 to establish a grades 7–10 "common school" with a concentration on core subjects.
- State stipends for students in grades 11 and 12 to choose from alternative educational programs offered by their school district or by other state-approved public or private vendors.
- Decentralized authority for school governance, management, and curriculum to the school site.
- Reorganized teaching roles and instructional management.
- Constant real—i.e., inflation-adjusted—spending levels while program is being implemented over a seven to ten year period (Minnesota Business Partnership 1984).

Besides the proposals of the Partnership, other reform-oriented reports injected recommendations into the policy arena, including those from the Governor's Commission on Education for Economic Growth (1984), the Higher Education Coordinating Board (1984), and the Minnesota Education Association (1984). None of these actors, however, could rival the Governor's Office in setting the policy agenda for a legislative session. By the end of 1984, Perpich had decided to take such a role on the issue of educational quality. Appearing before the Citizens League on January 4, 1985, Governor Perpich announced his plan for "Access to Excellence" (Perpich 1985). Perpich underscored its significance by proposing the plan several days prior to his State of the State address.

The theme of accountability running through the governor's message, a theme having some marked similarities to the proposals of the Minnesota Business Partnership, envisioned that, to quote one editorial commentary (*Minneapolis Star and Tribune* 1985):

> The state would be responsible to pay much more than now toward local-school expenses and to set statewide expectations for student learning. School districts would be responsible for meeting those expectations with curriculums, faculties, courses and methods responsive to local preferences and values. Families would be responsible for choosing the public schools they want for their children, whether in or out of the districts where they live.

The most far-reaching of the governor's recommendations is granting every Minnesota student by 1988–89 the right to attend any of the state's public schools, regardless of district boundaries. State school funding—and in the Perpich plan the state would pay the costs for all basic foundation aid—would follow the student. This public school choice system would begin in 1986–87 with eleventh and twelfth grade students.

Any sort of choice bill, even one confined to the public schools, seems to galvanize many Minnesota educational organizations in their opposition. The powerful teacher unions have given increased attention to private school voucher stands in screening legislative candidates. (The Minnesota Education Association in 1984 withdrew its endorsement of Representative Brandl; he was re-elected.) A new organization, The Minnesota Friends of Public Education (1984), has come into being. Having prominent policy leaders among its directors, along with individuals linked to the main public school groups, the Friends has become the focal organization in opposing "tax diversion" to private school parents and in opposing education voucher proposals, such as the Brandl bill, that would enlarge state support for nonpublic schools. On the other side of the issue, the Minnesota Catholic Conference is intensifying its statewide efforts to persuade citizens on the merits of these proposals (Minnesota Catholic Conference 1984).

Taken together, impressive power resources are commanded in Minnesota by the policy actors who are challenging the incremental strategy of educational reform. Mobilization of these resources is taking place around the restructuring issue, coalescing particularly around the governor's public school choice proposal. The decision arena, however, is congested, fluid, and amorphous. There are many more participants in the current debate about Minnesota education than the restructuring proponents and their adversaries, and many more options than those aimed at structural change (Peek, Duren, and Wells 1985). Those who cluster under the restructuring banner do not constitute a political coalition, though an umbrella organization is being formed to support the principles of Perpich's open enrollment plan. Basic tensions and points of disagreement exist, especially over extending the choice idea to nonpublic schools. Alignments undoubtedly will fluctuate as proposals are clarified, bill specifics become known, and organizational interests prove to be incompatible.

United or not, restructuring advocates are going to lever the Minnesota Legislature into more educational reform than would be the case if this pressure were not present. How much leverage they achieve in the 1985 session appears to hinge on such factors as the

- amount of the state budget remaining to fund costly proposals after prior claims (e.g., school aid entitlements) have been met and after lawmakers, with an eye toward the 1986 elections, have resolved the tax relief controversy, certain to be the dominant issue of the session;
- public and professional backing that Governor Perpich and legislative leaders perceive to exist for instituting structural reform in Minnesota's K-12 system;
- willingness of Governor Perpich to invest substantial political resources in fighting for public school choice and his other change proposals;
- initiating role (if any) of the Legislative Commission on Public Education, a body comprising most education policy leaders in the House and Senate;
- political party rivalry extending to educational reform issues (Independent Republicans will control the House in 1985);
- agreement among the main restructuring proponents as to some common agenda (e.g., to support the Perpich plan) and their capacity to answer implementation questions persuasively for lawmakers;
- commitment by the Minnesota Business Partnership to mobilizing legislative support for its restructuring proposals; and
- extent of unified and determined opposition to structural change by the public school lobby.

Legislative dynamics are hard to predict. Conceivably these factors could converge to produce major restructuring enactments in the 1985 session. More probable is that the new educational reforms—and there are likely to be some in such areas as testing, staffing, and choice—will continue over the next year to be modest in scope and incremental in character. Although two of its members are no longer committee chairpersons, the four DFL education legislators who have given direction to this policy do not intend to relinquish leadership. They, too, have announced a program for the upcoming session, one that aims at "improving Minnesota education by integrating new initiatives with past legislative accomplishments" (Pehler, Nelson, McEachern, and Nelson 1985: 2). No matter how these political forces play out in the 1985 session, educational restructuring with its base of organized support appears to be on a longer issue cycle in Minnesota than other reform enthusiams, a cycle that might not be complete until several election campaigns and legislative sessions have run their course.

APPENDIX
KEY REFORM PROVISIONS

Minnesota school reform initiatives can be grouped for the purpose of description under three headings: (1) educational improvement; (2) technology usage; and (3) early childhood and family education. Key provisions of selected initiatives are presented, with the initiatives being chosen because of the size of anticipated funding or because they appear to be particularly innovative.

Education Improvement

Subject area inservice. The Education Department is to establish a program of in-service training for school district staff. Emphasis is given to academic content of subject areas; the first year to be science, mathematics, and social science. After the initial year, the Commissioner of Education is to recommend subject areas to the legislature.

Instructional effectiveness. This provision encourages classroom application of instructional effectiveness literature through five steps: (1) Commissioner of Education is to develop a statewide plan for improving instructional effectiveness; (2) a state task force is to be established to help develop an implementation model; (3) pilot models are to be established and evaluated in at least twenty sites; (4) assistance in implementing effectiveness models is to be available through regional education service agencies; and (5) "building-level leadership teams" are to provide instructional effectiveness training to other school staff.

Minnesota Academic Excellence Foundation. A foundation is to be established as a public-private partnership to promote academic excellence through recognition of programs, teachers, and students who demonstrate accomplishments; summer institute programs for talented students; and summer mentorship programs (with business) for students who have special career interests and demonstrated high achievement.

Programs of excellence. The Commissioner of Education is to designate selected secondary school programs as "programs if excellence"; then to choose up to 100 pupils statewide to participate in these programs. Selection of students may be based on criteria such as "academic ability, future career plans, and lack of academic opportunity in the pupil's current school."

Summer educational improvement. A "summer program and aid levy" is authorized to begin in 1985. Besides instruction, proceeds from the local levy and state aid may "be used for expenditures during the summer for curriculum development, staff development, parent or community involvement, experimental educational delivery systems, and other measures designed to improve education in the district."

Research and development grants. The Council on Quality Education (CQE) is to "support research on alternative educational structures and practices within public schools and to develop alternatives that are based on research." Research topics to be considered include school-site management, individualized education plans, alternative delivery systems, and outcome-based education.

Planning, evaluation, reporting and assessment. This provision revises the Planning, Evaluating, and Reporting (PER) law. School districts are to establish instructional goals, measurable learner objectives, instructional plans, and annual evaluations, and to prepare annual reports for their communities. Districts are required to conduct assessments, using state tests, for at least one curriculum area in at least three grade levels each year. The Education Department is authorized to develop an "assessment item bank" to help districts comply with the testing requirements. The provision establishes PER and assessment aid of the greater of $1,500 per district or $1 per student.

School Management Assessment Center. A task force is to be appointed by the Commissioner of Education "to make recommen-

School Management Assessment Center. A task force is to be appointed by the Commissioner of Education "to make recommendations about an assessment center and in-service training for principals and assistant principals."

Technology Usage

Utilization plan. This provision encourages planning for technology in schools. A district receives 75¢ per student if it agrees to develop a "technology utilization plan." The Department of Education is to develop support documents and model plans, provide in-service to participating districts, and formulate criteria for evaluation distrist plans.

In-service training. School staff is to be prepared to apply technology. Funds are to be provided to be used by the Department of Education to offer workshops. (A separate appropriation for the Minnesota Educational Computing Consortium (MECC) is intended for similar purposes, i.e., offering workshops and consultation.) School districts with an approved technology utilization plan are eligible for staff training aid.

Demonstration sites. Funding is provided for fifteen sites. Exemplary sites in school districts, selected competitively, to demonstrate the uses of technology to other districts are to be established.

Courseware evaluation and subsidy. The Department of Education and an evaluation team are to assess available computer "courseware" and develop a list of quality products for school districts to review. Districts are not required to buy list items but will be reimbursed for 25 percent of the cost (up to $1.60 per student) if they do.

Courseware duplication rights. The Department of Education is given authority to purchase rights to duplicate courseware and establish volume purchase agreements. Courseware packages purchased in this manner are to be distributed to school districts through MECC.

Courseware development. MECC, in consultation with the Education Department, is to "develop and design courseware packages which will meet the needs of school districts and which otherwise are unavailable or too expensive for individual districts or the state to purchase."

Early Childhood and Family Education

Establishes an early childhood and family education program supported by revenue from both state and local levies. Beginning in 1985–86, the program may be offered by any school district that provides community education, with offerings directed toward newborn to kindergarten-age children and for parents of such children. Acceptable program characteristics include:

- programs to educate parents about the physical, mental, and emotional development of children;
- programs to enhance the skills of parents in providing for their children's learning and development;
- learning experiences for children and parents;
- activities to detect children's physical, mental, emotional, or behavioral problems;
- borrowing educational materials for home use; and
- giving information on related community resources.

NOTES TO CHAPTER 7

1. Both the U.S. Department of Education and the Task Force on Education for Economic Growth (Education Commission of the States) presented state-by-state assessments in 1984 based on their respective "excellence" criteria. On each, Minnesota's reform accomplishments appeared to rank in the bottom half of the states. See U.S. Department of Education (1984) and Ordovensky (1984).
2. In January-March 1984, interviews were held with 15 legislators and 10 lobbyists, with respondents in both groups being identified by position in the state school policy system and/or by reputation for being influential in deciding state school policy. In September-December 1984 interviews were held with legislators (3), legislative staff (5), Education Department specialists (5), education lobbyists (5), and other advocacy group representatives (12). Interviews focused on one of three issue areas: "Article 8" initiatives, early childhood and the family education, or education vouchers. All interviewees were guaranteed anonymity and confidentiality with respect to their information; hence, they are only cited by the cate-

gory of the respondent. In addition to the two authors, interviews were conducted by DeeDee Carpenter and Clark Evans. Support for this research came from the Center for Urban and Regional Affairs (CURA) and from the Center for Education Policy Studies, University of Minnesota.

3. From a poll conducted in Spring 1984 by the University of Minnesota Center for Social research. A random sample of 2,003 adult citizens of Minnesota were interviewed. Results for the average response are accurate with ±2 percent, 95 percent of the time. Poll questions on education were designed and paid for by the Center for Urban and Regional Affairs, University of Minnesota. See Craig and Pederson (1985: 7).
4. These findings are drawn primarily from The Minnesota Poll conducted in February 1984 of 1,222 randomly selected persons (accuracy of ±4). See Paulu (1984: 12A).
5. Public School Incentives had three questions on education vouchers included in the poll conducted by the Center for Social Research. The findings reported here are based on the question: "In some nations, the government allots a certain amount of money for each student's education. The parents can then send the child to any public, parochial, or private school they choose. This is called the 'voucher system.' Would you favor or oppose such a program in Minnesota, or do you have no opinion?" See Craig and Pederson (1985: 21).
6. This is from The Minnesota Poll. The exact question asked is not presented. See Paulu (1984: 1A, 12A).
7. These questions are from the Center for Social Research Poll. One queston asked, "In general, how would you rate Minnesota public schools . . . excellent, good, fair, or poor?" A second question asked, "Is the quality of Minnesota public schools better, the same, or worse than it was ten years ago?" See Craig and Pederson (1985: 9, 10).
8. Personal correspondence to the author, January 13, 1985.
9. Ibid.
10. The classic statement of policy incrementalism as a strategy for decision-making is found in Braybrooke and Lindblom (1963: 81–110). For its appropriateness to educational policymaking, see particularly Helms (1981).
11. A persuasive case for the bottom-up, capability building approach is found in Elmore (1980).

REFERENCES

Alnes, Stephen. 1984. "Perpich's High-Activity Level Draws Comment" *Minnesota Journal* 1, no. 22 (October): 1, 4.

Berman, Paul, and Sara Peterson. 1984. *An Assessment of Minnesota K-12 Education: The Cost of Public Education.* Berkeley: Berman, Weiler Associates.

Berman, P., R. Clugston, K. Dooley, D. Elsass, S. Peterson, and D. Weiler. 1984. *The Minnesota Plan: The Design of a New Educational System.* Vol. 1. Berkeley: Berman, Weiler Associates.

Brandl, John. 1984. "Educational System Needs Major Change, Not Mere Tinkering," *Minneapolis Star and Tribune*, August 2: 19A.

Braybrooke, David, and Charles E. Lindbloom. 1963. *A Strategy of Decision.* New York: Free Press.

Citizens for Educational Freedom. 1984. "Education Vouchers." Brochure prepared by Citizens for Educational Freedom, St. Paul, Minn., September 18.

Citizens League. 1982. *Rebuilding Education to Make It Work.* Minneapolis, Minn.: Citizens League.

———. 1983. *Understanding the Quality of Public Life: An Anthology About Minnesota's Political Culture.* Minneapolis: Citizens League.

Craig, William J., and Shane Pederson. 1985. "Minnesota Citizen Attitudes Towards Public Education." Minneapolis, Minn.: Center for Urban and Regional Affairs, University of Minnesota.

Elazar, Daniel J. 1966. *American Federalism: A View from the States.* New York: Crowell.

Elmore, Richard F. 1980. *Complexity and Control: What Legislators Can Do About Implementing Public Policy.* Washington, D.C.: National Institute of Education.

Gieske, Millard L., and Edward R. Brandt, eds. 1977. *Perspectives on Minnesota Government and Politics.* Dubuque, Iowa: Kendall/Hunt.

Governor's Commission on Education for Economic Growth. 1984. "Report to the Governor." St. Paul, Minnesota: Governor's Commission on Education for Economic Growth.

Helms, Lelia B. 1981. "Policy Analysis in Education: The Case for Incrementalism," *The Executive Review* 1, no. 6 (May): 2–6.

Higher Education Coordinating Board. 1984. "Staff Report and Recommendations on Teacher Education." St. Paul, Minn.: Higher Education Coordinating Board, November.

Kingdon, John W. 1984. *Agendas, Alternatives, and Public Policies.* Boston: Little, Brown & Co.

Kolderie, Ted. 1982. "Many Providers, Many Producers: A New View of the Public Service Industry." Unpublished paper prepared for the Humphrey Institute, University of Minnesota, April.

———. 1984. "Two Alternative Routes to the Improvement of Education: Part II," *Public Services Redesign Project.* Minneapolis: Humphrey Institute, University of Minnesota, May.

Krupey, Joyce. 1984. "Present State Support for Education." Unpublished memorandum, Senate Counsel and Research, St. Paul, Minn., January 18.

Mazzoni, Tim L. 1980. "Decodomg State School Policy in Minnesota." Unpublished monograph, Department of Educational Administration, University of Minnesota, December.

Minneapolis Star and Tribune. 1984. "U.S. Reports 'Tidal Wave of School Reform,' But Minnesota Contribution May Be Trickle." May 12: 1A, 11A.

Minneapolis Star and Tribune. 1985. "A Powerful Promise for the 'Brainpower State'." January 5: 10A.

Minnesota Business Partnership. 1984. "Educating Students for the 21st Century." Brochure prepared by the Minnesota Business Partnership, Minneapolis, Minn.

Minnesota Catholic Conference. 1984. "Minnesota Education Vouchers." Brochure prepared by the Education Department, Minnesota Catholic Conference, St. Paul, Minn.

Minnesota Education Association. 1984. *Agenda for Educational Excellence.* St. Paul: Minnesota Education Association.

Minnesota Department of Education. 1982a. *The Condition of Education, 1982.* St. Paul: Minnesota Department of Education.

____. 1982b. "Summary of Findings on Minnesota's Investment in Public Elementary and Secondary Education." Unpublished paper, Minnesota Department of Education, St. Paul, Minn.

____. 1984a. *Minnesota Dialogue on Education Report.* St. Paul, Minn.: Minnesota Department of Education.

____. 1984b. "Teachers Honored for Work on Restructuring Task Forces," *Education Update* 18, no. 8 (May-June): 5.

Minnesota House of Representatives. 1983. "New Subcommittee Looks at PER Requirements," *Interim* (October): 26.

____. 1984. "Technology and Educational Improvement, 1983 and 1984 Education Finance Bills." Unpublished summary, Education Finance Division, Minnesota House of Representatives, April 23.

Nathan, Joe. 1983. *Free to Teach.* New York: Pilgrim.

____. 1984. "Improving the Parent's Choice Can Improve the Child's Education." *Minneapolis Star and Tribune* October 25: 31A.

National Commission on Excellence in Education. 1983. *A Nation at Risk.* Washington, D.C.: U.S. Government Printing Office.

Nelson, Ken. 1984a. "Minnesota Seeks to Improve Public Education in Many Ways." *Minneapolis Star and Tribune.* June 28: 23A.

____. 1984b. "An Action Plan for Improving Minnesota K–12 Education." Unpublished paper, Minnesota House of Representatives.

Ordovensky, Pat. 1984. "School Reform Grows, States Ranked, Challenged." *USA TODAY* July 31: 4A.

Paulu, Nancy. 1984. "Minnesotans Want Better Schools Without More Sacrifice." *Minneapolis Tribune* May 13: 1A, 12A, 13A.

Peddie, Sandra. 1984. "3 Bids Boost High School for Arts." *St. Paul Pioneer Press* December 6: 3C.

Peek, Thomas R., and Douglas S. Wilson. 1983. *Economic Conditions and Changing Government Policies.* St. Paul, Minn.: Center for Urban and Regional Affairs, University of Minnesota, January.

———. 1984. *Local Perspectives on Minnesota's Intergovernmental System.* Minneapolis: Center for Urban and Regional Affairs.

Peek, T., E. Duren, and L. Wells. 1985. *Minnesota K-12 Education: The Current Debate, The Present Condition.* Minneapolis: Center for Urban and Regional Affairs.

Pehler, J., T. Nelson, B. McEachern, and K. Nelson. 1985. "Initiatives for Excellence." St. Paul, Minn.: Minnesota Senate, January.

Peirce, Neal R., and Jerry Hagstrom. 1983. *The Book of America: Inside Fifty State Today*, Norton.

Perpich, Gov. Rudy. 1985. "Proposed Governor's Remarks to Citizens League." St. Paul, Minn.: Governor's Office, January 4.

Pinney, Gregor W. 1983. "Randall's Goals Help Education Agency Shed Its Low Profile." *Minneapolis Star and Tribune.* November 14: 1A, 8A–10A.

———. 1984a. "Tougher High-School Graduation Rules Not Expected Soon." *Minneapolis Star and Tribune.* March 27: 1A, 6A.

———. 1984b. "'Excellence' Push Hasn't Changed State's Schools." *Minneapolis Star and Tribune* April 23: 7A, 9A.

Public School Incentives. 1984. "What is Public School Incentives." Unpublished Paper, Public School Incentives, St. Paul, Minnesota.

Randall, Ruth. 1983. *Commissioner's Report on Need for Curriculum Changes* St. Paul, Minn.: Minnesota Department of Education, October.

———. 1984. "Education in the '80s in Minnesota." Unpublished State of the State Address on Education, Excellence in Education Conference, Bemidji State University, February 24.

St. Paul Pioneer Press. 1984. "Perpich: Putting People Back to Work is No. 1. Priority." January 1: 9A.

Salisbury, Bill. 1983. "Perpich Program Ready for Testing." *St. Paul Sunday Pioneer Press.* May 29: 3C.

Smetanka, Mary Jane. 1984. "Schools Due For Critical Scrutiny by Legislature." *Minneapolis Star and Tribune.* December 3: 7A.

Sutter, Joel A. 1983. "Major Trends in Minnesota Public School Spending, 1970 Through 1982." Unpublished Plan B Paper, Department of Public Affairs, University of Minnesota, January.

Task Force on Education for Economic Growth. 1983. *Action for Excellence.* Denver: Education Commission of the States.

The Minnesota Friends of Public Education. 1984. "An Urgent Message." Brochure prepared by the Minnesota Friends of Public Education, Minneapolis, July 31.

U.S. Department of Education. 1984. *The Nation Responds: Recent Efforts To Improve Education.* Washington, D.C.: U.S. Department of Education.

Valdez, Gilbert. 1984. "Minnesota's Recent Educational Initiatives." Unpublished paper, Minnesota Department of Education, June 11.

Wilhelm, Patricia M. 1984. "The Involvement and Perceived Impact of the Citizens League on Minnesota State School Policymaking, 1969–1984." Unpublished Ph.D. dissertation, Department of Educational Policy and Administration, University of Minnesota, November.

8 THE POLITICAL ECONOMY OF EDUCATIONAL REFORM IN NEW YORK

James G. Ward and Charles J. Santelli

New York was originally called the Empire State because of the diversity and richness of its geography and because of the preeminent position it held in the economy of the nascent nation. Until New York lost its first place ranking among the states in population to California in the early 1960s, New York was clearly regarded as first in the nation in economics and in politics, as well as in the number of people. Likewise, New York has been regarded as a national leader in the field of public education. While Massachusetts and Connecticut began building state systems of common schools before New York and many of the Midwestern or Western states led New York in developing state university systems, New York was recognized across the United States for the quality of its public education system and for leadership in educational innovation.

It is no surprise that the course of educational reform has followed a different path in New York than in other states. New York does not have the very low teacher salary levels and the low school expenditures per pupil that prompted educational and financial reform in many states with low spending levels and low teacher salaries. New York has ranked near the top of the nation on both of those measures. New York has not had its state school finance system invalidated by the courts, a factor that has facilitated reform efforts in some places.

Educational reform in New York stems as much as anything from the unique governance structure of public education in the state. While educational reform was initiated by gubernatorial or legislative leadership in most states, the impetus for academic reform in New York came from the state Board of Regents, the quasi-independent body with responsibility for overseeing all education in the state.

STATE SCHOOL GOVERNANCE

The New York State Constitution (article XI, section 1) states that, "The Legislature shall provide for the maintenance and support of a system of free common schools, wherein all the children of this state may be educated." The state legislature created the Board of Regents in 1784 to have control over education in the state, and the Regents have had constitutional status since 1894. The Board of Regents is the governing body for the State University of New York, which includes all public and private education kindergarten through graduate school level. The Regents are elected by the legislature for seven year terms and the Regents in turn appoint the state commissioner of education. The commissioner is the chief administrative officer of the state Education Department, the administrative arm of the Regents (Zimmerman 1981).

As in all other states except Hawaii, the state legislature in New York has delegated responsibility for operating public elementary and secondary schools to local school districts governed by boards of education. The Board of Regents promulgates rules and regulations that control the discretionary and ministerial powers of local boards.

New York consolidated its school districts earlier than most other states. In 1931, there were over 9,000 school districts in the state, but this number had been reduced to below 2,000 by 1956 and below 1,000 by 1965. Today there are approximately 700 operating elementary and secondary school districts in the state (New York State Statistical Yearbook 1983).

DEMOGRAPHIC AND FISCAL TRENDS

Until the mid-1850s, the public elementary and secondary schools of New York enrolled more pupils than the public schools in any

Table 8-1. Enrollment Trends and Number of Teachers in New York State Public Elementary and Secondary Schools.

School Year	*Enrollment*	*Number of Teachers*	*Students/Teachers*
1960-61	2,700,824	118,883	23.3
1965-66	3,176,574	146,441	21.7
1970-71	3,506,303	188,817	18.6
1975-76	3,406,015	182,772	18.6
1976-77	3,328,551	173,975	19.1
1977-78	3,211,849	175,879	18.3
1978-79	3,083,800	176,141	17.5
1979-80	2,958,725	172,803	17.1
1980-81	2,860,371	169,189	16.9
1981-82	2,770,640	168,516	16.4
1982-83	2,705,413	167,172	16.2
1983-84	2,661,041	168,944	15.8
Percent Change:			
1960-61 to 70-71	+26.5	+58.8	-20.2
1970-71 to 80-81	-18.4	-10.4	-9.1
1980-81 to 83-84	-7.0	-0.1	-6.5

Source: New York State Department of Education.

other state. After the mid-1950s, California surpassed New York in total enrollment. Table 8-1 shows New York enrollment patterns since the 1960-61 school year. Public school enrollment peaked in the state in the early 1970s at over 3.5 million pupils. The beginning of the enrollment decline occurred in New York at about the same time it did nationally. By 1979-1980, the state public school enrollment had fallen below 3 million and by 1983-84 it stood at 2.7 million. Over a period of about ten years, New York state public schools had lost over 800,000 pupils, or almost one quarter of their enrollment. Total public school enrollment in 1983-84 was slightly below what it had been in 1960-61.

The number of public school classroom teachers peaked at just under 190,000 at the same time as the enrollment peak was reached. The number of teachers fell more slowly than the number of pupils, causing decreases in the ratio of students to teachers. This decrease in the student-teacher ratio was due in part to new mandates in special education to serve children who were previously unserved or

Table 8-2. Revenue Receipts for New York State Public Elementary and Secondary Schools (*dollar amounts in millions*).

School Year	*Federal Revenue*		*State Revenue*		*Local and Other Revenue*	
	Amount	*Change*[a]	*Amount*	*Change*[a]	*Amount*	*Change*[a]
1959-60	$ 20	$ –	$ 636	$ –	$ 964	$ –
1964-65	22	2	1079	443	1438	474
1969-70	190	168	2048	969	2313	875
1974-75	376	186	2993	945	4094	1781
1975-76	336	-40	3070	77	4219	125
1976-77	339	3	3094	24	4468	249
1977-78	388	49	3143	49	4823	355
1978-79	420	32	3367	224	4900	77
1979-80	503	83	3595	228	5141	241
1980-81	473	-30	3958	363	5538	397
1981-82	427	-46	4272	314	6180	642
1982-83	425	-2	4587	315	6529	349

a. Dollar change from previous period.
Source: New York State Department of Education.

inappropriately served. By 1983-84, there were about 169,000 classroom teachers in New York state public schools and the student-teacher ratio was 15.8, a drop from 18.6 in 1975-76.

Public education in New York has always been well-supported financially. In the 1920s, New York was a leader in enacting school finance legislation to equalize school district capacity to offer educational services (Crockett 1983; Johns, Morphet, and Alexander 1983). New York state public schools were "held harmless" in 1944 from the adverse financial impact of declining enrollments. A school finance formula revision in the early 1960s further refined the state system to make it more responsive to variations in local property wealth (Crockett 1983). Tremendous increases in financing public schools occurred during the years when Nelson Rockefeller was governor of New York. From 1960 to 1972, state spending for education increased nearly 400 percent. Rockefeller also assumed an activist role in educational management and policy matters and challenged the Regents and State Education Department for leadership in public education issues (Usdan 1974; McClelland and Magdovitz, 1981).

Table 8-3. Relation of Selected New York State Fiscal and Demographic Variables to National Average.

Variable	*New York State as Percent of National Average*	
	1971-72	*1981-82*
Per Capita Income	117	111
State/Local School Tax Effort	120	109
Education's Share of State/Local Expenditures	88	87
Public School Students as Percent of Population	84	87
Current Expenditures per Pupil	156	146

Source: U.S., Department of Education, National Center for Education Statistics, *The Condition of Education*, 1984, Table 1.15.

Table 8-2 shows the trend over the last twenty years in federal, state, and local funding of New York state schools. It is important to note that while there have been very large increases in state funding in various years, in many of those years the increase in local funding has been larger. The net effect has been a shifting of the fiscal responsibility for public schools away from the state to the local jurisdictions.

As the data in Table 8-3 indicate, educational trends in New York are consistent with the national phenomenon of movement toward the national average in many social and economic indicators. In per capita income (a wealth measure), state and local tax effort for education, and current public school expenditures per pupil, New York exceeded the national average in both 1971-72 and 1981-82. However, on all three measures the state moved closer to the national average over the ten year period. In both years, New York was below the national average in education's share of total state and local expenditures and in public school students as a percent of the state's population.

POLITICAL CULTURE OF STATE EDUCATION POLICYMAKING

The long tenures of James Allen and Ewald Nyquist as state commissioners of education in the 1960s and 1970s produced a number of controversial decisions and policies and abetted the process of politicization of education. For example, a number of decisions relating to school desegregation made by Nyquist caused the state legislature in 1976 to pass legislation allowing appeal of administrative decisions of the commissioner to the state judiciary (Zimmerman 1983). Also, in 1973, Governor Rockefeller proposed the creation of an office of Education Inspector General to review the operations of the state education department and to evaluate the performance of the state educational system. This independent office under the control of the state executive was seen as a threat to the Regents and was opposed by them and the Commissioner of Education. The office was created by executive order in mid-1973 and continued until it was eliminated by Governor Hugh Carey in 1975 (Zimmerman 1983; Usdan 1974). These actions made the Regents more active in their exercise of educational policymaking authority and made them more vigilant in protecting their power and leadership position. The Regents discarded the "rubber stamp" they had used for so many years in accepting the decisions of the commissioner of education and his staff and shifted power from the educational bureaucracy to themselves.

Since its creation in the late 1930s, the New York State Education Conference Board has been an important power in state school financing policy. The Conference Board is a coalition of statewide organizations representing teachers, school boards, superintendents, principals, school business officials, and parents. Each year the Conference Board members confer and develop a joint proposal for state aid to public schools. Even during the years of teacher militancy and collective bargaining, the Conference Board has remained a respected and powerful force.

Another unique element in the educational politics of New York has been the existence of a strong and powerful union, the New York State United Teachers (NYSUT), which represents over 90 percent of the public elementary and secondary school teachers in the state. NYSUT was formed in 1972 when the state affiliates of the American Federation of Teachers (AFT) and the National Education Association (NEA) merged into one statewide group. When relations with the NEA were severed in 1976, a few local teacher organizations rejoined the NEA. However, almost all of New York's teachers remained with NYSUT/AFT, and the organization has remained a political power group representing the interests of urban, suburban, rural schools, and postsecondary education. NYSUT/AFT has been particularly successful in building effective coalitions with other educational and labor groups to pursue its educational policies. NYSUT/AFT has been notably active and influential in such areas as teacher education and certification, special education, in-service education, and school financing policies.

LEVITTOWN: JUDICIAL OR LEGISLATIVE ROUTE TO REFORM

By the 1970s, it was clear that the early 1960s revision of the state school financing formula was not achieving its purpose of equalizing public school resources. In 1973, the report of the New York State Commission on the Quality, Cost, and Financing of Elementary and Secondary Education recommended that the state be responsible for funding the schools. Its recommendations were never implemented. In 1974, another task force proposed a new equalizing formula, which was enacted by the state legislature. Both pupil-save-harmless and total-save-harmless provisions served to counteract the equity effects of the new formula, and by the early 1980s, only a handful of the state's school districts were actually on formula and not receiving state aid under the same harmless provisions (Crockett 1983).

A number of school districts, later joined by the state's largest city districts, challenged the state's system of financing schools on both state and federal constitutional grounds in the late 1970s in *Levittown v. Nyquist.* In anticipation of the decision, the state legislature altered the state school financing formula in 1978 to aid low-wealth districts and reduce the save-harmless effects (Crockett 1983). The state lower court ruled for the plaintiffs against the state (*Levittown v. Nyquist* 1978), and the Appellate Division of the state Supreme Court largely concurred with the lower court ruling (*Levittown* 1981). The New York Court of Appeals, the highest state court, however, overturned the lower court decision (*Levittown* 1982) and found no constitutional violation. The U.S. Supreme Court refused to consider the matter, finding no substantial federal issue involved (*Levittown* 1983). The final *Levittown* decision has been described as one of the "most shattering defeats" for school financing reformers (Cambron-McCabe 1984: 106). Another writer observed that the plaintiffs most likely erred in not claiming that the quality and quantity of education services in property-poor school districts had fallen below state standards (Crockett 1983). The legislature has continued to make minor alternations in the state formula, but major reforms do not seem to be forthcoming.

The most notable feature of New York's school financing system is not structural reform but increases in funding. In the wake of the *Levittown* case, in 1984 the educational lobby in the state, led by NYSUT/AFT, secured an educational increase of $630 million in state aid from the legislature, the largest one year dollar increase in state aid to education in the state's history. While reform of the system has been piecemeal, the level of funding by the state has continued to increase at a rapid rate. Such incremental reform may well achieve the equity goals of those who pursued school financing reform litigation quicker than protracted formula reform following litigation would have, because this increased state funding has helped low-wealth school districts. An important question left from this experience is whether reform is best achieved through the regular channels of the political system or through external pressure on the legislature and governor from the judiciary. The political route does seem most successful when there are present powerful political forces who act on behalf of additional state funding and reform.

ANTECEDENTS TO REFORM

Educational reform activities in New York predated the report of the National Commission on Excellence in Education and the other reform reports by a number of years. The spirit of educational innovation and reform has always been strong in the state. In the early 1970s, New York reevaluated and reformed its system for educating and certifying teachers and seriously discussed the professionalization of teaching. In the mid-1970s, state curriculum requirements and minimum graduation requirements were reevaluated and strengthened. New York has been administering a statewide basic competency testing program for students since 1973. This Regents Competency Testing program has been integrated with the more traditional state Regents Examination program to provide a comprehensive program for student assessment and school accountability. Results of the program have been used since 1978 as a basis for implementation of the states' Resource Allocation Plan to reallocate the state's resources and to improve pupil performance (New York State United Teachers 1984).

While in many states education reform has involved a shift in education decisionmaking and control away from local education agencies to the state, the Board of Regents in New York has long occupied a central position in setting and enforcing state standards for schools. In New York, the process of reform has been ongoing for over ten years and does not represent an initiative by the governor and legislature to upgrade substandard educational programs and policies as has occurred in other states. Instead, educational reform in New York has resulted from the continuing efforts of an activist Board of Regents to maintain and ensure the highest quality standards in the state.

DEVELOPING THE ACTION PLAN

The Board of Regents began work in 1981 on an Action Plan to Improve Elementary and Secondary Education Results in New York State (Action Plan). While the development of the Action Plan was influenced by events outside of the state, the impetus for the plan came from a desire to coordinate and integrate a variety of programs already begun by the Regents and from the focus on public education in New York occasioned by the bicentennial of the Board of Regents and the University of the State of New York (New York State United Teachers 1984).

New York Commissioner of Education Gordon M. Ambach has described the initiatives of the Action Plan in the following manner (Ambach 1984: 202):

> In many cases those changes reinforce the practices and reforms already in place at the local level. But our plan recognizes that effective reform requires action throughout the education system. To have any meaning, a reform must reach each classroom and each child, but successfully reforming an enterprise as education also requires that a clear statement of purpose and direction be established throughout the system. And that responsibility clearly rests with the state.

The role of the state in educational reform in New York is that of initiator, goalsetter, coordinator, and monitor. The Regents and the commissioner have continually stressed that the Action Plan does not alter traditional state and local responsibilities, but strengthens the state-local partnership. However, some observers of educational politics in the state have speculated that the Action Plan does take control from local school districts.

The Process

The process of the development of the Action Plan was complex, but fairly open. Various proposals and ideas generated by the Regents themselves and the staff of the state Education Department were subject to broad public debate through the media, in conferences and hearings sponsored by the Regents and the Education Department, and through meetings sponsored by various educational groups in New York. The proposals of the Action Plan were widely debated throughout most of the 1983–84 school year, and the process culminated in May 1984 when the Regents formally adopted the Action Plan (New York State United Teachers 1984). The process was described as the "result of 2½ years of discussion, consultation, and review by more than 10,000 educators and citizens across the state" (Ambach 1984: 203).

In some ways, this was only the beginning of the process. Once the Action Plan had been adopted, the lengthy and laborious task of developing detailed regulations for its implementation began. Many who agreed on broad goals and statements of policy disagreed on implementation details. The New York State United Teachers described this phase in the following manner (New York State United Teachers 1984: 15):

> By its very nature, the process of translating the Plan into action is a more mundane process. It lends itself less well to media attention and fanfare than did the process of developing and approving the Plan. Yet this is the critical phase—the phase in which real and specific changes will be crafted and implemented. The Plan that was adopted in March of 1984 is only the blueprint. Actual construction is now in the offing.

In October 1984 the Board of Regents adopted Part 100 of the commissioner's regulations, which formally implemented the Action Plan. Most became effective September 1, 1985, for implementation in local school districts during the 1985–86 school year.

The Role of Teachers in the Process

Since its creation in 1972, NYSUT/AFT has been very active in state education policymaking with both the legislature and the Regents and state Education Department. NYSUT/AFT has been politically active in endorsing and supporting candidates for state offices, has maintained a visible lobbying presence in the legislature, has become a source of dependable and useful policy research, and has generally played a highly sophisticated game of educational politics.

When in 1983 the Regents first put forth a proposed Action Plan, the NYSUT/AFT president called for a statewide education summit conference to bring all educational interest groups together along with business, labor, and governmental leaders to address the issues in the Action Plan. Although the summit did not take place as proposed, the NYSUT/AFT president's action started a process that focused wide attention on the Regents' proposal.

Thus, maximum participation was secured in the hearings and regional conferences on the Action Plan sponsored by the Regents. In March 1984, the state convention of NYSUT/AFT adopted a position on educational reform that went even beyond the Action Plan (New York Teacher 1984b: 3).

> The NYSUT plan supported the Action Plan's call for rigorous changes in curriculum, but added proposals to insure teacher quality, to increase teacher salaries substantially, to strengthen discipline in the schools, to reduce class sizes, to relieve teachers of noninstructional duties, and other measures of vital concern to teachers in meeting their professional responsibilities.

The emphasis of NYSUT/AFT was articulated in testimony before the Regents, which stressed that the Regents must work to attract and retain the best teachers through:

- ensuring that teachers gain some control over discharging their professional responsibilities;
- using teachers as resources in curriculum development and selection of instructional materials; and
- promoting meaningful and ongoing in-service education opportunities for teachers and insuring that in-service education and staff development be determined, designed, and implemented for and by teachers (New York Teacher 1984a: 6).

In its testimony, the New York State School Board Association reiterated these concerns and supported NYSUT/AFT's position. Unlike teacher organizations in other states like Arkansas and Tennessee, which opposed education reform, organized teachers in New York supported reform and urged state policymakers to go further in achieving reform.

THE REGENTS' ACTION PLAN

The Action Plan of the Board of Regents presents a comprehensive program for school improvement that affects both public and private schools in the state. Its provisions relate to students, teachers, and the processes of school management, and they can be described under a number of broad categories.

Curriculum Standards and Graduation Requirements

The Action Plan increases requirements for high school graduation in the state by increasing the total number of credits required for a diploma, mandating foreign language requirements for a Regents diploma, and increasing requirements in mathematics, science, and social studies. New courses in technology and home and career skills will replace current practical arts courses in grades seven and eight.

Student Testing and Accountability

New Regents Competency tests are required in the areas of social studies and science and would be phased-in as a graduation requirement over a period of years, in order to allow students sufficient notice to prepare. These tests are required in addition to the current Regents Competency Tests in reading, writing, and mathematics. A foreign language proficiency examination would be required for graduation, and districts who use the examination and reach certain proficiency levels would receive state financial incentives and students who pass the test would be given credit toward graduation. Each public school district and private school will be required to submit to the state on an annual basis a Comprehensive Assessment Report containing data on student progress, including trend data, attendance, and retention rates.

Teacher Evaluation and Teacher Quality

Beginning with the 1985–86 school year, each school district will be required to conduct an annual review of every professional staff member. The specific procedures and number of evaluations are not specified. Provision is made to phase-in the requirement with the negotiation of new collective bargaining contracts for school employees after the implementation date.

While the proposal is not in the Action Plan, the Regents have requested the legislature to provide state aid incentives for local school districts to add additional staff development days. The state has already provided new funding for scholarship and fellowships to attract new science and mathematics teachers.

Beginning in 1984–85, beginning teachers who desire state certification must achieve a minimum score set by the state on the core battery of the National Teachers Examination. Additional tests may be required of prospective teachers but there are no plans to test practicing teachers in the state who are already certified.

Additional Resources and Remediation

The Resource Allocation Plan of the state, a program already in existence, provides additional resources to school districts that exhibit low rates of student achievement. These additional resources are in the form of state technical assistance. The Action Plan contains provisions for remediation work offered by a certified teacher for pupils who demonstrate a need for it.

SOME UNADDRESSED POLICY ISSUES

A number of policy issues either raised in New York during the development of the Regents' Action Plan, but not addressed in the final Action Plan, or addressed in other states, but not in New York, remain outstanding. For example, in New York, issues related to imposing additional mandates in the area of elementary school curriculum and instructional mandates were opposed by many on the argument that great flexibility is needed at the elementary level and that program details are best left to local determination. As a result, the Action Plan contains no provisions in this area.

Likewise, the Action Plan does not contain provisions for career ladders for teachers or master teacher plans. These proposals have arisen in other states partially in response to the generally low level of teacher salaries. This argument was used to support such plans in states like Tennessee and Arkansas and the meritorious school program in Florida. The thrust of the argument appears to be that such plans can provide for tremendous salary boosts needed to keep some high quality teachers in the classroom. New York presents a differing set of circumstances. While there is a great need for teacher salary improvement in the state, the average teacher salary in New York has traditionally ranked the state near the top of the nation. For example, in 1983–84 the median classroom teacher salary in New York was $27,319, according to the state Education Department, compared to a national average teacher salary of about $21,900. The average teacher salary is above average in the state for a number of reasons including the militance and effectiveness of NYSUT/AFT, the high percentage of teachers with advanced degrees, and the higher salary levels in the public and private sectors in the state. While the subject of teacher salaries was not addressed in the Action Plan, the Regents made it the major priority in its state aid proposal to the legislature.

However, in New York the median beginning salary in 1983–84 was only $14,000, thus qualifying a beginning teacher in many districts for government subsidized lunches. In New York City, where it has been virtually impossible to recruit sufficient numbers of certified teachers over the past five years, teacher salary levels have slipped below those of many surrounding suburban school districts due, in part, to the losses incurred during the city's financial crisis in the mid-1970s. New York City teachers have never recovered from the financial losses they were forced to take in that period.

Class size was another subject that was not addressed in the Action Plan, but it was afforded the second highest priority by the Regents in their state aid proposal. Some argue that attempting to increase pupil achievement through curriculum changes and increasing graduation requirements will not bear fruit if, at the same time, class sizes are not decreased. Teacher salaries, class size, and staff development are key issues in the Regents' $634 million proposal for increased state aid for schools.

PROSPECTS FOR SUCCESSFUL IMPLEMENTATION

The prospects for successful implementation of the Regents' Action Plan and educational reform in New York will depend on the outcome of the interplay between the political system, which emphasizes public preferences and power exchanges, and the economic system, which concentrates on the production of resources (Bidwell and Friedkin 1979). This political economy view of reform prospects was echoed by Commissioner Ambach when he wrote that (Ambach 1984: 204):

> The ultimate prospects for success of our Action Plan and of the other reform efforts under way in U.S. education will depend on two closely related factors. The first is a continuing commitment by state legislatures and governors to sustaining the reform efforts through continued increases in education funding. The second factor is our ability to recruit, prepare, and retain a talented teaching force.

In order for reform to succeed, the desire and commitment must exist to take such actions as are necessary to effectuate reform and to provide the necessary financial resources. The lack of either one will doom the reform effort in New York and every other state. The test of commitment will be the ability of the education system to attract and retain a sufficient cadre of high quality teachers to staff the public schools. This is particularly pertinent to New York where the average public school teacher in 1983–84 was forty years old and had fifteen years of teaching experience. Within the next decade large numbers of experienced teachers will retire and new teachers must be hired to replace them. The kind of individuals hired may well be the test of educational reform in the state.

The Politics of Implementation

Teachers and others have warned that an emphasis on changing state requirements without altering the fundamental culture of the school and its working environment may not lead to any educational improvements, but only to increased bureaucratization of the schools. Wise (1979: 211) has written that

> The rationalistic visions of the educational system has strong implications for education leadership. The system would require managers who are good bureaucrats rather than strong educational leaders. The system would value those able to manage a process without being disturbed by larger questions of the role of education in society. Those best able to manage rules and procedures would be preferred over those who worry about the direction of education.

Wise's comments were written in the context of his concern about trying to alter the schools from the federal and state levels through increased rules, regulations, and requirements through "hyperrationalization" of the education process. This sentiment was echoed by the NYSUT/AFT president when he expressed his concern that, "We haven't dealt with our administrative system in New York State in which teachers do not have a full professional role" (New York Teacher 1984c: 3). NYSUT/AFT has called for the professionalizing of teaching with full professional rewards, authority, and status for teachers. The union has not rejected the Regents' efforts to upgrade standards and requirements but has accepted them, with some questions about the efficacy of certain proposals, and called for a more complete and far reaching reform, including recommendations for:

- additional increases in state aid for public schools;
- a statewide minimum teacher salary of $19,000;
- action on student discipline through alternative schools and intensive pupil-personnel programs;
- programs for professional staff development;
- a talented teacher scholarship program for highly qualified undergraduate and graduate students;
- an internship program for teachers without previous classroom experience;
- expansion of other programs designed to upgrade special educational services in a variety of areas; and
- expanded and improved programs in higher education in the state (New York Teacher 1984c: 5).

The organized teachers in the state see this comprehensive approach to educational reform as one that will address the major educational problems of the state in a way that the Regent's Action Plan does not and that can be politically viable.

1986 is an election year in New York. Election years traditionally have been good years for increased educational funding. If the Regents continue to advocate increased funding for elementary and secondary education in the state, and indications are that they will, then it would appear that the 1986 session of the legislature will include educational reforms. While the Regents will continue to implement their Action Plan, their effectiveness is tempered by their inability to make budget decisions. That power still rests with the governor and legislature. As one member of the Board of Regents was quoted as saying, "We've never been autonomous. All our major decisions involve money" (McClelland and Magdovitz 1981: 174).

The Economics of Implementation

At the beginning of the 1980s, a standard work on the politics of education views the upcoming years as "a steady state . . . with expenditures [for education] lagging slightly behind inflation" (Wirt and Kirst 1982: 250). In the early 1980s, educational expenditures exceeded inflation in New York and other states because of the large decrease in the rate of inflation that occurred after 1981. The national recession of the early 1980s, however, greatly impaired the revenue raising ability of state and local government. At the time of this writing (early 1985) inflation remains relatively low and the national economy is growing sufficiently so that the revenue picture in the Northeastern and Great Lake states is much more optimistic than it was in late 1983 and early 1984.

An improved New York state economy coupled with the politics of an election year could provide the implementation of the Regents' Action Plan concurrently with increased state aid for public schools and legislative enactment of key elements of NYSUT/AFT's comprehensive program for professionalization and reform. If the funding is not forthcoming, reform will be incomplete with mounting political pressure among teachers, school boards, administrators, and the public to resist further intrusion of the Regents into local education policy. Individual regents have stated publicly that if sufficient funds are not made available, they will support a review of the new regulations and standards.

The Action Plan, Reform, and Educational Quality

The goal of any educational reform is improved quality and quantity of educational services and improved educational outcomes. The risk of state-initiated reform is that the result of well-intentioned educational policies will be not improvement in education but only an increase in mandates, state-required programs, and bureaucratic, rule-bound behavior (Wise 1979). In New York, organized teachers, one element of the educational environment, have a vision of a restructured and more effective education system that requires changes and reforms that even exceed the broad program of the Regents. They, as represented by NYSUT/AFT, are as concerned with continued public support for public schools and with program quality and accountability as they are with their own working conditions and welfare. They also realize, however, that the latter is critical to attracting and retaining a high quality school staff into the 21st century.

Key elements in the process of implementing reform will be the degree of acceptance among local educational leaders of the details of the Regents' Action Plan, the future trends in state financial aid, and the degree to which teachers achieve professionalization. If all three are achieved, then educational reform can make real improvements in New York public schools. If any element does not emerge, reform could become just more rhetoric.

PARTNERSHIP OR CENTRALIZATION?

This analysis suggests that the political culture in New York is important for understanding educational reform efforts. The state Board of Regents and the Education Department possess tremendous power in promulgating mandates, requirements, and standards for schools. Budget determination and fiscal control rest squarely with the governor and the legislature. The development of educational policy depends upon the relationships among these political institutions and the influences on them. New York has a strong, almost over-exaggerated, tradition of local control of schools; state intrusion is often resisted if it is not seen as beneficial and supportive of local prerogatives. School boards and teachers are politically powerful groups in the state and must be reckoned with. The combination of these elements made predicting the outcome of New York education politics a risky enterprise.

If the complete program of reform is enacted, a possible outcome is increasing centralization of decisionmaking at the state level. The Commissioner of Education stresses the state-local partnership, but increased centralization is a potential. A second issue that merits watching is that increased state funding, with proper modifications in the state-aid formula, could accomplish what the school financing reform litigation could not achieve. A third issue is whether teachers in New York are able to move toward professionalization. With the strength of NYSUT/AFT and its dominance among the states' public school teachers, it is an element that could be key in making New York the first state to go the full distance down the road to educational reform and emerge with a fully professional teaching force in control of its own members and destiny. This could be the most significant result of reform in New York. When this chapter was written, proposals to professionalize teaching and to improve salary levels for teachers were just beginning. Reform in New York State will fail if these elements are not funded and implemented.

REFERENCES

Ambach, Gordon M. 1984. "State and Local Action for Education in New York." *Phi Delta Kappan* 66, no. 3 (November): 202–204.

Bidwell, Charles E., and Noah E. Friedkin. 1979. "The Political Economy of Local School Districts: Intergovernmental Relations and Local Process in the Distribution of Educational Goods and Services." Paper prepared for a conference of the U.S. Department of Health, Education, and Welfare on Resource Allocation, Service Delivery, and School Effectiveness, September 18–19, Washington, D.C.

Board of Educ., *Levittown Union Free School Dist. v. Nyquist*, 408 N.Y.S.2d 606 (1978); 443 N.Y.S.2d 843 (N.Y. App. Div. 1981); 453 N.Y.S.2d 643 (N.Y. 1982); *cert. denied*, 103 S. Ct. 775 (1983).

Cambron-McCabe, Nelda H. 1984. "The Changing School Finance Scene: Local, State, and Federal Issues." In *School Law Update*, edited by Thomas N. Jones and Darel P. Semler, pp. 106–123. Topeka, Kans.: National Organization on Legal Problems of Education.

Crockett, Ulysses S. 1983. "Financing Public Education in New York State." The *Levittown* Decision and Its Challenge to the State Legislature." *The Urban Lawyer* 15, no. 1 (Winter): 29–73.

Johns, Roe L., Edgar L. Morphet, and Kern Alexander. 1983. *The Economics and Financing of Education.* Englewood Cliffs, N.J.: Prentice-Hall, Inc.

McClelland, Peter D., and Alan L. Magdovitz. 1981. *Crisis in the Making: The Political Economy of New York State since 1945.* New York: Cambridge University Press.

New York State Statistical Yearbook, 1983–84 Edition. 1983. Albany: The Nelson Rockefeller Institute of Government, State University of New York.

New York State United Teachers. 1984. *Local Leaders Guide to Research and Educational Issues.* Albaby: NYSUT.

New York Teacher. 1984a. "NYSUT to Regents: Focus on Teachers Professional Needs." (October): 6–7.

____. 1984b. "United Teachers Pressed Regents on Teacher Concerns, Sees More Work Ahead to Gain Real Reform." (December): 3.

____. 1984c. "United Teachers' Top Goal in 1985: Education Reform in New York State." (December): 3–5.

Usdan, Michael. 1974. "Elementary and Secondary Education." In *Governing New York State: The Rockefeller Years*, edited by Connery and Gerald Benjamin, pp. 225–238. New York: The Academy of Political Science.

Wirt, Frederick N., and Michael W. Kirst. 1982. *Schools in Conflict: The Politics of Education.* Berkeley: McCutchan Publishing Corp.

Wise, Arthur E. 1979. *Legislated Learning: The Bureaucratization of the American Classroom.* Berkeley: University of California Press.

Zimmerman, Joseph F. 1981. *The Government and Politics of New York State.* New York: New York University Press.

9 TENNESSEE EDUCATIONAL REFORM
Gubernatorial Advocacy

Charles M. Achilles, Zelma Lansford, and William H. Payne

INTRODUCTION, BACKGROUND AND CONTEXT

The early 1980s were a period of dramatic educational emphasis in Tennessee. Educational reform, begun in earnest in 1981, moved into high gear in 1984. By 1980–81, Tennesseans were spending the largest share of their public funds, 47.2 percent, for public education. Yet there had been no serious study of public elementary and secondary education since *Public Education in Tennessee: Grades 1–12* (Gibbs 1957).

A quarter of a century later, the Tennessee General Assembly, led by the lieutenant governor and speaker of the House, passed Senate Joint Resolution No. 56, which Governor Lamar Alexander signed into law in June 1981. This legislation and a subsequent appropriation initiated a comprehensive study of Tennessee education, kindergarten through higher education. The study focused on development and analysis of educational goals, governance, and organizational structures; instructional quality; and fund distribution for three levels, elementary and secondary, vocational education, and higher education (including professional schools of medicine, dentistry, law, and veterinary medicine) (Tennessee Comprehensive Education Study 1982: 3).

The *Tennessee Comprehensive Education Study* (TCES) and two other studies have aided the preparation of this case study. Tennessee was one of twelve states studied in the 1970s during the Educational Governance Project directed by Campbell and Mazzoni (1975). Lansford (1984) completed a study to document key participants and factors, and especially the elements of conflict, in Tennessee's current educational reform.

This report of Tennessee's current educational reform is not a case study in the usual sense of the word. The authors have chronicled selected events by synthesizing information and describing phenomena to provide a narrative about the reform effort. This report has many of the shortcomings of state governance case studies as described by Burlingame and Geske (1979). The authors did not collect new data; there were no predetermined sampling procedures or analysis plans. There is no substantive rationale for sample size or representativeness; there is no attempt to generate or test theoretical propositions, and at best, it is a third-hand accounting of events (Burlingame and Geske 1979: 63 and 66). Much information was derived from public, published accounts and from interviews. Many of the interviewees held office and influential positions in the state. Burlingame and Geske alert us to potential skewing of data when relying heavily on interviews. They state that "governors, legislators, chief state school officers, and educational interest group leaders are as adept as disseminating their own point of view as they are at concealing information the interviewer might seek" (Burlingame and Geske 1979: 64).

Tennessee education relies primarily on state sales and local property taxes for funds. Tennessee has ranked at or near the bottom in state and local expenditures for education when compared to other states. Table 9–1 shows Tennessee's consistently low support for education.

One TCES goal was to develop a long-range educational plan for Tennessee, including an educational, economic, and financial forecast and a review of present procedures in the distribution of funds to each level of public education (Tennessee Comprehensive Education Study 1982). Enrollment projections and corresponding anticipated revenue needs were computed on the assumption that programs and admission policies would remain the same and also on assumptions that included additional programs (such as mandatory kindergarten) and with changed admission policies in post-secondary education.

Table 9-1. Per Capita Total Expenditures of State and Local Governments for All Education: 1976-77, 1979-80, and 1980-81.

	Per Pupil Expenditure		*Rank*
Year	*US Average*	*Tennessee*	*(of 50)*
1976-77	$475.22	$370.71	48
1979-80	588.11	460.33	50
1980-81	634.51	478.52	50

Source: Tennessee Education Association, *Where Tennessee Ranks, 1979, 1982, and 1983* (Nashville: Tennessee Education Association), pp. 20-21.

Key factors considered in formulating school enrollment projections included the size and composition of the total state population. Birth rates and statewide population shifts were used to project population growth by county. Tennessee reflected the sunbelt growth trend by recording an 11 percent increase in total population between 1970 and 1978. Almost one-half of the growth, 5.3 percent, was due to net migration increase.

During 1981-82, Tennessee's economy was static. Unemployment in 1981 was 8.5 percent, the gross state product growth was slightly less than the gross national product, and personal income reflected little growth in constant dollars. In 1981, the 9.2 percent inflation and high interest rates contributed greatly to the state's economic condition (Fox 1982).

Education in Tennessee receives the largest proportional share of general fund revenues. Education received 54.9 percent of general fund disbursements in 1970-71 and 47.2 percent in 1980-81. In constant 1972 dollars, the total general fund disbursements amounted to $876,219,479 in fiscal year 1970-71 and $1,455,674,518 in fiscal year 1980-81, an increase of $579,455,039. In 1972 dollars, the overall general fund increase between 1970-71 and 1980-81 was 66.1 percent and the increase for education was 42.8 percent. Although education continued to receive the greater proportional share of general fund revenues, its relative share had decreased over the decade preceding the TCES. Although the state's proportional share of funding for public education decreased during the decade, disbursements in current dollars recorded a dramatic increase. In fiscal year

1970–71, the total disbursement for education was $849,056,675; in 1980–81, the total was $2,719,200,000.

Historically in Tennessee, the state has contributed a greater proportion of funding to grades K-12 programs than local or federal sources. The gap between state and local contributions closed during the 1971–81 decade to a point where local contributions almost matched the state. Disparities in local funds that are in addition to the state-funded Tennessee Foundation Program reflect varying wealth and differences in revenue per pupil between the average low of $582 in fifteen poor districts and the average high of $1,115 in the four wealthiest districts. The TCES recommended that the measure of the relative taxpaying ability of Tennessee counties used in the foundation program to determine each county's local contribution be revised to help resolve the equity problem. A bill passed the General Assembly regarding equalizing property assessed value in determining the local contribution to the foundation program, to be effective July 1, 1985.

Legal Structure, Political Culture, and Ethos

A synopsis of the state's ethos or culture for education helps explain educational reform in Tennessee. Education and politics are closely intertwined and nowhere is it more evident than in Tennessee that "the general political culture—the ways of doing things in a given state—influences the governmental agencies of that state" (Burlingame and Geske 1979: 57). Tennessee education's traditions, politics, and governance prior to 1984 clearly influenced the current reform. Two acts marked the formal change.

Although the governor's commitment to education and some formal action preceeded it, passage of the Comprehensive Education Reform Act (CERA) in late February 1984 officially started Tennessee's educational reform. In April 1984, state governance and, to a degree, state politics of education changed with enactment of the Public Education Governance Reform Act. This act was to "clarify the duties and responsibilities of the State Board of Education and the State Commissioner of Education and to amend or repeal applicable provisions of the Tennessee Code Annotated" (Senate Bill No. 16).

Tennessee education is governed by three boards: the State Board of Education/State Board for Vocational Education (grades K–12, including vocational education; area vocational schools; technical institutes); the Board of Trustees of The University of Tennessee System; the State Board of Regents (State Universities and Community Colleges). The Tennessee Higher Education Commission was established to provide coordination between The University of Tennessee System and the State Board of Regents System.

Prior to 1984, Tennessee's elementary and secondary education and vocational education was headed solely by a commissioner of education who wore many hats: administrative head and chief executive officer of the State Department of Education (SDE), executive officer of the State Board for Vocational Education (SBVE), and a member of the governor's Cabinet. The commissioner of education serves, ex officio, in other important capacities (TCES 1982). The commissioner of education is appointed by the governor and serves at the pleasure of the governor for a term not to exceed the term of the appointing governor (Tennessee Code Annotated §49-103-105). Harris (1973) drawing on material from Hansen and Morphet (1970) comments on the merits and problems of the appointed Chief State School Officer (CSSO):

> . . . Arguments in favor of appointment by the Governor usually begin with the assumption that the Governor can appoint and give full support to a competent leader. Other arguments mentioned are that (1) general control of State government by the appointing Governor tends to facilitate state-wide planning and coordination and (2) a chief State school officer appointed for a term longer than that of the governor and removable only for cause is somewhat free from short-term political pressures.
>
> Critics of the gubernatorial appointment method contend that it makes the chief State school officer politically dependent on the Governor. As a result of such dependence, a chief State school officer may benefit from the Governor's influence on behalf of education or, conversely, suffer from the Governor's unenthusiastic attitude toward it, or an opposition legislature's general hostility toward the Governor's programs. In addition, the State board of education in such a situation may tend to lose influence and at best become a weak advisory body."

In 1984, Tennessee was one of five states where the CSSO was appointed by the governor. From 1900–1984, fourteen states have used this method and only three (New Jersey, Pennsylvania and Tennessee) have used it continuously. The trend is away from gubernatorial appointment (and also from selection by popular election) and toward appointment of the CSSO by the SBE (Achilles and Buckley 1983).

The Tennessee governor has also appointed the members of the SBE, most recently for nine-year overlapping terms. In early 1984, the State Board of Education (SBE) consisted of the governor, executive director of the Tennessee Higher Education Commission (THEC), the commissioner of education, and twelve persons appointed by the governor. Appointments to the SBE have been governed by geographic considerations (four persons form each of the state's three Grand Divisions), by political considerations (at least three representatives from each of the two major political parties), and with attention to vocational education since the SBE serves also as the State Board of Vocational Education (SBVE).

Although the pervasive influence of politics on Tennessee education is evident from the fact that more than half of the state's 141 local school superintendents are elected to office by popular ballot, the far-reaching power of the governor to appoint the chief state school officer, members of the state board of education and other important groups epitomizes the state's political culture for education. This structure offers the potential for partisan politics to hinder the exercise of long-term, bold educational leadership. On the other hand, this structure also is most receptive to a governor's strong initiatives to influence education. Early in his second four-year term, Governor Lamar Alexander advocated educational reform.

Through the Public Education Governance Reform Act of 1984, the Tennessee General Assembly dismantled the fifteen-member state board of education and established a new nine-person board to be appointed by the governor (subject to legislative confirmation). The board then appointed its own chief executive officer in the late summer of 1984. At this point, the state had a governor-appointed chief state school officer (primarily responsible for administration) and a board-appointed executive director (primarily responsible for policy). The Public Education Governance Reform Act seemed to be a step to strengthen the state board of education and limit the power of the chief state school officer. Table 9–2 compares governance structures before and after the 1984 act.

Mazzoni and Campbell (1976) noted that in most their project's twelve states, "the type of education politics that Iannaccone termed 'state-wide fragmented' had come into being." They noted that only in Tennessee (91 percent), Georgia (77 percent), and Texas (60 percent) did a majority of legislative leaders interviewed describe the educator groups as being united on "nearly all" or on "most" issues. In only three states, and especially in Tennessee, did Mazzoni and

Table 9-2. Summary Comparison of Major Elements of Tennessee State Governance Structure for Education, Pre-1984 and After April 1984 as Derived from the Public Education Governance Reform Act of 1984.

	Pre-1984	*After April 1984*
State Board of Education (SBE)	*Appointed by Governor.* Twelve members; with at least 3 from each of 2 major political parties and 4 from each of Tennessee's 3 "Grand Divisions." Nine-year overlapping terms. *Ex Officio* (3): Governor, CSSO and Executive Director of Tennessee Higher Education Commission (THEC) as voting members.	*Appointed by Governor.* Nine members subject to confirmation by Senate and House; one from each Congressional District and at least 3 from each of 2 major political parties; at least one minority member. Nine-year overlapping terms. One public high school student appointed for one-year term. *Ex Officio* (1): Executive Director, THEC as nonvoting member (TCA: 49-106). SBE is housed in Department of Education, but "this shall not allow the Commissioner of Education any administrative or supervisory authority over the Board or its staff" (TCA: 49-107). Responsible for policy and governance (TCA: 49-106, 108).
Chief State School Officer (CSSO)	*Appointed by Governor.* Executive Officer of SBE. Responsible for policy *and* implementation.	*Appointed by Governor.* Implement law or policies of General Assembly or SBE; attend SBE meetings and "may speak at such meetings and make recommendations" (TCA: 49-105). (Implementation only.)
Executive Director, SBE.	*None.* The CSSO formerly acted in this capacity.	*Appointed by the SBE.* There is provision for a staff to be controlled by SBE and Executive Director. No civil service status. Housed in the Department of Education. "The Executive Director and staff shall have no responsibility for administering policies, rules or regulations, or the education laws of the state" (TCA: 49-104).

Campbell find Iannaccone's (1967) "statewide monolithic" influence structure, which is characterized by strong coalitions and unity among educator groups.

For many years Tennessee enjoyed considerable unity among its educator groups. This solidarity was a source of strength and influence for education. Mazzoni and Campbell (1976) found that all participating Tennessee legislators said that the chief state school officer was successful in getting a legislative program adopted. A corresponding high level of chief state school officer success was noted by educator interest-group leaders. This chief state school officer success has been helped by the localistic nature of the state department of education staff. There is little today to invalidate the Campbell and Mazzoni observation that "the composition of department personnel looks much as it did some thirty years ago. Frequently, staff additions have rural backgrounds, have been teachers and administrators . . . and are instate residents" (1975: 77).

The perceived success (or influence) of the Tennessee chief state school officer probably evolved through the unity of Tennessee educators and gubernatorial appointment of the chief state school officer, thus virtually assuring selection of an in-state educator and often a practicing superintendent who had been elected by popular ballot. Campbell and Mazzoni (1975) noted that of the 12 states in their study, the most effective educational coalitions existed in Colorado and Tennessee—two nonurban states with relatively little history of labor-management strife. The person selected as chief state school officer in Tennessee had typically been well-known in the state and could represent the interests of large coalitions of educators to the legislature. That solidarity and unity among educational groups, the harmonious coalitions observed during the early and mid-1970s, changed when the legislature, pressured strongly by the Tennessee Education Association (TEA) with help from the National Education Association (NEA), enacted a professional negotiations bill in Tennessee (1978).

The aura and atmosphere of access and support still exist today in day-to-day dealings in education. When major issues surface (such as Governor Alexander's Better Schools Program), however, educational interest groups tend not to coalesce into a single unit as before, but into two groups. One coalition is sparked by the Tennessee Education Association; the other often includes administrator, school board, and some higher education groups. Tennessee seems to have moved from Iannaccone's (1967) statewide monolithic entity to the state-wide fragmented entity, a more politically active and pluralistic pattern (Mazzoni and Campbell 1976; McGivney 1984).

Activity in Tennessee, in part led by the TEA, did delay CERA passage for some time. This gives rise to one speculation. Tennessee previously was firmly classified as a "statewide monolithic" with its harmonious education coalitions. If there had been no professional negotiations bill and attendant fragmentation of the coalitions, would the CERA have been delayed longer, changed more, or possibly not passed? Speculation aside, reform did come, but not without conflict and compromise.

POLICY MAKING ACTORS, PROCESSES, AND REFORM OUTCOMES

The Comprehensive Education Reform Act of 1984 (CERA) is lengthy and complex legislation developed to ameliorate a century of problems in Tennessee education. A history of education in Tennessee is a story of inadequacy. State and local appropriations have been inadequate, often reflecting a lag in the state's economic development. Teacher salaries, pupil performance, and numbers of high school graduates are but a few areas in which Tennessee's ranking has been low compared with other states (TEA 1983: Knoxville Journal 1985).

Tennessee's educational reform efforts occurred at a time when the United States was experiencing an improving economy, an absence of major military conflict, and growing national pride. The nation was led by a popular Republican president. Attention turned to education. Numerous national studies fueled an increased awareness of the need to improve education. These factors contributed to a favorable environment for an educational reform effort in Tennessee led by a popular Republican governor.

Initiating Conditions and Actors

In 1978, Lamar Alexander succeeded the tempestuous administration of Democrat Ray Blanton. With resolve to foster Tennessean's pride in their state, the new governor's first major effort was in attracting new business and industries and in nurturing economic development. During those efforts, the governor recognized the implications of the state's lagging education system. Emphasizing the relationship between economic development and education, the governor influenced the development of a Basic Skills Program for the public schools. After a decisive victory in his campaign for a second term, the governor seized the mandate and opportunity for major educational reform.

Only thirteen days after his second-term inauguration, Governor Alexander launched his ten-part Better Schools Program during a state-wide televised speech to the Tennessee Press Association on January 28, 1983. Nine of the program's ten points could be traced to the December 1982 Tennessee Comprehensive Education Study, the legislature's own study of Tennessee education.

Begun in June 1981, the Tennessee Comprehensive Education Study was a logical basis for Alexander's plan. The governor had made numerous appointments to the Tennessee Comprehensive Education Policy Task Force and was informed of its progress and findings. But any major reform would require legislative support. Thus, the governor drew recommendations from the Tennessee Comprehensive Education Study, embellished them with recommendations of others, and presented them as a cumulative effort.

The governor had surrounded himself with a staff of energetic professionals. This team proved to be a major factor in the outcome of his proposals. Chief among his team was the commissioner of education. The governor's administrative aides and others orchestrated his plans. Support for the commissioner's team at the State Department of Education was augmented by two University of Tennessee education professors, one who became Executive Director of the Interim Certification Commission, and was responsible for developing a teacher certification and evaluation system; while the other was responsible for the administrator-supervisor evaluation system.

One of the governor's earliest actions was to seek the involvement of the Democratic Speaker of the House, a frequently mentioned candidate for the 1986 gubernatorial election. Although not originally a CERA advocate, the lieutenant governor became active in the legislative proceedings and voted for the CERA. From the outset a few Democrats (in the Democrat-controlled legislature) enthusiastically supported the Republican governor's reform plans. Although one senator cast the deciding vote to delay the governor's Master

Teacher Bill when it was first considered in the Senate Education Committee, this senator later became a vocal supporter for the reform effort. Sister of a former governor and chairman of the TCES Task Force, the senator was an influential legislator.

By appealing to their parallel concerns for education, the governor attracted the support of long-term, influential Democrats and newly emerging Democratic leaders. He established educational reform and the tax increase needed to implement that reform as a bi-partisan effort in the legislature.

Some legislators were long-term, loyal supporters of the TEA and were not swayed from that position. The century-old TEA had high visibility in the state and aggressively influenced education policy in Tennessee. The TEA was proud of its accomplishments and comfortable in its state-wide role. In the CERA conflict, the TEA was a powerful opponent of the governor's efforts. Although there was no change from the basic TEA position, in July 1984 the new TEA president and the TEA legislative liaison worked to establish an environment to foster communication and negotiation.

The CERA policymaking participants were thus divided into three major groups: the administration and the SDE, the General Assembly, and the TEA. Others, such as the Tennessee School Boards Association (which did pass a supporting resolution), higher education, an administrator groups were not extremely active, but they generally supported the need for reform.

Major Reform Issues, Competing Goals, and Priorities

One issue that pervaded educational reform was *control* of education. The TEA had a long-established practice of deciding what was good for Tennessee education and how much money was needed. TEA's major focus, however, had been on what was good for Tennessee teachers. That focus, with little attention to other educational needs (such as higher education) and the 1978 passage of the Professional Negotiations Act, helped to diminish TEA's credibility. As Governor Alexander struggled to move his program through the commissioner and SDE, the TEA fought to retain control of its superior position.

Additional issues separating the governor and TEA included how monies should be spent for education and how the teaching profession should be improved. The TEA advocated higher salaries for *all* teachers, lower pupil/teacher ratios, and more money for existing programs; the governor insisted on incentive pay based on performance evaluation, a career ladder, and educational improvement through basic skills, computer skills, and new curricula. The governor was Republican; the TEA had strong loyalties to the Democratic party (Lansford 1984).

Other policymaking participants, the legislators, were largely influenced by their loyalties to either the governor or the TEA. Legislators also had to deal with a tax increase to fund the educational reform, their loyalties to special interest groups, and constituent reactions; all of this occurred in an election year.

All of the actors held the goal of improving educational quality in Tennessee. They differed on how much improvement was needed and where, who would control that improvement, how much money would be needed, and sources of that money. The governor's commitments to the future of the state and an improved educational system to support economic development were competing with such TEA goals as increases in teacher salaries and benefits; improvements in teacher working conditions, protection of the collective bargaining process; tenure and certification issues; and other membership concerns. The major difference in the two sets of goals was in the apparent beneficiaries.

Alignment: Coalitions Around Reform Issues. In early 1981, the lieutenant governor and others fostered the idea of a comprehensive study of education. After being convinced of the merits of a study, the governor, the speaker of the house, and other legislative leaders supported the study and its recommendations. Attitudes toward the TCES helped establish the basic bi-partisan alignment upon which the governor later built a coalition to support CERA.

One notable alliance involved organized labor. The governor and his supporters frequently criticized the TEA as being more of a union than a professional organization, but they apparently did so without offending organized labor. Although about 19 percent of Tennessee's nonfarm workers were union members, and the governor had a distinctly pro-management image, he nevertheless courted and received the favor of the American Federation of Teachers (AFT), an AFL–CIO affiliate. Although AFT membership in Tennessee was small, it provided an alliance of some consequence.

Power and Influence in Decision Processes. The ultimate power in policy decisions rests with the Tennessee General Assembly. Dominated by Democrats and known for its receptiveness to special interest groups, the legislature was a formidable challenge for the governor, who drew upon his personal resources and those of the governor's office to achieve enactment of the CERA (*Knoxville Journal* 1984).

Utilizing his positions in the National Governor's Association, the Task Force on Education for Economic Growth, and the Southern Education Board, Governor Alexander frequently invited key legislators to accompany him to national meetings. The legislators could observe what other states were doing and see that, for once, Tennessee could be a leader in education.

Governor Alexander was intense in his efforts to raise public awareness. He made considerable use of reference power, capitalizing on his popularity and state-wide network of supporters. He launched a ten-month travel agenda throughout the state and the nation to encourage educational reform. His staff described this educational effort as more intense than the election campaigns. He and his team members spoke to every civic group that offered an invitation. He addressed several national meetings, including the AFT convention, and appeared on national television.

Along with the constant stream of public appearances, the governor and his staff used or established organizations to support their efforts. The State Department of Education disseminated information and solicited feedback on various aspects of the program through the Principals' Study Council. A similar network, the Teachers' Study Council, was established. To finance these activities, Tennesseans for Better Schools was established. The governor's mother, a former teacher, and the son of a former Democratic governor participated in the supporting television commercials. Tennesseans for Better Schools raised more than $400,000 to finance the Campaign for Better Schools. Using an idea borrowed from Governor Winters of Arkansas, seven "bean suppers" were held across the state. Those well-attended events raised thousands of dollars to purchase computers for local schools. In addition to his personal campaign, the governor's efforts were aided by visits to Tennessee by President Reagan and Secretary of Education Terrel Bell.

These high-intensity levels of energy, pressure, power, and influence undermined TEA's resistance. During most of 1983 and 1984,

TEA relied on its past power and alliances with certain legislators. Instead of seeking to form new alliances or upstaging the governor's proposals with fresh and bold considerations, TEA tended to be defensive and to issue claims that the governor's plans would not work. The TEA's difficulty in establishing a centralized power base within the organization and the trouble with communications led to diminished influence in the news media.

The TEA exerted its most effective use of power with the legislature. Its well-practiced lobbying was successful in stalling 1983 reform attempts and in complicating the 1984 efforts. The TEA's pressure was responsible for numerous compromises regarding implementation procedures and nomenclature; TEA was not successful, however, in making major alterations in the original proposal (Lansford 1984).

Legal Nature of Major Reform Actions

When Lamar Alexander announced his Better Schools Program on January 28, 1983, he outlined ten points:

1. *Basic Skills First*—A reading and math competency program.
2. *Computer Skills Next*—A computer literacy program.
3. *Kindergarten for Every Child.*
4. *More High School Math and Science*—Double the required credits and appropriate money for the extra teachers.
5. *Residential Summer Schools for Gifted Juniors and Seniors.*
6. *Redefine High School Vocational Education Curriculum.*
7. *Classroom Discipline*—Create alternatives for disruptive students. Pay liability insurance of all school personnel.
8. *Put Adult Job Skill Training Under the Board of Regents*—Consolidate management of community colleges, technical institutes, and area vocational schools.
9. *Centers of Excellence at Universities*—Funding for special programs in higher education to stimulate excellence and research.
10. *Master Teacher and Master Principal Program*—Incentive pay based on performance evaluation and a career ladder.

Most proposals had some roots in the TCES, with the exception of item seven, discipline and state-paid liability insurance. Although liability insurance did not receive as much public opposition from TEA as the Master Teacher Program. it was an obvious threat. For many years, inclusion of a $1 million liability insurance package had been a strong motivation for teachers to join TEA. The insurance provisuib was eventually dropped from the CERA.

The governor's program had nine other parts, but the controversy and ensuing campaign highlighted the Master Teacher plan. After the January, 1983 speech, the governor's staff, consultants, and others began translating the proposals into legislation. Although the area vocational-technical schools and the technical institutes were moved to the Board of Regents, not one of the other proposals was passed during the 1983 legislative session. Controversy over the Master Teacher concept and fear of a tax increase to fund the reform stalled other action.

To avoid further delay, Governor Alexander appointed an Interim Certification Commission on April 1, 1983. Although it had no basis in law, the Commission was appointed according to requirements in the Master Teacher legislation. That move had special significance when, on April 12, 1983, the Senate Education Committee voted five to four to study all reform proposals until the 1984 session. With the aid of legislative leaders, $40,000 was appropriated to support the Interim Commission's work, an action that allowed the development of a teacher evaluation procedure to continue. Another move to maintain impetus was the appointment of a Joint Senate and House Select Committee to study the reform proposals and to draft a bill for the 1984 legislative session that would encompass the concerns of various constituencies.

Led by a Democrat, the Select Committee covered an even broader area for its study than the governor's original Master Teacher proposal. The Select Committee also reviewed teacher compensation, teacher training, and instructional development. Although a normal outcome of many issues sent into legislative study is a dilution of the original content, the Select Committee's bill to the legislature reflected refinement and a broadened scope. Thus the Master Teacher Program, the tenth point of the governor's Better Schools Program, became part of CERA. The CERA, passed by the legislature on February 23, 1984, included the following provisions.

- *Teacher Training.* All new teachers must pass the California Achievement Test. Colleges that have 30 percent or more of students fail the test lose accreditation.
- *Beginning Teachers.* All new teachers serve a one-year period of probation.
- *Apprentice Teachers.* Teachers with one, two, and three years of experience, and successful evaluation, receive a $500 supplement.
- *Career Ladder.* Levels I, II, and III are based on evaluation of performance; pay incentives range from $1,000 to $7,000 per year. Ten-, eleven-, or twelve-month contracts are options. Tenure may be granted after the fourth year by the local system.
- *Principal and Supervisor Career Ladder.* A three-rung ladder with up to $7,000 in performance-based pay.
- *Evaluation and Certification.* Five-year certification for career-level teachers, principals, and supervisors.
- *State Certification Commission.* Composed of eleven educators and two lay persons, appointed by the governor and confirmed by the legislature, the Commission is responsible for all certification and evaluation.
- *Teacher Aides for Grades 1–3.* Funds to hire an aide for each three teachers in grades 1–3 in 1984–85, $6.5 million for aides in 1984–85, $13 million in 1985–86, and $20 million in 1986–87.
- *In-Service Training.* Five days each year, focused upon skills measured in evaluations.
- *Length of School Year.* School year increased from 175 days to 180 days by converting five in-service days to instructional days.
- *State Salary Increases.* Across-the-board increase of 10 percent (1984–85).
- *Computers.* Nine million dollars appropriated for computers—one for every 30 students in grades 7 and 8.
- *Math and Science Teachers.* Appropriations of $3.5 million for math and science teachers; college scholarships to education majors who study math and science and promise to teach in Tennessee.
- *Discipline and Behavior.* Appropriations of $1.2 million for the creation of state-funded schools for disruptive students.

- *Basic Skills.* Appropriations for computer equipment to score basic skills tests and aid teacher efficiency.
- *Gifted Students.* Appropriations of $450,000 for special residential summer schools for the gifted.
- *Centers of Excellence at Universities.* Appropriations of $10 million to encourage quality teaching and research.
- *Textbooks.* Appropriations of $2.4 million, in recurring funds for textbooks and instructional supplies with an additional $3.4 million appropriated just for the 1984–85 year. The Textbook Commission was placed under the new State Board of Education.

Additionally, CERA indicated that full-time college of education faculty, including deans, have direct personal involvement with the grades K-12 public school setting on a periodic basis. The act also established training programs for principals and administrators with each principal and administrator attending a training session at least once every five years. To increase student involvement, CERA provided for the establishment of a student advisory council composed of six senior high students.

To monitor the progress of reform, the legislature established an oversight committee to monitor proceedings, appropriations, and improvements. One CERA component established a series of five-year goals. The act outlined an expectation for higher education that indicated specific achievements in student performance, numbers of graduates, graduate test scores, and research activities. An intent was also included for a reduction in developmental programs at the college level, especially in the four-year institutions.

Goals for grades K-12 included a 50 percent reduction in the number of teachers who leave the profession due to job dissatisfaction, a 20 percent decrease in high school drop-out rates, a 10 percent decrease in the percent of students failing the state proficiency test in each subject at grades 9 and 12, and a 15 percent increase in the number of students mastering each skill in reading and math as measured on the Basic Skills criterion-referenced tests in grades 3, 6, and 8. Additional goals were directed at increased performance on other standardized tests.

Another part of educational reform during 1984, but not a part of the governor's original proposal, was the Public Education Governance Reform Act. This Act, sponsored by the lieutenant governor, was to establish a strong, independent state board of education and to diminish somewhat the influence of the governor and commissioner of Education. The focus on educational reform and the governor's eagerness for passage of CERA made it possible for the lieutenant governor to obtain the governor's support and subsequent passage of his act.

While the commissioner had been a loyal and productive member of the governor's team, the increased mandate, the new energy, and the greater involvement of the public in school leadership made the change in governance attractive to the governor and to the legislature. Because Governor Alexander appointed the new state board of education, problems for the commissioner were not anticipated. The act did, however, create the vehicle for possible conflicts between future commissioners and SBE executive directors.

Fiscal Implications of Major Reform Actions

In April 1983, the results of a state-wide poll indicated that Tennesseans strongly supported Governor Alexander and his education proposals, and were willing to pay for education improvements. The legislators, however, were much more reserved. Although a comprehensive study of tax reform was not due for completion until 1985, the governor and some legislators favored proceeding with increases in several taxes. Other legislators felt that increases in taxes for education should be part of an overall tax reform. Without a state personal income tax, the main source of state revenue was the sales tax (*Knoxville Journal* 1985b).

An increase of 1¢ in the state sales tax was expected to produce $281 million the first year. An increase in the state corporate franchise tax was anticipated to generate $40 million. A gross premium tax on casualty and property insurance was expected to raise $7 million and a lowered vendor compensation for sales tax collection was expected to generate $5 million. A 5.5 percent amusement tax, expected to generate $25 million, was the most difficult and controversial tax to pass the legislature.

With all details in place, plans for implementation were begun. Although there were anticipated and unanticipated problems, considerable progress is already evident.

IMPLEMENTATION AND IMPACT

Implementation of Tennessee's educational reform began in earnest in 1984 and expanded in 1985. Key to implementation was the 1984 passage of three acts: CERA, the new education governance law, and a state sales tax increase from 4.5 to 5.5 percent. Unless it is renewed, a state sales tax passed specifically to fund the CERA will automatically expire in July 1985, causing an estimated loss of $300 million. The 1984 sales tax increase for education is extremely important since it fueled the fires for total tax reform. A special legislative task force on tax reform recently reported on its study to seek new, more equitable, and elastic revenue sources, including a personal income tax.

Implementation of the CERA has been the responsibility of the State Department of Education and has been so much the sole province of the SDE that, in a December 13, 1984, meeting in Nashville to generate Tennessee educational needs statements to be used in Appalachia Educational Laboratory planning, four of the thirty-nine highest priority responses dealt with the topic "need for more cooperation among all levels of education." Three additional high-priority items related directly to educational reform (Achilles 1984). These items reflected some frustration with the perception that the SDE is playing the implementation cards very close to the vest.

Detailed information about impact is sparse, probably due to the newness of the reform. Activities are proceeding. An Administrator's Academy was held in the summer of 1984; persons have been selected and trained as evaluators for the Master Teacher and Master Principal program; and persons are being trained in the Tennessee Instructional Model.

On January 7, 1985, Governor Lamar Alexander released a statement about education. He said, "In less than a year since the CERA was passed, there is virtually a new status quo in education in Tennessee . . . the program is here to stay and is working" (*Knoxville Journal* 1985a). The same article notes that the governor cited other accomplishments for CERA's first year:

- over 39,000 teachers had volunteered for the Career Ladder plan;
- over 900 teachers had been trained in computer skills;

- funding for about 250 new science and math teachers was available;
- discipline alternatives were available for about 80 percent of the state's high school students;
- over 6,400 computers were delivered to schools; and
- there was a basic skills emphasis—reading and math programs in 1,435 elementary schools.

The 1984-85 appropriation for grades K-12 education was $973,972,100. This represented a 23 percent increase over the 1983-84 appropriation, the largest increase for education in the state's history. One must believe that this increase resulted, at least in part, from the governor's commitment, the bipartisan effort of the select legislative committee, and the results of the TCES. The U.S. Department of Education, through the Secretary's Discretionary Fund, supported a project to study Tennessee's implementation of educational reform. The study team had already noted some results. Much political support is needed for change of this magnitude and the governor and legislature must work in concert. The highly complex effort requires well-informed legislators and competent State Department of Education staff (Handler and Carlson 1984). The study team will continue to monitor the implementation effort.

Educational reform in Tennessee has moved education into the spotlight. Considerable changes have been documented. The 1984-85 appropriations for grades K-12 education showed the largest percentage increase in the state's history. Legislation has been enacted to improve equity in distributing state foundation program funds. Indeed, it is probable that education reform hastened, if not precipitated, action on state tax reform.

The times and the political culture of the state provided the background. The willingness of key actors to seek bipartisan support and solutions opened the door. But it seems that the energy and commitment of the governor provided the sparkplug to start and drive the machinery of educational reform in Tennessee.

REFERENCES

Achilles, C.M. 1984. *AEL-Tennessee State Meeting*. Unpublished paper prepared for Appalachia Educational Laboratory, Charleston, W.Va. December.

Achilles, C.M., and M.R. Buckley. 1983. "Issues in State Governance of Elementary and Secondary Education: Focus on Tennessee," *Tennessee Education* 12, no. 3 (Winter): 3–8.

Branson, G.V., and D.J. Steel, Jr. 1974. *State Policy Making for the Public Schools of Tennessee.* Prepared for Educational Governance Project, Columbus, Ohio.

Burlingame, M., and T.C. Geske. 1979. "State Politics and Education: An Examination of Selected Multiple-State Case Studies," *Educational Administration Quarterly* 15, no. 2 (Spring): 50–75.

Campbell, Roald F., and Tim L. Mazzoni, Jr. 1975. "State Governance of the Public Schools," *Planning and Changing* 6, no. 2 (Summer): 67–80.

Fox, R.F. 1982. "State and National Outlooks," *An Economic Report to the Governor of the State of Tennessee*, Center for Business and Economic Research, University of Tennessee, Knoxville in cooperation with the Tennessee State Planning Office, Nashville.

Gibbs, James. 1957. *Report to the Education Survey Subcommittee of the Tennessee Legislative Council.* Nashville, Tenn.: The Tennessee State Department of Education.

Harris, Sam P. 1973. *State Departments of Education, State Boards of Education, and Chief State School Officers.* Washington, D.C.: U.S. Government Printing Office.

Handler, J.R. and D.L. Carlson. 1984. "Shaping Tennessee's Career Ladder Program. Part I: Overview. Improving Teacher Quality Through Incentives." Knoxville, Tenn.: The University of Tennessee.

Hansen, K.H. and E.L. Morphet. 1970. "State Organization for Education: Some Emerging Alternatives." In *Emerging State Responsibilities for Education*, edited by E.L. Morphet and D.L. Jesser, pp. 37–63. Improving State Leadership in Education Project.

Iannaccone, L. 1967, *Politics in Education.* New York: The Center for Applied Research.

Knoxville *Journal.* 1984. "Governor Planned to Quit Over School Bill." October 1: C6.

____. 1985. "South Ranks Lowest in Academic Poll." January 2: A1, A16.

____. 1985a. "Governor: Education Plan New Status Quo." January 7: B6.

____. 1985b. "It's High Noon For Legislature on State Taxes." January 8: C1.

Lansford, Zelma. 1984. *A Study of Conflict Related to the Development of Tennessee's Comprehensive Education Reform Act of 1984.* Unpublished Doctoral Dissertation, University of Tennessee, Knoxville.

Government Relations Staff, Tennessee Higher Education Commission. *Legislation Affecting Higher Education in Tennessee.* 1984. Nashville: The Ninety-Third General Assembly.

Mazzoni, Tim L. Jr., and R.F. Campbell. 1976. "Influentials in State Policymaking for the Public Schools," *Educational Administration Quarterly* 12, no. 1 (Winter): 1–26.

McGivney, J.H. 1984. "State Educational Governance Patterns," *Educational Administration Quarterly* 20, no. 2 (Spring): 43–63.

Morphet, E.L., and D.L. Jesser, eds. 1970. *Emerging State Responsibilities for Education.* Denver: Improving State Leadership in Education Project.

State of Tennessee. 1984. Public Chapter No. 7, First Extraordinary Session of the 93d General Assembly as Amended by Chapter 829, Public Acts of 1984: The Comprehensive Education Reform Act of 1984.

———. 1984. Public Chapter No. 6, Senate Bill No. 16: Public Education Governance Reform Act of 1984.

Tennessee Comprehensive Education Study: 1981–1982. 1982. Nashville, Tenn.: The Tennessee General Assembly.

Tennessee Education Association. 1979. *Where Tennessee Ranks, 1979.* Nashville: Tennessee Education Association.

———. 1982. *Where Tennessee Ranks, 1982.* Nashville: Tennessee Education Association.

———. 1983. *Where Tennessee Ranks, 1983.* Nashville: Tennessee Education Association.

Will, Robert F. 1964. *State Education Structure and Organization.* Washington, D.C.: U.S. Government Printing Office.

10 PUBLIC SCHOOL REFORM IN UTAH
Enacting Career Ladder Legislation

Betty Malen and Roald F. Campbell

In 1984, the Utah Legislature enacted a career ladder bill. The statute, substantively and financially, constitutes the state's primary response to the current call for reform. This chapter focuses on the political process resulting in career ladder legislation and the fiscal and legal implications of this new provision for Utah.

The conceptual framework combined the general orientation of political systems theory with analytical categories drawn from the power-influence perspective (Campbell and Mazzoni 1976). Legislative policymaking was viewed as an interactive process through which inputs, including demands for change, are converted into outputs, including governmental decisions. The dynamic of the process resides in the interplay of influence among competing participants at each stage of policymaking: interest articulation, alternative formulation, and decisional enactment. Participants have influence when they select, modify, or attain decisional benefits; they have power to exercise influence when they command and choose to deploy resources to obtain influence in the political arena.[1] This power-based process is characterized by conflict, exchange, and accommodation. It is regulated and constrained by institutional features and by the broader environmental context.

Data were acquired from official documents, interest group files, secondary materials (including a preliminary investigation of the career ladder decision dynamic), and eighteen in-depth interviews conducted in person between September and December 1984.[2]

The career ladder statute authorized local districts to develop (through consultation with parents and professional educators but subject to State Board of Education approval), plans that would restructure the compensation and promotion options of teachers.[3] District plans could include extended contracts for curriculum development, in-service, and summer teaching; differentiated staffing; and evaluation systems that incorporate student progress as one measure of teacher effectiveness. District plans must include provisions to distribute at least 50 percent of the funds for professional advancement on the basis of teacher performance. The Legislature appropriated $15.3 million (about 3 percent of total state aid dollars) to career ladder programs.

THE SETTING FOR REFORM

The forces that shape a state's political activity are numerous and complex. Only the cultural, fiscal, and structural features most directly related to public school reform efforts are discussed in this chapter.

Political Culture

Elazar's analysis of political cultures provides a useful construct for this sketch of Utah's political heritage (Elazar 1972). He identifies three subcultures, each closely associated with geographic areas, migration patterns, and ethnic-religious legacies. While no state completely embodies any of the subcultures, Utah mirrors the moralistic orientation.

The major source of Utah's moralistic orientation is the Mormon Church (officially, the Church of Jesus Christ of Latter Day Saints). Mormons settled Utah in order to protect their beliefs. While other groups are now present, the Mormon Church is still dominant, embracing, at least nominally, about 70 percent of the state's population and about 50 percent of the Salt Lake City population.[4] It is important to recognize that some Mormons are devout practitioners, others are not. Further, some are rural and some are urban; some are Republicans and some are Democrats; some are conservative and some are liberal. The culture is not as monolithic as first exposure might suggest.

The major sign of Utah's moralistic orientation is the presence of what Elazar terms a commonwealth concept of government, an outlook that values public service and fosters citizen involvement, issue emphasis, and policy innovation. Power, from a commonwealth perspective, is to be activated to advance the public good. Communal, preferably nongovernmental, problem solving approaches are sought. Governmental responses are respected, however, as legitimate, efficacious options. Utah has a long tradition of people working together in both private and public sectors; this is vividly illustrated in the comprehensive welfare programs of the Mormon Church and the swift responses to calls for flood relief volunteers. Citizen involvement is also evident in high voter turnout, the presence of advisory committees at both state and local levels of government, and the frequent use of polls to gauge citizen sentiment.

The issue versus partisan emphasis is difficult to unravel given the numerical superiority of the Republican Party at this time. Though the perceptual data may be normatively tainted, evidence suggests the educational issues are usually treated as nonpartisan issues (Campbell 1981). The concern for an effective and efficient system of public education seems to transcend party lines.

In some areas of public policy, Utah may be considered parochial. In educational policy, however, Utah has been receptive to reform. The state, early on, adopted a very sophisticated finance equalization formula. The state recognized sizeable special need categories well before Public Law 94-142. The state has funded for some time, albeit modestly, experimental programs and, more recently, productivity studies.[5] Although conservatism is present, openness to educational innovation is also apparent.

Fiscal Capacity

A state's ability to support its schools is contingent on a variety of factors including demographic developments, economic conditions, educational aspirations, and funding arrangement.

Demographic Developments. In 1983, for the first time in over a decade, Utah experienced a slight reduction in the number of births and a net outmigration. Yet the state's population (1,587,500) continues to grow at twice the national rate. Newly revised estimates project a population of two million by 1992 (Utah Office of Planning and Budget 1984).

Utah's population is characterized by a disproportionate number of school age children—more per household than any other state (Utah State Board of Education 1984–85). Only 1.2 percent of all elementary-secondary students attend private institutions (Utah Foundation 1983). A small but growing number utilize the home school option.[6] The vast majority depend on the public system. In 1982, the Legislature redefined kindergarten entrance requirements, reducing the eligible population by 4000; but, the 1983–84 public school enrollments still increased by 8,870 students to a total of 378,208 (Utah State Office of Education 1984). Enrollments are expected to increase by 20 percent over the next five years and by 32 percent over the next ten years (Utah Foundation 1983).

The enrollment boom has not been uniformly distributed. In 1983–84, for example, thirty-one districts had a net gain, but nine had a net reduction in students. School district rates of growth ranged from 1–15 percent (Utah State Office of Education 1984).

Utah's demographic profiles and projections generate troublesome policy issues. Teacher shortages in specialized areas are already present (Utah Education Reform Steering Committee 1983). Even though per pupil expenditures are low (49th on national rankings), the cost of simply extending existing levels of service to the additional clients represents a sizeable budget increase (Utah Office of Planning and Budget 1983).

Economic Conditions. The level and distribution of economic resources, along with their growth potential, are useful indices of fiscal capacity. On the basis of comparative family income measures, Utah is an average state, neither rich nor poor. Family income levels hug the national norm. A relatively high proportion of families cluster in the middle income range; a small proportion fall in the low and high categories (Utah Office of Planning and Budget 1983). On the basis of per capita measures, however, Utah is a poor state. Per capita income ($8,875) is only 79.9 percent of the national norm. Using this wealth index, Utah ranks forty-fifth in the country (Utah Foundation 1984). Economic circumstances suggest that this position will be sustained, not improved.

Utah is slowly rebounding from its "longest and deepest recession in 40 years" (Robson 1982). The 1980–83 period was marked by high levels of unemployment; sharp incidences of personal and business bankruptcy; negligible, uneven rates of economic growth; and recurrent budget cutbacks. Expansion in defense-supported industries, select private businesses, and special service occupations was offset by depressions in mining, agriculture, and energy-related sectors. Real revenue gains were virtually nonexistent. Basic governmental operations and flood and mudslide damages strained the available resources. The state budget was revised and reduced seven times during this three-year period (Utah Office of Planning and Budget 1983). Although year-end surpluses were recorded, the favorable balance sheet reflected austere appropriations, not abundant reserves. By late 1983, the economy showed signs of recovery (Macdonald 1984), but even with intensive and extensive campaigns to strengthen the economic base through special development incentives and regionally low corporate tax rates, steady, not substantial, growth is anticipated. Since the legislature tends to resist major tax rate increases, the state budget is likely to be a continuation budget, of modest incremental adjustments and greater productivity-efficiency requirements (Mathews and Arrington 1984).

Educational Aspirations. Utahns express confidence in and impose high expectations on their public schools. As indicated, nearly all elementary-secondary students are enrolled in public schools. A large proportion graduate.[7] Many "go beyond" the high school diploma. Residents invest a relatively high percentage of their personal income (9.8 percent) in public education, an investment effort surpassed by only three states (Utah Foundation 1983). A 1983 survey, sponsored by the governor-appointed Education Reform Steering Committee, revealed that 71 percent of the respondents would support a tax increase for public school improvements.[8]

Funding Arrangements. The basic educational program in Utah public schools is financed through a foundation plan that places approximately 72 percent of the responsibility on the state and 29 percent on the local districts. Weighted Pupil Units reflect adjustments for variation in school size, professional staff profiles, client needs, and program costs. Under a scaled and capped power equalizing formula, the state permits and modestly supports a voted leeway that districts can activate for services beyond the minimum level. In addition, the state pays the full cost of transportation to and from school (with a few exceptions), contributes categorical supplements for pilot projects or mandates programs, and shares marginally in capital expenditures. When these provisions are included, the public school funding scheme places about 55 percent of the burden on the state and 40 percent on the local districts. The remainder is covered by federal dollars.[9] In 1982, voters removed the 75 percent constitutional limitation on the state share of public education funding. A higher state ratio is now possible but not imminent.

State revenues are acquired primarily from the sales and personal income taxes. The sales tax is comprehensive, exempting only prescription drugs. Since indexes on the personal income tax have not been updated since 1973, most Utahns (53 percent) fall in the highest bracket (Mathews 1984). These features make the state school revenue structures high in yield but regressive in effect.[10] Local revenues are acquired primarily from the property tax. Although the legislature recently adjusted valuation fromulas and revised collection and equalization procedures, the 6 percent limitation (applicable the first year following adjusted assessments) was retained. This tax remains a restricted and controversial source of school revenues.

Public School Governance Structures

Educational policymaking is essentially a state function. The formal structures responsible for governing public grades K-12 schools include the legislature, the Office of the Governor, and the Utah State Education Agency. Like many states, Utah has created school districts (forty) managed by locally elected boards that have only those powers delegated to them by the legislature.

Legislature. The 104 member legislature (twenty-nine senators, seventy-five representatives) meets annually. Until 1985, a sixty day general session was held in odd numbered years and a twenty day budget session was held in even numbered years.[11] Each chamber has eleven standing committees—one in each chamber focuses on higher education and one focuses on public education. Between sessions there are joint interim committee meetings. The Joint Public Education Interim Committee meets one day a month. The Appropriations Committee is composed of all senators and representatives headed by an Executive Committee (seven senators, nine representatives) and divided into nine subcommittees, one for public education. Every member of the legislature is assigned to a joint appropriations subcommittee. Given the tendency to turn all issues into money issues, the senator and representative who chair the Joint Appropriations Committee are in a position to exercise considerable influence.

Staff support for legislators has improved in Utah as in most states.[12] Staff assistance is supplied by four offices: Legislative Research, Legislative Fiscal Analyst, Legal Counsel, and Legislative Auditor General. These data sources reduce the reliance on State Office of Education and interest group information banks and increase the capacity for oversight activities. There is, however, a love-hate relationship between legislators and staff in education (Campbell 1981). There is a recognized need for and appreciation of quality assistance but some resentment at being dependent on such help.

The 1983–84 Legislature was predominantly Republican. Twenty-four of the twenty-nine Senators and fifty-eight of the seventy-five Representatives were members of the majority party. While education is usually treated as a nonpartisan concern, "in the crunch" the party caucus position is a deciding factor (Campbell 1981). As has been the case for decades, 90 percent of the lawmakers were members of—many were active officials in—the Mormon Church.[13] Occasionally the General Authorities of the Mormon Church will take a public stand on issues (i.e., opposition to ERA and state supervision of private schools). Such explicit instruction is, however, rarely needed. Church preferences are protected through the firmly engrained positions held by individual legislators who may have been encouraged by Mormon officials to seek public office. Occupationally, business professions were prevalent in 1983–84. Twelve senators and thirty-two representatives held business-related jobs.[14] The common partisan, religious, and professional affiliations make the legislature very homogeneous. The norm is to settle disputes with the subtle side of power, through a composed, informed, civil search for consensus.

As one might predict, public education leaders in the legislature are majority party members in visible committee positions. Frequently they are directly linked with the Mormon Church and credibly aligned with owners and managers of independent and corporate businesses. In contrast to trends identified in some state settings (Rosenthal and Fuhrman 1981), educational leadership posts are desired positions in Utah, not only because education controls the budget but also because education constitutes, in the minds of many Utahns, the most important function performed by state government (Campbell 1981). The opportunity to effect reform and protect regional interests adds to the attractiveness of these posts.

Office of the Governor. The formal powers of this office are impressive but their convertability is constrained by contextual features. On the Combined Index of Formal Power used by Gray, Jacob, and Vines, this office has tenure potential; appointment prerogatives; organizational capacity, particularly evident in an independent staff and a comprehensive state bureaucracy; veto power; and budget control. These resources rank the power of the Utah Office of Governor second only to the New York Office of Governor (Gray, Jacob and Vines 1983).

Since legislative sessions are relatively short, and since the governor has formal authority to call special sessions, vetoes are structurally difficult to counter. Since the legislature is 80 percent Republican, vetoes are politically difficult to invoke. The governor's primary power resource—budget control—has been somewhat diluted by the Board of Examiners (made up of the governor, secretary of state, attorney general), which must approve certain types of expenditures. The distribution of power between the governor and the legislature is a live issue. Democrats have held the office for two decades (until the November, 1984 election). Partisanship may be an instigating and complicating factor in the discussion of plans to redefine executive-legislative relationships.

Utah State Education Agency. This agency encompasses the State Board of Education, the State Superintendent of Public Instruction, and the State Office of Education. The State Board of Education is composed of nine members elected from designated regions for four year overlapping terms. This board has general jurisdiction over the local school districts and the special schools for the deaf and blind. It also acts as the State Board for Vocational Education. The legislature appropriates dollars to the board for guided but discretionary distribution. Local districts can apply for the special program funds. The career ladder statute was financed as a special program, subject to the allocation decisions of this board. Board influence is limited by part-time member status but enhanced by the tendency to have a recognized constituency in the forty local boards and their superintendents. The State Superintendent of Public Instruction is the chief executive officer of the State Board of Education and the administrative head of the Utah State Office of Education. The Superintendent is selected by the State Board of Education. The Utah State Office of Education provides the Superintendent with advisors, specialists, data banks, and other resources that can be used to effect education policymaking.

THE PROCESS OF REFORM

The process that resulted in career ladder legislation is analyzed through an assessment of actor roles and influence efforts at each stage of policymaking. Since most of the political activity occurred before the legislature convened, and since the presession activity laid the base for in-session negotiations, the initial stage of the process is given greatest attention.

Interest Articulation

This stage marks the threshold phase of policymaking wherein select demands are translated into policy options, embraced by officials, and framed in bills to be considered by the legislature. Two career ladder bills were introduced. While the house members who sponsored these bills were the officials initiators, four other actors (the governor, the Education Reform Steering Committee, the Commission for Educational Excellence and the State Articulation and Planning for Education organization) provided the impetus for career ladder legislation. Two participants (the Utah Education Association, and the Republican Caucus), for quite different reasons, resisted this legislation.

The Governor. In June of 1983, Governor Scott Matheson appointed an Education Reform Steering Committee and directed the committee to develop a program of "essential reforms." He specifically requested that suggestions for "improving the attractiveness of the teaching profession, including a pay performance plan" be considered.[15] The governor appointed this task force and provided this explicit directive for at least three reasons.

First, the governor wanted major changes in education. His comprehensive plans for "Solving the School Crises" in 1982 and 1983 had been sharply cutback by the legislature.[16] As one executive office representative explained, "He was frustrated. He wanted to get the power brokers together to do something dramatic, something substantial."

Second, influential individuals requested the formation of a steering committee. Having conferred with the president of the Senate and the speaker of the House, Senator Warren Pugh, a seasoned, respected educational leader in the Legislature and co-chairperson of the Joint Appropriations Committee; Representative Robert Garff, House Majority Leader; and Neil Maxwell, a member of the Board of Regents (higher education governing board) and one of the Twelve Apostles in the Mormon Church, met with Governor Matheson. They suggested a commission that reflected the weight of the governor and the leadership of the legislature be created to develop appropriate responses to the demand for public school reform.

Third, the time was right. *A Nation at Risk*, directed and endorsed by to native sons—David Gardner, then President of the University of Utah, and Terrell Bell, then Secretary of Education—had captured the attention and legitimated the conviction of many Utahns (National Commission on Excellence in Education 1983). Public schools could and should be revamped. Even though revenues were right, all informants agreed with this legislative staff observation: "People were hyped. The national reports, the declining test scores, the teacher shortages . . . all created a fervor. . . . The media were pounding away about the deterioration in the quality of the teaching force. . . . There was a strong feeling that we better fix schools and fix them now." Public education was a center-stage issue. The "political winds" were more favorable than they had been in a long time.

Education Reform Steering Committee (ERSC). This bipartisan, governor-appointed group developed a $150 million package of proposals ($79.2 million to maintain public and higher education programs and $71.4 million to reform them.) The "lead" reform was a

$41.4 million career ladder plan for public school teachers (Utah Reform Steering Committee 1983).

Besides ambitious goals, the ERSC brought formidible resources to the policymaking arena. Emmanuel Floor, a well-known Democrat and president of one of the largest corporations in the state was named chair. A native Utahn, Floor was described as "bright . . . smooth . . . a superior speaker . . . an astute and trusted operator" by virtually all informants. He is reputed to be one of the most influential individuals in Salt Lake City.[17] The ERSC included representatives of the Governor's Office, key legislators from the House and Senate Public Education Committees and Joint Appropriations Committees, the Superintendent of Public Instruction, the Commissioner of Higher Education, heads and members of the State Board of Education and the Board of Regents. This group had stature; expertise; money to finance polls and publications; a forum from which to speak; access to executive and legislative staff; and linkages with the legislature, the governor, the Mormon Church, and the business community. Noticeably and intentionally absent, however, was a representative of or a direct conduit to the Utah Education Association (UEA).

The data suggest several plausible explanations for this omission. First, the governor wanted a small, cohesive commission, one that would zero in on and provide unanimous endorsement for his specific directive—a pay performance plan. If the UEA were given membership status, then other public school organizations would need to be included as well. The task force could become unwieldly. More importantly, UEA presence on the ERSC might disrupt and delay the commission's work. An executive office spokesperson noted, "The UEA always wants to study what they don't like, and we didn't need another study, we needed an action plan."

Second, the ERSC had substantial power resources of its own. If those resources were narrowly focused and skillfully deployed, UEA opposition might be effectively countered.

Third, formal identification with special interest groups like the UEA could be liability with legislators who held anti-UEA sentiments. An "objective" task force, one comprising community leaders and professional educators but not tied to specific public education interest groups, was consistent with the espoused norms of the Utah Legislature.

Informants generally agreed that the ERSC was committed to its task. Members were described as "eager," "serious," and "willing to really work at it." Informants specifically noted the commitment of Emmanuel Floor and Senator Warren Pugh. Improving the public schools, as one legislator stated, "helps Manny's goals for his business, but there is also a strong personal conviction there too. Manny is a product of the Salt Lake Schools and he cares what happens to them." Interview sources from all perspectives described Pugh as "the father of education in the Legislature" and "one who . . . really wanted to make a lasting contribution to Utah schools."

There was some concern that the ERSC would be controlled by the governor and consequently limited in its ability to garner support from Republican legislators. This concern was partially offset by the involvement of legislators in the selection of the commission and by the "open hearing" planning process incorporated by the commission. Despite the partisan, executive, legislative tensions, the ERSC was an actor with ambitious aims, impressive resources, political skill, and strong will.

Commission on Educational Excellence (CEE). Appointed by the State Board of Education just days after the ERCs was announced, the commission developed twenty-four recommendations for school improvement. A salary incentive program and an "opportunity ladder" for public school teachers topped the lengthy list of proposed reforms (Utah Commission of Educational Excellence 1983). Composed of legislators, Governor's Office staff, business leaders, college administrators, and members of all public school interest groups, including the UEA, this commission was, in the words of a state education agency official, "pretty motivated because they understood that the window was open, it was the time to request big money increases for education."

State Articulation and Planning for Education (SAPE). This organization (originally called Self-Appointed Prestigious Educators and since renamed Consortium for the Study of Education Issues in Utah) was composed of college deans of education, select school district superintendents, and individuals from the State Office of Education. In addition to respected positions, recognized expertise, and presumed objectivity, SAPE had the time and the ability to produce focused, documented policy action plans. During the spring and summer of 1983, SAPE generated a series of legislative proposals designed to improve the recruitment, preparation, performance, and retention of teachers. A career ladder plan was a major portion of SAPE's "teacher-oriented" educational reform package. Like the ERSC and the CEE, SAPE was, in the words of one of its members, "anxious to capitalize on the favorable political climate."

Overlapping memberships, compatible policy recommendations, and complementary role orientations enabled these actors to develop an early, stable alignment. Individuals within each group were members of, or knew members in, the other groups. Informal, candid exchanges on substance and strategy occurred frequently and easily. All at least publicly agreed that career ladder plans were partial but potent responses to the call for excellence in education. Further, SAPE and CEE were willing to let the ERSC be the "outfront player." SAPE was content to "feed" both task forces. Since SAPE was perceived to be knowledgeable, and, since it was "the only group with anything really spelled out, anything really down on paper," this "unofficial" organization could exert substantial influence by shaping the recommendations of the other two groups. CEE was also amenable to a less visible role. Its report was not progressing was quickly as that of the ERSC. The official publication would not be ready for the opening legislative session. CEE was in no position to compete for the spotlight. All informants agreed with the apt remark of a CEE member, "We were going to be outclassed. We needed to tie our tails to the governor's steering committee."

There are a number of reasons why these actors focused on a career ladder plan. First, it was an available alternative, reasonably well-defined by SAPE. Second, it was a credible alternative, endorsed by national reports, proposed in other state legislatures, and promoted persuasively, some even noted "inspirationally," by Tennessee Governor Lamar Alexander during his invitational presentation to and informal discussion with the ERSC in August of 1983. Third, it was relevant to the Utah setting. The availability of qualified teachers was a genuine concern. A program which might address this need would be pertinent. Finally, it was saleable in the Utah setting. The program could be framed in terms consistent with the fiscally conservative outlook of the Legislature. Economic incentives for greater productivity and economic rewards for exceptional performance were engrained and salient principles for many legislators. Whether individuals within each group were openly enthusiastic or simply pragmatic, the dominant perception was the these participants firmly supported career ladder plans as an initial but critical step toward excellence and efficiency in education and a potentially controversial but politically compelling rubric for major monetary requests.

Utah Education Association (UEA). Since the American Federation of Teachers has only one chapter in Utah, the UEA is clearly the major teacher organization in the state. Although the UEA's House of Delegates included "responsible pilot programs" to test the feasibility of career ladder plans in its legislative program, a statewide, mandated career ladder statute was unacceptable for at least three reasons. First, career ladder plans were viewed as synonyms for merit pay plans, opposed by most teacher associations as unworkable on the evaluation side and divisive on the morale side. Second, the UEA did not want money diverted from its primary preferences: across the board salary increases and meaningful class size reduction provisions. Third, the UEA was angry because it had not been recognized as a power broker worthy of inclusion on the ERSC. Informants maintained that the UEA "was miffed" and, as one legislator stated, "needed to repudiate the steering committee's recommendations to establish that they could not be ignored."

An inventory of the UEA's power resources indicates that it could be a decisive force: a membership of over 14,000, a campaign warchest of approximately $120,000, seven full-time staff, an established communications network with local organizations, a reputation for being able to "impact but not control" elections, and a reputation for being able to block legislation. As most acknowledged, but one state agency official stated, "The UEA can't pass a bill if other members of the education community are opposed, but they can disrupt it. . . . They can stop it if they put their mind to it." The ability to mobilize these resources for optimum influence, however, was constrained by several organizational and contextual factors.

First, the UEA's sizeable membership was a valuable asset but not cohesive entity. All informants confirmed the observation made by an interest group representative: "Many teachers don't think they belong in the political arena. Utah is behind most states in that regard." Among those willing to be politically active, there was division on the career ladder issue. Individuals from diverse perspectives reiterated the claim made by one legislator, "Teachers didn't speak with a singular voice. . . . Some supported the idea and others did not. . . . There were a lot of contradictory messages." Division on the propriety of political action and the propriety of career ladder legislation, then, diluted the resources of the UEA.

Second, the organization was, or was perceived to be, in transition. The UEA had hired a new executive director who did not arrive in the state until August. SAPE, CEE and ERSC had been underway for months. The UEA's capacity to focus on the career ladder issue was delayed and diminished by the need to concentrate on the internal, structural changes. The organization's credibility was also suspect because the new executive director was a non-Utahn, an "outsider" without established or trusted linkages in the legislative arena.

Third, the UEA's posture at times seemed to conflict with the Utah ethos. Utah policymakers espouse a harmonious, cooperative, decision making style. The perceived "militant," "aggressive," union-like," "combative" approach of the UEA tended to alienate legislators. Informants from all perspectives concurred with the statement of one legislator, "There is a lot of anti-UEA sentiment. It's hard to take them on, but they are sometimes rough and abrasive and that doesn't win friends in Utah." Concern for tactics fueled suspicion of intent. The UEA was viewed as one of its representatives put it, "wholly and simply worried about money. We were seen as trying only to feather our own nest."

Republican Caucus. This participant had numerical superiority in the Utah Legislature. It could, if unified, control decision outcomes. Within the caucus, some members claimed that public education was "already too fat." A few maintained that "an infusion of money was needed to improve the schools." Though members disagreed on funding levels, they agreed on funding rationales. Increased expenditures had to be tied to school reforms. All informants concurred with this executive staff assessment, "There would be nothing but a bare-bones cost of living adjustment [for public education] unless there were major changes." All informants also claimed that given the reluctance to raise tax rates, any division in the education family would be a convenient reasons, despite the contextual clamor for reform, to adopt an incrementalist stance.

The major limitation for the Republican Caucus was the absence of a well-defined, defensible alternative to career ladder legislation. As one legislative staff explained, "They needed to look like they were doing something, but they didn't know what to do, and they didn't want to spend a lot of money." The difficulty of developing a compelling response to the call for reform without appropriating substantial monies for reform, constituted a problem for the Republic Caucus and a dilemma for individual legislators who did not want to accept the recommendations of the governor's Commission.

Both the issue initiators and resisters attempted to influence the legislative process long before the session was underway.

Advocates' Influence Efforts. The advocates employed a number of strategies to enlarge the base of support. In preparing its recommendations, the ERSC solicited testimony "from everybody we could think of who might be remotely interested in our task, including the UEA," and conveyed information to the Interim Public Education Committee. The ERSC sponsored a poll designed to acquire resident views regarding both the viability of tax rate increases and the popularity of career ladder plans. The ERSC publication, *Education in Utah: A Call to Action*, was printed and widely distributed. In addition, the ERSC, in the words of a member, "took its platform on the road." Town meetings were planned and coordinated from a "war room" set up at the State Office of Education. Individuals from ERSC, CEE, and SAPE plotted out areas, sites, and strategies. They, along with the governor, traveled across the state to meet with citizens in open forums and cultivate the media coverage stimulated by these sessions.[18]

There were less flamboyant strategies as well. Individuals sought endorsements from all public school interest groups, private businesses, and the Chamber of Commerce. The governor contacted Mormon Church officials and requested a "keynote endorsement" at the churches' annual fall conference. Legislators were also approached informally through "a lot of preliminary, private politicking."

Opponents' Influence Efforts. According to a UEA spokesperson, the organization essentially "set itself up as an obstacle." It contacted the local chapters and encouraged members to "stack" the community meetings, raise questions about the fairness of the UEA's "exclusion" from membership on the ERSC, and express concern for the "lack of clear evidence on the effectiveness of career ladders." The UEA conducted its own polls and directed members to visit, write, or phone their legislators.[19]

The data suggest that the Republican legislators, with the exception of those on the steering committee, were involved in what one legislator described as "their own revolution. Everybody thought they (sic) had a cure, until they (sic) tried to write the bills. Then they weren't so all knowing. . . . Almost by default the focus was going to be career ladders. . . . Nobody had a better idea, at least not one they could get pulled together in bill form." But the repeated aversion to major tax increases and the presence of "counter cures" made the public education groups concerned about both the direction of and the dollars for public school reform.

Assessment of Influence Relationships. Both advocates and opponents perceived that their initial influence efforts secured mixed results. The advocates were able to secure endorsements from all members of the public school lobby, including the UEA. Since SAPE was perceived to be an objective organization, officials from the State Office of Education asked that organization to host a meeting of public school interest groups. All groups agreed to publicize their commonalities in a Joint Statement of Educational Reform, because they recognized that an adversarial posture would jeopardize funding levels. The UEA, the Utah Society of Superintendents, the Utah Association of Elementary School Principals, the Utah Association of Secondary School Principals, the Utah School Boards Association, the Utah Congress of Parents and Teachers, the Utah Deans of Colleges of Education, the Council of Utah Associations of School Administrators, and the Superintendent of Public Instruction pledged to work cooperatively with the ERSC for the principle of a "multilevel career ladder salary program for teachers and administrators" and for "substantial increases in the funding for education." This agreement was signed, shared with the media and presented to the legislature (Scarlet 1983). This agreement was reinforced by the publication of an addendum to the original ERSC report. The addendum highlighted the economic plight of Utah teachers, revised the initial career ladder proposal, and embraced, in the form of new recommendations, the class size and work environment issues salient to the UEA (Utah Education Reform Steering Committee 1984). An initial but fragile compromise had been secured. The advocates understood that the UEA was more committed to its own proposals than it was to the career ladder proposition. There was a paper coalition, not a policy agreement.[20]

The advocates were able to secure "tacit approval" from some businesses, but executive staff reported, "They weren't really in line either."[21] The Mormon officials, executive staff reported, "gave us five minutes." More importantly, several confirmed the church hierarchy "pulled in the reins of Maxwell [a member of the ERSC]. He was not allowed to testify. His prior speeches could not be circulated." That retrenchment was viewed as a serious setback for the proponents. As one explained, "We were counting on him to bring the church along. You can't get anywhere without that, but he got called in. They put the clamps on him and that really hurt." The reasons for this change in church position, beyond the observation that "the church can't let taxes get out of hand," cannot be gleaned from the data.

Although the poll results showed support for both a tax increase and a career ladder concept, legislator commitments were tenuous. The UEA had not managed to reverse the recommendations of ERSC, CEE, and SAPE, but it had managed to "disrupt and monopolize" the town meetings and create doubt and dissent among citizens and lawmakers. In short, the UEA had tarnished the proposed cure and dramatized the division within the public education lobby. The UEA would have to be accommodated in order to counter the Republican Caucus, in order to present a consensus proposal to a consensus-oriented legislature.

Alternative Formulation

The presession activities of the central power players set the parameters for this mediating phase of the policymaking process. Given the norm of harmony, the dominance of the Republican Caucus and its "default" decision to look primarily at career ladder plans as instruments of reform and justifications for expenditures, actors who wanted substantial allocations for public schools had better cooperate. Within those dictates, interdependent actors with competing program priorities but complementary financial stakes moved reluctantly and unsteadily toward a concilliatory position. That process is described through an analysis of the resultant content adjustments.

Conflicting Demands. The ERSC, CEE, and SAPE wanted a statewide career ladder plan that allowed extended contracts but emphasized performance promotions. The "merit" pay component was still viewed as substantively appropriate and politically persuasive. It was a prominent proposal, consistent with the push for a judicious and efficient use of tax revenues. The UEA still preferred a locally developed pilot program with multiple, "objective" advancement criteria and minimum reliance on performance standards.[22] If performance were to be included, then the UEA would insist on carefully defined teacher evaluation safeguards.

Delay Tactics. While the UEA testified and lobbied, its primary strategy was delay. All confirmed the observation that "The UEA relied on the stretch-it-out and water-it-down ploy." This approach was reasonably effective. It put pressure on the career ladder proponents. They had to reach out to "quiet and appease" the UEA. And, they had to "bring the UEA along quickly" since the legislative session was only twenty days long. Although Pugh "was holding the line in the Senate," Republican members of the ERSC were having trouble in the House. Republicans were suggesting that Majority Leader Garff had let the ERSC "get out of hand." This chamber was, as one legislative staff remarked, "almost out of the leadership's control. There were splinter groups holding ad hoc committee meetings in the hallways. The formal committee structure wasn't containing the division. Garff and Bangerter (Speaker of the House) had a lot of disruption to manage." A resolution was sorely and promptly needed.

Counter Moves. The proponents did not adopt a passive stance. They publicly testified and individually lobbied. More importantly, they privately pressured and collectively "boxed" the UEA. Legislators, members of SAPE, CEE, and ERSC, along with legislative staff, state department staff, and representatives of the Governor's Office made the contingency very clear. If the UEA didn't "buy in," there would be no major increases in public school appropriations, and, the UEA would be held responsible. As one state agency official expressed it, "We kept telling them that if we didn't come together, we'd all go down together and the blame would fall squarely on their shoulders."[23] Furthermore, the UEA leadership was told directly and repeatedly that if the public educational associations could not articulate their own reforms, the legislature would mandate those reforms. The words of an interest group representative capture the prevailing perception: "If we [UEA] didn't come on board, the legislature could have rammed anything down our throats. . . . There were diversionary bills worse than the career ladder bills. . . . When we saw those witches on the woodwork we knew we had to negotiate." There were virtually "hundreds of personal conversations and confrontations behind the scenes." These informal exchanges laid the groundwork for a private, marathon meeting involving representatives of the Governor's Office, the State Office of Education, ERSC, SAPE, CEE, the UEA, the Society of Superintendents, and legislative staff. Pugh, echoed by other legislators, had conveyed a believeable message. As one state office official recalled, "We were told we better sit down and not come out until we had an agreement. We were running out of time and the House especially, was running out of patience." In this session, Floor did what all described as a "yeoman's job of fringing together intense personalities and diverse views." The resultant compromises are reflected in the content of the statute.

Content Compromises. The proponents secured a comprehensive as opposed to a pilot career ladder bill, but district participation was to be voluntary, not mandatory. The proponents also maintained a requirement that at least 50 percent of the funds must be used for professional advancement and distributed on the basis of teacher performance. Anything less than that would result in defeat by the Republican Caucus. Teacher performance was to be gauged, at least in part, by student progress. The UEA secured specification of standards for teacher evaluation. It also secured a provision for career ladder plans to be developed by the local districts in collaboration with teachers, administrators, and parents. Although plans would have to be approved by the State Board of Education, this provision allowed for ongoing UEA input in the development of district plans. This allowance diminished the role of the legislature but appealed to the accepted principle of local autonomy and local control. It was thus viewed as a saleable concession.

The bill was eventually drafted by legislative staff. It was typically described as a "hodgepodge," a "pig in the polk," a "confusing and on face contradictory" piece of legislation. It was also described, however, as an "inevitable compromise" between adamant and resourceful power players who needed to put forth a unified position in order to secure a respectable share of the state's scarce revenues.

Decision Enactment

As is so often the case, enactment was pro forma. The substantive considerations had been handled through the private bargaining meetings previously described. The financial allocations were ultimately resolved in the closed meetings of the Republican Caucus. By the time the bill hit the floor, passage was assured. There was a UEA sponsored amendment that made one section of the bill permissive rather than mandatory, but the major provisions regarding merit pay and State Board of Education authority remained intact. In the closing hours of the 1984 Budget Session, the Utah Legislature authorized $15.3 million, less than half the original $40 million request, for a career ladder program.

Interpretation of the Process

This brief treatment of decision dynamics provides support for several observations about the politics of public school reform in Utah. Four major themes warrant explication.

Official Initiation Through Task Force Creation. While informants consistently noted that a wide array of factors contributed to the enactment of career ladder legislation, they also maintained that a key factor was the creation of the Education Reform Steering Committee. Even though, in retrospect, most respondents claimed that the steering committee might have reduced some of the UEA resistence by granting that organization membership status, the ERSC was able to accomplish a number of important political objectives.[24]

The ERSC served a symbolic function. It publicly distanced the governor from specific policy recommendations. It muted the executive-partisan tensions by becoming an umbrella organization for Democrats and Republicans, legislative and executive officials. It reinforced the perception of citizen involvement, "objective" analysis, and broad-based endorsements in policymaking. These symbolic reassurances were perceived to be important, particularly in a legislature dominated by Republicans and in a culture that expects and commends constituency participation, issue emphasis, and rational-consensual deliberation.

The ERSC served a dramatist function. Through a variety of techniques including special sessions with innovative individuals like Lamar Alexander, open hearings, town meetings, resident polls, and concrete, concise publications, the ERSC could call attention to and arouse support for a salient value-educational reform through improvement in the quality, availability, and accountability of the teaching force.

The ERSC served a strategist function. Members of the steering committee possessed intimate knowledge of the legislative process, its action channels, and its distinctive personalities. Members understood the consensual norm and persisted until they secured at least the illusion of a unified "education family." Members had access to Republican Caucus concerns and countered them initially with poll data and routinely with compromise adjustments. Members had trusted relationships and bargaining skills. They knew how to negotiate a saleable compromise and they could convince their resisters of the need for exchange and accommodation.

Whenever one assesses the role of power players, it is easy to confuse foresight and visibility with actual influence and decisional impact.[25] In this setting, the ERSC may have followed public opinion. The context was clearly ripe for and replete with teacher-oriented reform proposals. The ERSC was certainly the benefactor of SAPE's substantive contributions and CEE's concurrent endorsements. But there is also evidence to suggest that the ERSC exerted considerable influence. A policy precedent, albeit in modified form, was enacted. Attributional data merged with resource inventories and influence efforts to substantiate the central role of the ERSC in the policymaking process.[26] And, an analysis of the ERSC's capacity to perform crucial political functions suggests that official initiation through task force creation was a sound, effective approach to public school reform in Utah.

Early, Strategic Investment Versus Belated, Frenetic Reaction. When the influence efforts of the advocates and the opponents are juxtaposed, there is a noticeable difference in timing. Although both engaged in presession activities, the advocates entered the policymaking process months ahead of the resisters. They had a concrete definition of the issue to present and promote. Neither the UEA nor the Republican Caucus had a credible, innovative counter ready. Both were preempted by the advocates' ability to articulate policy options early on.

There is also an apparent difference in approach. The advocates appeared to be both more systematic and more culturally congruent in their choice of influence tactics. The data indicate that the ERSC and its allies carefully orchestrated a public information campaign and a private alignment agenda. While the desired outcomes of these strategies were not fully realized, the strategies themselves were favorably received. In contrast, the more spontaneous, reactive, combative style of the UEA reportedly detracted from the organization's concerns. While most informants noted that the UEA had to get the attention of decisionmakers, they also maintained that the strategies selected alienated legislators. The UEA certainly secured concessions. One can only speculate on the ultimate price of those temporary concessions. But one can confidently underscore the perceived importance of early, strategic investment as a more palatable and perhaps more persuasive approach to the policymaking process in arenas that prefer to see only the subtle side of power.

Fragmentation Versus Cohesion. Actors on both sides of the issue affirmed the importance of unity within and across organizations. The proponents, for example, kept the ERSC small to enhance cohesion. They perceived the slippage in their alignment with the Mormon church to be problematic. They indicated they were surprised they secured such favorable decision benefits, in light of the disagreements within the "education family." Likewise, opponents were limited by a Republican Caucus mildly divided on purse levels and openly diffused on policy focus and a UEA membership divided on both the propriety of political action and the desirability of career ladder legislation. Opponents indicated that the anticipated financial repercussions of further opposition prompted a compromise position.

In these comments, participants consistently echo a familiar political axiom: A unified organization or coalition can wield greater power than a fragmented one, particularly when the financial condition is characterized by scarcity and the dominant partisan is characterized by frugality. Whether a more unified public school lobby would have materially altered the financial allocations is a matter of conjecture. But informants from all perspectives recognized fragmentation as a liability. To secure major fiscal appropriations, unity, at least within and across the public education associations, may need to come out of the ranks of conventional political wisdom and into the ranks of consistent political practice.

Favorable Opportunity Structure. Virtually all informants reiterated that the 1984 legislative session was the time to seek major increases in public school appropriations. Although the quality of public education has been an important issue in previous sessions, a variety of forces converged to make it an imperative issue in this session. Those forces interacted to create an opportunity structure that favored career ladder proponents. There were supportive officials in both branches and both parties. There were multiple, credible organizations aligned on behalf of the legislation. The resisters were not aligned, they had no credible counter reform, and their decisions on timing and tactics reportedly alienated rather than ingratiated legislators. There were concrete indications that citizens would pay for public school reforms, particularly those that might address the pressing need to attract and retain quality teachers. And, there were clear indications that Utahns identified with their nationally visible educational leaders. While *Nation at Risk* could spawn dialogue in many states, it could spur action in this state. The national momentum permeated the Utah context and provided impetus for the "Utah response" to public school reform.

THE IMPLEMENTATION AND IMPACT OF REFORM

House Bill 110 directed the Utah State Office of Education to develop guidelines for career ladder plans. These guidelines were disseminated to the state's forty local and six special districts (five Area Vocational Centers and one School for the Deaf and Blind) on March 2, 1984. Although participation in this program was voluntary, all districts submitted proposals. In June, thirty-one plans were approved by the State Office of Education. The remainder were revised and approved August 3, 1984.[27] The State Board of Education funded proposals on the basis of the number of students enrolled in, teachers employed by, and Weighted Pupil Units allotted to the districts (Utah State Office of Education 1984).

Data regarding the extent to which district operations conform to district proposals are limited. Although the State Office of Education commissioned six district specific studies of career ladder development and implementation, only two have been completed. Data regarding the impact of career ladder programs on teacher performance, work relationships, and student achievement have not been acquired. Conclusions about policy implementation and impact are, therefore, premature, but several preliminary observations can be made.

Extended Contract Emphasis and Modest Salary Supplements

An analysis of district plans indicates that while each has unique features, forty-two incorporate the extended contract option for all, or nearly all, teachers. Most fund this provision at or near the statutory limit (50 percent of career ladder appropriations). The manner in which districts comply with the requirement that 50 percent of the appropriations must be used for career advancement varies. Nineteen provide merit increments for superior teaching; the remainder utilize additional assignments or a combination of job enlargement and teaching performance as criteria for career advancement.[28] Since only four districts supplemented state allocations with voted leeway revenue, and since most districts relied on uniform rather than targeted distribution schemes, the financial impact for teachers appears modest. Estimates of annual salary increases from extended contract provisions range from $119 to $1070, by school districts, and average $403 for the state. Estimates of annual salary increases from promotional provisions are not available. (Most district plans do not specify the number of teachers encompassed by the level of stipend attached to particular advancement steps.) Because advancement is often tied to job enlargement and extended time contract requirements, career ladder plans tend to adjust the amount, but not the rate, of pay. Salary increases are essentially the result of extra work days and additional work responsibilities.[29]

Revised-Expanded Teacher Evaluation Systems

Through the process of designing career ladder programs, most districts (85 percent) redefined teacher evaluation procedures. The new systems make procedures more explicit and increase the number of people involved in and the types of data collected for the evaluation of teacher performance.[30] The revised systems often incorporate committee assessment structures; peer reviews; concrete evidence of student progress; at times, parent and student appraisals; and administrator "ratings."

Unresolved Substantive-Financial Issues

The experimental status of career ladder plans, the diverse reactions of career ladder participants, and the revenue limitations of the state generate important but unanswered questions. For example, should plans focus on more dollars for more work or more dollars for "better" work? Should districts be allowed to maintain diverse plans or should the state seek a uniform, "exemplar" model? Will the competition for promotional positions help or hinder the teaching-learning process? Are the economic incentives attractive enough to recruit and retain the quality teachers needed? These and other policy issues require thoughtful attention and systematic investigation.

Probable Continuation-Incremental Expansion

The Legislature will probably retain the career ladder approach to educational reform. It would be difficult to admit a $15 million mistake. More importantly, while there are signs of teacher opposition there are also signs of teacher acceptance, especially in districts that initiated career ladder plans prior to legislative action, supported those plans with substantial district monies, and involved teachers in the development of plans from the outset.[31] The UEA has joined other educational groups in a formal request for increased career ladder funding. The "education family" is projecting a unified posture, a consistent appeal for "a fair trial" and a "careful evaluation" of career ladder programs.[32] In the Utah setting, this policy may well remain the most persuasive way to demand increased aid for pubiic schools because it focuses on a contextual concern, the availability of quality teachers, and it responded to a contextual requirement, the judicious investment of scarce resources.

NOTES TO CHAPTER 10

1. This definition of influence follows that of Terry Clark, 1968, "The Concept of Power," in *Community Structure and Decision Making*, edited by T. Clark, pp. 45–81, San Francisco: Chandler, p. 4, and Robert Dahl, 1984, *Modern Political Analysis*, 4th ed., Englewood Cliffs, N.J.: Prentice-Hall, p. 51. The distinction between influence (the actual exercise) and power (the potential) is made by several authors. See, for example, Daniel Katz and Robert Kahn, 1966, *The Social Psychology of Organization*, New York: John Wiley, pp. 218–222.
2. A graduate seminar, under the direction of Roald F. Campbell, completed a study of the career ladder decision in June 1984. Data for the seminar study were acquired primarily from structured interviews with thirty-four policy actors. The report is available through the Department of Educational Administration, University of Utah, Salt Lake City, Utah.

   Informants for the current study were selected on the basis of five criteria: proximity to the decision making process, potential for diverse perspectives, reputation for knowledge and candor, accessibility, and willingness to participate. Balanced by policy position and issue stance, the pool included legislators, legislative staff, executive office representatives, state agency officials, interest group representatives, and members of the Career Ladder Research Group, contracted by the Utah State Office of Education and comprised of state office staff and graduate faculty and students from the Department of Educational Administration, University of Utah.

   Interviews averaged one hour. Field notes were validated on the basis of position and certainty of source; clarity, detail, plausability of content; ability to corroborate information from sources within the interview method; ability to triangulate information across methods; and ability to verify information from interviewees reflecting different perspectives.
3. See House Bill 110, 1984 Budget Session of the Legislature of the State of Utah.
4. See, for example, Helen Papanikolas, ed., 1981, *The Peoples of Utah*, Salt Lake City: Utah State Historical Society.
5. For a discussion of Utah's early response to financing equity issues, see Craig Wentz, 1972, "Educational Financing in Utah," *Utah Law Review* (Summer): 228–246. Productivity studies in Utah primarily support efforts to revise staffing assignments, improve building utilization, incorporate proficiency-based instructional programs, and apply technology to managerial functions.
6. The Utah State Office of Education does not collect home school enrollment data. The President of the Utah Home Education Association, in a telephone interview, November 8, 1984, estimated that 500 families exer-

cise the home school option. He noted that the average number of children per home school household is four or five. On that basis, 2000–2500 children are part of this alternative.

7. In 1980, for example, 80 percent of Utah's population twenty-five years and older had completed high school. The national average was 66 percent. Utah Education Association, 1983, "Teacher Salary Schedules," *Research Bulletin*, Salt Lake City: Utah Education Association, and Ken Wells, 1984, "Utah Gets Youngsters Thanks to Mormons," *Wall Street Journal*, November 7: 22.
8. The poll was conducted by Dan Jones and Associates of Salt Lake City in August 1983.
9. Utah State Office of Education, 1983, *Utah School Finance Reference Manual*, Salt Lake City: Utah State Office of Education. See also, Utah State Office of Education, 1983, *Utah Elementary and Secondary School Finance Program 1983-84*, Salt Lake City: Utah State Office of Education.
10. See, for example, J. Paul Nielson, 1980, "The Utah State-Local Tax Structure," *Utah Economic and Business Review* 40, nos. 7–8 (July/August) 1–12.
11. A proposition passed on November 6, 1984, changed the legislative sessions. Beginning in 1985 the Legislature will meet for forty-five day annual sessions.
12. Several have described these changes. See, for example, Alan Rosenthal, 1981, *Legislative Life*, New York: Harper & Row.
13. Robert Gottlieb and Peter Wiley, 1984, *American's Saints*, New York: G.P. Putnam's Sons, p. 82. For the historical reference, consult Harmon Zielger and Michael A. Baer, 1969, *Lobbying: Interaction and Influence in American State Legislatures*, Belmont, Calif.: Wadsworth Publishing Co.
14. Remaining categories included Senate: agriculture-5, law-4, education-4, other-4; and House: education-11, agriculture-8, law-7, other-17.
15. Governor Scott Matheson, in a speech delivered to a meeting of the ERSC.
16. See Governor's Action Plan for Quality Elementary and Secondary Education, *Solving the School Crises Phase I* January, 1982; *Solving the School Crises Phase II* January 1983; and Utah State Office of Education, *Utah Elementary and Secondary School Finance Program 1983-84*, op. cit.
17. Robert Gottlieb and Peter Wiley, op. cit., pp. 115–117.
18. Newspapers throughout the state covered the town meetings. See, for example, "Consensus Fails School Reform Hearings Held Across State," 1983, *Salt Lake Tribune*, December 1: B2; "Education Reform Proposals Batted About," 1983, *West Valley View*, November 17: 1; "Governor Speaks on Education," 1983, *Beaver Press*, November 17: 3; "Meet Educators, Legislators," 1983, *Davis News Journal*, November 30: 2; and

"Town hearings tonight give John Q. Public chance to speak on school reforms," 1983, *Deseret News*, November 30: 61.

19. See, Vicki Valera, "Poll shows teachers don't want merit pay," 1983, *Deseret News* October 22: B1.
20. Newspaper accounts corroborate the fragile nature of the public school lobby alignment. See, for example, "Consensus Fails School Reform Hearings Held Across State," 1983, *Salt Lake Tribune*, December 1: B2; "Educators Work to Patch Rift," 1983, *Salt Lake Tribune*, December 10: B2; "Governor's Panel, School Officials Hope to Smooth Reform Plan Differences," 1983, *Salt Lake Tribune*, December 6: B1.
21. Newspaper accounts also substantiate that perception. See, Max B. Knudson, "Education sparks Salt Lake area Chamber debate," 1983, *Deseret News*, December 20: D9, and David Jonsson, "Matheson Asks Businesses to Support Education," 1983, *Salt Lake Tribune*, December 28: B1.
22. The rationale for that position is described by Peter Scarlet, "Teachers Ask For Experimental Career Ladder," 1983, *Salt Lake Tribune*, December 5: B1.
23. The press also carried stories indicating that the adversarial position of the UEA was jeopardizing funding levels. See, for example, "Group calls on UEA leaders to back education reform plan," 1983, *Deseret News*, December 14: B1, B2, and Vicki Varella, 1983, "State school board criticizes UEA budget demands," *Deseret News*, December 3: A9.
24. A similar description of the role of commissions in educational policymaking is provided by Paul E. Peterson, "Did the Education Commissions Say Anything?", 1983, *The Brookings Review* 2 (Winter): 3–11.
25. This complication is discussed by several authors, including J. Pfeffer, 1981, *Power in Organizations*, Marshfield, Mass.: Pitman Publishing Inc., pp. 44–47.
26. Here we follow William A. Gamson, 1968, *Power and Discontent*, Homewood, Ill.: Dorsey, p. 67.
27. G. Leland Burningham, 1985, "Superintendent's Message-Career Ladder Progress," *Utah Schools* 7, no. 1: 3, and Utah State Office of Education, 1984, *Career Ladders for Teachers in Utah*, Salt Lake City: Utah State Office of Education, p. 1.
28. See Utah State Office of Education, *Career Ladders for Teachers in Utah*, op. cit., and Career Ladder Research Group, *Analusis of Career Ladder Plans*, in progress report prepared for the Utah State Office of Education.
29. Ibid.
30. Ibid.
31. See the in-depth study of the Provo District, prepared for the Utah State Office of Education by Ann W. Hart and the press reports of Peter Scarlet, 1984, "Teachers Rap Career Ladders," *Salt Lake Tribune*, August 22: G3; "Most Provo Teachers Like Career-Ladder Program," 1984, *Salt Lake*

Tribune September 10: B1, B3; "UEA Survey-Career Ladders Receive a Mixed Review," 1984, *Salt Lake Tribune*, October 30: 8G.

32. See, for example, "Education Leader Calls for Legislative Summit," 1984, *Salt Lake Tribune*, October 11: B6, and "Educators Agree to Work Together," 1984, *Salt Lake Tribune*, October 19: B5.

REFERENCES

Campbell, Roald F. 1981. "Utah" In *Shaping Educational Policy in the States*, edited by S. Fuhrman and A. Rosenthal, pp. 101–112. Washington, D.C.: The Institute for Educational Leadership.

Campbell, Roald F., and Tim L. Mazzoni, Jr. 1976. *State Policymaking for the Public Schools*, pp. 5–13. Berkeley: McCutcheon.

Elazar, Daniel. 1972. *American Federalism: A View From the States*, 2d ed., pp. 84–154. New York: Harper & Row.

Gray, V., H. Jacob, and K.N. Vines, eds. 1983. *Politics in the American States: A Comparative Analysis*, 4th ed., pp. 454–58. Boston: Little, Brown.

Macdonald, Douglas. 1984. "The Utah Economic Recovery of 1983–84, *Utah Economic and Business Review* 44, no. 1 (January): 1–9.

Mathews, Anne. 1984. "Utahns Find Indexing Very Taxing." *Salt Lake Tribune.* October 18: B1, B4.

Mathews, John, and Paulette Arrington. 1984. *Utah Job Outlook for Occupations.* Salt Lake City: Utah Department of Employment Security.

National Commission on Excellence in Education. 1983. *A Nation at Risk.* Washington, D.C.: U.S. Department of Education.

Robson, R. Thayne. 1982. "Utah: An Economic Review and Outlook," *Utah Economic and Business Review* 42, no. 11–12 (November-December): 1–12.

Rosenthal, Alan, and Susan Fuhrman. 1981. *Legislative Education Leadership.* Washington, D.C.: The Institute for Educational Leadership.

Scarlet, Peter. 1983. "Educator's Unified Efforts Produces Joint Statement of Goals." *Salt Lake Tribune.* November 30: C1.

Utah Commission on Educational Excellence. 1983. *Report of the Utah Commission on Educational Excellence.* Salt Lake City: Utah State Board of Education.

Utah Education Reform Steering Committee. 1983. *Education in Utah: A Call to Action.* Salt Lake City: Utah Education Reform Steering Committee.

____. 1984. *Addendum to Education in Utah: A Call to Action.* Salt Lake City: Utah Education Reform Steering Committee.

Utah Foundation. 1983. "Utah School Enrollment Projections 1983–1993," *Research Briefs*, no. 82–23 (December): 1–2.

____. 1984. *Statistical Review of Government in Utah.* Salt Lake City: Utah Foundation.

Utah State Board of Education. 1984. *Utah Schools* 7, no. 1: 1.

_____. 1984a. *Fall Enrollment Report of Utah School Districts Annual Report.* Salt Lake City: Utah State Office of Education.

_____. 1984b. *Allocation of Career Ladder Funds.* Salt Lake City: Utah State Office of Education.

Utah Office of Planning Budget. 1983. *State of Utah Operations Budget 1984–85.* Salt Lake City: Office of Planning and Budget.

_____. 1984. *Utah Current Conditions*, Annual Report. Salt Lake City: Office of Planning and Budget.

11 A COMPREHENSIVE SHIFT IN EDUCATIONAL POLICYMAKING
Texas Educational Reform Legislation

Deborah A. Verstegen, Richard Hooker, and Nolan Estes

Declaring in his inaugural address, "Texas is the State of the Future . . . standing on the very edge of greatness," Governor Mark White (1983a) outlined the foundations that were necessary for Texas to become the industrial and financial leader of the United States. The first foundation for greatness was education. According to the governor, significant reform in the system of public education was the cornerstone for future economic vitality in a technological society and an investment in the state's most valuable resource—human potential (1983a); (1984a); (1984b). "Today Texas is in the midst of a great period of transition. . . . Today Texas is at the crossroads," White said. "[A] strong educational foundation is the only true basis for progress . . . for higher human achievement . . . and for greater economic growth" (1984c).

EDUCATIONAL REFORM: THE CONTEXT

This section describes the economic, political, and legal setting in Texas and provides a necessary backdrop for considering educational reform actions.

Economic Trends. The economic foundation of Texas' past, oil and gas, is gradually receding with the depletion of those resources;

the age of information and high technology has arrived with lightening speed (White, 1984c: 7). With the decline of mining gross product projected at 1.1 percent annually from 1982 to 2007, although Texas' real gross product is expected to increase from $104.4 billion to $247.2 billion—an annual average increase of 3.5 percent—future economic growth will not keep pace with the extremely high rates of the past decade—5.7 percent per year. The population of Texas is also expected to grow from 15.1 million to 22.1 million over the twenty-five year period (1982 to 2007), an annual average growth rate of 1.5 percent compared to 2.6 percent from 1973 to 1981. If current trends continue, Taxes will pass New York to become the nation's second largest state by the late 1980s (see Mahoney 1984; Plaut et al. 1984; Texas Past and Future 1981). Economic and population forecasts, together with projections of a downturn in the ratio of government revenues to expenditures undergird the conclusion that a major adjustment in revenues or expenditures is on the horizon if substantial new economic growth is not forthcoming.

Manufacturing and agriculture are expected to be the fastest growing sectors in the Texas economy in terms of output from 1982 to 2007. Within manufacturing, however, that almost half the growth in the state over the next twenty-five years will be caused by the rapid growth of the state's second largest industry—nonelectrical machinery, which includes computers and other high technology equipment—and by the moderate growth of the state's largest industry, chemicals, which is dominated by petrochemicals (Palut et al., 1984).

"We are living through a technological revolution," White explained. "Tomorrow's economy will have no place for the unskilled and the semi-skilled. It will demand a constant supply of well-educated men and women. And it will require the best research our universities can produce" (1983a).

Legal Imperatives. Before World War II, 30 percent of the labor force in Texas was employed in agriculture; by 1985, the proportion had been cut in half. To cope with the rapid transition from an agricultural to an industrial economy, the legislature created the Gilmer-Aikin Study Committee in 1947 to restructure the Texas public school system (Barnes 1984). The result was enactment of the Gilmer-Aikin ACt of 1949, which provided the basis for the state education system and established the Minimum Foundation Program (now the Foundation School Program [FSP], based on the Strayer-Haig model.

Minimum Foundation Program. The Gilmer-Aikin Commitee rejected the simplest form of a foundation program (an amount per student) and instead funded a minimum list of school services translated into dollar terms through the use of a classroom-teacher unit system. The salary cost of the program for each district was determined by applying the state salary schedule to the FSP personnel employed. Added to these costs was another $400 per classroom teaching unit for operating expenses and an amount for transportation of students living two miles or more from school. The program was intended to equalize the ability of school districts to provide a quality, basic education. For districts with a property-poor tax base, the local fund assignment was relatively low with the state providing a proportionately larger share of the cost; a wealthy district would pay a larger portion of the FSP with the state funding a smaller share. Several factors, however, diminished the foundation program's equalizing ability (see House Study Group [HSG] 1984a: 11–13; Texas Research League 1984a, 1984b).

First, local districts were not required to raise their local fund assignment [LFA] but could, and did, "enrich" their basic FSP by raising more local revenue than required to meet the local share cost. In fact, more than 95 percent of Texas' school districts raised additional enrichment funds, with property-rich districts spending many times the FSP level with lower tax rates than poorer districts with higher tax rates.

Second, wealthy districts, whose enrichment funds enabled them to provide substantial salary supplements, attracted and retained a larger share of experienced teachers and had the state support their spending advantage over poorer districts under this system.

Program Revisions. Continuing dissatisfaction with the state's school finance system led to several studies and revisions of the Minimum Foundation Program since its inception (see Augenblick and Adams 1979; Berne and Stiefel 1983; Lindahl 1984; Sunderman and Hinely 1979; Texas Research League 1984a, 1984b; Thomas and Walker 1982; Walker 1982). In 1961, several changes were made and teachers' salaries were raised. From 1965 to 1969, the Governor's Committee on Public School Education, chaired by Houston attorney Leon Jaworski, conducted one of the most comprehensive studies of a state system to date. The multivolume report, *The Challenge and the Chance*, was presented in 1969, when state aid to education was expanded, teacher salaries raised, and public kindergarten added;

but the legislature was largely unresponsive to the extensive reform advocated in the report.

Shortly thereafter, in 1971, a federal district court ruled that the Texas school financing system was unconstitutional because of the wide disparity in funding-per-student. Subsequently, the U.S. Supreme Court's decision in *San Antonio Independent School District v. Rodriguez* (1973) reversed the lower court's decision by a five-to-four vote, ruling that the Texas system was "chaotic and unjust" but that solutions to the inequities "must come from the lawmakers and the democratic pressures that elect them."

To correct some of the deficiencies at issue in *Rodriguez*, Governor Dolph Briscoe created an Office of Educational Research and Planning in 1973 and study committees were formed to propose changes. Significant changes in the school financing system resulted in 1975, including:

- the adition of a new program granting extra equalization aid to poorer school districts in an attempt to offset wealthy districts' enrichment funds;
- a weighted personnel unit (PU) system for fund allocation;
- a single wealth factor based on property values utilized for computing state aid;
- compensatory and bilingual education funding;
- a $760 million increase in foundation program aid; and
- the near doubling of the local fund assignment.

In compromising the measure, however, a minimum aid clause providing each school district with at least a 5 percent increase in state aid and a hold harmless clause limiting the increase of the local share to 120 percent of the prior year was included.

Increasing the local share and changing the measure of local wealth resulted in higher local property taxes and larger enrichment revenue; thus, in a 1977 special session, the FLA was reduced by almost one-half and $998 million in state funds were added. Only one in seven districts reduced taxes, however, spurning the public demand for fiscal containment. In 1979, the legislature responded with state-mandated exemptions in local school property taxes and provided $1.2 billion in state aid (Barnes 1984). With this complete, in 1981 the sixty-seventh Legislature turned its attention to curriculum and enacted a mandated state curriculum, H.B. 246 (see Killian 1984). Thus, nearly a decade after *Rodriguez*, despite the state's efforts, progress toward achieving school financing equalization had been limited. In fact, the revenue disparity between the poorest and wealthiest districts had widened (see Lindahl 1984; Texas Research League 1984a, 1984b).

Political Context. In the fall of 1982, amid the milieu of economic transition and school financing disparity, aspirant Governor Mark White was engaged in an uphill battle with the incumbent Republican governor, Bill Clements. White had mobilized the teachers of the state, particularly the members of the Texas State Teachers Association (the largest of four statewide teacher organizations), and aggressively campaigned on a platform of broadly improving public education and particularly increasing teachers' salaries and equalization aid with no new taxes. Having won the election in an upset, he gave a large part of the credit to teachers. Anticipating 21 percent in additional state revenues from current tax sources for the 1984–85 biennium—over $4 billion—he promised a 24 percent increase in teachers' salaries (White 1983b). As the sixty-eighth Legislature session convened, however, the Comptroller began a series of estimates revising projected revenue downward. By March 1983, the picture had dramatically changed from one of "How are we going to set priorities in allocating this new revenue among competing demands" (White 1983c) to "[How can we] hold taxes down and keep Texas strong until better economic times return?" (White 1983b: 15).

Consequently, Governor White's biennial budget proposal of $32.9 billion contained a $3 billion increase in overall expenditures for education—including (1) a $1.6 billion increase for teachers' salaries (a minimum 24 percent), (2) $170 million for equalization of financial resources for poor school districts, and (3) an additional $10 million for bilingual education—along with a tax hike on such items as cigarettes, liquor, and amusement machines (HSG 1984b; White 1983b). The House of Representatives, however, refused to support new taxes to fund the increases. The resulting General Appropriations Act (S.B. 179) funded no pay raises for teachers other than the usual grade and step increases based on length of employment and educational level. At the close of the 1983 session, a movement led by the governor, lieutenant governor and speaker of the House supported a comprehensive, in-depth study of public education prior to the passage of a tax bill. The result was the passage of House Concurrent

Resolution (H.C.R.) 275 in the waning hours of the session, and the creation of the Select Committee on Public Education (SCOPE), which was charged to report as quickly as possible regarding the status of public education in Texas and the recommendations necessary to "carry the Texas educational system into the 21st Century as a quality, effective system" (H.C.R. 275). Governor White, Lieutenant Governor Hobby, Speaker Lewis, Chairpersons of the House and Senate Education Committees and the State Board of Education Chairperson, Joe Butler, were among the committee's members. The governor named H. Ross Perot, head of Electronic Data Systems of Dallas, as chair of SCOPE, a task that he undertook with missionary zeal to make Texas the national model for reform of elementary and secondary public education.

The Select Committee. The Perot committee held its first meetings in July 1983, just as a spate of national reports on education appeared. The most influential, *A Nation at Risk: The Imperative for Educational Reform* (National Commission on Excellence in Education 1983) warned that the "educational foundations of our society are being eroded by a rising tide of mediocrity," and that low educational quality was a threat to future economic development. The report offered a number of recommendations that influenced SCOPE, including: a strengthened core curriculum, a longer school day and school year, more time actually devoted to learning, better teacher training, higher teacher salaries and a career-ladder system with the highest compensation for master teachers, a grant and loan program to attract higher calibre students to teaching, and higher spending on education (House Study Group 1984a).

A report issued to the U.S. Department of Education, which ranked the states by several criteria from the period of 1972 to 1982, followed the commission's report. According to the report, of the twenty-two states that administer the Scholastic Aptitude Test, Texas ranked sixteenth in 1982, down from fourteenth in 1972. With an average pupil-teacher ratio of 18:1, Texas placed twenty-fifth out of the fifty states; it was forty-second with regard to high school graduation rates, thirtieth in average teachers' salaries, and thirty-eighth in expenditures-per-pupil (Boyd 1984).

An additional inducement to reform, which was increasingly gaining momentum, was provided by property-poor school districts. According to State Comptroller of Public Accounts Bob Bullock, ". . . Texas is threatened with a major lawsuit challenging our state education aid system and if we don't change it, some judge will step in and do it for us" (1984).

With these and other concerns in mind, the Perot committee traveled throughout the state, visiting the public schools and talking with school board members, administrators, teachers, and the public at large. It then held wide-ranging hearings on the problems of public education, asking for alternative solutions that should be considered by SCOPE and, ultimately, the legislature.

In April 1984, SCOPE issued its final recommendations. The top priority for new spending was given to a new equalization aid system ($400 million in FY 1985). A career-ladder program and teacher raise ($350 million), a lengthened school year by five days ($47.5 million), a limitation in class size fo twenty pupils in grades one and two ($120.8 million), annual student testing with nationally normed tests ($7 million), voluntary prekindergarten for disadvantaged four-year-olds ($53.3 million), and various governance and administrative changes, such as an appointed State Board of Education, followed (SCOPE 1984). Since Representative Haley, Chairperson of the House Education Committee and a member of SCOPE, could not support several of the proposals, he began a series of hearings to develop an alternate education bill. The State Board of Education responded to SCOPE's proposals by approving legislative recommendations favoring the current school financing system based on personnel units, in contrast to the SCOPE recommendation for a weighted pupil system.

The Special Session

With the SCOPE agenda complete, the governor called a special session of the legislature designating three specific topics: (1) public educational reform, including school financing revision and increased teacher compensation, (2) measures to provide adequate highway funding, and (3) appropriation measures to raise funds for these purposes and to meet future state needs.

As a result of concerns raised by the SCOPE committee, the national reports, and the property poor districts and their representatives, the legislative leadership was committeed to comprehensive reform and the new taxes necessary to fund it but also made it clear that there would be no new taxes just to increase funding of the status quo. "A million dollars for reform but not a penny for the status quo" had been the familiar adage heard across the state of H. Ross Perot traveled to muster support for SCOPE's proposals during the weeks preceding the special session (House Study Group 1984a: 10).

Rodriguez II. Immediately prior to convening the special session, the Mexican American Legal Defense Education Fund (MALDEF) on behalf of the parents of children in property-poor school districts and the districts themselves filed a lawsuit, *Edgewood v. Bynum*, challenging in state district court the constitutionality of the state system of school financing under the Texas Constitution. MALDEF argued that the state was not providing children in poor school districts with an "efficient system of public free schools" (Texas Consitution, art. III, § 1) or with programs and services "that are substantially equal to those available to any similar student" (Texas Education Code, § 16.001). MALDEF also charged that since there was a concentration of low income and Mexican-American residents in poor school districts, the state was discriminating against them on the basis of poverty and national origin, thus violating the equal protection provision of the State Constitution (art. I, § 3), which states: "All free men, when they form a social compact, have equal rights, and no man, or set of men, is entitled to exclusive separate public emoluments, or privileges, but in consideration of public services" (House Study Group 1984a: 19).

A few days after MALDEF filed suit, the attorney general of Texas issued a statement concluding that the state was guilty as charged and advised plea bargaining negotiations to develop an equitable plan of school finance.

Legislative Action. The omnibus SCOPE proposals were introduced in the House by Representative Hammond (House Bill 1) and in the Senate by Jones et al. (Senate Bill 4). Chairperson of the House Education Committee, Representative Haley, with SCOPE opponents, introduced House Bill 72 and led his committee in opposition to House Speaker Lewis, who supported his own modified version of SCOPE's proposals. Subsequently, the House committee reported out a substantially amended version of Haley's measure, House Bill 72, which largely reflected the status quo but spent more on teachers' salaries. The speaker responded by having Haley insert the speaker's modification of SCOPE's proposals as a substitute amendment to House Bill 72 on the House floor. Opposition was knocked off the track by what the press corps called the "Speaker's train."

Lieutenant Governor Hobby, committed to SCOPE proposals, used a very unusual approach to directing action in the Senate. Rather than refer the educational bills to the Education Committee, chaired by Senator Parker, who had voiced his opposition to many of the SCOPE proposals and had, like Haley, developed his own bill, the Committee of the Whole was utilized and divided into issue subcommittees with the chairpersons and all members named by the lieutenant governor. The subcommittee reports were very similar to Senate Bill 4, the purest expression of the SCOPE proposals; however, Senator Parker's bill number, Senate Bill 1, was utilized. When the Committee of the Whole adjourned and reconvened as the Senate, passage came quickly (Texas Legislative Council 1984; House Study Group 1984c).

The House had completed deliberations prior to Senate action; thus, when House Bill 72 was taken up in the Senate, it substituted Senate Bill 1, as amended. The House responded by calling for a conference. In conference, Senate conferees became convinced that the House version (1) was substantially less costly thereby requiring less state revenue and (2) would require a lower local share thereby creating less local taxpayer opposition. Thus House Bill 72, as passed, reflected mainly the House version with SCOPE structures and principles, but it was greatly reduced in cost from SCOPE recommendation levels to a $2.8 billion state increase over three years.

Association Support. Initially, the Equity Center, composed of the lowest third of property-poor school districts, and the Urban Council, representing the "big eight" urban districts, were the only educational organizations supporting SCOPE's proposals. They were soon joined by the Texas Elementary Principals and Supervisors Association and the Texas Association of Secondary School Principals. After it became clear that a reform bill would pass, however, the Texas Association of School Boards and the Texas Federation of Teachers joined a press conference called by the legislative leadership to promote the final passage of the bill. All other educational organizations—including the three other major teacher organizations—and the State Board of Education were in opposition, with the Commissioner of Education, the Texas Association of School Administrators, and the Texas Association of Suburban Schools most active.

REFORM OUTCOMES: EDUCATION

The Second Called Session of the Sixty-eighth Legislature enacted legislation that addressed the dual educational priorities of the special session—equalization and an increase in salaries for teachers. Beyond this, it passed the state's first major tax bill in thirteen years—raising more than $4.6 billion over the next three years—and committeed $2.8 billion to education. The omnibus tax bill (House Bill 122) raised the rates on the sales tax; franchise tax; motor fuels taxes; motor vehicle sales and the use tax; the liquor, beer, ale, wine, and mixed drinks taxes; the cigarette tax; the hotel-motel tax; the amusement machine tax; and the motor carriers sales tax. In addition, the vehicle registration fees and tuition for out-of-state and foreign students were increased, the sales tax base was expanded, and procedural changes in the collection of sales, franchise, and insurance taxes were implemented (House Study Group 1984d: 2).

Administration and Management. Under House Bill 72, a comprehensive change in all asepcts of educational policy including governance, finance, and teacher and student standards was enacted. The elected State Board of Education was abolished and a smaller, appointed state board was established. The board, appointed from fifteen districts created by the legislature, functions as the primary policymaking body for public education in Texas. The commissioner serves at the will of the board; under prior law, the commissioner served a set of four years, with removal only for cause. Requirements for the commissioner to be a five year state resident, have the highest school administrator's certificate, or hold a master's degree were removed.

Appointment to the board is a two stage process with a newly created Legislative Education Board (LEB)—composed of the lieutenant governor, four senators, the speaker and four House members—nominating three persons from each of the fifteen state board districts. From these nominees, the governor appoints fifteen members to the state board and the chairperson. The LEB is charged with conducting oversight of the implementation of educational law and making recommendations to the legislature concerning needed changes in educational policy. Because the opposition was strong enough to prevent a permanently appointed State Board of Education, a compromise evolved whereby the board will revert to an elected status in four years.

Financing: State-Local Shared Foundation Program Cost Elements. The adopted Foundation School Program (FSP) replaces the personnel unit system and related statutory formulas with a weighted program cost differential system consisting of a basic entitlement and six special allotments.

Basic Allotment. The level of 1.00 in the system, the basic allotment, is the level of funding for "regular" education, exclusive of transportation, determined upon the basis of the best four weeks of average daily attendance among eight weeks selected by the state board, with full-time-equivalent students (FTEs) in special and vocational education subtracted. The amount is $1,290 in 1984–85, $1,350 in 1985–86, and the amount established in the appropriations bill thereafter. Formerly, provision for the Foundation School Program was made under a sum sufficient revenue bill in contrast to this sum certain measure with pro rata reduction if entitlements exceed appropriations.

Price Differential Index (PDI). The basic allotment is adjusted by a price differential index that is intended to reflect for 1984–85 the variance in purchasing power of the dollar as it relates to the recruitment and retention of teachers. The following formula resulted in an FSP cost element in the amount of $600 million:

$$\text{PDI} = \frac{\text{CATS}}{\text{CFTS}} + (.10 \times \text{DED})$$

where:

PDI is the price differential index applicable to a district;

CATS is the total of salaries paid in the preceding year to classroom teachers (not including federally funded teachers) in other districts in the same county as the district for which the calculation is made, except that if there are fewer than three districts assigned to that county by the Central Education Agency for administrative purposes;

CATS is the total of salaries paid in the preceding year to those teachers in districts contiguous to the district for which the calculation is made.

A district with territory in or contiguous to a county with a population of 1.5 million or more may elect to have CATS calculated for the district on the basis of salaries in both the county to which it is assigned for administrative purposes and the county with a population of 1.5 million or more; a district with territory in two counties may elect to have CATS calculated for the district on the basis of salaries in both counties;

CFTS is the total minimum salary portion of salaries paid in the preceding year to the classroom teachers used to determine CATS; and

DED is the percentage of the district's students who are educationally disadvantaged.

On an interim basis, the econometric model proposed by SCOPE (Augenblick, 1979) was rejected in favor of this model. In FY 1985, the index has a floor and a ceiling at the fifth and ninety-fifth percentiles, respectively, and adjusts 75 percent of the basic allotment.

The law requires the establishment of a PDI advisory committee to the State Board of Education that is responsible for recommending an index to be based on an econometric model reflecting the variance in purchasing power of the dollar among school districts as they purchase goods and services to maintain an accredited program.

Small/Sparse and Small District Adjustments. An additional adjustment of the adjusted basic allotment was enacted for small/sparse and small school districts, as follows:

$$AA = (1 + [(1{,}600 - ADA) \times .004]) \times ABA$$

where:

AA is the district's adjusted allotment per student;

ADA is the district's average daily attendance; and

ABA is the adjusted basic allotment determined under the PDI.

The .004 modifier is for districts containing at least 300 square miles with no more than 1,600 students in ADA. If the district contains less than 300 square miles with no more than 1,600 students in ADA, the modifier is changed from .004 to .0025.

The adjusted allotment provides a reduced modifier for small districts; also, school districts having fewer than 130 students in ADA are provided an additional adjustment.

The legislature intended to modify the basic allotment with the PDI and the resulting adjusted basic allotment with the small/sparse adjustment to create a final adjusted allotment. It would function as a base level for eligible school districts; all program and pupil weights for special programs would be applied to the final adjusted allotment. This FSP cost element has been estimated at $171 million.

Special Education. Special education for 1985–86 and thereafter is funded on the basis of FTEs by instructional arrangement with twelve arrangements including indirect costs. The assumption is that the instructional arrangement, not the handicapping condition, drives costs to schools. Since House Bill 72 was enacted in July and the school year began in late August, the legislature chose to have special education funded for the 1984–85 school year on the personnel unit basis with this FSP cost element estimated at $435 million, a 0.4 percent increase over prior law. The state board is mandated to conduct a study of weights by instructional arrangement and to recommend adjustments to the weights enacted into law for 1985–86 and thereafter. The following weights will become operative unless the legislature amends the law in its regular session that begins in January 1985: homebound 5.0; hospital class 5.0; speech therapy 10.0; resource room 2.7; self-contained, mild and moderate, regular campus 2.3; self-contained, severe, regular campus 3.5; self-contained, separate campus 2.7; multidistrict class 3.5; nonpublic day school 3.5; vocational adjustment class 2.3; community class 3.5; self-contained, pregnant 2.0. These weights were computed on a $1715 base; therefore, the $1290 finally adopted by the legislature would substantially reduce special education funding below estimated requirements.

Vocational Education. Vocational education is to be funded on a basis similar to special education; however, the legislature chose to establish an interim weight of 1.45 for all FTEs generated by vocational education in the 1984–85 school year, with one FTE defined as 30 hours of class contact per week. The 1.45 weights was calculated to reflect the aggregate statewide funding level of $239 million used in 1983–84, which excluded salary increases and indirect cost considerations. The state board is required to study program weights and report to the legislature in spring 1985.

Compensatory Education. Compensatory education is a 0.2 add-on weight for each student in a federally subsidized free and reduced price lunch program. Free and reduced price lunch had been the basis for the distribution of a $51.6 million allotment under prior law and adequate alternative education data were unavailable for distribution of this $319.4 million FSP cost element (519 percent change). In the legislatively required weighted program cost differential study, the state board is seeking information regarding FTEs by instructional arrangement for compensatory education and the costs associated therewith to produce a more appropriate basis for the distribution of state aid.

Bilingual and English as a Second Language (ESL). Bilingual and ESL programs are an add-on weight on 0.1 applied to each student who qualifies for the programs based on testing. The inconsistency between compensatory and bilingual weights resulted in the inclusion of this program in the study of cost differentials associated with instructional arrangements. The program cost increased from $10 million under prior law to $35 million under House Bill 72 (256 percent change).

Educational Improvement and Career Ladder Allotment. An Education Improvement and Career Ladder Allotment was added to the system based on the demands of the teacher lobby that was being asked to accept a merit pay system with no guarantee within the weighted pupil system that designated money would be available for the supplements. As a result of negotiations, a $100 per ADA, $291 million FSP cost element was designated for 1984–85, in addition to money generated by the weighted pupil system, with $120 per ADA in 1985–86 and $140 per ADA in 1986–87. A minimum of $30, then $40, and then $50 of the allotment must be spent on career ladder supplements; 25 percent is to be used for supplementing the salaries of persons other than classroom teachers; the remainder can be utilized for any legal purpose.

Transportation. Since the 1979 linear density formulas for transportation were viewed as being a reasonably equitable distribution of funds, although inadequate, 10 percent adjustments of all rates per mile and limits were enacted.

State/Local Shares. The cost elements described above are to be shared between the state and local school districts based on the following formula:

$$LFA = \frac{DPV}{SPV} \times (N \times FSP)$$

where:

LFA is the district's local share;

DPV is the taxable value of property in the district for the prior tax year;

The State Property Tax Board is responsible for producing the estimates of value based on sales/ratio studies, sample appraisals, and other techniques used in monitoring the countywide appraisal districts' practices; therefore, independent, uniform procedures executed by a state agency becomes the basis for the local share;

SPV is the total of the taxable values of property in the state for the prior tax year;

N is a percentage, which for the 1984–85 schol year is 30 percent, and which for each school year thereafter is 33.3 percent; and

FSP is the total cost of the Foundation School Program, not including experienced teacher allotments or enrichment equalization allotments.

This provision replaces a local fund assignment, fixed at a specific rate, e.g., eleven cents per $100 of equalized valuation in 1983–84, with a variable amount dependent on costs of the state program and state property values (Walker and Kirby 1984). In 1983–84, the aggregate local share of the FSP was approximately 12.7 percent of the cost of a much lower level FSP. The 30 percent local share for 1984–85 and 33.3 percent for 1985–86 and thereafter represents a dramatic increase for property rich school districts.

The equity that results from requiring property rich districts to support a higher share of an increased FSP cost was made possible by a 1979 property tax reform law, Senate Bill 621 (the Jones-Peveto bill). The law called for the establishment of county-wide appraisal units, certification of all persons working in the appraisal process, development of uniform appraisal guidelines for all classes of property, development of uniform record keeping and accounting systems, and creation of the State Property Tax Board to monitor the process and estimate true values by school districts.

State Supported Programs. In addition to the shared state-local portion of the FSP, several fully supported state programs were enacted or continued. Total state FSP aid—state and local shared costs plus fully funded state programs—was intended to provide sufficient district revenue to meet accreditation standards previously adopted to implement House Bill 246—the state-mandated curriculum. Because data were not available to determine the actual cost of an accredited program, new budgeting and reporting requirements were mandated by House Bill 72 and statutory provisions for an accountable cost advisory committee to the state board were included in the legislation.

Equalization Transition Fund. The big losers of state aid can be generally described as affluent, suburban school districts with stable or declining enrollments and rapidly escalating property values. In a compromise measure, the Equalization Transition Fund was created to aid losing districts in adjusting their local expenditures and/or local tax effort over a period of three years. The 1984–85 amount was set at \$70 million, 1985–86 at \$35 million, and 1986–87 at \$17.5 million, after which it expires. The formula is as follows:

$$\text{ETE} = \text{N} \times \text{DL} \times \frac{\text{DETR}}{\text{SETR}}$$

where:

- ETE is the equalization transition entitlement;
- N is a percentage, which for the 1984–85 school year is 60 percent, for the 1985–86 school year is 40 percent, and for the 1986–87 school year is 20 percent;
- DL is the amount of the district's lost state aid;
- DETR is the district's effective tax rate for the prior year; and
- SETR is the statewide average effective tax rate for the prior year.

If DETR is less than SETR, a value of 1.0 is used in the formula. If a district's lost state aid (DL) minus the equalization transition entitlement (ETE) is greater than the total amount by which the district's 1984 tax levy exceeds its 1983 tax levy, the district's equalization entitlement is adjusted (AETE) in accordance with the following formula (where DTI is the district tax levy increase):

$$\text{AETE} = [\text{DTI}/(\text{DL} - \text{ETE})] \times \text{ETE}$$

If DTI is greater than DL minus ETE, then a value of 1.0 is used. If DTI is less than DL minus ETE, then ETE is adjusted downward, as the district did not raise its full loss of state aid above ETE to be received. The formula rewards increased tax effort on the part of local school districts to make up their losses in state aid under the FSP and provides a "bonus" for those school districts which are exceeding the statewide average effective tax rate. It replaces the minimum aid and hold harmless provisions of prior law.

Enrichment Equalization Allotment. Texas has had an enrichment equalization aid component since its School Finance Reform Act of 1975 (House Bill 1126), and the maximum entitlement would have been $346 per-student in ADA for 1984–85. Initially, the Equity Center-Urban Council coalition recommended a much higher level FSP floor with a local share set at 40 percent, thereby making a 15 percent of FSP cost maximum entitlement all that was needed, in its view. However, the basic allotment was significantly lowered from the recommended $1,850 to $1,290 per ADA and the local share was reduced; therefore, equalization aid was increased to a maximum of 35 percent of FSP cost in 1984–85 and 30 percent in 1985–86 and thereafter. The total estimated cost of this component increased from approximately $275 million under prior law to $499.5 million (84 percent change). The formula is as follows:

$$\text{EEA} = [1 - \frac{\text{DPV/ADA}}{\text{SPV/ADA} \times 1.10)]} \times \text{ADA} \times \text{MAXENT} \times \frac{\text{DTRT}}{\text{BTRT}}$$

where:

EEA is the enrichment equalization allotment to the district;

DPV/ADA is the district's taxable value of property divided by the number of students in average daily attendance in the district;

SPV/ADA is the total statewide taxable value of property divided by the total number of students in average daily attendance in the state;

MAXENT is the maximum entitlement per ADA, which is a percentage of the total of the district's other FSP allocations per ADA, which percentage for the 1984–85 school year is 35 percent and for each school year thereafter is 30 percent;

ADA is the number of students in average daily attendance in the district.

If a district's tax effort exceeds the statewide average, then the DTRT/BTRT is set to equal one; if the district's tax effort is less than the statewide average, its equalization aid is proportionately reduced. Tax effort is the greater of two ratios under this formula: (1) the ratio of the district's effective maintenance tax rate to the effective maintenance tax rate necessary for a district at 110 percent of SPV/ADA to raise its local share plus an amount equal to MAXENT (.35 times the district's FSP cost per student); or (2) the ratio of the district's total effective tax rate to the sum of: The effective maintenance tax rate necessary to a district at 110 percent of SPV/ADA to raise its local share plus an amount equal to MAXENT, plus the statewide average effective tax rate for debt service.

Enrichment equalization is designed to provide poorer school districts with additional state aid to supplement the cost of the FSP as wealthier districts may do with additional enrichment funds generated through tax levies. The decrease in enrichment equalization in 1985–86 corresponds with the statutory increase in the basic allotment and the local share cost that move in tandem.

Reformers had three primary objectives in enrichment equalization: (1) to lift the floor of the FSP program to a level where enrichment equalization was not really necessary, (2) to eliminate enrichment equalization for school districts that were above average in wealth per pupil, and (3) to insert a local school district tax effort qualifier. The formula reflects that reformers lost two out of three. School districts with up to 110 percent of state average wealth-per-pupil can receive benefits. Rather than a 15 percent of FSP cost maximum entitlement, 35 percent was necessary and actually inadequate to accomplish the objective of creating an average opportunity to spend for an average effective tax rate. The reform lobby was successful in inserting Texas' first tax effort factor, however.

Experienced Teacher Allotment. The teacher lobby managed to extract an experienced teacher modifier from the political process. Teachers were losing a base-plus-fourteen-step, twenty-year longevity salary increase guarantee that was the basis of flowing state money to school districts. The teacher lobby feared the loss of competitiveness for experienced teachers in district hiring practices if the state did not offset most, if not all, of the additional cost. The following formula resulted that distributes $37 million:

$$\text{EXP} = \frac{\text{DAS}}{\text{SAS}} - 1 \times 1 - \frac{\text{LFA}}{\text{DFSP}} \times [.75 \times (\text{DFSP} - \text{TA})]$$

where:

EXP is the experience allotment;

DAS is the district's average classroom teacher's minimum salary required;

SAS is the statewide average classroom teacher's minimum salary;
LFA is the district's local share of the FSP;
DFSP is the total of the district's other FSP allotments, not including any enrichment equalization allotment; and
TA is the district's transportation allotment.

If the formula results in a negative amount, the district is not entitled to an experienced teacher allotment.

Other Funding Implications. House Bill 72 mandated three new programs, two of which were granted partial funding.

First, the high priority on improving early childhood education was reflected in the addition of a prekindergarten program for four-year-olds, operated for a half day with state support on the same basis as state-local sharing of the FSP cost in the district. The state obligated itself for expenditures not to exceed $50 million per year; program eligibility is limited to the economically disadvantaged and limited English proficient students.

Second, the state will also share the costs for summer programs which are to operate for a half day for eight weeks of prekindergarten and pre-first grade, for students with limited English proficiency. However, only $6 million per year was appropriated. It is questionable whether these funds will meet the demands of a state with a substantial and growing hispanic population.

Third, the kindergarten program was inadvertently increased in the omnibus measure from half day for all eligible students, to a full day, at a cost of approximately $58 million for 1984–85.

A measure that impacts local financing requirements without specific state funding is the specification of a maximum class size of twenty-two for grades K–4, with implementation in 1984–85 for grades K–2, and in 1988 for grades 3–4. The personnel and facilities implications of maximum class size have probably created more concern than any financing provision enacted within House Bill 72. Both Houston ISD and Dallas ISD are projecting the need for at least 400 additional teachers and a similar number of new classrooms in order to meet this requirement.

Also, without special funding, the legislature enacted laws related to discipline that create a strong obligation for the development of alternative schools to serve students who in many cases would have been suspended or expelled in the past, and the addition of after school tutorial programs to be offered to students who are failing. The current adequacy of all districts to fund the additional costs of new programs is questionable; it may require larger local enrichment subsidies thus diluting equalization objectives.

Additional equalization was achieved, however, through a transfer of revenue from the Available School Fund, which is distributed on a per-capita basis to all school districts regardless of wealth, to the Foundation School Fund, which equalizes payments among wealthy and poor districts. It is estimated that prior to the transfer of monies, all students received $530 each; under the new distribution students receive $230 each (Legislative Budget Board 1984). Also, provisions for equalization and transition aid remove, for three years, prior statutory limitations permitting local referendum on tax initiatives exceeding 8 percent of the previous year's tax rate. This allows property poor districts an opportunity to maximize equalization aid and possibly decrease the revenue gap that has been held constant or, at best, slowed by the statutory fiscal containment requirement. If both wealthy and poor districts take advantage of this provision, however, inflation rather than equalization may result.

Cost Savings. In an effort to contain expenditures and to promote further equalization, the legislature has withdrawn its willingness to meet teacher retirement contributions for salaries that exceed the state minimum adjusted by the school district's price differential index. Property-rich local school districts that have substantially enriched salaries above that minimum level will be expected to pay the state share (8.5 percent) on the amount of local salary enrichment in 1985–86. School districts that exceed 125 percent of the state average effective tax rates are exempt. Special state funding for educational television, teacher sick leave, and student teacher supervision were all repealed.

Teacher Reform. As previously noted, the state salary policy has been significantly changed—no money flows through the current minimum salary schedule. As a part of the compromise with the teacher lobby, however, a one-line minimum salary law was put in place with ten annual steps that range from $1,520 to $2,660 per month—a 36 percent increase in the minimum salary guaranteed to the beginning teacher under prior law. Since most Texas teachers are ln a ten month contract, the guaranteed minimum increase under the FSP amounts to approximately $4,000 per year. However, as in the past, districts can pay teachers at higher than minimum levels. No separate salary provisions were enacted for administrators, counselors, supervisors, or paraprofessionals.

House Bill 72 also provides for a four step career ladder with increments of $2,000 per year beginning at level two. Districts may reduce the supplements up to 25 percent or provide more challenging performance criteria for placement than those specified in the law, if the FSP does not provide sufficient funding within this component. Under the new law, all teachers and administrators are required to pass a competency test on subject matter and basic skills by June 1986; duties, qualifications, and alternative certification routes for principals and superintendents are specified.

Educational Quality. Under the provisions of House Bill 72, students will be required to pass an exit level test to receive a high school diploma; they will also take basic skills tests in the first, third, fifth, seventh ninth, and eleventh grades. Students currently take tests in third, fifth, and ninth grades. Advance placement tests will allow students to skip an elementary grade or receive credit for a course beginning in grade 6. Schools are prohibited from granting "social promotions"; a grade average of at least 70 percent must be maintained to be advanced from one grade level to the next or to receive credit for a course.

Less than five unexcused absences are necessary to receive class credit. Students are required to attend school through the year in which their sixteenth birthday occurs, in contrast to the mandatory attendance requirement of age seventeen in prior law.

The State Board of Education, by rule, will limit extracurricular activities during the school day. A student who receives a failing grade in any academic class for a grading period will be suspended from extra-curricular activities for the next grading period. Announcements are limited to one time each day except for emergencies. Students are required to have a discipline management program, approved by the state board. The district must train teachers in discipline management and have a parent-training workshop for home reinforcement of academic skills; school board training is also required. The accreditation cycle has been reduced from a visit every five years to one every three years. School districts found deficient will experience action from the commissioner in four states: private notice, public notice, appointment of an agency to monitor and report on local activities, and appointment of a master to oversee operations who has final authority over the board and superintendent. Finally, the Texas Education Agency is authorized to develop a program to reduce the state drop-out rate to 5 percent from the current 32 percent.

A number of issues have been raised concerning the new legislative requirements (Bernal 1984). Particular issues are related to the requirement that disallows social promotions, in a system with multilevel grouping grades K–12, and to competency testing of professionals who have been in the field a number of years. With regard to the latter, those that score well on the test may not necessarily be "good" teachers/administrators. The possible legal implications that could arise from failure on a test resulting in dismissal of teachers/administrators holding lifetime certificates and continuing contracts has caused this provision to be dubbed the "lawyer's section." Concerning financing, the lack of state aid for school building construction and renovation, the continued operation of extremely small school districts, and the understatement of the true cost of education are issues of continuing interest.

IMPACT OF REFORM

Enactment of House Bill 72 in the Second Called Session of the Sixty-eighth Legislature authorized increased appropriations for the Foundation School Program from \$4.016 billion to \$5.598 billion in FY 1985, an increase of \$1.582 billion (39.4 percent) over FY 1985 appropriations under prior law (Senate Bill 179). This provided \$747,158,665 (19.1 percent) in new FSP state aid, for which a total of \$4.654 billion was appropriated under the reform measure. With regard to the state-local shared FSP costs, the local share, set at an aggregate 30 percent in FY 1985 compared to 12.7 percent under Senate Bill 179, increased \$1.096 billion, from \$510 million to \$1,606 billion (214 percent); this compared to an increase of \$486.3 million (13.87 percent) in the state share portion of the FSP. The upward adjustment of the local share cost of the FSP, distributed among school districts in direct proportion to taxable property wealthy districts, while releasing more state FSP aid to districts with the least property wealth.

Net Changes. Under the new school financing system, one-fourth (266) of the state's 1068 school districts received less total state aid in 1984-85 than they would have received in the absence of the initiative; the large majority (802) of Texas' local education agencies (LEAs) were provided with additional revenue.

In general, urban areas, i.e., Houston and Dallas and their surrounding suburban areas, had lower gains in total state aid than nonmetropolitan or rural districts. Districts with average daily attendance (ADA) under 100 tended to lose aid; all other ADA categories gained funds with LEAs ranging in size from 100 to 1,500 ADA recording the largest increases in per-pupil revenue. Wealthy districts sustained the largest average losses in per-pupil revenue ($196.50); poor districts gained the most aid per student ($692.70).

The reductions in aid by size and type of district may be accounted for, in part, by the high property wealth of those districts. Differences in funding for urban and suburban districts would have been more pronounced, however, without the mitigating effect of the Price Differential Index (PDI); this and the substantial growth in compensatory, bilingual and English as a Second Language funding, prevented Houston and Dallas from being substantial losers.

Price Differential Index (PDI). Major urban districts and their surrounding suburban LEA's tended to have higher PDIs than cities, nonmetropolitan, and rural areas. Generally, wealthy districts recorded higher indices than poor districts. According to the PDI Advisory Committee to the State Board of Education, the salary enrichment factor utilized in 1984-85 for the cost index calculations provided higher indices in areas of the state with large salary enrichment differentials—major metropolitan areas, urban areas, accompanying suburban areas, and wealthy West Texas areas—areas that had the property tax base to fund the increments. All data are based on Texas Education Agency impact model figures utilizing ADA estimates for September 1984. Actual reimbursement figures or district tax rates are not available.

During 1984-85, the average district PDI was 1.1895, which provided a mean adjustment to the basic allotment of $185 (14.25 percent). This resulted in an average adjusted basic allotment of $1,474. For 53 districts (5 percent) the index was the minimum—1.00; 53 districts (5 percent) were assigned the maximum value of 1.29. An additional 50 local education agencies (LEAs) qualified for the maximum index rate through statutory provision that Austin and Bryan Independent School Districts had secured in the bill. The districts at the bottom of the scale received no adjustment; the districts at the top were provided an additional $280 per student.

Equalization. In total state aid, the 71 poorest Texas districts—those with less than $83,000 per pupil in property values—received an additional $220.1 million or an average increase of 46.3 percent in per-pupil funds; the 176 wealthiest districts—with property wealth of $431,000 or more per-pupil—lost $21.6 million, a 20.5 percent decrease in per-pupil revenue. Under House Bill 72 the range in total state aid between the poorest and wealthiest districts increased by 164 percent. Those districts with the least per-pupil property wealth received an average $2,188 in per-pupil state aid, whereas wealthy districts received $757 per pupil—the poorest districts received 2.9 times more state aid per-pupil than the wealthiest districts. Under Senate Bill 179, the poorest districts would have received an additional $542 or 1.6 times more state aid per pupil than the wealthiest districts (see also McCulley 1984). Univariate measures of range, restricted range, and federal range ratio underscored the trend toward an increased range under House Bill 72 (Table 11-1). The rationale for an increased range providing more equalization, maintains that state aid is distributed in unequal amounts to allow the combination of state and local resources to be more equal (Texas Research League 1984a; Barnes 1984).

The largest percentage change in range and restricted range occurred under the local share portion of the FSP (65 percent and 124 percent respectively). This resulted from the increased dollar costs to wealthy districts at or above the ninety-fifth percentile, compared to lower dollar increases for poor districts, clustered at or below the fifth percentile. The reduction in the federal range ratio for local costs is accounted for by the proportionately larger percentage increase at the fifth versus the ninety-fifth percentile (Table 11–2).

The increased range, restricted range, and federal range ratio for state aid resulted from reductions in funds for districts at the lower percentiles, with increases at the higher percentiles. It might be noted that percentage increases in total state aid and the state share cost of the FSP were largely confined to those districts above the median, generally favoring poor districts; wealthy districts below the fifth

Table 11-1. Measures of the Variation in the Distribution of Foundation School Program Funds per Student, Fiscal Year 1985, under Prior Law, S.B. 179, and Current Law, H.B. 72.

	Total Local FSP Revenue:		*Total State FSP Revenue:*		*Total State Revenue:*	
Measure	*S.B. 179*	*H.B. 72*	*S.B. 179*	*H.B. 72*	*S.B. 179*	*H.B. 72*
Range	2362	3918	5019	6253	5019	6108
Restricted Range	866	1939	1442	2016	1396	2048
Federal Range Ratio	14.0	9.68	1.98	8.9	1.582	3.29
Mean	188	576	1210	1350	1322	1550

Table 11-2. Percentile Distributions of Local Foundation School Program Revenue, State Foundation School Program Revenue, and Total State Aid, per Student, Fiscal Year 1985, under Prior Law, S.B. 179, and Current Law, H.B. 72 (*dollars*).

	Total Local FSP Revenue:			Total State FSP Revenue:			Total State Revenue:		
Percentile	*S.B. 179*	*H.B. 72*	*% Change*	*S.B. 179*	*H.B. 72*	*% Change*	*S.B. 179*	*H.B. 72*	*% Change*
99th	1724.8	2980.2	73	2758.6	2899.4	5	2980.0	3207.0	8
95th	927.9	2139.4	131	2169.3	2242.0	3	2279.5	2670.9	17
75th	271.9	841.5	209	1505.6	1867.0	24	1602.3	2206.3	38
50th (median)	159.6	480.5	201	1331.4	1599.7	20	1464.5	1819.8	24
25th	105.3	317.3	201	1211.9	1273.8	(5)	1302.6	1392.0	6
5th	61.7	200.7	225	727.4	226.1	(69)	883.4	623.0	(29)
1st	38.5	127.0	229	479.5	215.1	(55)	483.3	358.3	(26)

percentile generally lost state aid. An intervening factor of district size however, distorts the relationship between wealth and state-local share costs, for districts at or above the ninety-ninth percentile. Eight of the ten districts at this percentile were above the state average in taxable property wealth, while all of these districts had less than 105 in ADA. This was altered somewhat in favor of property poor districts under the total state aid portion. The formula, however, may overadjust for districts under 135 ADA, or the LFA, calculated on aggregate versus per pupil property wealth to state total wealth may in some cases have resulted in small FLAs, thus larger state share costs, to districts with small geographic areas.

The achievement of school financing equalization, under any state schema, however, is ultimately determined by both the proportion of total educational revenues the program represents and by the ability of the program to provide an equal opportunity for quality education to all students regardless of the property wealth of the district in which they reside. Under House Bill 72, both considerations were addressed. By substantially increasing the local fund assignment, local enrichment revenue may be absorbed into the foundation program cost; by designing the program to cover more of the cost of education, a basic education may be available to all students, regardless of additional district spending beyond that amount. In addition, equity is enhanced through the special allotment portion of the FSP, which provided additional funds for high cost students, by a price differential index that offsets differences in costs of purchasing goods and services among districts; and by formulas that provide additional funds to adjust for diseconomies of scale incurred by small/sparse districts.

As in the past, however, local districts are not required to raise their local share of the Foundation School Program cost and they are permitted to raise their local revenues beyond the FSP level. If a district does not raise enough revenue to meet its local share, then its ability to provide a basic educational program may be substantially impaired. On the other hand, if the actions of local boards broadly increase local enrichment revenue, thus providing substantial unequalized aid, then equalization will be defeated. Given these considerations, the dual factors of financing equalization and unbridled local discretion appear incompatible under pure foundation program financing systems.

While the Texas educational legislation signals a comprehensive shift in educational policymaking from the local to the state level resulting in increased state centralization, particularly in the areas of pupil and teacher standards, curriculum, and oversight, state fiscal policy permits substantial local discretion. These consideration, notwithstanding, the reform of education will ultimately be determined by those who implement the new law—teachers, administrators, local boards—and the democratic pressures that elect them.

REFERENCES

Augenblick, John, and Kathleen Adams. 1979. *An Analysis of the Impact of Changes in the Funding of Elementary and Secondary Education in Texas: 1974-75 to 1977-78.* Austin: The Texas Legislative Commission on Public School Finance.

Barnes, Alan. 1984. "Address to Texas Research League Annual Meeting." Paper presented at the Annual Meeting of the Texas Research League, Austin, Tex., November 9.

Bernal, Jesse R. 1984. "A Report on Results of a Survey Conducted Among Superintendents in Senatorial Districts 20." Austin: Senator Truan's Office, Texas State Capitol.

Berne, Robert, and Leanna Stiefel. 1983. "Changes in School Finance Equity: A National Perspective," *Journal of Education Finance* 8, no. 4 (Spring): 419-435.

Boyd, Gerald M. 1984. "Drop out Rate is Up Sharply in U.S. Schools, Surveys Say." *The New York Times* (January 6): Section D, p. 13.

Bullock, Robert D. 1984. News Release, January 23. Austin: Comptroller of Public Accounts, Texas State Capitol.

Edgewood Independent School District v. Raymon L. Bynum, 250th District Court of Travis County, Texas, Cause no. 362, 156, May 23, 1984.

House Bill 246. 1981. 67th Texas Legislature. Texas State Capitol, Austin, Tex.

House Bill 1. 1984. 68th Legislature, 2d Called Session. Texas State Capitol, Austin, Tex.

House Bill 72. 1984. 68th Legislature, 2d Called Session. Texas State Capitol, Austin, Tex.

House Bill 122. 1984. 68th Legislature, 2nd Called Session, Texas State Capitol, Austin, Tex.

House Concurrent Resolution 275. 1983. 68th Texas Legislature, Regular Session. Texas State Capitol, Austin, Tex.

House Study Group. 1984a. *The June 1984 Special Session: A Preview*, no. 103 (July 16). Texas House of Representatives, Austin, Tex.

____. 1984b. *Raising State Taxes*. no. 102 (May 30). Texas House of Representatives, Austin, Tex.

____. 1984c. *Daily Floor Report* (June 15). The Texas House of Representatives, Austin, Tex.

____. 1984d. *Key Issues in the June 1984 Special Session*, no. 104 (July 16). Texas House of Representatives, Austin, Tex.

Killian, Michael G. 1984. "Local Control—The Vanishing Myth in Texas." *Phi Delta Kappan* 66, no. 3 (November): 192–195.

Legislative Budget Board. 1984. Fiscal Note on Conference Committee Report On House Bill No. 72, Second Called Session, 68th Legislature. Texas State Capitol, Austin, Tex.

Lindahl, Ronald A. 1984. "Equity in the Financing of Public Education: A Look at the State of Texas One Decade After Rodriguez v. San Antonio." Paper presented at the Annual Meeting of the American Education Finance Association, Orlando, Fla., March 15–17.

McCulley, Madeline D. 1984. *Analysis of Changes in Public School Finance Resulting from H.B. 72, Second Called Session, Sixty-Eighth Legislature*. Austin: Legislative Budget Board.

Mahoney, Leo G., Claude A. Talley, Jr., and Benjamin H. Alvarez. 1984. "Technological Change: Its Impact on Texas Public School Budgets." Paper presented at the Annual Conference of the American Education Finance Association, Orlando, Fla., March 15–17.

National Commission on Excellence in Education. 1983. *A Nation at Risk: The Imperative for Educational Reform*. Washington, D.C.: Department of Education.

Plaut, Thomas R., Susan M. Tully, and Patrick J. Henaff. 1984. *Texas Economic Outlook: Long-term Forecast Summary*. Austin: Bureau of Business Research, University of Texas.

Price Differential Advisory Committee. 1984. *Report of the Price Differential Index Advisory Committee to the State Board of Education*. Austin: Texas Education Agency.

San Antonio Independent School District v. Rodriguez, 411 U.S. 1 (1973).

Select Committee on Public Education. 1984. "Recommendations" (April 19). Texas State Capitol, Austin, Tex. Mimeo.

Senate Bill 621. 66th Legislature, Texas State Capitol, Austin, Tex.

Senate Bill 179. 1983. 68th Legislature, Texas State Capitol, Austin, Tex.

Senate Bill 1. 1984. 68th Legislature, 2d called session. Texas State Capitol, Austin, Tex.

Senate Bill 4. 1984. 68th Legislature, 2d called session. Texas State Capitol, Austin, Tex.

Sunderman, Harold and Reg Hinely. 1979. "Toward Equality of Educational Opportunity: A Case Study and Projection," *Journal of Education Finance* 4, no. 4 (Spring): 436–450.

Texas Constitution. Texas State Capitol, Austin, Tex.

Texas Education Code. See *Texas School Law Bulletin.* 1980.

Texas Legislative Council. 1984. "Bill History Report." Texas State Capitol, Austin, Tex.

Texas Past and Future: A Survey. 1981. Office of the Governor, Texas 2000 Commission, Austin, Tex.

Texas School Law Bulletin. 1980. Texas Education Agency, Austin, Tex.

Texas Research League. 1984a. "School Finance Equalization: How? Why?," *Analysis* 5, no. 5 (May): 1–8. Austin, Tex.

____. 1984b. *Bench Marks for 1984–85 School District Budgets in Texas.* Austin: Texas Research League.

Thomas, Stephen B. and Billy D. Walker. 1982. "Texas School Finance," *Journal of Education Finance* 8, no. 2 (Fall): 223–281.

Walker, Billy D. 1982. *The Basics of Texas Public School Finance*, 2d ed. Austin, Tex.: Texas Association of School Boards.

Walker, Billy D., and William Kirby. 1984. *The Basics of Texas Public School Finance*, 3rd ed. Austin: Texas Association of School Boards.

White, Mark W., Jr. 1983a. "Inaugural Address," January 16. Office of the Governor, Texas State Capitol, Austin, Tex.

____. 1983b. "Governor Mark White's Budget Message to 68th (sic) Texas Legislature," March 9. Office of the Governor, Texas State Capitol, Austin, Tex.

____. 1983c. "Governor Mark White's First Speech to the Legislature," January 27. Office of the Governor, Texas State Capitol, Austin, Tex.

____. 1984a. "Remarks by Governor Mark White at a Joint Press Conference," [Announcing the Second Called Special Session of the 68th Legislature] May 11. Office of the Governor, Texas State Capitaol, Austin, Tex.

____. 1984b. "Address by the Governor to the Texas Legislature," June 4. Office of the Governor, Texas State Capitol, Austin, Tex.

____. 1984c. "Address by the Governor to the Texas Legislature," June 4. Office of the Governor, Texas State Capital, Austin, Tex.

III STATE REFORM ISSUES
Implications for the Future

12 IMPLICATIONS FOR FUTURE REFORM
A State Perspective

Kent McGuire

INTRODUCTION

Without question, the last two years have been eventful for public elementary and secondary education. Beginning in 1983 with an outpouring of reports, books, and articles investigating the condition of the nation's schools, public education climbed to the top of the policy agenda in almost every state. Since that time, virtually every state has attempted to change and improve the quality of their education systems. Although differences exist as to specific strategies for reform, whether to extend the school year and/or day, increase graduation requirements, reform school curriculum, or to implement various programs to improve teacher quality, the states have, in a manner not seen since the school finance reforms of the 1970s, taken significant steps to influence the scope and character of elementary and secondary education.

The educational reform movement has stimulated the participation of new participants in the educational policymaking process, garnered support for tax increases to fund new programs, and raised public expectations for measurable improvements in student achievement. The specific impact of reform on school districts, teachers, and students cannot be determined at this time. It will be several years before the introduction of teacher quality provisions will have a demonstrable effect on either the current stock of teachers or the career choices of high school graduates and college students. It will also be some time before student test scores reflect the impact of reform. But it is important to develop ways of determining the short-term and intermediate impact of reform if meaningful improvements in education are to be realized.

The question is whether there is anything that one can say at this time about current state educational reform initiatives that might provide insights for the direction and focus of future state education policy. The focus and content of current reform efforts is well documented, and there are a number of questions that should be addressed regarding the anticipated and unanticipated consequences of these efforts. This in turn gives rise to a number of new issues, new challenges for policymakers, and new policy research questions. These issues need to be expanded on for consideration by state policymakers, and strategies must be developed for dealing with them. A number of issues related to equity and adequacy (traditional school financing issues) re-emerge in the context of excellence, and the implications of these issues for improving schools need to be clearly stated. The issues are: (1) the current focus of reform and the manner in which specific reform initiatives are likely to impact teachers and students; (2) the complexities associated with improving education and the challenges these complexities create for state policy makers; and (3) the problems related to equity and adequacy that undergird the current education reform scene, and they are the focus of this chapter.

THE FOCUS OF CURRENT REFORM EFFORTS

The current public debate about education reveals an almost unidimensional preoccupation with academic achievement and accountability. Reformers pointing to declining international competitiveness abroad and declining test scores at home call attention to the economic and cultural dangers of failing to improve the schools. As evidence, note that the blueprints for action that have emerged are quite similar from state to state. A recent summary of state education initiatives indicates that between 1980 and 1984, forty states and the District of Columbia have raised graduation requirements, primarily in math and science; ten states have lengthened the school day, seven have extended the school year; thirty-five have tightened teacher preparation and certification requirements; twenty-one have enacted some type of performance-based teacher incentive program fifteen of the career ladder/merit pay type; and thirty-three some type of academic enrichment program. Statewide testing and evaluation programs have been either established or expanded in thirty-six states (U.S. Department of Education 1984).

From a policy perspective, states are placing the greatest emphasis on regulations, either in the form of tests to be passed or educational procedures to be followed. This "gate-keeping" function is characteristic of a traditional state role in many public policy areas, and it is not surprising that it represents the dominant strategy for state educational reform. It is instructive to take a few examples of what is currently being proposed or implemented in the states and flesh out some of the likely impacts of these initiatives. The major impacts appear to be on teachers and students.

Impact on Teachers

A major focus of current reform efforts has centered on teachers. This makes intuitive sense, since teachers are central actors in the educational process. Of late, the push for improving teacher quality has focused on minimum standards, primarily through competency tests and tougher certification requirements and on the introduction of system incentives to attract and retain high quality people in the profession. Of these two types of policy instruments, the former (tests, new certification requirements, and other screening mechanisms) are most prevalent.

During 1984, eleven states initiated tests for new teachers and four states adopted tests for granting promotions or tenure (Siegel 1985). There is already some evidence available regarding the likely impact of these policies. Based on a series of interviews with teachers, Darling-Hammond and Wise (1985) argue that efforts to improve the quality of education with new standards for teachers may have certain unintended consequences. Most important is that such policies might make teaching more standardized and less attractive for both prospective and currently employed teachers. Policy instruments such as competency-based testing for certification or recertification are viewed with suspicion by teachers, primarily because they do not perceive them to be appropriate indicators of their ability to teach.

There is some question whether testing and certification policies will improve, over the long term, teaching. Studies have found no consistent relationship between scores on teacher competency tests and measures of teacher performance in classrooms (Andrews, Blackmon, and Mackey 1980; Ayers and Quail 1979).

Ekstrom and Goertz (1985) point out that state policies requiring prospective teachers who have already completed teacher-training programs to take competency tests fail to address the central issue—developing the talents associated with effective teaching. And, they find that the current focus on screening for competence impacts disproportionately on minority teachers.

What can be said about these policies is that they are likely to have a significant impact on the traits of persons in the teaching profession, both good and bad. Teachers will possess higher grade point averages and test scores, but they may also be less ethnically, racially, and socioeconomically diverse. This is because the focus of such policies is on rewarding the traits of individuals and only indirectly on the improvement of teaching. Moreover, states will need to watch carefully the impact of these policies on the supply of teachers since raising entrance requirements (usually considered a supply-constraining device) may be at odds with efforts also underway in a number of states (e.g., loan forgiveness programs) to attract new people into the teaching profession.

Regarding policies that focus more directly on improving teaching practice, the most popular approach is the career ladder program. Florida, Tennessee, and Texas have enacted statewide programs. Georgia will implement a career ladder program during the 1986–87 school year. Other states have provided grants to local school districts to develop their own programs (Arizona, Idaho, Pennsylvania, and Utah). Still other states are experimenting with the idea on a pilot basis. A typical career ladder plan has at least three steps (the plan in Tennessee has five), which include an apprentice or probationary teacher, one or more levels of professional teacher, and one or more levels of advanced teaching status (senior or master teacher).

There are several observations to be made regarding these programs with implications for subsequent state involvement in this area. The first is that many of these programs are very expensive and all the costs associated with their implementation may not yet be known. The Tennessee career ladder program had a FY 1985 price tag of $50 million (Odden and Dougherty 1984). California's Mentor

Teacher program cost $30.8 million during the 1983–84 school year (Massell and Kirst 1985). Texas has set aside $225 million for a career ladder program, the specifics of which remain to be determined (Odden and Dougherty 1984). In each of these states, the revenues to finance these programs derive entirely from state sources. The long-term success of such efforts will hinge in large measure on state capacity to fund them at adequate levels.

Second, there is considerable disagreement as to what constitutes movement from the lower to higher rungs on the ladder and over the percentages of teachers needed on various rungs for adequate staffing. In some states, teacher willingness to assume additional responsibility is the basis of promotion. In others, moving to higher status is based strictly on superior performance. Unfortunately, there is little research to guide policy in this area. Jung (1984) suggests that promotions be granted only when job performance has met or exceeded some predetermined standard. Yet it is possible that the teachers who score highest on performance evaluations are not the best for performing the duties associated with master or mentor teacher status. What this might mean for future policy in this area is that states should leave the determination of criteria for promotion up to local school districts so that such programs can be structured to meet local personnel and program needs. Unfortunately, some of the state programs that have emerged are rather specific in both the number of rungs on the ladder and the process by which individual teachers move up the ladder.

Third, such programs imply changing the organization of schools if they are to represent significant and meaningful departures from current practice (Bird 1984). Unlike policies focusing on the traits of teachers (e.g., new certification requirements), which can be implemented within the existing structure, reorganizing schools to deal with differentiated pay and responsibilities among teachers can present thorny implementation problems. Future state policy regarding career ladder programs and other policy interventions directed toward improving teacher performance will need to be sensitive to these complexities. Money alone will not solve them. Nor will uniform state implementation policies across school districts. The strategy that may prove most successful, that of leaving the specifics of implementation up to the districts (while providing technical assistance and other resources), is the strategy state policymakers often tend to have difficulty with. In the interest of accountability, they tend to favor prescribing the details over delegating authority and training to local administrators.

Impact on Students

A number of reform measures can be expected to have an immediate impact on students. The emphasis in most state reform efforts appears to be on a return to more traditional academic curricula, with an added measure of computer literacy, more standardized tests, additional course requirements, firm criteria for grade to grade promotion, and higher graduation standards.

During 1984, thirty-four states report having increased high school graduation requirements (Seigel 1985). There are several issues raised by this reform strategy. First, it is important to note that very few states have provided extra funding to implement these additional requirements (Odden and Dougherty 1984). Apparently, policy makers assume that such courses should be funded out of new local revenues or that trades should be made between these courses and others now viewed as marginal. Preliminary evidence suggests that trades between the basics and electives are being made. Seigel (1985) reports on a survey of local school board members asked about the impact of tougher curriculum standards. Twelve percent of those responding to the survey reported cutbacks in music, art, industrial arts, health, and physical education courses over the past two years.

The underlying issue concerns the role of the comprehensive high school and whether this institution can continue to address the needs of students in an increasingly complex world. On the one hand, policies pushing for a return to the basics have emerged with particularly emphasis on math and science. These subjects are linked to developments in the economy. At the same time however, several governors are now advocating public school voucher programs, the point of which is to provide greater choice for individual students.

In the future, it seems clear that more attention will need to be focused on the identification and articulation of local or community needs and strategies identified for satisfying those that the comprehensive high school cannot adequately address. Forcing students to make choices they are not comfortable with, either by requiring more of certain courses for graduation or by removing certain courses from the curriculum may push more students out of the system.

Indeed, another issue is the impact of these tougher requirements on "at-risk" student populations. While it is not generally believed that tougher curriculum and increased high school graduation requirements will create problems for average and above average students, there is some concern that pressure will be placed on marginal students, possibly forcing greater numbers of these students to drop-out (Howe 1984). And it is with respect to these marginal students that the current reform pays the least attention.

A recent report by the National Coalition of Advocates for Students (NCAS) contains some alarming statistics concerning "at-risk" student populations.

- Tracking and sorting policies have a resegregating effect resulting in predominantly white upper level courses and predominantly black and hispanic lower level courses in which students experience lower self-esteem, more misconduct, and higher rates of dropping out.
- The national drop-out rate for Blacks is nearly twice that of Whites and in urban high schools, drop-out rates have reached 80 percent for Puerto Rican students and 85 percent for Native American students.
- Only one-third of the 2.7 million students with limited English receive any special help. That figure falls to 10 percent for Hispanic students.
- Only half of the almost 10 million students eligible for federal compensatory education services actually receive these services.
- Males and females have equal achievement in most major subjects at age nine, but at age thirteen females begin a decline that by age seventeen places them behind males in math, reading, science and social studies.
- The average child from a bottom quarter income family receives four fewer years of education than the child from a top quarter income family (NCAS 1985).

Unfortunately, there is little contained in most state reform strategies directed toward the conditions and trends outlined above. Moreover, it is not at all clear that simply raising standards will address these problems. In fact, they might exacerbate them. Preschool education, day care for young children, and strategies to make school more relevant and to motivate students have not received much attention in current proposals to improve schools. But the statistics suggest that these are issues that states will have to address in the very near term.

How these issues are addressed is another challenge for future state education policy. It may be that the traditional "programmatic" responses will not work. At a minimum, the current political climate suggests that they will not be vigorously pursued. More likely are "nonprogram" responses involving tax incentives and other strategies. One advantage to this approach is the possibility for specialized educational experiences tailored to specific needs. But even here, the state role will need to be carefully considered.

First, states will need to know what the various problems are for at-risk populations.

Second, the state should play a role in educating parents and students as to what choices are available to address their needs and the trade-offs associated with making particular choices.

Third, the state may want to perform its traditional gate-keeping function for those who provide services to at-risk populations, particularly for third-party service providers.

Finally, the increased emphasis on student testing should be monitored closely. On the one hand, greater attention to testing and assessment is a positive development. States and school districts will have more and better information about how well the schools are doing. At the same time however, teachers often view standardized tests as altering the curriculum (Darling-Hammond & Wise 1985: 331). They begin to emphasize what they know will be tested, and what is not tested may not be taught. The incentives to do this are stronger when student performance is used as a measure of teacher performance. The challenge for states will be to maximize the positive aspects of testing and assesment while minimizing the negative or unintended outcomes.

Future state policy related to testing in assessment should move in at least two directions. First, states should be clear about the objectives of their testing programs. Indication that such programs are directed toward minimal levels of achievement, not the maximum, is important. It is also important to stress the limited scope of such programs. The fact that only math and reading might be assessed does not mean that only math and reading are important.

Second, attempts should be made to link test results to curriculum development, staff development, planning, evaluation, and technical assistance. Test results have a potential beyond an indication of how well schools are doing. They can be used to identify gaps in the curriculum, monitor the impact of reform on different student populations, and target assistance to at-risk students and school districts.

SIMPLE SOLUTIONS TO COMPLEX PROBLEMS

As the preceding discussion indicates, the business of improving the quality of education is fraught with complexities and unintended side-effects. The focus of most reform efforts at the state level has been additive. The message has been to provide more math and science, to increase graduation requirements for students and certification requirements for teachers. There is a logical explanation for the focus and content of current reform initiatives and a case can probably be made for some of this, but we know that many improvements in education are predicated on finding solutions to relatively complex problems and devising policies that will work in a variety of contexts. The problems identified in the national and state reports may not have solutions as straightforward as those contained in most state reform initiatives.

There are several reasons for this. First, understanding the range of problems associated with improving the quality of education is difficult. They show up at different points in the system (district, building, and classroom). Some are caused by or related to internal factors (e.g., organization and management) and others by external factors (e.g., demographics, resource constraints, etc.). Some problems are within the direct control of policymakers while others are not.

Second, the connections between the many goals of educational reform and the policy instruments states have selected to achieve these goals are not straightforward. Evaluations of federal educational interventions such as Head Start clarify this point. The dominant paradigm associated with this effort was that a given strategy or model could be identified that would lead to measurable gains in student achievement. Once specified, and given adequate planning, training, and resources, this model could be applied in a variety of contexts. But as subsequent evaluations illustrated, no consistent patterns of success emerged either by type of intervention or by educational setting (Bermn 1981). Evaluators found that many factors unique to a given school or district combined to facilitate or impede successful implementation of the program. What this implies for state educational policy is that a variety of different and seemingly unrelated policies may need to be combined in the quest for excellence. It will not be enough to know *what* strategies work. State policymakers will need to learn more about *how* they work in different contexts.

Third, there are examples where state policy-instruments are only marginally related to the stated objectives of reform. A good example is improving the quality of classroom teaching. Here, a stated objective is to improve the on-the-job performance of classroom teachers. The policy-instruments employed in a number of states are paper and pencil tests of teacher competency and/or new certification requirements. No research to date shows a consistent relationship between either test scores on such exams or training and experience and classroom performance. So while the use of examinations, certification, or recertification may raise the status of teaching in the public's eye, which is itself a legitimate reform objective, such policies will not provide insights into how to improve the quality of teaching classrooms.

In conclusion, there is a gap between what is currently known about school effectiveness and about implementation and change in education and the content/structure of many state reform initiatives. It is true that new and important linkages are emerging between state educational policy/practice and the research on effective teaching and effective schools. McLaughlin (1983) catalogs a number of state initiatives directed at local educational improvement. For the most part, these efforts precede the reform movement. Examples include Minnesota's Essential Learner Outcomes (SELOs) initiative, which combines curriculum development, testing, technical assistance, evaluation, and staff development into a single program, or New Jersey's quality improvement initiative, which links local planning processes to the state's minimum basic skills program. Odden and Dougherty (1982) have identified seven general state strategies for improving schools, which include training, program review, dissemination, and technical assistance. But these phenomena have gone almost unnoticed by governors, state legislators, and the business community—the principle participants in this most recent round of educational reform.

The issue is how to close this gap. One place policymakers can look is to the research on effective schools and effective teaching. For example, the school effectiveness literature suggests that programmatic and/or structural changes likely to improve academic achievement are uniquely local in character. The characteristics of effective schools are found in the attitudes and behaviors of their staffs. All students, regardless of family background, are seen as being capable of academic achievement. School culture, defined to include the mix of norms, values, and roles existing within the school, is said to strongly affect student performance. Reviews of this growing literature are numerous (see Cohen 1983; Purkey and Smith 1983; Rowan, Bossert, and Dwyer 1983; Madaus, Airasian, and Kellaghan 1980). For a review of state programs of school improvement, see Odden and Dougherty (1982).

Recent attempts have been made to flesh out the implications of this research for policy. The suggestions Purkey and Smith (1985) provide for school districts have some value for states as well. Resources can be made available for planning processes, evaluation and staff development. Incentive structures for teachers and administrators can be changed to encourage participation in in-service and staff development programs linked to identified district and school problems/needs.

Yet it would be naive to assume that concrete solutions to all the complexities of improving schools can be found in this research. As Fullan (1985) suggests, there is more that needs to be learned about the process of change and of how to transplant the conditions leading to improvement in some educational settings to others. Moreover, for what has essentially been described as a local process of improvement, strategies for state involvement need to be developed that both satisfy the desire for state control over educational affairs without creating impediments to effective local action and innovation. By implication, this means that policymakers may find themselves in the uncomfortable position of having to leave the details of educational improvement to educators. States may have an important role to play in setting standards and in providing leadership for sustained attention to educational problems. But state policymakers may also have to accept the fact that solutions to current weaknesses may not look the same in every school district.

SCHOOL FINANCE AND SCHOOL IMPROVEMENT

An assessment of the anticipated and unanticipated consequences of education reform would be incomplete without paying some attention to traditional school finance issues that emerge in the context of excellence. With a few notable exceptions, states continue to address school finance issues separately from issues of school improvement. The funding associated with recent reform initiatives has generally been allocated independently of school finance formulas. Yet there are a number of reasons why school finance and school improvement may converge in the near term.

First, failure to link school improvement to school finance may over the long run jeopardize sustained support for these initiatives. As Augenblick (1984) points out, legislators will be looking for measurable results from the funds they are providing for improvement. If these results are not available within a politically acceptable time frame, resources for improvement may disappear.

Second, some states have tied the funding of reform initiatives to newly earmarked sources of revenue. The long-term availability of these revenues depends on the performance of state and local economies. A return to the economic climate of the first two and one-half years of this decade could leave reform initiatives without a fiscal base.

Finally, it is clear that school districts begin the process of improvement from very different points of departure. Failure to address the resource disparities that lie beneath the push for excellence will result in at the very least an uneven distribution of the benefits associated with reform.

This is not to suggest that there is no relationship between school financing and the day-to-day operation of schools. A review of current school financing systems reveals a number of these relationships. It is very common to find features such as training and experience factors for teachers included in school financing systems, either as a means of compensating school districts for the higher costs of more experienced teaching staffs or as a direct incentive for districts to hire more highly trained and experienced teachers. It is the practice in 29 states to adjust guaranteed revenues by grade level differences (McGuire and Dougherty 1983). The objective is to compensate districts for the higher costs of instruction at the secondary level and to provide incentives to reduce class size (and focus more resources) in the early grades. These policies focus on the inputs to the system. What has been learned recently, however, is that while inputs are important, how they are combined and used in the educational process are also important. It is in this sense that the linkages between school financing and school improvement are weakest.

Some of the developments stemming from educational reform have the potential to strengthen these new and important linkages. Career ladder programs, for example, built upon the early focus on training and experience of teachers by emphasizing the need to put these resources to work in new and different ways. Direct incentives are provided for improved teacher performance. State funding to support such efforts create, in essence, a new linkage between school financing and school improvement. However, the way these programs are designed and funded will bear significantly on their long-term success. While implementing these programs, states would do well to focus not only on rewarding teachers for superior performance but also on the teacher salary equity problems (and the associated staffing problems these create) that may be present at the time. The consequences of ignoring this could be an unfair distribution of master teachers across school districts. The state will have in effect created a new equity problem at cross-purposes with the goal of improving quality.

A similar caution is warranted with respect to state mandates to increase course offerings at the secondary level and/or increasing graduation requirements. In this case there has been little or no attempt by states to link these new standards to school finance. The assumption has been that these are either low cost or no cost items and that if costs are involved that they can be funded out of local resources. It will be important to know the cost implications of such requirements. Where they are significant and where no support is available to assist school districts in meeting these requirements, states may force some school districts into difficult trade-offs between these new state standards and other important education objectives.

In short, school financing considerations must go hand in hand with school improvement if reform goals are to be met in a majority of school districts. This means that states must continue to "fine-tune" their basic aid systems to make them more sensitive to the differing needs and circumstances of school districts. Efforts to reduce gross resources disparities and tax burdens among school districts must continue. These disparities translate into differences in program offerings; instructional materials and equipment; class size; teacher salaries; and availability of counselors, aides, and other special personnel. And, they limit the capacity of school districts to embrace reform initiatives.

States will also need to pay attention to new financing issues raised by educational reform. It will be important to monitor the implementation of specific reform initiatives in different types of school district (e.g., high wealth versus low wealth, high spending versus low spending, urban versus rural) to learn about the factors that contribute to or detract from successful implementation. Over time it will be important to monitor the true costs of specific initiatives to be sure that resources are allocated in relation to actual program needs. This information should be combined with information on the effectiveness of specific initiatives so that resources can be reconfigured to produce desired results more efficiently. Finally, it may be that intradistrict resource allocation issues will become as important as the reforms of interdistrict allocation issues, which increasingly have to do with matters of time, materials, content, and teacher variables (Kirst 1983: 13). Linking school financing to school improvement by way of the micro issues of curriculum and instruction and of school-site budgeting may indeed signal a "new era" for school financing.

REFERENCES

Augenblick, J. 1984. "The States and School Finance: Looking Back and Looking Ahead," *Phi Delta Kappan* 66, no. 3 (November): 196–201.

Ayers, J.B., and G.S. Quails. 1979. "Concurrent and Predictive Validity of the National Teacher Examination," *Journal of Education Research* 73, no. 2 (November-December): 96–92.

Andrews, J.W., C.R. Blackmon, and J.A. Mackey. 1980. "Preservice Performance and the National Teacher Examinations," *Phi Delta Kappan* 61, no. 5 (January): 358–359.

Berman, P. 1981. "Educational Change: An Implementation Paradigm." In *Improving Schools*, edited by Rolf Lehming and Michael Kane, pp. 253–286. Beverly Hills: Sage Publications.

Bird, T. 1984. *School Organization and the Rewards of Teaching.* Denver: Education Commission of the States.

Cohen, M. 1981. "Effective Schools Research: Toward Useful Interpretations." A paper prepared for the 1981 Summer Instructional Leadership Conference of the American Association of School Administrators.

Darling-Hammond, L., and A. Wise. 1985. "Beyond Standardization: State Standards and School Improvement," *The Elementary School Journal* 85, no. 3 (January): 315–336.

Fullan, M. 1985. "Change Processes and Strategies at the Local Level," *The Elementary School Journal* 85, no. 3 (January): 391–421.

Howe, H. 1984. "Giving Equity a Chance in the Excellence Game," *NASSP Bulletin* 69, no. 473 (September): 75–90.

Jung, S.M. 1984. *Guidelines for Evaluating Teacher Incentive Systems.* Denver: Education Commission of the States.

Kirst, M.W. 1983. "A New School Finance For a New Era of Fiscal Constraint." In *School Finance and School Improvement Linkages for the 1980s*, edited by Allan Odden and L. Dean Webb, pp. 1–16. Cambridge, Mass.: Ballinger Publishing Co.

Madaus, G.E., P.N. Airasian, and T. Kelloghan. 1980. *School Effectiveness: A Reassessment of the Evidence.* New York: McGraw-Hill.

Massell, D., and M. Kirst. 1985. *State Policymaking for Educational Excellence: School Reform in California.* Palo Alto: Stanford University, School of Education.

McGuire, K., and M.V. Dougherty. 1983. *School Finance at a Glance: 1983–84.* Denver: Education Commission of the States, Education Finance Center.

McLaughlin, M.W. 1983. "State Involvement in Local Educational Quality." In *School Finance and School Improvement Linkages for the 1980s*, edited by Allan Odden and L. Dean Webb, pp. 51–68. Cambridge, Mass.: Ballinger Publishing Co.

National Coalition of Advocates for Students. 1985. *Barriers to Excellence: Our Children at Risk.* Boston: National Coalition of Advocates For Children.

Odden, A., and E. Odden. 1984. "Education Reform, School Improvement and State Policy," *Educational Leadership* 42, no. 2 (October): 13–19.

Odden, A., and M.V. Dougherty. 1984. *Education Finance in the States: 1984.* Denver: Education Commission of the States.

Purkey, S.C., and M.S. Smith. 1985. "School Reform: The District Policy Implications of the Effective Schools Literature," *The Elementary School Journal* 85, no. 3 (January): 353–390.

Rowan, B., S.T. Bossert, and D.C. Dwyer. 1983. "Research on Effective Schools: A Cautionary Note," *Educational Researcher* 12, no. 4 (April): 24–31.

Siegal, Peggy M. 1985. "School Reform Momentum Continues," *State Legislatures* 11, no. 3 (March): 11–15.

U.S. Department of Education. 1984. *State Profiles Update: 1984.* Washington, D.C.: U.S. Department of Education.

13 AN EQUITY PERSPECTIVE ON EDUCATIONAL REFORM

David C. Long

INTRODUCTION

The recent flood of suggestions for improving the nation's schools has generated new movement for educational reform. Some suggestions for reform emanate from research on effective schools and classrooms. Others stem from broader critiques of the failings of schools to adequately prepare students for a rapidly changing high technology future and of the declining academic caliber of the teaching profession.

Although some educational researchers have argued that educational reform can be cost-free (Walberg 1983 and Somers 1980), most states implementing these recommendations recognize that systemic educational reform requires additional funding, often in substantial amounts. For example, to make teachers' salaries competitive with other occupations requiring a similar level of education is likely to be costly. During the last several years, this recognition of the costs of educational reform has led a number of states to increase their appropriations for public education after several years of relative decline (Odden 1984).

Earlier chapters describe recent state education reform initiatives and their funding. This chapter considers some of the equity issues that popular education reform initiatives raise. Reform proposals considered here include raising teachers' salaries, extending instructional time, increasing writing assignments, expanding course offerings, and promotion and graduation requirements.

Since little actual data are available on the effects of recent reform initiatives on the equity of school financing systems, this chapter will be more conceptual than empirical. Recent studies of growing inequities in school financing systems in a number of states, however, form a backdrop to the issues discussed (Goertz and Hickrod 1983a and 1983b). In many states, the bleak economic climate during the late 1970s and early 1980s resulted in a reduced state share of educational funding and increased funding from the widely disparate tax bases of school districts (Odden 1984: 3). In states such as Illinois (Hickrod, Chaudhari, and Hubbard 1983), this was accompanied by statutory changes that made state aid systems less equalizing. In a number of states, the unfortunate result has been an increase in inequality among school districts in per pupil funding.

Many states are allocating, or proposing to allocate, additional funds to school districts to implement educational reform. Odden (1984) found that some states have addressed equity and excellence concerns simultaneously. What effect will increased state funding for educational reform have on the equitability of state-wide school financing systems? Will it mitigate, exacerbate, or leave untouched the effects of current expenditure disparities among school districts in a state? If fiscal disparities are ignored in the distribution of state funds for educational reform, they will remain wide and may continue to grow in spite of new infusions of state aid.

How will state funds appropriated for educational reform affect inequalities among school districts in educational programs, services, and facilities that result from unequal funding? Will state educational reform initiatives reduce inequalities in educational opportunities? The literature on school financing contains little information on the extent to which unequal funding of school districts produces inequalities in educational opportunities. The best information on educational resource disparities has been developed for cases challenging school financing systems as unconstitutionally unequal or inadequate. In these suits, many courts, even those holding school financing systems constitutional, have concluded that unequal funding resulted in unequal staffing, programs, services, facilities, materials, and supplies (Long and McMullen 1982). This chapter draws heavily upon the facts in these cases.

Reports such as *A Nation at Risk* (1983), which have inspired much of the current educational reform activity, largely ignore fiscal and educational inequalities among school districts. They also largely disregard the fact that poor and minority children, who tend to be far more at risk than other children, tend to be concentrated in fiscally distressed central city and poor rural school districts. The major focus of the current movement for educational reform is on "excellence" rather than on equity and access. An irony of this movement is that it had its genesis in research that grew from a concern for low-income and minority children (Odden 1983: xvii and Odden 1984: vi).

One issue discussed in this chapter is whether these fiscal and educational disparities prevent poor low-spending districts from implementing educational reform to the same extent as wealthy high-spending districts. A further issue considered here is whether children who are at academic risk will benefit from reforms that require them to pass tests or take additional courses for promotion or graduation.

EQUITY ISSUES RAISED BY EDUCATION REFORM PROPOSALS

Raising Teachers' Salaries

Recent reports have called for increased teachers salaries (National Commission on Excellence 1983). Salaries for educators have not kept pace with inflation (Corcoran and Hansen 1983), and there has been a relative decline in teachers' salaries (Doyle and Hartle 1984: 21). As a result, teachers are increasingly drawn from a pool of the least academically able college students (National Commission on Excellence 1983: 21); Ward 1983: 164). This is occurring at a time when there is a shortage of teachers in subjects such as math, science, and vocational education and where the competition for employees with the private sector is particularly intense (Doyle and Hartle 1984: 55–57). The predicted increase in public school enrollments means that the problem of attracting and retaining well-qualified teachers is likely to grow (Schlechty and Vance 1983). Since the assumption that there is an intelligent, well-trained, and adaptable cadre of teachers and administrators is the keystone of most educational reform proposals, the decline in the number and intellectual caliber of teachers looms as a major problem states must address.

To make teaching more competitive with other careers, substantial increases in teachers' salaries have been proposed (U.S. Department of Education 1984). Master teacher and career ladder plans are also being implemented to create additional incentives for attracting and retaining good teachers.

Proposals to increase teachers' salaries are inherently costly. Staff salaries and benefits make up the largest share of school district budgets. In most states these costs are the staple of state equalization programs. Consequently, state proposals to mandate, and to provide aid for, increased teachers' salaries are educational reforms that can have great impact on the equity issues: First, is state aid for salary increases equitably distributed among school districts; Second, do the ripple effects of state salary mandates mitigate or exacerbate expenditure and educational disparities among school districts?

The threshhold issue for a state that proposes to assist school districts to increase teachers' salaries is whether to provide this aid within or outside its existing equalization formula. Odden (1984) reports that some states such as Arkansas, which accompanied educational reform with school financing reform, provide aid for increased teacher compensation within the equalization formula. However, others such as California and New Jersey have adopted or proposed nonequalizing categorical grants to fund the full cost of raising entry level salaries from their current level in each district up to the state mandates level of $18,000 per year (Odden 1984; Bridgman 1985). States have also adopted or proposed financing plans obligating the state to pay the full incremental cost in each school district of implementing other educational reforms. For example, Odden (1984) found that all of the recent merit pay and career ladder proposals he analyzed provided state aid for full incremental funding.

State funding of the full cost of increasing the entry level salary in each school district to the state mandated level is likely to have some equalizing effects. In most states, poorer low-spending districts tend to pay lower salaries at each rung of the salary ladder than do more affluent high-spending districts. Poor districts with low entry-level salaries will receive more state aid per entering teacher than will high-spending districts, whose entry-level salaries are closer to the new state mandate.

In other common situations, however, this method of funding acts to disequalize. Wealthy districts that have chosen to make little tax effort for education and to keep salaries low receive a state aid windfall, allowing them to remain low-tax enclaves. Other wealthy districts may be so attractive to teachers that they may not have had to pay high entry-level salaries (even when salaries for experienced teachers are high) and may have chosen to use their additional local resources to provide more favorable staff ratios than poorer districts.

These nonneedy wealthy districts would receive substantial benefits under this plan. A wealthy district that keeps entry level salaries low and employs more staff per 1000 students receives a double windfall. It not only receives more aid per teacher to close the gap between its low entry-level salaries and the state minimum, but it also receives aid for more teachers than does a poorer district that has a less favorable staff ratio.

Some poor low-spending districts may have chosen to compete for staff with their more affluent neighboring districts by offering a high entry level salary, which they pay for by enlarging classes and reducing programs and services. Under this plan, such poor districts receive little or no aid. Poor districts with few entry level teachers also receive little benefit under this plan. At best, full state funding of the cost in every district to increase entry-level teachers' salaries to a common level is likely to lead to capricious and wasteful allocations of state funds.

Plans such as those adopted in California and proposed in New Jersey only mandate and provide state aid for increasing *entry level* salaries of teachers. However, any increase in entry level salaries is sure to have a substantial ripple effect, pushing up the salaries of more experienced teachers, who will demand that existing salary differentials be maintained. Under these plans the fiscal burdens of the ripple effect are borne by local districts. These plans allow states to push all teachers' salaries up at a relatively small short run cost to the state treasury. However, by pushing down onto local school districts the costs of paying for the ripple effect of higher salary costs of more experienced teachers, these plans are likely to exacerbate fiscal and educational inequalities among school districts within the state.

The ripple effect of state mandates to increase entry level salaries is likely to be greater for poor school districts since their salaries, across the board, are often lower than those of better endowed districts. If entry level salaries increase the most in poor school districts, these districts will be under the great pressure to grant substantial salary increases to more experienced teachers. In contrast, more affluent districts, whose higher entry level salaries are least affected by the state mandate, will be under less pressure to increase substantially the salaries of experienced teachers. As a result, those districts least fiscally able to increase salaries from general revenues will be under the greatest pressure to do so.

The disequalizing effects of these unequal pressures will probably be less in states which have state aid systems that substantially equalize the effects of district wealth differences. In a highly equalized system the increased costs to poor districts of increasing teachers' salaries across the board would eventually be paid for within the state equalization formula. However, many state systems, which purport to be highly equalizing for district wealth differences, provide no current aid for a district's annual budget increases. This results from calculating state aid on a district's prior year expenditures—the prior year reimbursement system. In a prior year reimbursement system, all of this year's increased expenditure for higher teachers' salaries (except increases paid by the state for entry level teachers) must be funded from the unequal tax bases of school districts. In poorer districts this means higher taxes in the current year or reductions in other expenditures, irrespective of how equalizing the subsequent state reimbursement will be. Of course, in state aid systems where later reimbursements are not substantially equalizing, the unequal impact on rich and poor districts of these ripple effects is even greater.

State mandates and state aid to increase the salaries of entry level teachers are intended to make teaching a more attractive profession. The failure to address the adverse fiscal effects of these mandates on poorer school districts could substantially interfere with accomplishing this objective. The disproportionate fiscal burdens on poorer districts presents them with the dilemma of having to decide between reducing salary differentials between entry-level and experienced teachers, reducing the number of teachers, reducing programs and services, increasing class sizes or raising taxes, and risking a taxpayer revolt. For poor districts the outcome of this dilemma could be a reduction in staff morale and more difficult working conditions, the exact opposite of the intended objective of education reform.

Improving Working Conditions for Teachers

Recent reports indicate that teachers are frequently unhappy with working conditions and that such conditions deter the best students from entering teaching and causing some of the better teachers to leaving the profession (National Commission on Excellence 1983). Research also indicates that intrinsic rewards for teachers may be as important as salary (Doyle and Hartle 1984: 22). Although recent critiques of working conditions in the schools have largely focused on the professional status and role of teachers—for example, interpersonal relations, lack of career ladders, and the isolation of the classroom environment—this criticism applies equally to the physical condition and lack of resources in many schools, particularly those in central cities and poor rural areas. It may be difficult to measure the precise affects on student achievement of deteriorated school buildings, large classes, few support services, and inadequate instructional materials. However, these certainly affect the ability of a school district to attract and retain staff (Murnane 1983). Where the students in the district are perceived as difficult to educate, the problem is compounded.

Evidence in school finance cases has shown that the conditions under which teachers work in central cities such as Baltimore and New York City and in poor rural areas such as those in West Virginia and New Hampshire are substantially different than in more affluent school districts in those states. This is not simply because central city and rural poor children have greater learning problems but also because of old, deteriorated school facilities and fewer instructional resources and support services. A state study of school facilities in New Jersey found that it would cost over $3 billion to bring schools in the state up to contemporary standards, in large part because of the deteriorated condition of school facilities in poor urban centers such as Newark and Camden. These hard-pressed urban and rural districts tend to have fewer applicants per staff vacancy and to draw from a narrower applicant pool. They also tend to have a high turnover of inexperienced teachers and to retain teachers who have few other options.

Recent reports on educational reform deal with the issue of attracting more qualified persons into teaching as if this were a single problem. They largely ignore that school districts that are perceived as having more adverse working conditions have greater difficulty attracting and retaining the most qualified applicants than other districts such as those in the suburbs, in which working conditions are seen as more positive. They also ignore that these working conditions are more adverse, in part, because facilities are deteriorated and educational resources are inadequate. Even if teachers' salaries were substantially increased these disadvantages in attracting and retaining staff would remain.

Increasing Instructional Time

Many states have proposed or sought to implement reforms that increase instructional time. Some states have specified instructional time requirements within the existing school day and year; however, a number of states have proposed to increase the length of the school day and the school year (U.S. Department of Education 1984). These proposals to lengthen the school day and school year typically require increased expenditures since teachers and other school staff must be paid for additional hours of work (Odden 1984: 14). The two major equity issues that these proposals raise relate to the extent of state aid and the manner of its distribution to school districts.

The failure of a state aid system to take into account the full incremental costs of increasing the school calendar places poor districts on the horns of a fiscal dilemma similar to that discussed in connection with state salary mandates. To pay for the unaided portion of this reform a district must reduce other services or raise taxes.

Arkansas and Texas distributed additional funds to lengthen the school day and year within new equalization formulas. However, other states that have implemented school reform separate from general school finance issues have tended to provide state aid to lengthen teacher contracts through categorical grants (Odden 1984: 14). In several states, only school districts that voluntarily agree to lengthen the school day or year receive this state aid, which is distributed as a categorical grant. Because these categorical programs appear small in comparison to general equalizing aid, their disequalizing effects will probably be small. They could have, however, a substantial adverse effect on equalization formulas if they become precedent for funding teachers' salaries outside of equalization mechanisms.

The California state aid program to increase the school day or year bears watching for an additional reason: It also provides aid to school districts that already have a longer school day or year. This raises an equity issue because the most fiscally hard-pressed California districts reportedly shortened their school days to save money (Kirst 1983: 9). If higher spending districts generally have longer school days than lower spending districts, this aid program will largely maintain existing resource inequalities. Lower spending districts must use the funds to lengthen their shortened school days, and higher spending districts that never shortened their school days will have extra funds for educational programs and services.

This illustrates the danger of creating even small unequalized funding programs for educational reform. Political considerations may require that funds be widely distributed beyond the specific need for them, and the small amount of funds involved may not appear to warrant great concern about the disequalizing effects of the distribution. These programs, however, when piled on top of one another over time, can largely destroy a state aid equalization system. This has happened in the past. In Arkansas, many years of flat grants to fund annual increases in teachers' salaries, coupled with hold harmless guarantees, rendered ineffective the equalization mechanism in the Arkansas school finance system, which was held unconstitutional by the Arkansas courts (*DuPree v. Alma School District No. 30* (1983)).

Reforming Instructional and Administrative Practices

Research on effective schools suggests that certain instructional and administrative practices can lead to increased educational effectiveness. These include well-organized and prepared lessons, increased homework and writing assignments that are evaluated by teachers, orderly classrooms, use of new technologies such as computers, and principals that act as instructional leaders (Cohen 1983). Implementation of such reforms often focuses on additional staff training, which is acknowledged to require additional resources (Odden 1984: 18). However, there has been little recognition that resource inequities among school districts will interfere with implementation of these reforms. More affluent higher spending districts may already have put these instructional and administrative practices in place or, because of the flexibility provided by additional resources, may be able to implement change with fewer problems. Poorer, lower spending districts often require additional resources to implement them. This is particularly the case when resource poor districts have large concentrations of children with educational problems. Ignoring these differences will lead to inequalities in implementation of these reforms. States, however, have not provided substantial additional funds for implementation of these school improvement reforms; consequently, this discussion will focus on the effects of overlaying these reforms on school districts having unequal resources.

Reform proposals have called for better organized and prepared lessons and increased homework and writing assignments. These require that teachers spend additional time preparing for class and evaluating student work. This is time that cannot come from periods of active classroom work, since that time is used for interaction with students. Nor can it come from times when teachers are expected to perform other duties such as monitoring lunch rooms or supervising extracurricular activities. It must be done during preparation periods made available to teachers during the school day or during evenings and weekends.

Preparation periods require that other staff be available to relieve the classroom teacher. Even when preparation time is equal, the quality of preparation time can be substantially different depending on the resources available in a school. In poorer districts it is common for elementary art, music, and physical education to be conducted in the classroom because no special purpose rooms exist in the schools. During these free periods, the classroom teacher must either stay in the classroom or flee to the typically cramped and smoke-filled teachers' lounge. More affluent schools frequently have art and music rooms and gymnasiums, as well as teacher preparation rooms with office equipment and clerical staff to assist teachers with lesson preparation. These resource-related details may have a great deal to do with the success of instructional reform, yet they appear to be largely ignored in current implementation efforts.

Reforms that made demands on the evenings and weekends of teachers can also be thwarted by lack of educational resources. The task of evaluating student writing assignments and other homework is greater when the teaching load is 150 students as compared to 100 students. In recognition of this, Florida accompanied an expanded writing program with a requirement that high school English teachers have responsibility for no more than 100 students (Odden 1984: 16). Low teachers' salaries that force teachers to take second jobs also diminish the time for out-of-school preparation and student evaluation and the professional inclination of teachers to devote this time to school work.

Research points to the obvious conclusion that orderly classrooms are more effective than those in which the flow of instruction is constantly disrupted (Cohen 1983: 26). All else being equal, orderly classrooms may be a product of effective classroom instructional and management practices. Differences in resources and in concentrations of children with learning and discipline problems, however, often mean that all is not equal. Large classes may not create serious problems where children are educationally motivated; but they may increase the difficulty of managing classrooms of heterogeneous students who have learning or motivation problems. In these situations, maintenance of orderly classrooms may also depend on the availability of adequate special education diagnostic and treatment services, of remedial education services, of home and school liaison staff, and of administrative support.

Access to new instructional technologies such as those made available through computers are also highly dependent on resources. The cost of computers, software and training usually must be funded at the margin of school district budgets since most of the budget is usually already committed to pay for existing programs and services. Wealthy, high spending districts typically have more flexibility at the margin than do poor, low spending districts, and thus they have an advantage in implementing new instructional technologies (Odden 1984: 21). This advantage is compounded by the greater access that children of affluent families have to computers in the home, and by the different experiences with computers that low income and affluent children have with computers in the schools. Schools tend to use computers as sophisticated page turners to teach basic skills to low income children. More affluent children are more likely to learn higher order math skills, computer languages, and more sophisticated computer applications.

There is a tendency for states to ignore unequal access to new instructional technologies. New York, for example, reimburses school districts on a flat grant basis for the purchase of computer hardware (Bridgman 1985: 8). Although the amount of state aid per student is small, such programs are not likely to close this technology access gap. A categorical program with specific program and access criteria for distribution, although less politically popular, would be a better use of small amounts of state funds for this purpose.

Increasing the principal's role as an instructional leader is a major tenet of school improvement reforms. States such as Arkansas and South Carolina have recently funded state programs to provide greater in-service training to principals (Odden 1984: 18); however, principals may need more than management and instructional leadership skills to perform the leadership role contemplated by the school effectiveness research (Cohen 1983). The additional ingredient is time. The activities of the effective instructional leader are time consuming. The principal must observe classrooms, make notes and written evaluations of teachers, and meet with teachers individually to discuss evaluations and suggestions for improvement. Instructional leadership also assumes time for planning.

Principal time to perform leadership activities is an important resource issue. Principals must be freed from many of the tasks that they commonly perform such as extensive paperwork, student discipline, and welter of administrative details. Career ladder and merit pay proposals rely heavily on evaluations of teachers by principals, and some of these proposals recognize the additional costs required for good evaluations. For example, nearly 20 percent of the costs of Tennessee's career ladder program are for teacher evaluation and program administration (Odden 1984: 13). Evidence in school financing cases has shown that welahty higher spending districts are able to free principals from administrative detail in ways that are denied poorer lower spending districts. These higher spending districts tend to provide more clerical support and office equipment, counselors and other administrative support necessary to give the principal time to perform leadership functions. Existing inequalities in the ability of districts to support the principal's enhanced role as instructional leader are likely to lead to differences in the meaning of this concept at the school level.

Increasing Requirements for Promotion and Graduation

Increased requirements for promotion and graduation are also popular education reforms. The U.S. Department of Education (1984) reports that the majority of states have increased course requirements for graduation and have required students to pass tests for promotion or graduation. A number or states have also raised college admission standards, which indirectly mandate additional requirements for high school graduation. These promotion and graduation mandates raise serious equity issues. They may impose substantial additional costs on local districts that must provide additional courses and find qualified teachers for them. Increased academic standards also mean that more at-risk children, who are often poor and minority, will fail or drop out. Fiscally hard-pressed districts serving at-risk children will have difficulty providing the remedial and other services required to respond to the academic failures identified by these requirements. Absent appropriate educational programs and services, these requirements may simply stigmatize more children as educational failures without promise of educational improvement. Unfortunately, additional resources for an appropriate educational response appear to be largely absent from current state reform efforts. Odden (1974: 17) found that states have provided few additional funds to assist school districts to meet new promotion and graduation requirements.

Increasing Course Requirements for Graduation. Evidence in school financing cases has documented that school districts with fewer funds per pupil tend to offer a narrower range of courses, and this is particularly the case for poor small rural districts. Their offerings are truncated in math, science, and foreign languages as well as in fine arts and vocational programs, subject areas that *A Nation at Risk* (1983) and other reports seek to strengthen. But state mandates requiring high school students to take additional courses for graduation are likely to be implemented in different ways in poor low spending districts and wealthy high spending districts.

Course mandates are likely to have little effect on the programs of wealthy districts, particularly those that now serve relatively affluent college-bound students. Most students in those districts probably already take the necessary courses. If they do not, these districts tend to have the fiscal and staff flexibility to expand or modify course offerings. Poorer districts, particularly if they are small, have less flexibility. To offer more math or science courses, for example, would require such districts to reduce other programs and services. These districts also have the greatest difficulty attracting scarce teachers for these subjects. Consequently, they may resort to temporary certification of unqualified teachers or use teachers who are minimally qualified by courses taken in the distant past. These staff limitations, as well as inequalities in facilities and instructional materials and equipment, will result in poorer districts offering mandated courses with the same names as those in better funded districts but inferior in depth and scope.

Poorer districts serving concentrations of low-achieving children have an even greater incentive to water-down required courses. State requirements that students take more academically rigorous courses will cause more at-risk students to fail. A district can respond to this greater failure rate in at least three ways. It can maintain high academic standards and provide remedial programs for those who fail; it can maintain high academic standards and ignore the increased failure and drop-out rates; or it can water-down mandated courses for at-risk children to minimize failure. Limited resources act as a powerful incentive to reduce the academic standards of mandated courses, a result at odds with the objectives of educational reform.

Testing Requirements for Promotion and Graduation. During the 1970s, many states required school districts to administer tests to assess student performance. In more recent years, states have sought to increase the academic rigor of the public schools and the meaning of the high school diploma by requiring students to pass state specified tests as a condition for promotion and graduation. These testing requirements are intended, in theory, to ensure that children who are most at-risk academically will attain an acceptable minimum level of achievement. There is evidence, however, that the actual implementation of these requirements by states is having the opposite effect for large numbers of these children. Odden (1984: 17) reports that few states have provided additional resources to address the educational problems identified by the tests; of the states he studied only South Carolina acknowledged and provided additional funds for the remedial services needed for students who do not pass. By identifying more children as academic failures without ensuring an appropriate educational response, these tests are increasing the number of at-risk children who are dropping out of school (Ranbom 1984).

For at-risk children, testing mandates pose greater problems than increased course requirements. Tests classify and stratify children by academic achievement in ways that are more direct and stigmatizing than the failure to pass a particular course or the placement in a less challenging section of a required course. Without receipt of additional state funds, fiscally constrained school districts must choose between responding to increased student failure by cutting other educational services to expand remedial programs or by ignoring the higher incidence of academic failure and drop-outs.

In several states, minority children have sued to enjoin states from denying diplomas to children who fail state tests. In *Debra P. v. Turlington*, the federal courts enjoined Florida's minimum competency exam from being used to deny high school diplomas. The basis for these decisions is important for other states that seek to implement such diploma requirements. Black students disproportionately failed the Florida exam. The court found that this was, in part, because some of the black students in the state had received a portion of their education in racially segregated schools. Consequently, the court prevented the state from using the test to deny diplomas until black students had completed twelve years in desegregated schools. A federal court in Georgia issued a similar ruling (*Anderson v. Banks* 1981). The court of appeals in *Debra P.* also held that the test could not be used to deny diplomas to any student, minority or white, until the state showed that the test covered material that was actually taught in the classrooms in the state. Subsequently, in 1984, the Court of Appeals approved Florida's use of the graduation test after the state introduced evidence about its validity in measuring what was taught in the schools. Significantly, the court resolved its lingering doubts about the validity of the test on the basis of the state's extensive remedial efforts. The amount of notice students receive about test requirements for graduation has also been litigated. In *Brookhart v. Illinois State Board of Education*, a federal court of appeals prevented a school district from denying diplomas to handicapped students who had been given less than two years notice to prepare for the exam.

States that seek to implement testing requirements for graduation may face litigation if they or affected school districts have not fully disestablished formerly segregated educational systems. Similar issues may arise in states in which unequal school finance systems have been held unconstitutional but in which prior inequalities have not been eliminated. Most court decisions have also focused on the amount of advance notice of deficiencies students are given and the availability of remedial programs to prepare at-risk students for the exam. Thus, states that ignore the resources required for remediation may face litigation. Irrespective of the outcomes of such litigation, however, the equity issues remain. States that use tests to label poor and minority children as academic failures, but which do not ensure that appropriate educational services are provided in time to maximize their chances of graduating from high school, compound the problem of low achievement, which the tests were intended to address.

Administering Education Reform by State Education Agencies

State educational reform proposals often require state education agencies to carry out increased responsibilities. Legislatures frequently delegate to these agencies the tasks of selecting or developing state minimum-competency tests, approving courses, setting education standards, monitoring and evaluating school district reforms, approving school improvement plans submitted by districts, and deciding which school districts should receive state accreditation or sanctions based on compliance or noncompliance with state standards.

State departments of education are often aware of the unequal capacities of school districts to implement higher standards (McLaughlin 1983). This awareness typically is taken into account when state departments adopt educational standards pursuant to legislative mandate or when they monitor and evaluate school improvement efforts by school districts. Evidence in school financing cases has demonstrated that state agencies tend to adopt lowest common denominator standards, which even the poorest school districts can implement. When legislators set more stringent standards, state educational agencies tend to ignore violations by school districts that result from lack of educational resources and to go to great lengths to avoid denying accreditation to, or imposing other sanctions on, districts because of problems caused by lack of resources. This avoidance of criticism of districts for resource-based problems is understandable since poor districts may have little control over these inequalities. In addition, such criticism could put the agency in conflict with the state legislature over the amount and allocation of state aid needed to implement standards. In many states, however, this has created a "see no evil, speak no evil" approach by state educational agencies toward resource-related barriers to implementing education reform. This tendency to overlook such problems also reduces the incentive for poor school districts to speak out on these issues. As a result, there appears to be a policy vacuum on this issue in a number of states.

This policy vacuum may mean that these issues will remain dormant until groups outside of the educational establishment, for example, civil rights and citizen reform groups, raise or seek to litigate them. During the 1970s, school financing reform was often initiated by these groups rather than by the traditional educational interests such as school boards, teachers, and administrators' organizations, and state departments of education. In many states, outside pressure for change may also be required in order for the issues discussed in this chapter to be seriously addressed.

SUMMARY

Existing fiscal and educational inequalities among school districts cannot be ignored in state educational reform initiatives. These inequalities may be exacerbated by disequalizing allocations of state funds for educational reform. Furthermore, absent equalized state funding for educational reform, wealthy high spending districts will be able to implement education reforms in ways that are denied to poor low spending districts.

The failure of the reports recommending education reform to address interdistrict resource inequalities creates the impression that school districts are equally capable of implementing the prescribed reforms. There is little recognition in the "education reform" literature that school districts differ in their abilities, and need for additional funding, to implement these reforms. These reports, for example, leave the impression that all districts are equally affected by the economic disincentives for persons to enter and stay in the teaching profession. They ignore that low salaries and poor working conditions for teachers tend to be greater problems for poor school districts than for those endowed with large tax bases and that these factors may produce teaching staffs of unequal quality. Many of the interdistrict inequalities that affect the implementation of education reform are the result of years of accumulated resource disparities. This is particularly true of the quality of teaching and administrative staffs and of facilities. These inequalities cannot be eliminated quickly. Moreover, it is unlikely that these inequalities will ever be eliminated if they are ignored.

Failure to address present fiscal inequalities can result in the unequal implementation of educational reform by rich and poor districts. This is particularly the case where the state imposes additional requirements on districts without additional funding, or with only partial funding, to implement them. State requirements for additional instructional time, more courses, higher teachers' salaries, and testing requirements for promotion or graduation are examples of reform proposals that impose explicit or implicit additional costs on districts. Better endowed districts may nearly meet or exceed these requirements already. Low spending districts, in contrast, may have to reduce other programs and services to meet state mandates or may simply ignore the programs and services implied by the mandate, for example, remediation for students failing a state-mandated test. There is a danger that in future years we will look back in hindsight and conclude that state funds for educational reform were misdirected to those districts that could have funded reform on their own, while insufficient funding was provided to districts having the greatest need but the fewest resources to implement reform.

This last example illustrates another equity issue raised by state implementation of educational reform: Some children may be actually harmed by these reforms if equity issues are ignored. Higher educational standards, without more, are likely to result in more educational failures, more retentions in grade, and more drop-outs. And the children most affected are minority and poor. Few would argue for lower standards. The issue is whether the reforms assure that children who do not meet the higher standards are provided an educational "safety net" of programs and services that address the causes of failure or whether "reform" results in failing and pushing more poor and minority children out of school.

Many poor and minority children will certainly benefit if educational reform results in higher achievement. These reforms, if effective, however, are likely to help all schools, both those with few and with many resources and those serving the rich as well as the poor. These reforms by themselves do not promise any narrowing of the opportunity gap between rich and poor districts and between poor and minority children and those from affluent homes. Consequently, it cannot be assumed that there is some equalizing tendency in educational reform strategies that justifies ignoring the equity issues discussed here.

REFERENCES

Alexander, Kern, and Lee Shiver. 1983. "Equalization Among Florida School Districts," *Journal of Education Finance* 9, no. 1 (Summer): 53–62.

Anderson v. Banks. 649 F. Supp. 472 (S.D. Ga. 1981).

Bridgman, Anne. 1985. "Governors Outline Education Agendas as Legislators Convene," *Education Week* IV, no. 17 (January): 8-9.

Cohen, Michael. 1983. "Instructional Management, and Social Conditions in Effective Schools." In *School Finance and School Improvement Linkages for the 1980s*, edited by A. Odden and L.D. Webb, pp. 17-50. Cambridge, Mass.: Ballinger Publishing Co.

Corcoran, Thomas B., and Barbara J. Hansen. 1983. *Making Public Schools More Effective.* Trenton: New Jersey School Boards Association.

Cronk, Cynthia A., and Gary P. Johnson. 1983. "An Equity Analysis of Pennsylvania's Basic Instruction Subsidy Program," *Journal of Education Finance* 8, no. 4 (Spring): 502-510.

Doyle, D.P., and T.W. Hartle. 1984. "Excellence in Education: The States Respond." Paper for American Enterprise Institute Public Policy Week, Washington, D.C.

DuPree v. Alma School District No. 30. 279 Ark. 340, 651 S.W.2d 90 (1983).

Edlefson, Carla. 1983. "Progress Toward Equity in Ohio," *Journal of Education Finance* 8, no. 4 (Spring): 511-519.

Goertz, M.E., and G.A. Hickrod. 1983. "Introduction: Evaluating the School Finance Reform of the 1970s and Early 1980s," *Journal of Education Finance* 8, no. 3 (Winter): 415-424.

____. 1983b. "Introduction," *Journal of Education Finance* 9, no. 1 (Summer): 1-4.

Hickrod, G.A., R.B. Chaudhari, and B.C. Hubbard. 1983. "The Decline and Fall of School Finance Reform in Illinois," *Journal of Education Finance* 9, no. 1 (Summer): 17-38.

Kirst, Michael W. 1983. "A New School Finance in a New Era of Fiscal Constraint." In *School Finance and School Improvement Linkages for the 1980s*, edited by A. Odden and L.D. Webb, pp. 1-15. Cambridge, Mass.: Ballinger Publishing Co.

Kuprey, J.E., and A. Hopeman. 1983. "Minnesota School Finance Equity," *Journal of Education Finance* 8, no. 4 (Spring): 490-501.

Long, D.C., and S. McMullen. 1982. "Educational Productivity Issues in School Finance Litigation." In *New Directions for Testing and Measurement: Productivity Assessment in Education*, edited by A. Summers, pp. 112-126. San Francisco: Jossey-Bass.

McDonnell, Lorraine M. 1983. "School Improvement and Fiscal Retrenchment: How to Improve Education When Resources are Declining." In *School Finance and School Improvement Linkages for the 1980s*, edited by A. Odden and L.D. Webb, pp. 69-89. Cambridge, Mass.: Ballinger Publishing Co.

McLaughlin, Milbrey W. 1983. "State Involvement in Local Educational Quality." In *School Finance and School Improvement Linkages for the 1980s*, edited by A. Odden and L.D. Webb, pp. 51-69. Cambridge, Mass.: Ballinger Publishing Co.

Murnane, Richard J. 1983. "Qualitative Studies of Effective Schools: What Have We Learned." In *School Finance and School Improvement Linkages for the 1980s*, edited by A. Odden and L.D. Webb, pp. 193-209. Cambridge, Mass.: Ballinger Publishing Co.

National Commission on Excellence. 1983. *A Nation at Risk: The Imperative for Educational Reform.* Washington, D.C.: U.S. Government Printing Office.

National Board of Inquiry. 1985. *Barriers to Excellence: Our Children at Risk.* Boston: National Coalition of Advocates for Students.

Odden, Allan. 1984. *Education Finance in the States: 1984.* Denver: Education Commission of the States.

Odden, A., and L.D. Webb. 1983. "Introduction: The Linkages Between School Finance and School Improvement." In *School Finance and School Improvement Linkages for the 1980s*, edited by A. Odden and L.D. Webb, pp. xiii-xxi. Cambridge, Mass.: Ballinger Publishing Co.

Phelps, J.L., and Addonizio. 1983. "Michigan Public School Finance: The Last Ten Years," *Journal of Education Finance* 9, no. 1 (Summer): 5-16.

Ranbom, Sheppard. 1984. "Higher Standards Linked to Dropout Increase," *Education Week* 3, no. 30 (April): 1, 17.

Rydell, Lars H. 1983. "Equity for Taxpayers and Equal Opportunity for Students in Maine," *Journal of Education Finance* 9, no. 1 (Summer): 39-53.

Scheuer, Joan. 1983. "The Equity of New York State's System of Financing Schools: An Update," *Journal of Education Finance* 9, no. 1 (Summer): 79-93.

Schlechty, P.C., and V.S. Vance. 1983. "The Promotion of Quality in Teaching." In *School Finance and School Improvement Linkages for the 1980s*, edited by A. Odden and L.D. Webb, pp. 144-152. Cambridge, Mass.: Ballinger Publishing Co.

Summers, Anita. 1980. Testimony for Defendants in *Somerset County Board of Education v. Hornbeck*, No. A-58438, Circuit Court of Baltimore City, Maryland.

Toch, Thomas. 1984. "Teacher-Shortage Realities Seen Thwarting Reform," *Education Week* IV, no. 14 (December): 1, 14.

U.S. Department of Education. 1984. *The Nation Responds.* Washington, D.C.: U.S. Government Printing Office.

Walberg, Herbert J. 1983. Affidzvit in Support of Defendants' Motion for Summary Judgment in *Abbott v. Burke*, No. C-1893-80, Superior Court of New Jersey, Chancery Division, Mercer County.

Ward, James G. 1983. "On Teacher Quality." In *School Finance and School Improvement Linkages for the 1980s*, edited by A. Odden and L.D. Webb, pp. 163-170. Cambridge, Mass.: Ballinger Publishing Co.

Williams, Mary F. 1983. "Small Change: Maryland's Progress Toward Greater School Finance Equity," *Journal of Education Finance* 9, no. 1 (Summer): 97-115.

INDEX

ABOUT THE EDITORS

Van D. Mueller is Professor of Educational Administration at the University of Minnesota. He serves on the Board of Directors of AEFA, the Minnesota and National PTA, the board of editors of the *Journal of Education Finance*, and was co-editor of the Fifth Yearbook, *Managing Limited Resources: New Demands on Public School Management.* Dr. Mueller has participated in several state school finance studies (Indiana, Missouri, Minnesota) in addition to chairing a legislatively established commission studying the impact of declining school enrollment in Minnesota. He currently directs the Education Policy Fellowship Program of the Institute for Educational Leadership's Minnesota site and serves as a Vice President of the National PTA.

Mary P. McKeown is a financing analyst with the Maryland State Board for Higher Education. Previous professional positions include her being a financing analyst for the Illinois State Board of Education and faculty member at Sangamon State University, University of Illinois, and Eastern Michigan University. She has served on the Board of Directors of AEFA and will co-edit the 1986 AEFA Yearbook, *Values in Conflict: Funding Priorities for Higher Education.* Research and consulting interests include school transportation programs, management information systems, and systems analysis.

ABOUT THE CONTRIBUTORS

C.M. Achilles is Professor, Educational Leadership, and Coordinator of Field Services, Bureau of Educational Research and Services, College of Education, University of Tennessee, Knoxville, Tennessee. He served as a special consultant to the Tennessee Comprehensive Education Study (1981–82). He teaches courses in state and federal relations and has had research interests in state educational agencies for several years.

Kern Alexander is Professor of Educational Administration at the University of Florida and Executive Editor of the *Journal of Education Finance.* He served as an administrator in the U.S. Office of Education in Washington, D.C. during the Johnson years and was most recently, (1982–84), Florida Governor Robert Graham's Educational Policy Coordinator for the planning and budgeting for Florida's universities, community colleges and public schools. He has published nineteen books in the areas of educational financing and law including the standard texts *The Economics and Financing of Education* (1983), *The Law of Schools, Students, and Teachers* (1984), and *American Public School Law* (1985).

John Augenblick is a partner in Augenblick, Van de Water & Associates (AVA), a Denver-based consulting firm specializing in educational financing, governance, and planning. Prior to founding AVA, he served as director of the Education Finance Center at the Education Commission of the States. He has undertaken studies of school financing and higher education financing in numerous states.

Roald F. Campbell has been a teacher, a principal, and a superintendent in the public schools of Idaho. He completed his doctoral program at Stanford University. Dr. Campbell has held endowed chairs in Educational Administration at the University of Chicago and Ohio State University. At Chicago he also served as Dean of the Graduate School of Education. Author and co-author of numerous articles, monographs, and books in his field, Dr. Campbell is currently an adjunct professor at the University of Utah.

Nolas Estes is currently a Professor of Educational Administration and Coordinator of the Cooperative Superintendency Fellow Program at the University of Texas at Austin. He has been the General Superintendent for the Dallas Independent School District, Associate United States Commissioner of Education, and Director of the Division of Planning and Supplementary Centers of the United States Office of Education.

Susan Fuhrman is a senior research associate at the Eagleton Institute of Politics, Rutgers University. She had conducted numerous studies of state educational politics, educational policy, and school financing. She co-authored two monographs on state legislative educational leadership.

Richard Hooker is a professor of Educational Leadership at the University of Houston-University Park. As associate Executive Director of the Texas Association of School Boards, Governor's Assistant for Education, and Professor-consultant, he has been a leader in the Texas School Finance Reform Movement for 16 years. In 1984, as a consultant to the Texas Select Committee on Public Education he coordinated the development of the Finance Section of the proposed reform law functioned as the Technical Consultant to the Committee lobby.

Michael W. Kirst is a Professor of Education and Chair of Administration and Policy Analysis at Stanford University. He is a former president of the California State Board of Education. Dr. Kirst's research interests center upon school financing, educational policy, and the politics of education.

Zelma Lansford received a doctor of education degree in December 1984 from the University of Tennessee, Knoxville with a major in administration. Her doctoral study considered educational reform in Tennessee. She holds a master of special education for the gifted and is the principal of an elementary school in Chattanooga, Tennessee.

David C. Long is an attorney who has worked on school financing cases in many states including representing plaintiffs in Arkansas, Colorado, Georgia, New Jersey and West Virginia. He has also conducted legal policy analysis of federal educational programs and civil rights obligations. He is currently director of legislative research for the State Bar of California.

Betty Malen has been a teacher and administrator in secondary schools in Michigan and North Dakota. She completed her Ph.D. in educational administration at the University of Minnesota where she gave specific attention to the politics of education. Currently, she is assistant professor of educational administration at the University of Utah. Her teaching and research interests include politics and finance.

Diane Massell is a Ph.D. student in Education Policy Analysis at Stanford University. She is a former staff member of the National Conference of State Legislatures.

Tim L. Mazzoni is Associate Professor of Educational Policy and Administration, University of Minnesota. He is co-author, with Roald Campbell, of *State Policy Making for the Public Schools.* Research activities focus on state school governance with an emphasis on legislative lobbying, constituency mobilization, and the politics of educational reform.

Lorraine M. McDonnell is a political scientist at The Rand Corporation in Santa Monica, California. Her research and writing have focused on educational policy and the politics of education, particularly at the state level. She is currently interested in developing a better understanding of the conditions under which state policies are most likely to be linked to local practice in schools and classrooms.

Kent McGuire is a senior policy analyst with the Education Commission of States. He holds a B.A. from the University of Michigan in Economics and an M.A. in Educational Administration from Columbia University. During his tenure at ECS, Kent has conducted research on various aspects of school financing and he has participated in numerous consulting projects on school financing and related topics.

Julie Underwood O'Hara is assistant professor of educational administration and adjunct assistant professor of law at the University of North Dakota, Grand Forks, North Dakota. She received her J.D. from Indiana University School of Law and her Ph.D. from the University of Florida. She currently teaches education law courses both on-campus and off-campus in workshops, seminars and in-services. She has written a number of articles in the area of educational law and financing. She has served as Assistant Editor of and is now one of the Legislature Editors for the Journal of Education Finance.

William Payne has over twenty-five years of service in teaching and administering secondary and postsecondary education. For nine years, he was the North Area Superintendent in Memphis, responsible for 48 schools and 30,000 students. He was Executive Director of the Tennessee Comprehensive Education Study, grades K through graduate school. He has recently accepted a staff appointment with the Tennessee Higher Education Commission.

Charles J. Santelli is Director of Research and Educational Services for the New York State United Teachers, the statewide affiliate of the American Federation of Teachers, and the largest state teachers organization in the United States. He has previously taught on both the high school and college levels and has served as a college administrator in the State University of New York system. He is widely recognized in New York for his work in the area of school financing, teacher education and certification, and educational policy. He has been to educational reform issues in New York.

Arthur Steller is Superintendent of the Oklahoma City Public Schools. He previously served as superintendent for the Mercer County Public Schools in West Virginia and assistant superintendent for the Shaker Heights City Schools in Ohio. Other administrative positions he has held include Coordinator of Systemwide Planning in Montgomery County, Maryland; Director of Elementary Education in Beverly, Massachusetts; elementary principal in South Western City Schools in Ohio; and curriculum coordinator in Belpre, Ohio. He has taught at the elementary, secondary, and college levels as well as a summer special education program. In addition, he has been a coach, an intramural director, and a school bus driver.

Barry Sullivan is Assistant Director of Government Relations for the Minnesota Department of Education. His duties include interpretation of state and federal legislation. He received a Ph.D. in Educational Administration from the University of Minnesota in 1980.

Deborah A. Verstegen recently completed her Ph.D. at the University of Wisconsin-Madison and is currently assistant professor of educational administration at the University of Texas-Austin. She received the dissertation award from the American Education Finance Association in 1984. Her research interests center on educational finance, educational policy, and the politics of education.

James G. Ward is assistant professor of education administration at the University of Illinois at Urbana-Champagne. Formerly he was Director of Research for the American Federation of Teachers, a position he held since 1977. Previous to that he was Associate in Educational Services, New York State United Teachers, and a secondary school teacher. He is 1985–86 president-elect of the American Education Finance Association and is a member of the editorial advisory board of the *Journal of Education Finance.* He has published widely on issues in school finance, budgeting and business management, educational law, and educational policy. He earned a professional degree in public administration from the State University of New York at Albany and a doctorate in educational administration from Virginia Polytechnic Institute and State University.

AMERICAN EDUCATION FINANCE ASSOCIATION OFFICERS 1985-86